DIRECTORS OF DEVELOPMENT

Influences on the Development
of Children's Thinking

DIRECTORS OF DEVELOPMENT

Influences on the Development of Children's Thinking

Edited by
Lynn Okagaki
Robert J. Sternberg
Yale University

LEA LAWRENCE ERLBAUM ASSOCIATES, PUBLISHERS
1991 Hillsdale, New Jersey Hove and London

Lawrence Erlbaum Associates, Inc., Publishers
365 Broadway
Hillsdale, New Jersey 07642

Library of Congress Cataloging-in-Publication Data

Directors of development : influences on the development of the children's thinking / edited by Lynn Okagaki, Robert J. Sternberg.
p. cm.
Includes bibliographical references and index.
ISBN 0-8058-0627-X (hard). – ISBN 0-8058-0628-8 (pbk.)
1. Cognition in children. 2. Nature and nurture.
BF723.C5D57 1991
155.4'13–dc20 90-24667
CIP

Printed in the United States of America
10 9 8 7 6 5 4 3 2 1

Contents

Introduction: Influences on the Development of Children's Thinking

LYNN OKAGAKI
Yale University

Behavioral scientists continue to debate whether cognitive development is the function of nature or nurture or some complex interaction of the two. In this book, the various researchers consider the ways in which different factors—some biological, some social–environmental—influence the development of cognition and explicitly seek to address how these influences interact.

The book is divided into three sections. We first consider biological influences on cognitive development. Then we turn to cultural and familial influences and, finally, to educational and intervention programs designed to shape children's thinking. The authors represent a diversity of views, and the research reviewed in the book includes anthropological, educational, medical, neurological, psychological, and sociological perspectives.

The biological section begins with Sandra Scarr and Anne Ricciuti's (chap. 1) intriguing discussion of the effects parents have on children's development. They elaborate on Scarr's "genotype → phenotype" theory. According to Scarr and Ricciuti's thesis, children are the primary directors of their development, and the authors present an impressive array of empirical evidence to support this thesis. Not only do children contribute to their cognitive development by bringing innate abilities, but they also actively work to shape their environment, to evoke certain behaviors from parents and other caregivers, and to select the types of activities and experiences in which they want to participate. Yes, the authors argue, experiences help foster development, but it is the children who create the experiences from the environment.

According to Scarr and Ricciuti, the driving force that shapes the child's thinking is the child. On the positive side, they argue that this means parents do not need to try to be "super parents." Parents need only to be "good enough," that is, to provide an adequate environment in which the child can develop. On the down side, intervention to improve children's development is difficult unless their environments are outside the range of what is normal and adequate for human beings. This chapter sets a strong biological perspective from which to view the following chapters.

Next, Leila Beckwith and Carol Rodning (chap. 2) provide an extensive review of research on intellectual functioning in children born preterm. With Scarr and Ricciuti's thesis that children strongly control their cognitive development in mind, we direct the reader's attention to the section on process studies and the analysis of parent–child relationships and family environments. Beckwith and Rodning provide an example of how the characteristics and functioning of the child can shape the responses of caregivers. They note that early on, preterm infants differ from healthy term infants in their motor behaviors, visual attention, and state organization, and suggest that under those circumstances, the preterm infants "may be inadequate social partners in their natural role in initiating, maintaining, and promoting caregiving." Moreover, the accompanying medical problems of prematurity can affect the relationships between parents and infants. Parents face the difficulties of dealing with the infant's medical problems and, for some, conflicting emotions, such as guilt, uncertainty about the future, and decreased self-esteem.

But, despite the biological origin of many of the preterm infant's problems, Beckwith and Rodning conclude that the infant's environment plays an important role in determining long-term consequences. They observe that although a supportive and enhancing environment cannot eliminate serious neurological problems, it can ameliorate some deficits. They argue that the cognitive development of many children born preterm may be more closely tied to their environments than to prenatal and perinatal problems.

We conclude the first section with Henry Ricciuti's chapter (3) on malnutrition and cognitive development, which discusses research-policy linkages and current research directions. Ricciuti begins with a thought-provoking critique of the impact of the social–political environment in the United States during the 1960s on research dealing with the relation between malnutrition and cognitive development. He argues that for scientists and policymakers good intentions are not enough. Carefully conducted and reported science will better inform the design and implementation of policy than oversimplified and, perhaps, overstated claims. With this historical background on nutrition research, he proceeds to identify examples of good research and possible productive directions for researchers. Arguing that malnutrition cannot be isolated from the social environment that precipitates and surrounds it, he suggests that scientists focus on how malnutrition interacts with related socioenvironmental factors to affect development. Prospective studies of populations at risk for malnutrition that give careful attention to possible mediating variables (e.g., children's exploratory behavior, motivation, and curiosity) might increase our understanding of the processes by which nutritional status affects cognitive outcome, and subsequently, better inform developers of intervention strategies. Ricciuti's chapter is a unique examination of both an important research area and of the interplay between science and policy.

We want to call attention to two images drawn from these three chapters on biological influences on cognitive development. In the first chapter, Scarr and A. Ricciuti posit that children, drawing on biological givens, shape their own environments. Thus, children are influencing their development both through their own biological maturation and by evoking certain kinds of social interaction or stimulation from their environments. In Beckwith and Rodning's chapter, we have an excellent example of how a physical status (i.e., premature birth) can affect the child's biological maturation and the child's environment (i.e., parenting responses). Here is the image of the child shaping the environment. In contrast, Beckwith and Rodning also provide the image of the environment affecting the child's development. They present evidence that a supportive environment can ameliorate some of the negative consequences of the physical condition. Similarly, in H. Ricciuti's discussion of the consequences of malnutrition on development, it is not that the child's initial biological status shaped the environment to bring about the child's current malnourished status, but that environmental conditions, in this case, negatively affect the child's development. H. Ricciuti then posits that the consequences or influence of the physical condition (i.e., malnutrition) cannot be isolated from or understood apart from the social environment in which it occurs. His example illustrates the perspective that human development must be understood within its social context—even when one is attempting to understand the consequences of a biological condition.

From the biological emphasis, we turn to cultural and familial influences on cognitive development. The three chapters in this section each support the thesis that social–cultural factors—that people around the child—can shape the child's thinking. Edmund Gordon and Eleanor Armour-Thomas (chap. 4) posit that culture both describes and constrains human behavior. They examine different aspects of culture and suggest macrolevel mechanisms by which each aspect affects cognitive behavior. They then utilize neurological research and garner evidence indicating that the amount, type, and timing of early experiences affects brain development, which in turn affects cognitive performance. They argue for the interdependence of culture and cognition.

Following Gordon and Armour-Thomas's more general examination of cultural influences on cognition, Okagaki and Sternberg (chap. 5) focus on the family environment in their discussion of cultural and parental influences on the development of children's thinking. They propose that culture affects cognition by: (a) establishing what objects and ideas are thought about, (b) constraining the functions or ways in which these objects and ideas are normally used, (c) determining the social situations, the roles, and the expectations in which people act, and (d) specifying what responses are accepted as good answers or solutions to problems. They also review research that examines ways in which parenting and home environment are related to children's cognitive development. They argue that "when children learn a skill, which skills children learn, and even the level of expertise children achieve are influenced by parental action."

Also focusing on parental effects on cognitive development, Irving Sigel, Elizabeth Stinson, and Jan Flaugher (chap. 6) direct their attention toward one particular aspect of cognition in their chapter on socialization of representational competence in the family. Most research examining the relation between family environment and children's cognitive development have relied on global measures of intellectual functioning, such as IQ and school achievement test scores. In contrast, the work by Sigel and his colleagues at the Educational Testing Service has focused on one particular cognitive ability—representational competence—and at *theoretically related* parenting beliefs and behaviors in order to understand the role of the family environment in facilitating cognitive development. Representational competence is the ability to take information or experience and to transform it into mental symbols that can be used in thinking and reasoning processes. It is the fundamental cognitive ability to organize, integrate, and transform mental representations of external phenomena. In this chapter, the authors discuss the ways in which parental "distancing strategies"—that is, behaviors that require children to separate themselves from the immediate context (e.g., to think abstractly, to imagine a change in a given object)—affect children's representational competence.

The second section examines the informal ways in which familial and cultural factors influence cognitive development. The third section looks at formal curriculum—school and intervention programs—designed to change children's thinking. We begin this section with John Bransford, Susan Goldman, and Nancy Vye's (chap. 7) excellent review of current research on thinking and teaching thinking skills. The authors identify several principles from cognitive psychology that can be utilized to develop effective instruction for enhancing cognitive development. For example, they note that in the last 10 years more emphasis has been placed on recognizing the social nature of cognition and suggest that future programs will include greater efforts to involve parents in their children's education and will view parents as important mediators of learning. Similarly, they observe that studies of expert problem solving have led to a better understanding of different problem-solving strategies, of the role of domain-specific knowledge in problem solving, and of the interaction between knowledge and thinking strategies. The role of knowledge in teaching thinking skills has often been neglected in the past, and the authors predict that more effective programs will be developed in the 1990s that build on this better understanding of the role of knowledge. Finally, Bransford, Goldman, and Vye conclude with a hopeful look at directions researchers and educators may take to enhance the development of thinking skills.

The following two chapters consider two types of intervention programs. First, Kathleen McCartney and Elizabeth Howley (chap. 8) review research on home-based intervention programs and then, Richard Darlington (chap. 9) discusses center-based preschool programs.

McCartney and Howley begin by presenting a theoretical framework for home-based intervention programs that considers current knowledge of the relations between parental beliefs and parenting behaviors. From this framework, they then discuss the empirical evaluations of 12 home-intervention programs. Based on their consideration of the parental beliefs research and home-intervention programs, McCartney and Howley argue that home-intervention programs need to direct attention to changing parents' maladaptive beliefs rather than trying to get "disadvantaged parents to emulate the play behaviors of middle-class parents." Their analysis is an excellent reminder of the need to consider relevant research in the development of intervention strategies.

In the following chapter, Darlington recalls one of the most important U.S. evaluations of preschool intervention programs. He focuses on the Consortium for Longitudinal Studies' evaluation of 11 preschool programs that had originally been experimental models for the Head Start program in the 1960s. The Consortium's evaluation has been credited with saving Head Start by providing convincing evidence that early intervention helps children do better in school.

Up to this point, we have considered three types of environmental influences on cognitive development—family, school and early intervention programs, and general cultural factors. In the last three chapters, the authors discuss the integration of multiple social influences. Whereas all of the chapters to some degree have acknowledged the interaction of multiple factors influencing cognitive development, the final chapters specifically address this issue. Echoing Bransford, Goldman, and Vye's perspective that effective schooling needs to involve parents in the educational process,

Joseph Shimron (chap. 10) emphatically states that schools must relinquish the view of parents as adversaries and must work to involve parents as important collaborators in their children's schooling. Shimron first reviews educational theories of home–school relations and then provides two diverse examples to support his thesis that schools must see parents as allies in the educational process.

Second, Harold Stevenson, Chuansheng Chen, Shin-ying Lee, and Andrew Fuligni (chap. 11) present an intriguing study of the effects of schooling and culture on children's thinking. They argue that to understand the role of education on cognitive development, we must consider the social–cultural setting in which the schooling occurs. They describe two elegant studies of the effects of schooling in different cultural settings. The first study examines the school experiences and cognitive development of Quechua Indian children in Peru—one group in poor inner-city settlements, one group in small highland villages in which the Quechuas are the primary residents, and one group in remote, tropical rain forest villages in which they are a minority group. The results are interpreted in light of differences in cultural practices that have developed in these Quechuan communities. The second study takes us half-way around the world to Japan and Taiwan and compares the school experiences of children in these two countries with those of children in the United States. The authors point out that variables important in explaining school achievement in the three affluent countries may be quite different from those related to the achievement levels of children from impoverished communities. They also observe that whereas the level of cognitive development (as assessed, for example, by memory, concept formation, and seriation tasks) was fairly comparable across all four countries, the academic achievement was not, and conclude that the academic environment of the Peruvian children was not enabling them to academically achieve what they were capable of doing. This chapter provides a fascinating and unique look at schooling and culture in very different settings.

For the final chapter, Robert Sternberg (chap. 12) gives us a brief, but unique, overview of 30 years of answers to the nature versus nurture question. He argues that the ways in which scientists have asked how hereditary and environmental factors influence cognitive development have shaped their answers and suggests that scientific progress comes from the examination and reexamination of issues from multiple perspectives.

In conclusion, this book examines multiple influences on cognitive development. We have attempted to include a variety of perspectives and research methodologies that consider what motivates and directs cognitive development.

Part I

Biological Factors Influencing Cognitive Development

CHAPTER 1

What Effects *Do* Parents Have on Their Children?

SANDRA SCARR
ANNE RICCIUTI
University of Virginia

Most parents in most societies get children with the virtues they most admire and with the vices they are most willing to tolerate.

(LeVine, 1987, p. 25)

Given a normal human newborn, parents begin their long job of nurturing and guiding the baby toward adulthood. What difference does it make in children's development that parents in different cultures subscribe to quite different norms about proper infant care and child rearing? What difference does it make whether parents follow culturally prescribed norms of their own society about proper parenting?

In this chapter, we discuss the alleged effects of child-rearing environments and alternative ways of understanding the effects of parents on their children. We present the theory of genotype → environment effects and interpret the data on parent–child correlations as individual differences in the ways children construct their own experiences.

CONSTRUCTING EXPERIENCES FROM ENVIRONMENTS

The idea that people make their own environments (Scarr & McCartney, 1983) runs counter to the mainstream of developmental psychology. A large base of literature examining the relationships between familial, parental, and child characteristics has found that these characteristics are, indeed, related to each other. Developmental psychologists most often interpret these findings as evidence that the rearing conditions parents provide for their children make differences in the children's life chances and eventual adult statuses—both socioeconomic achievements and mental health. Thus, although some developmentalists have suggested that children may affect their environments as well as vice versa (Bell, 1968), the theory that children actually construct their own environments challenges the basic tenets of much of mainstream developmental psychology.

The idea that children create their own experiences from the environments they encounter also challenges parents' beliefs about the potential impact they can have on their children's development. After all, most parents invest tremendous efforts in rearing their children—efforts that involve emotional, personal, and financial sacrifices. If parents can be given accurate information about how much influence they might or might not have on their children's development, it might help alleviate needless sacrifices and emotional turmoil on their part.

Thus, from both psychologists' and parents' perspectives it is important to understand as much as possible about exactly what impact parents have on their children's development. It is important to examine the extent to which differences between families produce differences between children, and in what areas of development. Accurate information about the extent to which differences between families contribute to differences between children, is particularly important for the design and implementation of timely and effective intervention programs for at-risk children and families. Thus, although the theory that children construct their own environments challenges widely held ideas about families and children, it is important to consider and evaluate it, given available data.

Observations and Inferences

Both parents and psychologists observe pervasive correlations between characteristics of parents, the environments they provide, and their children's outcomes. Both parents and psychologists make causal attributions to those correlations: They believe that differences in parental behaviors and environments cause differences in children's outcomes. The construction of causal inferences from the web of parent–child correlations is fraught with logical and scientific problems (Scarr, 1985). Ever since Bell's (1968) seminal paper pointing out the possibility that children may affect their environments as well as vice versa, numerous studies have shown that, indeed, children do have an effect on the behavior of their caregivers (e.g., Bell &

Harper, 1977; Breitmayer & Ricciuti, 1988; Lytton, 1980; McCartney, Robeson, Jordan, & Mouradian, in press). Using a variety of research designs and outcome measures, these studies have all demonstrated that, rather than passive recipients of care, infants and children are active, influential partners in their interactions with the people around them. Thus, the notion that parental behaviors cause all observed differences among children is called into question.

Causal assumptions about the direction of effects between parental behavior and children's outcomes have been called into question even more strongly by research over the past 20 years in the field of developmental behavior genetics. Behavioral genetic methods are used to investigate the sources of individual variation in a population (Plomin, 1986). The focus is on what makes individuals different from one another, not on the causes of the particular mean value of a trait in a population. By studying family members with varying degrees of relatedness, estimates can be obtained of the proportion of observed variation in a population that is due to genetic variation. This estimate is referred to as heritability, and is limited to the particular population under study.

Behavior genetic research has shown that, for a wide variety of traits, including measures of intelligence, specific cognitive abilities, personality, and psychopathology in North American and European populations, there is as much, if not more, variation within families as there is between families (Plomin & Daniels, 1987). Being reared in one family rather than another makes few if any differences in children's personality and intellectual development. These data suggest that environments most parents provide for their children have few *differential effects* on the offspring. It is proposed here that each child constructs a reality from the opportunities afforded by the rearing environment, and the constructed reality does have considerable influence on variations among children and differences in their adult outcomes.

Means and Variances

The statement that parents have few differential effects on children does not mean that not having parents is just as good as having parents. It may not matter much that children have different parents, but it does matter that they have parent(s) or some supportive, affectionate person who is willing to be parentlike. This is essentially the distinction between examining sources of variation between individuals, and examining mean values in the population. The methods best suited to the former are not necessarily appropriate for the latter.

The distinction between causes of mean or average values with causes of variation around mean values can be confusing to both psychologists and parents. For some characteristics there is very little individual variation around the mean, but for other characteristics there is a broad distribution of results, for which a mean and a variance can be described. For example, there are some human characteristics for which there is no normal variation at the chosen level of analysis: for example, having bilateral limbs, two eyes, and a cerebral cortex. Every normal member of the species has these characteristics. At another level of analysis, however, all of these species-typical characteristics show variation (e.g., limb length, eye shape, brain size). The structural genes that cause the development of species-typical characteristics may have no normal variants; but there may be regulatory genes that influence the developmental patterns and the eventual amount of each characteristic in a given individual. There is no necessary association between the structural causes of species-typical characteristics and the regulatory causes of variation. Research on variation has no necessary implications for the causes of the average value of the population (but see Turkheimer, 1990).

As pointed out by Arthur Jensen (1989), this distinction is particularly important to remember when considering analyses of heritability:

> Hence, the results of any heritability analysis are necessarily limited to statements concerning variation around the overall *mean* of the group in which the analysis is performed, and it affords no information whatsoever about the factors responsible for the particular value of the group mean. (p. 241)

Similarly, as McGuffin and Gottesman (1985) emphasized, heritability estimates have no meaning for a given individual. Such estimates simply tell us the proportion of variance of some trait that is due to genetic variation in that particular population. They cannot tell us what percent of individual *A*'s limb length is due to genetic influences.

Along the same lines, research on family effects can be seen as similar to research on school effects. In studies of school effects on children's educational achievement (really, the study of differential school effects), we tend to forget that all of the children are in some sort of school. If schooling is a universal experience in the population under study, one cannot study the effects of schooling per se. For example, in some educational intervention studies, investigators have found that the control group was receiving services too similar to those experimentally provided to the children in the intervention (e.g., Ramey, Bryant, & Suarez, 1986). To see the effects of schooling, one would have to contrast schooled children with those who receive no schooling. For a study of this sort, one would have to go outside of the bounds of normal Western civilization, which presents many other problems (e.g., Cole, 1990; Stigler, Lee, & Stevenson, 1987).

To see the effects of no parents (or parent-surrogates), one would have to return to the orphanages of long ago (or study those in use today in the Soviet Union), or see children trapped in crack houses of inner cities, locked in basements and attics by vengeful, crazy relatives (see Clarke & Clarke, 1976). Really deprived, abusive, and neglectful environments do not support normal development for any child. Having no parental figures or being reared in terribly deprived circumstances have clear detrimental effects on child development, regardless of the child's genetic background (Dumaret & Stewart, 1985). It is important to point out here that *variations* among environments supporting normal human development are not very important as *determinants of variations* in children's outcomes.

Common and Uncommon Assumptions

Many psychologists and parents believe that variations in normal environments, particularly those provided by their families, (a) shape children's development and (b) determine their adult futures. It is also commonly assumed that parental characteristics and home environments are arbitrarily or even randomly associated with individual children's characteristics (Bandura, 1982). In this sense, parents are "the luck of the draw." The structure of experience is assumed to be given in the environment, which acts as stimuli that impinge and shape children, regardless of who they are. The uncorrelated nature of people and environments is challenged by constructivist views of how people determine their own experiences and by the hypothesis that experiences are largely correlated with people's own characteristics.

In fact, several lines of research in cognitive, clinical, and social psychology have been based on theories about individual differences in experience and on the idea that individual's responses to environments differ and they construct their own experiences. The following are some brief examples:

1. In cognitive psychology Bower pursued the idea that people construct their own experiences and personal histories (Bower, 1987). Faced with the same brief story, different individuals remembered and recalled different versions of the story.

2. Clinical psychology has found that people differ in their emotional responses to situations (e.g., Eysenck, 1982, 1983, on psychopaths versus normals in their emotional reactivity to punishment and reward; Wexler, Schwartz, Warrenburg, Servis, & Tarlatzis, 1986, on stress reactions) that shape their behaviors in those situations.

3. Social psychology has presented evidence that personal characteristics affect how others respond to the stimulus person (Langlois & Roggman,

1990). Physical attractiveness may be in the eye of the beholder, but there is a great deal of cultural consensus in judgments about what constitutes physical attractiveness. People judged to be physically attractive by others are more likely to be asked for dates, more likely to be hired for jobs, and, once hired, more likely to be promoted than others judged to be less physically attractive (Berscheid & Walster, 1974).

4. In personality psychology, Henry Murray (Kluckhohn, Murray, & Schneider, 1953) pursued for many years the idea that each person constructs a personal myth, which gives coherence to his life, just as larger cultural myths give coherence to a society. Personality characteristics that are moderately heritable (30%–50%) have been shown to influence how people react across time and situations. Sociable and outgoing people experience social interactions with strangers differently than shy, fearful people (Eysenck, 1983; Kagan, Reznick, & Gibbons, 1989). Optimistic, internally directed older adults cope much better with aging than others who are less optimistic and feel less in control of their lives. A twin study of older adults shows these life-outlook characteristics, like all personality variables, to be moderately heritable (Pedersen, Gatz, Plomin, & McClearn, 1989).

Cultural Psychology and Individual Differences

Although several areas within mainstream psychology have pursued the idea that people construct their own reality, the rather new field of cultural psychology is actually predicated on the assumption that no sociocultural environment exists apart from the meaning that human participants give it. According to Shweder (1990), "it is a principle of cultural psychology—the principle of intentional worlds—that nothing real 'just is,' and that realities are the product of the way things get represented, embedded, implemented, and reacted to" (p. 3). Shweder contrasted the aims of cultural psychology with those of general psychology.

> General psychology assumes that its subject matter is a presupposed central . . . processing mechanism inherent in human beings, which enables them to think . . . experience . . . , act . . . , and learn. . . . Since the central processing mechanism is presumed to be a transcendent, abstract, fixed, and universal property of the human psyche, general psychology has the look, taste, and smell of a Platonic undertaking. (pp. 3–4)

Cultural psychology is non-Platonic. It presupposes that reality and human experience are constructed by the human mind. The power of a particular stimulus to evoke a particular response is not independent of the way a person classifies it, responds to it, and reasons about it. And it is this attributed meaning and transaction between human and environment that is the major subject matter of psychology. Shweder (1990) commented on an article by Roger Shepherd (1987) on what he claimed to be "universal laws of generalization."

> Shepherd seems to think that something truly fundamental about the mind—an inherent central processing mechanism—can be divined only if we can transcend the noise and clutter of the environment by bleaching it of familiar things and impoverishing it of feedback, and by isolating the mind from its own mental supports.
>
> The alternative interpretation—the view from cultural psychology—is that the mind left to its own devices is mindless.
>
> The implication, of course, is that genuine success for psychological science will come when we stop trying to get beyond the 'noise' and start trying to say interesting things about some of the more interesting, robust and patterned varieties of it. (p. 10)

> Speaking from within the intentional world of cultural psychology, the virtue in general psychology is its concern with the organized nature of the mental life. Its vice is its conception of the mental as a central processing mechanism—abstract, interior (transcendent), universal, fixed, and content-free. (p. 17)

Although cultural psychology uses non-Platonic, philosophical constructivism to explore ethnic differences in personality, intelligence, and social behavior, the same ontological and epistemological principles apply to individual differences within cultures (Scarr, 1985). Different people, at different developmental stages, interpret and act on their environments in different ways that create different experiences for each person. In this view, human experience is the construction of reality, not a property of a physical world that imparts the same experience to everyone who encounters it.

Thus, there are contradictory theories in psychology about how people are influenced by their environments and how they construct their own experiences from those environments.

The Average Expectable Environment

A resolution of the seeming contradictions in theories about how parents affect their children can be found in the concept of the "average expectable environment" (Hartmann, 1958). Based on evolutionary theory, there are three components that describe normal organisms in normal environments (LeVine, 1987).

1. *Preadaptation.* Infants and children are preadapted by their human species genetic inheritance to respond to a specific *range* of environmental opportunities for stimulation and knowledge acquisition.

2. *Variation.* Within the genetically specified range of normal environments, a variety of environmental patterns of stimulation can all act to promote normal human developmental patterns. A wide variety of variations in environments within this normal range are "functionally equivalent" opportunities for people to construct their own experiences (Scarr & Weinberg, 1983).
3. *Limits.* Environments that fall outside of the species-normal range will not promote normal developmental patterns.

Thus, normal development does occur in a wide variety of human environments, but not in those that are abusive or neglectful or without "average expectable" conditions, in which the species has evolved. For infants, species-normal environments include parenting adults and a surrounding social group to which they will be socialized. The exact details and specifications of the socialization patterns are not crucial to normal development (although they are crucial to understanding the meaning people give to their experiences), but having a rearing environment that falls within the limits of normal environments is crucial to normal development. LeVine (1987) pointed out:

> Many of the environmental conditions of young children observed to be statistically average, culturally valued and socially expectable in other cultures are ones that would be considered prognostic of abnormal development by psychoanalytic clinicians in our own. . . . By their standards, the environments of Gusii, Japanese, and Hindu Indian children are abnormal, certainly beyond the average expectable environment that appears to promote normality in a Western context. Are these non-Western people to be classified as pathological in their development or is an average expectable environment specific to a culture? (pp. 21–22)

LeVine (1987) concluded, of course, that a wide variety of culturally different practices promotes normal human development. He suggested that theories of development should be revised to include an expanded view of what is normal in human rearing environments.

In addition to cultural psychology's theoretical emphasis on the importance of constructed reality, cross-cultural data has provided further evidence for the influence of children's characteristics on caregiving. In their excellent summary of two decades of research in Zinacantan, Greenfield, Brazelton, and Childs (1989) proposed that ethnic groups are both genetically different in their responsiveness to environments and cultures most often work with those biological differences to make rearing environments compatible and supportive of normal development. As an example, infant-care practices among the Zincantecos take advantage of the long attention spans and quiet motor activity of the babies. Babies are swaddled and seldom stimulated verbally or motorically, but are allowed to observe ongoing family activities for long periods. By contrast, infants of European descent are more often jittery and vigorously active; child-rearing practices among their parents include more vigorous social interactions, motor play, and encouragement of independent locomotion.

Each culture emphasizes only some aspects of development—Americans stress more socially engaged, talkative children, the Gusii more obedient, less socially demanding children—but all groups rear children, most of whom are normal members of the human species (LeVine, 1987).

Patterns of attachment between parents and infants are also culturally patterned by ideals and experiences. The meaning of separations and reunions between mothers and infants are culturally relative, showing very wide variations among groups (LeVine & Miller, in press). Japanese mothers are rarely separated from their infants; they are carried for much of the day and sleep with their mothers at night. Israeli infants in traditional kibbutzim are separated from their mothers for most of the day and at night in separate living quarters. But it would be specious to claim that the majority of infants in Japan and Israel are "insecurely attached" in the sense of having inferior relationships to their parents than North American infants, for whom Ainsworth and Wittig's (1969) Strange Situation was designed. It is true that the modal pattern of response to the Strange Situation is not the same for many cultures as the modal pattern of U.S. infants, whose experiences with separations and reunions with their mothers are vastly different from the other groups.[1]

Across cultures, then, there are possible variations in average genotypes that affect developmental patterns of responsiveness to rearing environments. Cultures are likely to map valued rearing techniques and conditions to what is appropriate to their living conditions and to their children's developmental patterns.

We propose that individual parents make exactly the same accommodations of rearing techniques to their own children and that on average parents take both developmental status and individual differences among their children into account as they work to rear them to normal adulthood. Furthermore, children tailor their experiences from the rearing environment to fit their own individual talents, interests, and personality.

---

[1]Within the United States, the meaning of the Strange Situation has been questioned for infants with extensive child-care experience, for the same reasons: Separations and reunions are familiar and predictable everyday occurrences in their lives and therefore not as stressful as the same events for infants who are less often and unpredictably separated and reunited with their mothers (Clarke-Stewart, 1989; Phillips, McCartney, Scarr, & Howes, 1987).

Organism and Environment: Interaction

At the same time that most of psychology assumed the environment shaped development and behaviors in much the same way for everyone, a number of investigators have stressed the importance of considering that different individuals may react quite differently to objectively "similar" environments. The theoretical importance of organism–environment interactive effects has been discussed by a number of authors in a wide variety of substantive areas. In their discussion of the possible role of interactive genotype–environment effects in development, McGuffin and Gottesman (1985) pointed out that

> some geneticists have tended to treat them as "nuisance factors." The biological reality of gene–environment interactions have, however, been amply demonstrated in laboratory animals, at least in which it is possible to breed genetically homogeneous strains and experimentally rear them in differing environments. . . . It seems probable that human beings will exhibit at least as much phenotypic plasticity and gene–environment effects of as much complexity as our laboratory mice. (p. 21)

In addition, they stress that "throughout infancy, childhood, adolescence, adulthood, and senescence, there is a dynamic epigenetic interplay between the changing environment and the changing genetic constitution. Each new stress may evoke latent genetic potentialities that reveal unknown strengths or weaknesses" (p. 30).

Although numerous authors discuss the potential importance of organism–environment interactions in development, there is a fair amount of variation in the conceptualization of the term *interaction*. Recently, a number of authors have attempted to differentiate among different types of organism–environment relationships in order to more clearly delineate what is meant by organism–environment interaction. For example, behavior genetic researchers have stressed the importance of distinguishing between genotype–environment correlation and genotype–environment interaction (Bergeman & Plomin, 1989; McGuffin & Gottesman, 1985; Scarr, 1989). In this sense, *interaction* is used to refer to the differential responses of individuals with different genotypes to a given environment. As discussed by McGuffin and Gottesman (1985), an example of genotype–environment correlation would be if the higher rates of schizophrenia found in lower socioeconomic status (SES) populations were due to a downward (SES) drift by those individuals with a high genetic liability for schizophrenia. However, if the higher rate of schizophrenia in low SES populations were due to the fact that only individuals with a high genetic liability experienced such environments as stressful, then we would have a genotype–environment interaction.

In order to guide the examination of genotype–environment interactions,

Bergeman and Plomin (1989) further distinguished three types of potential interactions. The first type occurs when the environment has a greater impact on individuals with a genotype to score low on a particular trait ("low G"). The second type occurs when the environment affects only those individuals with a genotype to score high on a certain trait ("high G"). The third type occurs when the environment effects both "high G" and "low G" individuals, but in opposite directions. The first two types of interactions are referred to as *ordinal interactions,* and the last type of interaction is referred to as a *disordinal interaction.*

A number of authors outside the field of behavior genetics have also attempted to differentiate among various types of organism–environment relationships (Rutter, 1983). For example, Wachs (1983) differentiated between three kinds of organism–environment relationships. The first is what he considered to be organism–environment interaction, and is defined as differential reactivity of organisms to similar environmental stimulation. An example of one way in which differential organismic reactivity might influence development of child–mother attachment relationship is suggested by Thompson (1986). Infants who are temperamentally difficult (those who cry a lot) will have a harder time picking up contingencies in their caretaking environment. It is much easier for an infant who only cries occasionally to pick up contingent responding by the caregiver. So, two infants could have caregivers rated by observers as equally sensitive, but might have subjectively very different experiences.

As mentioned by McGuffin and Gottesman (1985) and Bergeman and Plomin (1989), there is some fairly good evidence of organism–environment interaction in the animal literature. For example, Cooper and Zubek (1958) used selectively bred "maze dull" and "maze bright" rats raised in either restrictive, normal, or enriched environments. They found that the enriched environment had no effect on the performance of the "maze bright" rats, but improved that of the "maze dull" rats. In contrast, the restricted environment had no effect on the ability of the "maze dull" rats, but was detrimental to the performance of the "maze bright" rats.

More recently, Sackett and his colleagues (Sackett, 1984; Sackett, Ruppenthal, Fahrenbruch, Holm, & Greenough, 1981) found evidence of organism–environment interaction in the development of nonhuman primates. For example, in a series of studies, they found that the effects of social isolation rearing on later development depended on both the species and gender of the primate under investigation. Males appeared to be more affected by social isolation than females. In addition, three different species of macaques showed different behavioral patterns as a result of social isolation rearing. Thus, Sackett (1984) concluded that the "effects of poor rearing experiences can be understood only in interaction with genetic and prenatal variables" (p. 470).

Evidence for organism–environment interaction in human development comes from a number of substantive areas. For example, as discussed by Bergeman and Plomin (1989), behavior geneticists have proposed methods with which to test for genotype–environment interaction in twin and adoption studies. In the adoption method, *genotype* is estimated from the biological parents' scores on some measure of interest. *Environment* is estimated from a measure of the adoptive home environment. Hierarchical multiple regression analysis is then used to test the significance of the genotype–environment interaction term over and above the genotype and environment main effects. Using such methods, Plomin (1990) and his colleagues examined the role of genotype–environment interaction in development using data from two large studies—the Colorado Adoption Project (CAP) and the Swedish Adoption/Twin Study of Aging (SATSA). They found little evidence of genotype–environment interaction for measures of mental development, temperament, and behavior problems in infancy and early childhood. They did find that for a measure of language development, the HOME (Caldwell & Bradley, 1978) Encouraging Developmental Advance factor had a positive effect only for children who scored higher on measures of mental development, whereas a measure of "warmth" of the home had an effect on language development for children who scored lower on measures of mental development.

In addition, the SATSA analyses revealed some genotype–environment interaction effects for personality measures such as extraversion and neuroticism. With regard to the development of neuroticism, it appears that people with low genetic propensity ("low G") are more affected by their environment (as measured by socioeconomic factors) than those individuals with "high G." In addition, the development of extraversion appears to be influenced by measures of familial control only for those individuals with "low G."

Plomin (1990) cautioned that certain behavior genetic designs are more powerful in their ability to detect genotype–environment interaction, and although the percentage of variance accounted for may be small, the interactions they have found may be substantively very important.

A striking example of genotype–environment interaction has been reported by Gottesman and Bertelsen (1989) in their follow-up study of offspring of identical and fraternal twins discordant for schizophrenia. They found that the risk for schizophrenia in the offspring of schizophrenic fraternal twins was 17.4%, and those of their normal co-twins was 2.1%. However, the risk for the offspring of schizophrenic identical twins was 16.8%, and for those of their normal co-twins was 17.4%. Gottesman and Bertelsen thus concluded that "discordance in identical twins may primarily be explained by the capacity of a schizophrenic genotype or diathesis to be unexpressed unless it is released by some kinds of environmental, including nonfamilial, stressors" (p. 867).

Thus, it is clear from both the work in cultural psychology and the investigation of organism–environment interaction, that the environment does not necessarily have the same meaning for all individuals, regardless of who they are.

A TRIARCHIC THEORY OF EXPERIENCE

How might individuals create their own experiences? In earlier publications (McCartney et al., in press; Scarr, 1985; Scarr & McCartney, 1983; Scarr & Weinberg, 1983), we have proposed that people make their own environments in three ways: First, children's genes are necessarily correlated with their environments because parents provide both, so that their experiences are constructed from opportunities positively correlated with their personal characteristics; second, people evoke from others responses correlated with the person's own characteristics; and third, people actively select environments correlated with their interests, talents, and personality characteristics. Although the proposed theory is based on the idea that, given the same "objective" environment, individuals will react differently, Scarr (1989) argued that *genotype–environment correlations,* rather than gene–environment interactions, predominate in the construction of experiences. Many environmental opportunities are taken in by some individuals and not by others, depending on the individuals' characteristics. This selective use of environmental opportunities is better thought of as genotype–environment correlation than as genotype–environment interaction.

The theory of genotype → environment effects holds that genotypes drive experiences. Following Hayes (1962), we proposed that the state of development and the individual characteristics of people shape the experiences they gather from exposures to their environments. People are both individually different and developmentally different in the ways they encode and experience their environments. Experiences the person constructs from exposures to various environments are uniquely correlated to that person's perceptions, cognition, emotions, and more enduring characteristics of intelligence and personality.

General Theory

Following Plomin, DeFries, and Loehlin's (1977) analysis of variances in behavior genetic studies, we proposed that the same concepts could be used in our developmental theory of the determinants of development and individual differences. In this theory there are three ways by which genotypes and environments become correlated.

First, one must take into account the fact that most biological parents provide their children with both genes and home environments. The fact that parents provide both genes and environments means that the child's genes and environments will necessarily be positively correlated. For example, parents who read well and who like to read will be likely to subscribe to magazines and papers, buy and borrow books, take books from the local library, and read to the child. Parents who have reading problems are less likely to expose themselves to this world of literacy, so their children are likely to be reared in a less literate environment. Those same children are also more likely to have reading problems themselves and to prefer nonreading activities. Thus, the reading abilities of parents are likely to be correlated with the reading abilities of their children and with the environments parents provide for their children—a positive genotype–environment effect.

Second, each person at each developmental stage evokes from others responses that positively or negatively reinforce that person's behaviors. Evocative effects have profound effects on a person's self-image and self-esteem throughout the lifespan. Smiling, cheerful infants who evoke positive social interactions from parents and other adults (Wachs & Gruen, 1982) seem likely to form positive impressions of the social world and its attractions. Infants who are fussy, irritable, and who receive negative or neutral interactions with their caregivers and others would seem less likely to form the impression that social interactions are a wonderful source of reinforcement. School-age children from disadvantaged families who are more intelligent and more "spunky" (Garmezy, Masten, & Tellegen, 1984) are more likely to be given positive attention and encouragement by teachers than less intelligent or less spunky children. Adults who are considered physically attractive by others are more likely to be chosen as dates and mates than others considered less attractive. Attractive adults are also more likely to be hired for jobs and more likely to be promoted on those jobs than their less physically attractive peers. Thus, people's own characteristics evoke responses that are correlated with that person's developmental status and individual differences.

Third, each person makes choices about what environments to experience. Past infancy, people who are in a varied environment[2] choose what to

[2]The entire theory depends on people having a varied environment from which to choose and construct experiences. The theory does not apply, therefore, to people with few choices or few opportunities for experiences that match their genotypes. This caveat applies particularly to

attend to and what to ignore. Depending on their personal interests, talents, and personality, people choose pursuits, whether educational, occupational, or leisure activities.

The idea that people assort themselves into environments according to their interests, talents, and personality has a long history in industrial/organizational psychology. People choose occupational environments that correlate with their personal preferences for social interaction or solitary work, for independent or supervised work, salesmanship or social service. Preferences for one kind of work environment or another are correlated with other aspects of personality (Grotevant, Scarr, & Weinberg, 1977; Holland, 1973).

Differences in preferences for work environment turn out to be just as heritable as other aspects of personality (Bouchard, Scarr, & Weinberg, in preparation). Thus, differences in choices among various kinds of environments have been shown to be, in part, functions of the personal characteristics of the individual.

A test of the notion of gene–environment correlation can be seen in a study of reading (Hayes et al., 1989).

> Regression analyses detect a marginally significant skewing of book choices at age 12, but the effect is small. The predicted pattern is clearest among the 14 year olds, but those differences too are relatively small. This age-dependent pattern of skewing is consistent with Scarr and Weinberg's (1983) hypothesis that as children grow older, their experiences are increasingly of their own choosing. That implies that at age 10, children's leisure time book reading may have been influenced by parents, peers, librarians, and teachers, but at 12 and especially 14, reading was largely self-selected. The provisional conclusion is that genotype → experience relationship is weak during this 10 to 14 year period.
>
> By contrast, we found pervasive gender and age differences in book choice, at all ability levels—with all three measures of text difficulty and with both ability indicators. (p. 13)
>
> These measurements on popular children's books showed: (a) the most able British children read approximately 50 percent more than their less able peers (within that four week period), and (b) the average text grows more demanding (lexically) and longer in the older age cohorts. . . . The most able children not only read more books than their peers, those books were slightly more difficult. When this one month language experience is multiplied across years, the highest ability students must have accumulated a huge advantage over their less able peers. They encountered many more uncommon terms and

---

children reared in very disadvantaged circumstances and to adults with little or no choice about occupations and leisure activities.

> non-mundane topics from their reading. *Even if these most able children were no more efficient* in extracting, integrating and retrieving information from what they read than their less able peers, they would still have the much richer language experience from their book reading. If it can be shown that they are also more efficient, their advantage over their peers would be still greater. (p. 14)

Although age and gender differences in reading are large—girls read more than boys; boys read more difficult books than girls, and reading declines with adolescence—still, individual differences in amount of reading and to a lesser extent, difficulty of reading material chosen, are related to students' abilities. There is nothing in the genotype–environment correlation theory to imply that *developmental* differences are unimportant; on the contrary, developmental differences are predicted to be very important, pervasive, and large, based on the same principles as individual differences. For many behaviors, developmental changes, based on genotype–environment experiential correlations, will be much larger than individual variations at any one age.

All of this is in accord with the theory of individual differences in the selection and construction of experience.

Families as Environments

The idea of correlated personal and environmental characteristics has been ignored, and even opposed in developmental psychology (e.g., Rheingold & Cook, 1975). Most attention has been focused on differences among families in the opportunities they provide for their children. Beginning with family differences in social class, however measured, it has been assumed that observations of ubiquitous correlations between family education, occupational status, and income and children's intellectual and other outcomes were caused by differences among families' environments (Scarr, 1985). Clearly, there are family differences; it is not clear that most of those differences are environmental. In fact, among families in the mainstream of Western European and North American societies, differences in family environments seem to have little effect on intellectual and personality outcomes of the children.

This point is worth pondering. How can it be that parents have little effect on the intellectual or personality development of their children? As parents who care, it seems impossible that this could be the case. This is not to say that parents may not have effects on children's self-esteem, motivation, ambitiousness, and other important characteristics. It is to say that parental differences in rearing styles, social class, and income have small effects on the measurable differences in intelligence, interests, and personality among their children.

Family differences have been assumed to be *environmental* differences. However, research on adoptive families and on twins suggest that a proportion of differences between children from different families is related to genetic differences among parents, which is transmitted to their children. Thus, their children have different genes and different interests, talents, and personalities.

All of this is not to say that variations in environments are not related to differences in children's development. In fact, the same body of behavioral genetic literature that illustrates the importance of genetic variation also highlights the importance of environmental variation. As pointed out by Plomin (1990), "the majority of the variance for most behaviors is due to non-genetic factors, the environment" (p. 117). However, the behavior genetic literature points out that for a variety of traits, most of the environmental variance is contributed by nonshared environmental influences. Nonshared environmental influences are those that are not shared by members of a family, that is, they act to make members of a family different from one another. As Plomin and Thompson (1987) highlighted, the aforementioned finding "implies that the unit of environmental transmission is not the family, but rather micro-environments within families" (p. 20).

Good Enough Parents

Good enough, ordinary parents probably have the same effects on their children's development as culturally defined super-parents (Rowe, in press). This comforting idea gives parents a lot more freedom to care for their children in ways they find comfortable for them, and it gives them more freedom from guilt when they deviate (within the normal range) from culturally prescribed norms about parenting. As Richard Weinberg and I noted (Scarr & Weinberg, 1978), children's outcomes do not depend on whether parents take children to the ball game or to a museum so much as they depend on genetic transmission and having a good enough environment that supports children's development to become themselves.

The idea of good enough parents is a constructive step toward recognizing that parents do not have the power to make their children into whatever they want, or in John Watson's (1928) terms, to ruin them in so many ways. Fortunately, evolution has not left development of the human species, nor any other, at the easy mercy of variations in their environments. We are robust and able to adapt to wide-ranging circumstances—a lesson that seems lost on many ethnocentric psychologists. If we were so vulnerable as to be led off the normal developmental track by slight variations in our parenting, we would not have survived.

The flip side of this message proposes that it is not easy to intervene deliberately in children's lives to change their development unless their environments are outside the normal species range. We know how to rescue children from extremely bad circumstances and to return them to normal developmental pathways by providing rearing environments within a normal range. But for children whose development is on a normal trajectory and whose parents are providing a supportive environment, interventions have only temporary and limited effects (Clarke & Clarke, 1989). Should we be surprised? Feeding well-nourished but short children more and more will not make them into basketball players. Feeding average intellects more and more will not make them brilliant. Exposing shy children to socially demanding events will not make them feel less shy. The average intellects and the shy children may gain some specific skills and helpful knowledge of how to behave in specific situations, but they will not be fundamentally changed.

What psychologists need is more respect for individual differences among parents in the ways they rear their children. And we need to take our own textbook advice and actually believe that correlations are not causes. The associations between a child's characteristics, those of the parents, and the rearing environment they provide are neither accidental nor a likely source of fruitful intervention, unless the child's opportunities for normal development are quite limited. Given a wide range of opportunities, our research and that of the past 25 years in behavioral genetics supports the idea that people make their own environments based on their own heritable characteristics.

REFERENCES

Ainsworth, M. D. S., & Wittig, B. (1969). Attachment and exploratory behavior of one-year-olds in a strange situation. In B. Foss (Ed.), *Determinants of infant behavior* (Vol. 4, pp. 233–253). London: Methuen.

Bandura, A. (1982). The psychology of chance encounters and life paths. *American Psychologist, 37,* 747–755.

Bell, R. Q. (1968). A reinterpretation of the direction of effects in studies of socialization. *Psychological Review, 75,* 81–95.

Bell, R., & Harper, L. (1977). *Child effects on adults.* Lincoln, NB: University of Nebraska Press.

Bergeman, C. S., & Plomin, R. (1989). Genotype-environmental interaction. In M. H. Bornstein & J. S. Bruner (Eds.), *Interaction in human development* (pp. 157–171). Hillsdale, NJ: Lawrence Erlbaum Associates.

Berscheid, E., & Walster, E. (1974). Physical attractiveness. In L. Berkowitz (Ed.), *Advances in experimental social psychology* (pp. 157–215). New York: Academic Press.

Bouchard, T., Scarr, S., & Weinberg, R. (in preparation). *Vocational interests among relatives of varying genetic relatedness.*

Bower, G. H. (1987). Commentary on mood and memory. *Behavior Research and Therapy, 25,* 443–455.

Breitmayer, B. J., & Ricciuti, H. N. (1988). The effect of neonatal temperament on caregiver behavior in the newborn nursery. *Infant Mental Health Journal, 9(2),* 158–172.

Caldwell, B. M., & Bradley, R. H. (1978). *Home observation for measurement of the environment.* Little Rock, AR: University of Arkansas.

Clarke, A. M., & Clarke, A. D. B. (1976). *Early experience: Myth and evidence.* New York: Free Press.

Clarke, A. M., & Clarke, A. D. B. (1989). The later cognitive effects of early intervention. *Intelligence, 13,* 289–297.

Clarke-Stewart, A. (1989). Infant day care: Maligned or malignant? *American Psychologist, 44,* 266–273.

Cole, M. (1990). *Cultural psychology: A once and future discipline?* (Report No. 131). San Diego, La Jolla, CA: Center for Human Information Processing, University of California.

Cooper, R. M., & Zubek, J. P. (1958). Effects of enriched and restricted early environments on the learning ability of bright and dull rats. *Canadian Journal of Psychology, 12,* 159–164.

Dumaret, A., & Stewart, J. (1985). IQ, scholastic performance and behaviour of sibs raised in contrasting environments. *Journal of Child Psychology and Psychiatry and Allied Disciplines, 26,* 553–580.

Eysenck, H. J. (1982). Why do conditional responses show incrementation, while unconditional responses show habituation? *Behavioural Psychotherapy, 10,* 217–220.

Eysenck, H. J. (1983). Human learning and individual differences: The genetic dimension. *Educational Psychology, 3,* 169–188.

Garmezy, N., Masten, A., & Tellegen, A. (1984). The study of stress and competence in children: A building block for developmental psychopathology. *Child Development, 55,* 97–111.

Gottesman, I. I., & Bertelsen, A. (1989). Confirming unexpressed genotypes for schizophrenia. *Archives of General Psychiatry, 46,* 867–872.

Greenfield, P. M., Brazelton, T. B., & Childs, C. P. (1989). From birth to maturity in Zinacantan: Ontogenesis in cultural context. In V. Bricker & G. Gossen (Eds.) *Ethnographic encounters in Southern Mesoamerica: Celebratory essays in honor of Evon Z. Vogt* (pp. 177–216). Albany, NY: Institute of Mesoamerican Studies, State University of New York.

Grotevant, H. D., Scarr, S., & Weinberg, R. A. (1977). Patterns of interest similarity in adoptive and biological families. *Journal of Personality and Social Psychology, 35,* 667–676.

Hartmann, H. (1958). *Ego psychology and the problem of adaptation.* New York: International Universities Press.

Hayes, D., Whitehead, F., Wellings, A., Thompson, W., Marschlke, C., & Moran, M. (1989, November). *How strongly do genes drive children's choice of experiences?* (Tech. Rep. No. 89-13). Ithaca, NY: Cornell University.

Hayes, K. J. (1962). Genes, drives, and intellect. *Psychological Reports, 10,* 299–342.

Holland, J. L. (1973). *Making vocational choices: A theory of careers.* Englewood Cliffs, NJ: Prentice-Hall.

Jensen, A. R. (1989). Review. Raising IQ without increasing *g? Developmental Review, 9,* 234–258.

Kagan, J., Reznick, J. S., & Gibbons, J. (1989). Inhibited and uninhibited types of children. *Child Development, 60,* 838–845.

Kluckhohn, C., Murray, H. A., & Schneider, D. M. (Eds.). (1953). *Personality in nature, society, and culture* (2nd ed.). New York: Knopf.

Langlois, J. H., & Roggman, L. A. (1990). Attractive faces are only average. *Psychological Science, 1,* 115–121.

LeVine, R. A. (1987). *Beyond the "average expectable environment" of psychoanalysis: Cultural Differences in mother–infant interaction.* Paper presented at American Anthropological Association Meeting, Chicago, IL.

LeVine, R. A., & Miller, P. M. (in press). Strange situations in other cultures: An anthropological view of infant–mother attachment. *Human Development.*

Lytton, H. (1980). *Parent–child interaction.* New York: Plenum.

McCartney, K., Robeson, W. W., Jordan, E., & Mouradian, V. (in press). Mothers' language with first- and second-born children: A within-family study. In K. Pillemer & K. McCartney (Eds.), *Parent–child relations throughout life.* Hillsdale, NJ: Lawrence Erlbaum Associates.

McGuffin, P., & Gottesman, I. I. (1985). Genetic influences on normal and abnormal development. In M. Rutter & L. Hersov (Eds.), *Child and adolescent psychiatry* (pp. 17–33). Oxford: Blackwell Scientific.

Pedersen, N. L., Gatz, M., Plomin, R., & McClearn, G. E. (1989). Individual differences in locus of control during the second half of the life span for identical and fraternal twins reared apart and reared together. *Journals of Gerontology, 44*(4), 100–105.

Phillips, D., McCartney, K., Scarr, S., & Howes, C. (1987, February). Selective review of infant day care research: A cause for concern! *Zero to Three, 7,* 18–21.

Plomin, R. (1986). *Development, genetics, and psychology.* Hillsdale, NJ: Lawrence Erlbaum Associates.

Plomin, R. (1990). *Nature and nurture.* Pacific Grove, CA: Brooks/Cole.

Plomin, R., & Daniels, D. (1987). Why are children in the same family so different from one another? *Behavioral and Brain Sciences, 10,* 1–60.

Plomin, R., DeFries, J. C., & Loehlin, J. C. (1977). Genotype–environment interaction and correlation in the analysis of human behavior. *Psychological Bulletin, 84,* 309–322.

Plomin, R., & Thompson, R. (1987). Life-span developmental behavioral genetics. In P. B. Baltes, D. L. Featherman, & R. M. Lerner (Eds.), *Life-span development and behavior* (Vol. 8, pp. 1–31). Hillsdale, NJ: Lawrence Erlbaum Associates.

Ramey, C., Bryant, D. M., & Suarez, T. M. (1986). Preschool compensatory education and the modifiability of intelligence: A critical review. In D. Detterman (Ed.), *Current topics in human intelligence* (pp. 247–296). Norwood, NJ: Ablex.

Rheingold, H. L., & Cook, K. V. (1975). The contents of boys' and girls' rooms as an index of parents' behavior. *Child Development, 46,* 459–463.

Rowe, D. C. (in press). As the twig is bent?: The myth of child rearing influences on personality development. *Journal of Counseling and Development.*

Rutter, M. (1983). Statistical and personal interactions: Facets and perspectives. In D. Magnusson & V. L. Allen (Eds.), *Human development: An interactional perspective* (pp. 295–319). New York: Academic Press.

Sackett, G. P. (1984). A nonhuman primate model of risk for deviant development. *American Journal of Mental Deficiency, 88*(5), 469–476.

Sackett, G. P., Ruppenthal, G. C., Fahrenbruch, C. E., Holm, R. A., & Greenough, W. T. (1981). Social isolation rearing effects in monkeys vary with genotype. *Developmental Psychology, 17*(3), 313–318.

Scarr, S. (1985). Constructing psychology: Making facts and fables for our times. *American Psychologist, 40,* 499–512.

Scarr, S. (1989). How genotypes and environments combine: Development and individual differences. In G. Downey, A. Caspi, & N. Bolger (Eds.), *Interacting systems in human development* (pp. 217–244). New York: Cambridge University Press.

Scarr, S., & McCartney, K. (1983). How people make their own environments: A theory of genotype → environment effects. *Child Development, 54,* 424–435.

Scarr, S., & Weinberg, R. A. (1978). The influence of "family background" on intellectual attainment. *American Sociological Review, 43,* 674–692.

Scarr, S., & Weinberg, R. A. (1983). The Minnesota adoption studies: Genetic differences and malleability. *Child Development, 54,* 260–267.

Shepard, R. N. (1987). Toward a universal law of generalization for psychological science. *Science, 237,* 1317–1323.

Shweder, R. A. (1990). Cultural psychology—what is it? In J. W. Stigler, R. A. Shweder, & G. Herdt (Eds.), *Cultural psychology* (pp. 1–43). New York: Cambridge University Press.

Stigler, J. W., Lee, S., & Stevenson, H. W. (1987). Mathematics classrooms in Japan, Taiwan, and the United States. Special Issue: Schools and development. *Child Development, 58,* 1272–1285.

Thompson, R. A. (1986). Temperament, emotionality, and infant social cognition. In J. V. Lerner & R. M. Lerner (Eds.), *Temperament and social interaction in infants and children. New directions for child development, no. 31* (pp. 35–52). San Francisco: Jossey-Bass.

Turkheimer, E. (1990). *Individual and group differences in adoption studies of IQ: One (and only one) realm of development.* Manuscript submitted for publication.

Wachs, T. D. (1983). The use and abuse of environment in behavior-genetic research. *Child Development, 54,* 416–423.

Wachs, T. D., & Gruen, G. (1982). *Early experience and human development.* New York: Plenum.

Watson, J. (1928). *Psychological care of infant and child.* New York: Norton.

Wexler, B. E., Schwartz, G., Warrenburg, S., Servis, M., & Tarlatzis, I. (1986). Effects of emotion on perceptual asymmetry: Interactions with personality. *Neuropsychologia, 24,* 699–710.

CHAPTER 2

Intellectual Functioning in Children Born Preterm: Recent Research

LEILA BECKWITH
CAROL RODNING
University of California at Los Angeles

Prematurity exposes children to a wide range of biological and social vulnerabilities that have the potential to compromise normal developmental processes. The vast majority of studies find that children born preterm show an increased incidence of a range of cognitive difficulties from mental retardation to problems in learning and attention (Cohen, 1986; Kopp, 1983). Yet, all children are not affected in the same manner or to the same degree. Some children develop normally from the beginning; others seem to have transitory problems with delays that appear early then dissipate; still others appear to have subtle effects that interfere with effective learning throughout the school years and maybe into adulthood; and some are severely compromised. Therefore, children born preterm are a prototypic group for examining, in all its complexity, the influences of both normal and deviant early developmental abilities and experiences on outcome. It is also an opportunity to study the complex interrelationship between biological and social factors in development.

This chapter reviews primarily research published in the 1980s. The studies focus on the preterm infants who are most at risk, that is, those of lowest birthweight and shortest gestational age, and/or those with severe perinatal physiological derangements resulting in evident brain insult, or respiratory failure, requiring mechanical ventilation for survival. A few investigations were continuations into late childhood and adolescence of previously studied cohorts, born in previous decades, surviving with fewer technological interventions. This chapter addresses three major questions about preterm children:

1. What are the consequences of preterm birth for cognitive functioning?
2. Which children within the preterm group show deficits?
3. What are the processes by which normal or superior development versus poor development occur?

The first question has been called a *product question.* Studies addressed to the other two questions have been categorized as *process studies* (Hoy, Bill, & Sykes, 1988).

The ways in which these three questions are asked influence the information found and contribute to the conflicting conclusions made about the deleterious impact of prematurity. The product question, guided by the issue of whether these individuals will be able to function in adulthood, tends to focus on developmental handicaps known to interfere with adequate functioning such as cerebral palsy, severe sensory deficits, and mental retardation.

The second question is often construed as one of early identification or *prediction.* Prediction attempts to delineate risk and protective factors that will discriminate those children born preterm who will have cognitive or neurological problems from those who will not. The inclusion of multiple factors enhances prediction, so the work is often directed to determining a "cumulative risk index" (Broman, 1989; McCarton & Vaughan, 1984; Siegel et al., 1982; Stewart, 1983) that accounts for individual differences in subsequent development. One important goal is to be able to identify more accurately and earlier those children and their families who will need special services so as to make a more informed allocation of medical, social, and educational resources.

The third question tries to understand the process of developmental trajectories and environmental transactions in order to illuminate those principles that direct the development of normal as well as atypical children. Such studies of process collect data longitudinally, and assess the biological history of the child, the infants' own behavior, the social context of the family, attitudes of the parents, and the parent–child relationship (Cohen, Parmelee, Sigman, & Beckwith, 1988; Greenberg & Crnic, 1988). The research is predicated on a developmental model in which children's development is a result of reciprocal influences and mutual regulation between the rearing environment and the infants' own capacities, determined genetically, as well as by prenatal and perinatal biological factors (Sameroff & Chandler, 1975). Whereas identifying those preterm infants who are more at risk for later problems may determine who receives intervention, understanding how biological and social forces interact with one another guides the nature of the intervention. Although studies addressed to the second and third questions have somewhat different emphases, they often overlap methodologically and conceptually.

OUTCOME STUDIES

Medical Factors and Outcomes

Prematurity is not a single entity but a marker event associated with obstetrical and perinatal hazardous factors, and postnatally with increased risk for pulmonary disease, acute respiratory illness, serious and protracted illness, rehospitalizations, and stress on the stability of the family system (McCormick, 1985).

Infants born preterm are not a homogeneous group as to the nature or severity of biologic hazards experienced. Even when born at similar birthweights or gestational ages, they differ in the type and severity of physiological derangements that occur, and in the medical interventions received. The impact of prematurity on later cognitive functioning is influenced by the occurrence of multiple perinatal events in the context of birthweight and gestational age (McCarton & Vaughan, 1984). Moreover, the caregiving behaviors and environment within the intensive care unit have been shown to alter outcome (Als et al., 1986).

Physiological problems in the perinatal period often appear overwhelming. Yet some infants who experience serious perinatal complications go on to develop into competent children. Unraveling the effects of physiological disturbances during the perinatal period on later development has been difficult. It is only recently becoming clearer which of the many medical problems (e.g., apnea, hypoxia, intraventricular hemorrhage, respiratory distress syndrome, hydrocephalus) are hazardous to cognitive development.

We are now able to provide better medical care for smaller, sicker, and more immature neonates than before due to our improved physiological knowledge and ability to monitor crucial physiological processes such as blood gases and glucose levels, thus the preterm infants of 1,500 to 2,500 grams now suffer less physiological and brain insult. However, because we are now able to maintain survival for the more fragile, immature newborns who would not have survived previously, and because the extrauterine environment is hazardous to such immature organisms, they are more likely to be physiologically and neurologically compromised. Therefore, although the survival rate has increased for preterms, the rate of disability remains similar to previous decades (McCormick, 1985).

Birthweight Groups

Prematurity refers to early birth defined as gestational age of 37 weeks or less. Birthweight is often substituted for age because it is difficult to precisely measure gestational age. Prematurity then becomes defined as birthweight equal to or less than 2,500 grams. Advances in medicine and technology have made it possible for very young and small infants to survive, thus subdivisions within prematurity based on birthweight have emerged. Very low birthweight (VLBW) children are born under 1,500 grams and extremely low birthweight (ELBW) are under 1,000 grams.

There has been much recent interest in the outcomes of preterms born very early and very small. Improved medical technology and knowledge has resulted in a dramatic reduction in neonatal mortality within these groups. For example, in one study mortality rate of infants born under 1,000 grams was reported to be 75% for 1979–1980, and 58% in 1984 (Zubrick, McCartney, & Stanley, 1988). Although the survival rate has increased over the 4-year period, the majority of children born in the extremely low birthweight and gestational age group are not surviving even with the advances in medicine. Surprisingly, it appears that there has been no change in handicap rate over time; although the absolute number of impaired infants has increased, so has the absolute number of normal survivors.

Very Low Birthweight. Several investigations suggest that being born at very low birthweight increases the percentage of children with neurological damage, both when compared to other categories of prematurity and when compared to full-term children. For example, children born preterm, below and over 1,500 grams, were compared as preschoolers. The groups did not differ on IQ scores, but the two birthweight groups were statistically different as to neurological abnormalities, with a higher percentage of children with moderate or severe abnormalities in vision, hearing, and motor tone in those born under 1,500 grams (McCarton & Vaughan, 1984). Comparing the school performance of two groups of preterms, Grunau (1986) found that infants born under 1,750 grams had lower scores than heavier preterms weighing 1,751 to 2,041 grams in arithmetic and reading from kindergarten through sixth grade, even when social class and maternal education were controlled. When children with an IQ less than 80 or with evident neurological problems were excluded, differences between birthweight categories disappeared. Therefore, the effects of very low birthweight may be to increase the number of children with handicaps, rather than to decrease cognitive abilities in all children within the group.

However, other studies that compared the very low birthweight preterms to fullterms and excluded children with overt neurological handicaps still have found very low birthweight children to show decreased cognitive functioning. In one study by Lloyd and associates (Lloyd, Wheldall, & Perks, 1988) in which intelligence and school performance at age 7 of very low birthweight children were compared to a matched control group, very low birthweight children gained lower IQ scores (93.1 vs. 100.4). When very low and extremely low birthweight preterm groups are compared to a full-term group, there is a tendency for the distinction between the two preterm groups to be obscured by the much greater competence of the fullterms.

The increased neurological difficulties and decreased IQ scores appear to lead to increased difficulties in school achievement. Lloyd (1984) described the outcome of a group of very low birthweight infants at ages 3 to 7 years and compared with their full birthweight siblings. Whereas 49% of the very low birthweight children of school age were performing poorly at school, only 13% had poor school performance in the sibling group.

Extremely Low Birthweight. Infants born weighing less than 1,001 grams at birth show a survival rate of 36% to 51%, and of those, about 22% to 35% have severe handicaps and 40% to 66% are considered to be developing adequately by age 2 (Hack & Fanaroff, 1988; Hirata et al., 1983; Horgan, Perlman, Sonnekalb, & Testi, 1984; Kitchen, Ford, Rickards, Lissenden, & Ryan, 1987; Kitchen et al., 1987; Rothberg et al., 1983; Saigal, Rosenbaum, & Stoskopf, 1984; Skouteli, Dubowitz, Leven, & Miller, 1985).

There may be an inverse relationship between mortality and morbidity, however, with decreased survival rates linked to decreased morbidity in the survivors. Children who survive with fewer technological interventions of shorter duration have better cognitive outcomes. Intensive care techniques, even though they help increase survival, are themselves hazardous to the organization and coherence of central nervous system functioning. Thus, one study of infants born weighing less than 800 grams at birth was found to have a survival rate of only 20%, but of the babies who managed to survive, 81% were normal in development at least until age 3 (Bennett, Robinson, & Sells, 1983). At age 3, the mean IQ of the sample was 106, with a range from 90 to 127.

Unfortunately, even among those considered to be developing adequately and who appeared to have escaped the adverse sequelae of extremely low birthweight, a large percentage have school problems. In one study, for example, of school-age survivors of birthweights from 501 to 1,000 grams, 68% were found to be "unimpaired," that is, without cerebral palsy, hydrocephalus, hearing loss, and with IQ's above 85 (Lefebvre, Bard, Veilleux, & Martel, 1988). However, 57% were having difficulty in regular classes or needed special education. Another study of extremely low birthweight children at age 10 found only 28% functioning at average or above-average levels, because 64% were in special educational classes (Nickel, Bennett, & Lamson, 1982). The high incidence of school-related problems even with average or better IQ's illustrates the cognitive vulnerability in the very low birthweight groups.

Physiological Systems

The cardiopulmonary system and the brain are two interrelated physiological systems that are highly vulnerable to disturbance from premature birth and are therefore studied extensively. Derangements in the cardiovascular system lead to acute and chronic hypoxia and respiratory assistance with external mechanical procedures increases the incidence of brain hemorrhage for young preterms.

Respiratory Distress Syndrome. The most common physiological disorder of the young and light preterms is the inability to breathe on their own; they require external mechanical ventilatory assistance in order to survive. Respiratory distress syndrome (RDS) represents a continuum of impairment in pulmonary functioning from difficulties requiring short duration assistance to severe chronic bronchopulmonary dysplasia (BPD). Respiratory distress is most common in the smallest infants who are hospitalized the longest and they tend to suffer an increased incidence of the severest form, that is, bronchopulmonary dysplasia. The incidence of respiratory distress syndrome is greater than 50% in infants with birthweights less than 1,500 grams (Korones, 1981). Whereas approximately 30% of newborns born at weights less than 1,500 grams require mechanical ventilatory assistance, approximately 70% of those with birthweights less than 1,000 grams will need such assistance, and almost 70% of those will go on to have bronchopulmonary dysplasia or chronic lung disease.

Even preterm birthweight subgroups are not homogeneous in the nature and severity of physiological disorders, and it may be the specific physiological derangements rather than birthweights per se that are hazardous to development (Stewart, Reynolds, & Lipscomb, 1981), consequently researchers are beginning to compare medically distinct subgroups within the prematures (Meisels, Plunkett, Pasick, Stiefel, & Roloff, 1987). Meisels and associates compared three preterm groups differing in degree and length of respiratory illness as well as length of hospitalization and matched on social class, parity, or number of parents in the family. Those who had suffered respiratory illness that lasted more than 3 weeks (a condition that often precipitates BPD) compared to those who had not experienced respiratory illness and those with respiratory illness that had resolved within 3 weeks, had significantly lower scores on the Bayley Scales of Infant Development (Bayley, 1969) and the Uzgiris–Hunt Scales of Infant Psychological Development (Uzgiris & Hunt, 1975).

Similarly, other investigators have found decreased cognitive functioning mainly for the children with bronchopulmonary dysplasia and fewer cognitive deficits for children with less severe forms of respiratory distress syndrome. In toddlerhood when children with bronchopulmonary dysplasia were excluded there were no differences between toddlers born prematurely who had experienced respiratory distress syndrome, and toddlers born healthy and at term (Landry et al., 1984), even when differences had existed earlier in infancy. However, when children with bronchopulmonary dysplasia were included in the large study of 126 very low birthweight infants grouped by incidence of early medical complications (RDS with and without intraventricular hemorrhage or BPD), those children who had experienced respiratory distress syndrome performed within the average range by 2 years and showed much better Bayley scores than those with bronchopulmonary dysplasia. When follow-up was done at age 3, those with respiratory distress syndrome continued to score significantly higher as measured by the Stanford–Binet Intelligence Scale (Terman & Merrill, 1960) and the Sequenced Inventory of Communication Development than those with bronchopulmonary dysplasia. Furthermore, when the children with bronchopulmonary dysplasia were divided into those who were hospitalized for less than or more than 16 weeks, no child in the longer hospitalization group had age-appropriate scores on any measure, whereas the range of scores for children with shorter hospitalizations was wide, ranging from retarded to average (Landry, Chapieski, Fletcher, & Denson, 1988). In contrast to Landry's previously reported study, preterms in all subgroups scored significantly lower on standardized intelligence tests than the full birthweight controls.

Persistence into early childhood of abnormal cardiopulmonary function is characteristic of infants who require prolonged ventilatory support. By the age of 1 year, for example, about 40% of infants with respiratory distress syndrome born less than 1,500 grams have been rehospitalized in comparison to 8.7% of full-term infants (McCormick, 1985). The effects of repeated hospitalizations, and/or chronic illness and its attendant complications such as reduced energy and activity must be considered as potential additional hazards to development. Werner and Smith (1982) found that repeated or serious illnesses during infancy was one of the significant stressful life events associated with maladaptive outcomes in children.

Cerebral Intraventricular Hemorrhage (IVH). The most common serious brain insult encountered in preterms is periventricular-intraventricular hemorrhage. Computerized tomography (CT scans) and ultrasonography, noninvasive procedures, now make it possible to identify intracranial lesions in living infants, even when the hemorrhages are clinically silent. Hemorrhages have been reported in 40% to 50% of surviving very low birthweight infants born under 1,500 grams (Landry et al., 1984).

When intraventricular hemorrhages were first identified, it was assumed that this severe insult to the brain explained the increased incidence of cognitive deficits especially in the very low birthweight children. Studies investigating the effects of intraventricular hemorrhages show conflicting results, however. Although major handicaps are overrepresented in children who show brain hemorrhage, not all children with hemorrhages have difficulties, and the absence of a hemorrhage is no guarantee of good cognitive development. It may be that it is the degree of tissue damage that results from the hemorrhage rather than the bleeding itself that is related to later cognitive outcomes. When the tissue damage is so extensive that it can be detected with present techniques, major handicaps are found in a large percentage of children.

One study of 294 infants tested at the corrected age of 2 years, found that children with the most extensive hemorrhages had significantly more major and minor handicaps (52.9%) than children without cerebral bleeds (17.8%) (Van de Bor, Vanhorick, Baerts, Brand, & Ruys, 1988). A group of infants with and without intraventricular hemorrhages during the neonatal period were assessed at age 3 $\frac{1}{2}$ by the Stanford–Binet Intelligence Scale and the Reynell Developmental Language Scales. The mean IQ of preterm children without hemorrhage was 106, whereas those with hemorrhage was 95. The decreased functioning could not be ascribed to a few children with obvious neurological dysfunctioning because children with neonatal hemorrhages compared to those without were found to perform more poorly on the McCarthy Scales at age 5, despite normal Bayley Mental Development Index (MDI) scores at age 1.

Other studies indicate that cognitive problems are restricted to only those children with the most severe hemorrhages, those that result in ventricular dilatation, cerebral atrophy, and/or hydrocephalus (Daum, Danziger, Ruff, & Vaughan, 1983; Fawer, Diebold, & Calame, 1987). In a comparison of 198 surviving very low birthweight infants with and without cerebral intraventricular hemorrhage, major handicaps were found in 10% of infants without intraventricular hemorrhage and 28% of infants with intraventricular hemorrhage. Among infants with intraventricular hemorrhage, 76% of major handicaps were found for those with Grade 4, the most severe hemorrhage, 36% for Grade 3, whereas Grades 1 and 2, the least severe, did not increase infants' risk for major handicaps (Papile, Munsick-Bruno, & Schaefer, 1983). Similarly, infants without hemorrhage or uncomplicated periventricular hemorrhage showed an 11% incidence of neurodevelopmental disorder in comparison to 88% of those with hydrocephalus or cerebral atrophy (Stewart et al., 1987). At age 4 children with hydrocephalus and/or cerebral atrophy showed 56% major handicaps versus 7% for children without hemorrhages or with uncomplicated periventricular hemorrhages (Costello et al., 1988).

Other studies show that the relationship between perinatal hemorrhages and later developmental problems may dissipate over time. Bayley MDI scores of infants with Grade-4 bleeds were significantly lower than all other children at age 1; by age 2, there were no longer any significant differences. Moreover, there was substantial variability of scores within each intraventricular hemorrhage group (Sostek, Smith, Katz, & Grant, 1987).

Furthermore, because intraventricular hemorrhages rarely occur without respiratory distress syndrome, it is often unclear whether developmental disturbances, when found, are due to the hemorrhage, the respiratory distress, or the long hospitalizations resulting from the multiple and severe medical complications (Papile, Burstein, Burstein, & Koffler, 1978).

Landry (Landry et al., 1984) concluded that uncomplicated intraventricular hemorrhage, in the absence of chronic lung disease, does not impair cognition.

Summary of Medical Factors

In general, severe medical complications associated with preterm birth influence developmental outcome for at least the first 3 years (Landry et al., 1988). In the absence of catastrophic physiological derangements, differences in medical status among preterms has either a weak or no association with later development (Astbury, Orgill, Bajuk, & Yu, 1983; Cohen & Parmelee, 1983; Escalona, 1982; Greenberg & Crnic, 1988) or it explains only a small proportion of the variance in later competence (Bennett, Robinson, & Sells, 1982).

Cognitive Developmental Outcomes

Differential Abilities. Studies examining medical factors, such as those already reported, often are focused on evaluating the effectiveness of medical diagnostic or therapeutic procedures. For the purposes of such studies it is important to know the percentage of infants who are grossly or mildly handicapped. For the purposes of this chapter, those reports do not tell how successfully or with what difficulty children function in stage-salient, cognitive tasks. In addition, when studies report only the incidence of handicapping conditions without reporting the range of scores, the remarkable variability associated with the self-righting nature of development and the resiliency of many children and families are obscured.

The complexity of cognitive functioning requires that more than intelligence tests be used as the standard of the effect of prematurity. Studies that use multiple measures that test multiple functions are helpful in defining the specificity of effects within groups of children born preterm.

Visual Perceptual and Visual Motor Tasks. Very low birthweight children have significantly more problems with visual perceptual and visual motor tasks (Fitzhardinge & Ramsey, 1973; Francis-Williams & Davies, 1974; Hunt, Tooley, & Harvin, 1982; Siegel, 1983b) even when there is not a significant difference in IQ between preterms and the full birthweight controls. One study exemplifies the common findings. Very low birthweight children at age 5, selected to be neurologically normal and to have IQ's greater than 85, were compared to matched controls, full-term classmates. Despite the equality in general intelligence level for both groups, with a mean IQ of 108, the very low birthweight children performed significantly poorer in perceptual and visual motor function, but not on picture vocabulary, memory for sentences, visual auditory learning, and quantitative concepts. Their scores were lower on the Developmental Test of Visual Motor Integration (Beery, 1982) and the spatial relations subtest of the Woodcock–Johnson Psycho-Educational Battery (Klein, Hack, & Breslau, 1989; Klein, Hack, Gallagher, & Fanaroff, 1985).

Language. There is some evidence that language development is more likely to be delayed or disrupted in preterm children. There are conflicting findings as to whether the deficits endure or are transient, and whether they are specific to language or reflect more general intelligence. Because IQ assessments are so dependent on verbal skills, it is difficult to control for IQ level without also diminishing the variability in language ability.

Some studies find that preterm children (even when tested at corrected age) acquire language skills more slowly. Low birthweight infants compared to full-term infants at age 2 have shown significantly lower receptive and expressive scores on a variety of standardized measures, including the Peabody Picture Vocabulary Test and the Reynell Language Scales (Siegel et al., 1982; Vohr, Coll, & Oh, 1988). Additionally, in a systematic analysis of a taped sample, recorded during play between mother and child, preterms with respiratory distress at birth had shorter mean length of utterance and more limited vocabularies than full-term children (Field, Dempsey, & Shuman, 1981).

Preterm children may show poorer language skills past the infancy period into preschool and the early elementary school years. Very low birthweight children at age 3 when compared to their siblings and to a normal control group on language, memory, reasoning, and visual-motor integration performed more poorly on receptive vocabulary and on auditory sequential memory, from the Illinois Test of Psycholinguistic Ability (Klein, Raziel, Brish, & Birenbaum, 1987). At age 4, low birthweight children compared to full birthweight controls did more poorly in following oral directions in sequence, used fewer prepositions, conjunctives, and had shorter sentence length (Washington, McBurney, & Grunau, 1986) but did not differ in the easier tasks of pointing to named objects or in use of nouns, verbs, and adjectives (Washington et al., 1986). The groups were not comparable in full-scale IQ. A study in Scandinavia assessed very low birthweight children at age 9 (Michelsson, Lindahl, Parre, & Helenius, 1984). Even when the children with severe handicaps were excluded, the low birthweight children performed significantly less well than the controls on processes believed to underlie language, including visual reception, visual sequential memory, auditory association, and auditory closure, as measured by subtests of the Illinois Test of Psycholinguistic Ability. These groups also differed in general intelligence.

Other investigators, however, either report no differences or early differences that disappear over time (Bakeman & Brown, 1980; Greenberg & Crnic, 1988; O'Connor, 1980). Although, preterms scored significantly lower than fullterms at 12 months, (Crnic et al., 1983) the groups did not differ at 24 months in either receptive vocabulary or mean length of utterance (Dale, Greenberg, & Crnic, 1987). No differences between preterm and full-term children were found at age 3 (Bakeman & Brown, 1980). Most of the deficiencies of prematures in comparison to full-term infants were not evident on the Reynell Scale by the age of 3, although significant delays in language were apparent at age 2 (Ungerer & Sigman, 1983). At age 5, there were no differences on the Illinois Test of Psycholinguistic Ability or the Peabody Picture Vocabulary Test (Siegel, 1983a).

Language is one of the most complex cognitive abilities, is vulnerable to environmental influences, and is likely influenced by social and emotional factors within the individual. Disruptions to the language learning process are developmentally significant and require more investigation to reconcile the conflicting findings.

Unevenness of Functioning Within Individual Children. Whereas the previous studies looked for between group differences in specific cognitive functions, several investigators stress the importance of unevenness of functioning within individual preterms as evidence of cognitive dysfunction. When children with low IQ scores, or visual-motor disability, or children whose verbal IQ scores were significantly discrepant from performance IQ scores, either higher or lower by 15 points, were categorized as deviant, Hunt and her associates (Hunt, Cooper, & Tooley, 1988) identified only 36% of their sample of very low birthweight children as having adequate development. The results must be taken with caution because there was no comparison group, so that the percent of unevenness in functioning that exists in fullterms is unknown. However, in a study of 335 low birthweight children compared to full-term controls at age 6 ½, 18% low birthweight and only 7% controls were found to have significant discrepancies between verbal and performance IQ scores, or IQ and Goodenough–Harris drawing scores, or IQ and scores on the Bender–Gestalt test (Dunn et al., 1986). When the children were tested at age 13, on a battery of tests, including the Wechsler Intelligence Scale for Children (WISC), Bender–Gestalt, Porteus mazes, embedded figures, behavior rating scales, academic achievement tests, and psychiatric interviews, the preterm group identified 6 years previously with significant unevenness of functioning, scored significantly below other groups in IQ, academic achievement tests, perceptual tests, and visual-motor coordination. More of them were also judged to be abnormal psychiatrically (40% compared to 12% in the full-term group).

Attention Deficit Disorder/Problems in Focused Attention. There is some evidence that very low birthweight children have significantly more difficulty following directions and attending to tasks. A cluster of behaviors, low frustration tolerance, either hyperactivity or sluggishness, brief attention span, and distractibility were noted to occur more commonly in children born preterm versus fullterm, particularly in preterm males by Drillien (1964) and Neligan, Kolvin, Scott, and Garside, (1976). In a study in which very low birthweight children did not differ in IQ from their full birthweight classroom peers, teachers still rated the very low birthweight children as lower on task orientation, as well as visual/auditory skills, and verbal expression (Klein et al., 1989). Contrary to popular belief, the very low birthweight children were not rated as more active, impulsive, or disruptive; on the contrary, they were judged to be more passive.

School Achievement. Many studies agree that a high percentage of children born early and are of low birthweight have significant learning problems. The percentage of such children in special educational programs is very high. For children born under 1,000 grams, the rates range from 51% to 68% (Eilers, Desai, Wilson, & Cunningham, 1986; Nickel et al., 1982), and for children born under 1,500 grams the rate ranges from 28% to 54% (Lloyd, 1984; Vohr & Garcia-Coll, 1985) in comparison to a 3% rate reported for normal birthweight siblings (Lloyd, 1984) or 24% to 25% rate in the general school populations studied (Eilers et al., 1986; Grunau, 1986).

Part of the increased incidence of school problems can be attributed to the increased percentage of neurological problems, sensory deficits, and low IQ within the preterm population. However, excluding such children from analysis, or using IQ scores as a covariate, diminishes but does not erase the differences between preterm and full-term groups (Dunn et al., 1986). The poor educational achievements of many preterm children, therefore, cannot be attributed completely to decreased general intelligence.

Although there may be either no differences or only minor differences in intelligence at ages 2 and 3, differences may begin to emerge during the early school years as deficits become more evident in the developmental skills necessary for successful school achievement (Siegel, 1984). In the school setting it is not only IQ differences that become important, but difficulties in following directions, poorer task orientation, and problems in visual-motor integration (Klein et al., 1989).

Low birthweight infants, compared to matched classroom controls, were assessed at the end of first grade. Poor reading was identified for 18.6% of the full-term controls and 29% of the low birthweight children (Zubrick et al., 1988).

Very low birthweight children show even more problems in academic achievement than the low birthweight group. When classroom performance of very low birthweight children at ages 5 to 8 years was compared with peers (Eilers et al., 1986) approximately one half of the very low birthweight children required special education—either remedial instruction to perform at grade level or placement in special classes—as compared to 24% of the general school population. Another study also reported 54% of very low birthweight children at age 7 required special education or resource help (Vohr & Garcia-Coll, 1985).

Again at age 9, significantly more very low birthweight children, 40% in contrast to 11% of matched controls of normal birthweight, had repeated a grade. Additionally, the very low birthweight children scored significantly lower than the controls on WISC-R IQ scores, the Bender–Gestalt, and reading and mathematical achievement. Children with IQ's below 85 in the very low birthweight group (24%), accounted for the differences in WISC-R, Bender–Gestalt, and reading achievement, but did not explain the group differences in mathematical skills.

There is additional evidence that problems in mathematics may be more common and more severe than reading disabilities in preterm children, particularly in the later grades (Cohen et al., 1988; Dunn et al., 1986; Nickel et al., 1982). One study, for example, found that the greatest difference between the very low birthweight and normal controls was in mathematics, with 73% of the very low birthweight group and only 27% of the controls performing below average (Lloyd et al., 1988).

Stability of Cognitive Functioning From Infancy to Later Ages

There is a continuing controversy as to whether early identification of deficits in children born preterm is too pessimistic, and children outgrow or compensate for early problems; or whether early assessments are too optimistic, and hidden problems are revealed only after infancy and preschool when more complex, abstract thought is required. One perspective suggests that developmental problems arising from adverse perinatal events will be most evident in the performance of very young children, because as children grow older the impact of the environment becomes greater (Kopp & Parmelee, 1979). On the other hand, biological factors may become more evident as the child gets older and higher cortical processes emerge.

The question is often couched in terms of whether or when preterm children catch up with their full-term peers. Some investigators find deficits to be more common in the first year of infancy and for preterm children to show improvement or recovery so that differences between groups diminish or disappear by ages 3 to 5 (Greenberg & Crnic, 1988; Ross, Lipper, & Auld, 1985; Ungerer & Sigman, 1983). For example, a study of extremely low birthweight children assessed at both 2 and 5 years (Astbury, Orgill, & Bajuk, 1987), found that 4% declined in functioning, whereas 33% were judged to be less handicapped at age 5.

Other investigators find that problems, obvious in infancy, persist into childhood in some form (Stewart et al., 1981; Wallace, Escalona, McCarton-Daum, & Vaughan, 1982). Still other studies find increasing intellectual deficits with age, including problems that do not become apparent until school age (Hunt et al., 1982; Klein et al., 1985; Noble-Jamieson, Lukeman, Silverman, & Davies, 1982). There is even a suggestion that moderate mental retardation may be asymptomatic in the first year of life and abnormal neurological signs of mild cerebral palsy may disappear during the first year but may or may not recur later (Nelson & Ellenberg, 1982; Weisglas-Kuperus, Uleman-Vleeschdrager, & Baerts, 1987).

Except for some severely handicapped children, it is likely that mental processes among children born preterm show as much discontinuity and instability as among full-term children.

Assessments in Adolescence. In past decades, when less aggressive neonatal intervention techniques were available, preterm cohorts were of higher birthweight, experienced fewer medical complications, and received fewer medical interventions than cohorts born in the late 1980s. This raises the possibility that cognitive outcomes may differ because contemporary survivors differ from the preterm survivors from earlier periods. The issue is particularly important in trying to understand the effects of premature birth on long-term functioning. For instance, present reports of the impact of premature birth during adolescence or early adulthood cognition are based on the survival circumstances typical of the 1960s and 1970s. This information may change when studying the children who survive as a result of the extraordinary medical technology that has emerged since the 1970s.

There is a paucity of data about cognitive functioning during adolescence of children born preterm. From the few studies published to date, a 14-year follow-up of a cohort of 12,058 live births in 1966, of whom 524 were low birthweight infants (Rantakallio & Von Wendt, 1985), indicated that approximately 75% of the low birthweight infants were normal at the age of 14, with a significantly higher percentage of mental retardation, cerebral palsy, and severe hearing defects than full-term children. A longitudinal study of surviving children weighing less than 1,501 grams, born in 1966–1970, were also studied at 14 years of age (Rickards, Ryan, & Kitchen, 1988). Their average WISC-R Verbal score was 89.7 and 48% showed a delay in reading comprehension. In comparison to a group of normal birthweight children from similar social and cultural backgrounds, the very low birthweight children had significantly poorer performance.

In the 18-year follow-up of the Danish Prospective Perinatal Cohort of children born 1959–1961 when extraordinary techniques for survival were not used, there were 94 low birthweight children compared to 857 children in the cohort (Barker, Mednick, & Hunt, 1987). No differences between the low-risk preterm and full-term birthweight groups were found on teachers' ratings of proficiency in mathematics, reading, reasoning, or work organization, or mothers' perceptions of children's academic performance.

Another Scandinavian study examined military draft board conscripts at age 18 years and compared those who had been born of low birthweight to the total cohort (Nilsen, Finne, Bergsjo, & Stamnes, 1984). The low-risk, low birthweight group were indistinguishable from those of full-term birth except for stature and minor defects of vision.

Although the methodological and procedural difficulties associated with longitudinal research are extensive, the ultimate question of the impact of prematurity on cognition in adulthood cannot be answered until the data from such studies are forthcoming.

Methodological Considerations in Evaluating Outcomes

Some of the contradictions in findings presented in the previous sections are related to methodological issues.

Some studies compared the preterm sample to an hypothesized population norm such as an average IQ of 100 plus or minus one standard deviation. In this approach, the percentage of preterm children who performed less well than the norm was enumerated. In contrast, other studies compared the preterm sample to a full birthweight control group of similar demographic characteristics in order to determine significant between group differences.

Studies that compared preterms to a hypothesized population norm, and did so without a control group, may have underestimated or overestimated deficits. Deficits may have been overlooked when the preterm sample was middle class because the average IQ for middle-class full-term children is higher by 10 to 15 points than the hypothesized norm of 100. Problems caused by prematurity may also have been overestimated because prematurity is confounded with poverty and social disadvantage, which makes it difficult, without a control group, to disentangle the direct effects of sociocultural factors within the rearing environment from the biological effects of prematurity.

In addition to differences in design, the composition of the samples varies among studies. Samples defined only by birthweight may include infants born at term but at weights "small for gestational age" as well as preterms with weights "average-for-gestational age." There is some evidence that small-for-gestational age children may be significantly less skillful cognitively than randomly selected average-for-gestational age preterm children (Eilers et al., 1986; Neligan et al., 1976).

Correction for prematurity is another source of differences in conclusions between studies. Cognitive development depends in part on neurological maturation, which begins at conception, so when infants born preterm are tested at their chronological age—that is, their age from birth—they are more neurologically immature than their full-term comparisons. When tested by age from date of birth, the effect is to increase the apparent deficits ascribed to the premature group. When both the preterm and full-term groups are tested at the same age from conception, their development is found to be more similar to the full-term children. Some investigators argue that adjusting the age back to conception and thereby "correcting for prematurity" may give an unduly optimistic view because it has been shown that identification during infancy of children with later handicaps is more accurate when uncorrected scores are used (Barrera, Rosenbaum, & Cunningham, 1987; Miller, Dubowitz, & Palmer, 1984; Siegel, 1983a). Other investigators urge "correcting for prematurity" in order to differentiate true deficiencies from neurological immaturities that will disappear.

Differences in results also arise from variation in the severity of medical complications within the sample, the proportion of the sample born in the tertiary care hospital compared to the proportion of the sample that were born in different hospitals and then transferred to receive tertiary care, and the type of intensive care received.

Gender Differences

Although not all studies look for gender differences, most of those that do find that girls are less affected by preterm birth and its attendant medical complications. The ratio of males to females within each sample affects the results.

Survival has been found to be significantly greater in females than in males in the extremely low birthweight group (Horgan et al., 1984). Significantly more males than females were found to have abnormal neonatal ultrasound brain scans with more ventricular hemorrhages and hypoxic-ischaemic lesions (Weisglas-Kuperus et al., 1987).

Preterm males are at higher risk for developmental problems than their female peers (Broman, 1989; Meisels et al., 1987; Werner & Smith, 1982). The differences have been found at preschool and early school age in vocabulary and expressive language (Washington et al., 1986). In early elementary school, more school adjustment troubles were found for boys than girls (Grigoroiu-Serbanescu, 1984). A population study of a cohort of full-term and low birthweight infants born in Finland in 1966, when the children were age 14, found that mortality and percentage of handicapped children were significantly higher among boys than among girls (Rantakallio & Von Wendt, 1985).

PREDICTION AND IDENTIFICATION

The accurate prediction of which infants will be more likely to have subsequent cognitive problems is important both scientifically and clinically. Identifying those children who will be more at risk can determine who needs and can benefit from early intervention. The cluster of factors used for prediction varies among investigators with some using medical indices (McCarton & Vaughan, 1984), others using measures of the infants' own behaviors (Siegel, 1983b), and others using aspects of the family environment in combination with medical and child factors (Cohen et al., 1988; Werner, 1989).

Siegel (1983b) posited that it is possible to predict with reasonable certainty which preterm infants are likely to develop cognitive problems. In contrast to studies that use correlational or multiple regression analyses to predict outcome, Siegel suggested that prediction can be enhanced by using contingency analyses in which children are categorized as delayed or adequate on the basis of a cut-off score for successful performance. The accuracy of prediction would then be determined by comparing the percentages of children in four groups: (a) adequate functioning at infancy and later ages, (b) delayed at infancy and later ages, (c) falsely predicted to have later problems, (d) those whose later problems were not predicted. Using this approach, Siegel reports a 71% to 84% accuracy rate for prediction of later problems.

However, group percentages of accuracy can be misleading. Accuracy of prediction in individual cases is influenced by the overall rates of impairment and nonimpairment for the specific preterm cohort as a whole. For cohorts in which the overall rate of impairment is low, the risk of false positives in prediction is high. Furthermore, the sets of predictors differ depending on the circumstances specific to the cohort, that is, demographic variables, social variables, developmental functions selected for assessment, and duration of follow-up. Ironically, whereas the original intention is to identify the children who are likely to have problems so that early intervention services can be obtained, the accuracy tends to result from identifying children without problems, rather than a finely tuned ability to detect children with problems.

Cohen and her associates (1988) used two strategies to test the correctness of individual prediction from infancy of children who at age 12 would show cognitive problems; one prediction was based on developmental tests in infancy, the other used multiple measures in infancy, including the social environment of the family. On the basis of developmental test scores alone, prediction for IQ scores in the normal range was highly accurate, but identification of those with low IQ scores was not better than chance. Accuracy in identification increased when multiple predictors, including a measure of the family environment, neonatal neurobehavior, and infant developmental test performance were used. However, as the authors pointed out, even with multiple measures the rate of success was modest and prediction for individual children was subject to a number of misclassifications.

PROCESS STUDIES

To understand the development of children born preterm it is necessary to know more than birthweight, gestational age, or medical complications. The theoretical proposition that development proceeds from the transactions of individuals with their environments requires an examination of how perinatal events alter characteristics within their rearing environments as well as within the preterm infants themselves.

The nature of the parent–child relationship is of particular interest in understanding the development of children born preterm because the premature birth and its sequelae may alter the relationships between parents and infants. Parents of preterm infants face many problems, including the question of the survival and long-term health of their babies, and for some parents, guilt as well as loss of self-esteem because of their babies' problems (Barrera et al., 1987; Caplan, 1960; Minde, Whitelaw, Brown, & Fitzhardinge, 1983). Although most parents cope with their emotional distress concerning their infants, they may still find it difficult to maintain a gratifying relationship with them. Perinatal problems may so affect infants that they enter the relationship with altered or diminished behavioral capacities. During early infancy, preterm infants, as a group, differ from term healthy infants in motor patterns, state organization, and visual attention (Kopp, 1983). Under those circumstances, preterm infants may be inadequate social partners in their natural role in initiating, maintaining, and promoting caregiving (Field, 1980; Goldberg, 1977). During social interaction preterm infants and their parents show less joy and less pleasure in interaction with each other than term infants with their parents (Goldberg, Brachfield, & DiVitto, 1980).

Infant Neurobehavior

Advances in understanding the development of preterms have resulted from the assessment of infant neurobehavioral functioning in prediction and process studies. It has been found that measures of electroencephalogram (EEG) and organization of states of arousal, and infant attention enhance prediction of later cognitive functioning beyond that contributed by perinatal complications (Cohen et al., 1988). The EEG in the context of states of arousal has been used to measure neurological integrity and to determine whether and how much brain functioning is altered by preterm birth and attendant complications. Measures of infant attention depend less on the motor system than standard developmental tests and assess more directly basic processes of cognition and attention (Rose, 1989). How preterms differ from fullterms and how preterms differ among themselves in early brain functioning and attentional processes sheds light on the effects of premature birth on later cognition.

EEG and State Organization. Use of the EEG to assess altered or deviant brain function in preterm infants has demonstrated significant differences in EEG patterns between infants born preterm and full birthweight controls (Parmelee & Sigman, 1983; Schucard, Schucard, & Thomas, 1988). Moreover, within the preterm group, alterations in EEG patterns are associated with later neurological and/or cognitive problems (Als, Duffy, McAnulty, & Badian, 1989; Beckwith & Parmelee, 1986). Although the EEG has been an insightful source of information, it is important to point out that it has not been the conventional interpretation of EEGs according to discrete clinical pathology, such as seizures, that has been instructive in understanding prematurity. Rather, innovative analyses have identified developmental variations in EEG patterns within the normal range that are both particularly characteristic of prematurity and are linked to later cognitive functioning.

EEG assessments have been used past infancy, at school age and early adolescence, to identify a subgroup of low birthweight children with "minimal brain dysfunction" (Dunn, Auckland, & Low, 1986). The minimal brain dysfunction group had significantly more abnormal or borderline EEG patterns at both 6 $\frac{1}{2}$ and 13 years, and at age 13, showed reduced interaction within and between hemispheres during complex tasks. Children with abnormal EEG patterns had poorer cognitive performance at each age tested.

The Brain Electrical Activity Mapping technique, a computer-based tool that interprets electroencephalographic and evoked potential data was used at age 5 in conjunction with an extensive battery of neuropsychological tests to assess children who had been differentiated on the basis of their behavior as newborns (Als et al., 1989). Using the Assessment of Preterm Infants' Behavior Scale (Als, Lester, Tronick, & Brazelton, 1982) the infants were divided into three groups: low threshold, highly reactive infants; moderately well-modulated infants; and well-modulated infants. Independently, as 5-year-olds, the children were grouped by attention, achievement, and spatial ability. The concurrent EEG and evoked potential functioning differentiated the behavioral groups. Moreover, there was concordance between the cluster of low threshold reactive newborns, all of whom were preterms, and the cluster of 5-year-olds who had more difficulty in spatial organization, attentional capacity, and sequential processing.

In a prospective, longitudinal study from birth to early adolescence, infants' biological capacities for self-regulation were assessed through 1-hour polygraph recordings of their sleep states and EEG patterns at term date. The degree to which the infants could maintain the neurophysiological organization required for quiet sleep, which involves the suppression of body and eye movements and the maintenance of regular respiration, and coordinate it with the specific, developmentally appropriate EEG pattern of 407-trace alternant, was found to be significantly correlated with IQ scores at ages 2, 5, and 8, but not 12 years (Beckwith & Parmelee, 1986). Those children who were able to sustain the developmentally correct EEG pattern when they were in quiet sleep, performed better on intelligence tests from toddlerhood to school age. Additionally, children who showed more active sleep as neonates characterized by irregular respirations and heart rate, frequent body movements, and rapid eye movements, gained higher IQ scores during school age. Moreover, at age 12, children within the normal range of IQ who showed learning difficulties, either retention in grade, need for special educational services, or poor scores on the Wide Range Achievement Tests in reading or arithmetic, had demonstrated significantly less active sleep at term than had comparable children born preterm without learning problems (Cohen et al., 1988). The two sleep state measures did not correlate with each other, and appeared to be linked to somewhat different later cognitive processes. The percent of active sleep was associated with sustained attention, whereas 407 trace alternant in quiet sleep was correlated with perceptual organization (Sigman, Beckwith, Cohen, & Parmelee, 1989). These findings support the hypothesis that there are discrete cognitive processes that have differing early antecedents in brain functioning.

Visual and Auditory Attention Including Preference for Novelty. Measures of the neonates' and infants' own behavior, particularly the recruitment and shifting of focused visual attention, appear to be important antecedents to later intelligence (Bornstein & Sigman, 1986; Fagan & Singer, 1983; Rose, 1989). There is good evidence that measures of visual attention in infancy discriminate between preterm and full-term infants (Sigman, 1983) and are associated with later intellectual performance within the preterm group (Rose, 1989).

Using a paradigm in which a visual stimulus is exposed for a brief period of familiarization, followed by paired-comparison trials in which the previously exposed and a novel stimuli are presented simultaneously, Rose (1989) demonstrated that 6- and 12-month-old preterms, even when tested at corrected ages, showed less preference for novelty than full-term infants. However, when familiarization times were substantially increased, novelty preference for preterm infants improved dramatically. The fact that preterms could show novelty preference with long but not short familiarization times suggested that preterms are deficient in the speed with which they process and encode visual information. In three separate studies with different samples, novelty scores were found to be significantly related to cognitive measures from 2 to 6 years (Rose & Wallace, 1987).

Preterms also have greater difficulty than fullterms in intersensory functioning, that is, in dealing with manipulative and visual cues simultaneously (Rose, 1989). Preterms who had more difficulty with cross-modal information processing performed more poorly on measures of cognition through age 6.

Another group of investigators using length of first fixation and length of total fixation as the measure of visual attention found that preterm infants showed longer fixations at expected date of birth than did full-term newborns (Sigman, Cohen, Beckwith, & Parmelee, 1986). Sigman and her associates have hypothesized that the longer durations of fixation shown by preterm infants may reflect a slowness in rate of visual processing; or alternatively, a difficulty in modulating states of arousal such that the preterms are less able to inhibit looking at the unchanging visual stimulus. Length of first and total fixation was negatively associated with the children's IQ scores at 5, 8, and 12 years (Cohen & Parmelee, 1983; Sigman et al., 1989). Those newborns who showed longer fixations were later less competent cognitively. The association between neonatal attention and later cognition seemed to be based in part on genetic factors and to be global in nature, in that the early attention measures were modestly correlated to all three WISC-R factors at age 8, which included verbal comprehension, perceptual organization, and freedom from distractibility (Sigman et al., 1989).

It is not only visual attention, but how the child attended to auditory stimuli that discriminated preterm and full-term infants and within the preterm group also correlated to IQ scores at age 5 (O'Connor, 1980; O'Connor, Cohen, & Parmelee, 1984). The evidence suggests that preterms process information at slower rates because they show slower rates of habituation (Bornstein, 1989) and also have difficulty in shifting attention.

Recently, other investigators have looked at differences in visual attention among medically homogeneous subgroups within the preterm group. Landry and Chapieski (1988) compared preterms with more severe intraventricular hemorrhages and/or pulmonary disease to preterms with less severe cerebral bleeds and respiratory distress. At 6 months, when presented with a standard set of toys, preterms who had experienced the most severe medical complications spent less time looking at the toys. However, both preterm groups, when compared to the full-term group, made fewer shifts in gaze and examined fewer toys. It was the measure of number of shifts in looking (Landry, Leslie, Fletcher, & Francis, 1985) that was associated with toddler cognitive outcome at 24 months. Among very low birthweight preterms compared to full-term infants at 7 months of age, preterms with respiratory distress syndrome, especially those who had required prolonged mechanical ventilation, were least able to recruit and shift attention (Rose, 1989).

It is not clear yet why preterms have difficulty in shifting attention. It may be because their motor system is less functional (Landry et al., 1984), or there may be deficits in visual functioning, or longer latencies, on a neurological basis, in initiating responses to stimuli (Landry et al., 1984). Longer latencies decrease the efficiency with which a response is organized, and may as well decrease the arousal to novel stimuli (Ruff, 1986).

Influence of the Family Environment

The link between adverse perinatal status and long-term cognitive deficits can neither be predicted nor understood without taking into account the support for "self-righting" within the environment or the adversities posed by the environment that ameliorate or exacerbate the hazards of preterm birth (Sameroff & Chandler, 1975; Werner & Smith, 1982). The infant born preterm is not different from the normal infant in the effects of experience on the growth of cognitive skills. That is not to say that the environment can repair serious neurological or sensory problems, as in cerebral palsy or blindness. Nonetheless, it may compensate for more subtle neurological dysfunctioning. For children without neurological insults, the environment may seriously impede or enrich cognitive development. For many children born preterm, their cognitive outcomes will be more strongly related to their environments than to prenatal and perinatal difficulties (Drillien, 1964; Werner, Bierman, & French, 1971).

Numerous studies find that the deleterious influence of preterm birth on cognition is greater in a lower social class environment and seems to be mitigated by higher social status (Broman, Nichols, & Kennedy, 1975; Drillien, 1964; Werner et al., 1971; Wilson, 1985). It appears that the social environment can buffer the child against biologic risk or create a double hazard by compounding biological and social risks (Escalona, 1982). Thus, there appears to be a disproportionately severe effect of preterm birth for the most economically disadvantaged (Drillien, 1964; Grunau, 1986; Lasky et al., 1987; Werner et al., 1971).

For example, one study found that at 20 months, children in middle-class homes with the most severe perinatal complications performed on developmental tests almost comparably to children in poverty without perinatal problems. Differences in performance between those with the most severe perinatal stress and those without were larger for children in poverty then children in more advantaged homes. The most developmentally delayed were those with the greatest perinatal risk from poverty homes. Moreover, by age 10, children with and without severe perinatal stress growing up in middle-class homes achieved mean IQ scores above the average, whereas children from poverty had depressed scores, particularly for those who had experienced severe perinatal stress. This suggests that perinatal complications were related to later impairments only when combined with persistently poor environmental circumstances, unless there was severe central nervous system impairment (Werner & Smith, 1982).

More specific dimensions of the environment, particularly aspects of the parent–child relationship provide stronger associations to children's competence than maternal education or family socioeconomic status alone (Beckwith & Cohen, 1984, 1987; Bradley, Caldwell, & Rock, 1988; Dale et al., 1987; Siegel, 1984). For example, Beckwith and Cohen (1984, 1987) examined social interactions between parent and child during infancy in a sample in which parental occupations ranged from manual laborers to professors and physicians and found that the pattern of parental responsiveness altered the children's intellectual performance within social class. When parents were able to consistently engage in very interactive and contingent ways with their children during infancy, the children tended to achieve IQ scores at age 5 above the average, even within families from the lower social class. Conversely by age 8, children from higher social classes who had not experienced responsive caregiving in infancy performed on the average no differently than children from lower-class families; only the children who had received the more responsive caregiving in infancy and had families of middle or upper social class achieved the highest IQ scores and were significantly more skilled than all others.

Although preterm infants are more difficult to care for and their parents are more stressed than parents in healthy infant–parent dyads, there is as much variability in their relationships as with healthy, term infants. Many preterm infant–parent dyads are able to compensate for difficulties and to work out satisfying social interactions. Whereas it was initially thought that preterm birth, and perinatal illness would interfere with parental attachment to the child, a major discovery has been the existence of compensatory mechanisms within parents such that the smaller, those born earlier, and the sicker infants may receive decreased attention and responsiveness in the first month of life when the infant is still stabilizing (Davis & Thoman, 1988) and increased attention and responsiveness thereafter (Beckwith & Cohen, 1978; Greenberg & Crnic, 1988). In a very careful study that assessed severity of illness daily during neonatal intensive care stay, Minde and his associates (Minde et al., 1978) documented that parents were less attentive to those preterm infants who were the least sick, and more attentive to those who had experienced more medical complications. However, those infants who were most severely ill for the longest period of time received the least parental nurturance, as though the trauma for the parents exceeded their ability to compensate.

More positive attitudes toward the child and parenting, and more positive responsiveness tend to assist vulnerable infants in their development (Beckwith & Cohen, 1984; Werner & Smith, 1982), so the compensatory mechanisms involved in the parent–child relationship may operate to so alter cognitive development that infants at greater medical risk may actually become more competent than infants at lower medical risk. This startling finding demonstrates the bidirectional and transactional nature of the influences between parent and infant in which each contributes and is changed in the process of the relationship (Sameroff & Chandler, 1975). It also underscores the importance of determining the processes by which preterm birth influence later development.

In a study that found that development at age 2 was related to birthweight, gestational age, and perinatal illness such that the sicker, smaller infants, born earlier tended to have higher scores, analysis of mother–infant interaction at 8 months showed that mothers were more likely to support symbolic development by verbally responding to their child's signals, in the more vulnerable infants (Dale et al., 1987). Further illustrating the unexpected nature of compensation within relationships, preterms who were born earlier, weighing less, were more likely than their healthier preterm peers to have secure attachments (Goldberg, Perrotta, Minde, & Corter, 1986). Although it is possible that the parent–child relationship is able to have a compensatory influence, it must be remembered that this is not true in many cases (Barrera et al., 1987).

Mothers differ in their degree of stress; their ability to cope and adapt; their social support; their ability to provide a structured, organized environment versus a chaotic, unpredictable environment. Moreover, the birth and care of an at-risk infant may adversely affect family functioning.

A classic study of the joint influences of perinatal risk and quality of caregiving environment that set the model for other investigations, is the long-term investigation by Werner and associates of the entire cohort of births in 1955 on the island of Kauaii, studied prospectively from birth to adulthood. One of the major contributions of the study was to demonstrate that the cumulative balance between risk factors and protective factors within the child and the caregiving environment determines dysfunction or resiliency in development. The salience of specific risk and protective factors was different for boys and girls, and for children from higher or lower social status, or from psychotic or nonpsychotic parents, but key protective factors for most were: first-born status, fewer children in the family, 2 years or more spacing between the index child and the next born sibling, a great deal of attention given the child by the primary caregiver during infancy, emotional support from alternative caregivers, maternal positive attitudes toward the infant, cohesiveness and stability of the family, and the absence of chronic stressful life events experienced, including father absence, prolonged separation from the mother during infancy, parental mental health problems, repeated or serious illnesses during infancy, parental discord, and loss of a sibling through departure or death.

Based on the Kauaii study, later investigations looked even more intensely at the caregiver–infant relationship. Responsiveness is the dimension of parent–child relationships widely considered to be the most significant for children's development (Bornstein, 1989), one large, longitudinal study of more than 100 preterm children assessed parental responsiveness in three naturalistic home observations during infancy. Children who experienced more responsive social interactions from their primary caregiver during infancy showed higher intelligence test scores from age 2 through age 8. Moreover, parental responsiveness in infancy through toddlerhood, was found to be strongly and significantly related to school achievement, specifically competence in arithmetic at age 12. Responsive caregiving proved to be such a strong factor in buffering children against sequelae of biologic risk that it appeared to remediate early deficits in maturity of brain organization as shown by polygraphic recordings of EEG and state organization taken at term date (Beckwith & Parmelee, 1986). Whereas the least cognitively competent children were those with both altered EEG patterns and less responsive caregiving, the group with altered EEG patterns and more responsive caregiving was indistinguishable from those who had started out with more organized brain functioning. The study is one of the first to show the buffering effect of family environments in ameliorating early risk factors expressed in brain activity in young infants.

Crnic and Greenberg extended the work of Werner and Beckwith on the influence of the family environment. In an important study they found that preterm birth appears to have a sensitizing effect that actually potentiates the influence of the family environment (Greenberg & Crnic, 1988; Siegel et al., 1982). That is, more variance in IQ scores of children born preterm was explained by their home environment than was true for the fullterms. The passivity associated with prematurity may make preterm children more dependent on the environment as it is presented than are healthy fullterms who actively select, recruit, and organize their environment.

FUTURE DIRECTIONS

The findings from more than three decades of research on prematurity indicate that the prevalence of cognitive problems ranging from mental retardation to learning difficulties is greater in children born prematurely, but is far from universal. Conceptually and empirically, risks associated with prematurity are statements about the group, not about the individual. In the most hazardous combination of severe and numerous complications, the mortality rate escalates, and for those who survive, development is severely compromised for many. Some children are remarkably resilient even under the most hazardous circumstances. In less catastrophic biological circumstances, problems in cognitive development are increased, but only in a few samples have such problems been found in a majority of the children. Single factors are not likely to determine outcome. Studies to date indicate that even a single catastrophic event does not universally impair all children, and even in the absence of catastrophic events some preterms function poorly. Rather than single events, it is the combination of multiple risk factors, including conditions within the family and the specific nature of the parent–child relationship, that more powerfully influences outcomes.

The percentage of preterm children with difficulties varies widely and is influenced by the definition of *morbidity.* Increased morbidity in children born preterm results in part because a few children are severely affected and a greater number of children are mildly affected creating a downward shift in the distribution of scores. In most studies cognition appears adequate on intelligence tests for the majority of children but even for these children in the average range there is a higher prevalence of subtle learning problems and poor school achievement than in a normally developing population. Although the incidence of subtle cognitive problems, learning difficulties, and poor school achievement is true for less than the majority of children born preterm, the emotional cost to the individual child, and the cost to their families and the educational system cannot be overlooked.

Our understanding of the effect of prematurity on development is general and nonspecific. The primary measure of outcome has been a global score of intelligence. Measures of specific abilities have not been utilized sufficiently to identify and understand which cognitive functions are impaired and which are more resilient. Differentiating cognitive functions is necessary for understanding the association between prematurity and school achievement.

The focus has also been limited to a unidimensional interpretation of intelligence represented by the IQ score. Alternative conceptualizations of cognition are emerging that would be useful to investigate with preterm children. Sternberg (1985) identified several components of *cognition* that could advance understanding of the developmental processes in children born preterm. In Sternberg's conceptualization, cognition incorporates the ability to seek, to be curious about, and to prefer novelty. When novelty is encountered, cognition involves extracting relevant information and processing the information in meaningful ways. Cognition also includes insight that is dependent on the ability to differentiate relevant from irrelevant information and to make inductive leaps. Research has shown that preterms are slower to process information and show less preference for novelty in infancy, but it is not yet known whether this is true at later ages. If these difficulties persist at later ages it seems reasonable to hypothesize that these specific cognitive problems contribute to problems in school achievement.

Persistence of effects and the stability of individual cognitive processes is an open question; does the impact of prematurity dissipate over time or are there developmental sequelae that carry forward into adolescence and adulthood? At this time the evidence is conflicting and there are a paucity of data about adolescents and adults born preterm. It is necessary not only to identify the degree of stability, but to identify systematically the lawful processes that govern instability.

Finally, attention and cognition interact with social and emotional processes. Investigators have tended to study either cognition or the social-emotional domain, and the latter only in infancy, rather than studying the coherence of development across domains and across ages. To understand vulnerability and resiliency it is necessary to know how the interrelationship among domains exacerbates or compensates for the problems associated with prematurity.

ACKNOWLEDGMENTS

The preparation of this chapter was supported by the Prevention Research Branch, National Institute of Mental Health, Grant MH-36902.

REFERENCES

Als, H., Duffy, F. H., McAnulty, G. B., & Badian, N. (1989). Continuity of neurobehavioral functioning in preterm and fullterm newborns. In M. H. Bornstein & N. Krasnegor (Eds.), *Stability and continuity in mental development* (pp. 3–28). Hillsdale, NJ: Lawrence Erlbaum Associates.

Als, H., Lawhon, G., Brown, E., Gibes, R., Duffy, F. H., McAnulty, G., & Blickman, J. G. (1986). Individualized behavioral and environmental care for the very low birthweight preterm infant at high risk for bronchopulmonary dysplasia: Neonatal intensive care unit and developmental outcome. *Pediatrics, 78,* 1123–1132.

Als, H., Lester, B. M., Tronick, E. Z., & Brazelton, T. B. (1982). Towards a research instrument for the assessment of preterm infants' behavior (A.P.I.B.). In H. E. Fitzgerald, B. M. Lester, & M. W. Yogman (Eds.), *Theory and research in behavioral pediatrics* (Vol. 1, pp. 35–64). New York: Plenum.

Astbury, J., Orgill, A., & Bajuk, B. (1987). Relationship between two-year behavior and neurodevelopmental outcome at five years of very low birthweight survivors. *Developmental Medicine and Child Neurology, 29,* 370–379.

Astbury, J., Orgill, A. A., Bajuk, B., & Yu, V. Y. H. (1983). Determinants of developmental performance of very low birthweight survivors at one and two years of age. *Developmental Medicine and Child Neurology, 25,* 709–716.

Bakeman, R., & Brown, J. V. (1980). Early interaction: Consequences for social and emotional development at three years. *Child Development, 51,* 437–447.

Barker, R. L., Mednick, B. R., & Hunt, N. A. (1987) Academic and psychosocial characteristics of low-birthweight adolescents. *Social Biology, 34*(1–2), 94–109.

Barrera, M. E., Rosenbaum, P. L., & Cunningham, C. E. (1987). Corrected and uncorrected Bayley scores: Longitudinal developmental patterns in low and high birth weight preterm infants. *Infant Behavior and Development, 10,* 337–346.

Bayley, N. (1969). *Bayley scales of infant development.* New York: Psychological Corporation.

Beckwith, L., & Cohen, S. E. (1978). Preterm birth: Hazardous obstetrical and postnatal events as related to behavior. *Infant Behavior and Development, 1,* 403–411.

Beckwith, L., & Cohen, S. E. (1984). Home environment and cognitive competence in preterm children in the first five years. In A. W. Gottfried (Ed.), *Home environment and early mental development* (pp. 235–271). New York: Academic Press.

Beckwith, L., & Cohen, S. E. (1987). Social interaction with the parent during infancy and later intellectual competence in children born preterm. *Early Child Development and Care, 27,* 239–254.

Beckwith, L., & Parmelee, A. H. (1986). EEG patterns of preterm infants, home environment, and later IQ. *Child Development, 57,* 777–789.

Beery, K. E. (1982). *Developmental test of visual-motor integration.* Cleveland, Ohio: Modern Curriculum Press.

Bennett, F. C., Robinson, N. M., & Sells, C. J. (1982). Hyaline membrane disease, birthweight, and gestational age. *American Journal of Diseases of Children, 136,* 888–891.

Bennett, F. C., Robinson, N. M., & Sells, C. J. (1983). Growth and development of infants weighing less than 800 grams at birth. *Pediatrics, 71,* 319–323.

Bornstein, M. H. (1989). Information processing (habituation) in infancy and stability in cognitive development. *Human Development, 32,* 129–136.

Bornstein, M. H. (Ed.). (1989). *Maternal responsiveness: Characteristics and consequences. New directions in child development.* San Francisco: Jossey-Bass.

Bornstein, M. H., & Sigman, M. D. (1986). Continuity in mental development from infancy. *Child Development, 57,* 251–274.

Bradley, R. H., Caldwell, B. M., & Rock, S. L. (1988). Home environment and school performance: A ten-year follow-up and examination of three models of environmental action. *Child Development, 59,* 852–867.

Broman, S. H. (1989). Infant physical status and later cognitive development. In M. H. Bornstein & N. A. Krasnegor (Eds.), *Stability and continuity in mental development. Behavioral and biological perspectives* (pp. 45–62). Hillsdale, NJ: Lawrence Erlbaum Associates.

Broman, S. H., Nichols, P. L., & Kennedy, W. A. (1975). *Pre-school IQ: Prenatal and early developmental correlates.* Hillsdale, NJ: Lawrence Erlbaum Associates.

Caplan, G. (1960). Patterns of parental response to the crisis of premature birth. *Psychiatry, 23,* 365–374.

Cohen, S. E. (1986). The low birthweight infant and learning disabilities. In M. Lewis (Ed.), *Prenatal and perinatal factors relevant to learning disabilities* (pp. 153–193). Urbana, IL: University of Illinois Press.

Cohen, S. E., & Parmelee, A. H. (1983). Prediction of five-year Stanford–Binet scores in preterm infants. *Child Development, 54,* 1242–1253.

Cohen, S. E., Parmelee, A. H., Sigman, M., & Beckwith, L. (1988). Antecedents of school problems in children born preterm. *Journal of Pediatric Psychology, 13,* 493–508.

Costello, A. M., Hamilton, P. A., Baudin, J., Townsend, J., Bradford, B. C., Stewart, A. L., & Reynolds, E. O. R. (1988). Prediction of neurodevelopmental impairment at 4 years from brain ultrasound appearance of very preterm infants. *Developmental Medicine and Child Neurology, 30,* 711–722.

Crnic, K. A., Ragozin, A. S., Greenberg, M. T., Robinson, N. M., & Basham, R. B. (1983). Social interaction and developmental competence of preterm and fullterm infants during the first year of life. *Child Development, 54,* 1199–1210.

Dale, P. S., Greenberg, M. T., & Crnic, K. A. (1987). The multiple determinants of symbolic development: Evidence from preterm children. In D. Cicchetti & M. Beeghly (Eds.), *Symbolic development in atypical children. New directions for child development* (no. 36, pp. 69–86). San Francisco: Jossey-Bass.

Daum, C., Danziger, A., Ruff, H., & Vaughan, H. G. (1983). Periventricular low density as a predictor of neurobehavioral outcome in very low birthweight infants. *Developmental Medicine and Child Neurology, 25,* 559–565.

Davis, D. H., & Thoman, E. B. (1988). The early social environment of premature and fullterm infants. *Early Human Development, 17,* 221–232.

Drillien, C. M. (Ed.). (1964). *The growth and development of the prematurely born infant.* Edinburgh: Livingstone.

Dunn, H. G., Auckland, G., & Low, M. D. (1986). Electroencephalograms. *Clinics in Developmental Medicine,* 95–96. Sequelae of low birthweight: The Vancouver Study. (Chapter 13, pp. 219–237).

Dunn, H. G., Ho, H. H., Crichton, J. U., Robertson, A., McBurney, A. K., Grunau, R. V. E., & Penfold, P. S. (1986). Evolution of minimal brain dysfunctions to the age of 12–15 years. *Clinics in Developmental Medicine,* 95–96. Sequelae of low birthweight: The Vancouver Study. (Chapter 15, pp. 249–299).

Eilers, B. L., Desai, N. S., Wilson, M. A., & Cunningham, M. D. (1986). Classroom performance and social factors of children with birthweights of 1,250 grams or less: Follow-up at 5 to 8 years of age. *Pediatrics, 77,* 203–208.

Escalona, S. K. (1982). Babies at double hazard: Early development of infants at biologic and social risk. *Pediatrics, 70,* 670–676.

Fagan, J. F., & Singer, L. T. (1983). Infant recognition memory as a measure of intelligence. In L. P. Lipsett (Ed.), *Advances in infancy research* (Vol. 2, pp. 31–78). Norwood, NJ: Ablex.

Fawer, C. L., Diebold, P., & Calame, A. (1987). Periventricular leucomalacia and neurodevelopmental outcome in preterm infants. *Archives of Disease in Childhood, 62,* 30–36.

Field, T. (1980). Interaction of high-risk infants: Quantitative and qualitative differences. In D. B. Sawin, R. C. Hawkins, L. O. Walker, & J. H. Penticuff (Eds.), *Psychosocial risk in infant-environment transactions* (pp. 120–143). New York: Brunner/Mazel.

Field, T. M., Dempsey, J. R., & Shuman, H. H. (1981). Developmental follow-up of pre- and post-term infants. In S. L. Friedman & M. Sigman (Eds.), *Preterm birth and psychological development* (pp. 299–312). New York: Academic Press.

Fitzhardinge, P. M., & Ramsey, M. (1973). The improving outlook for the small prematurely born infant. *Developmental Medicine and Child Neurology, 15,* 447–459.

Francis-Williams, J., & Davies, P. A. (1974). Very low birthweight and later intelligence. *Developmental Medicine and Child Neurology, 16,* 709–728.

Goldberg, S. (1977). Social competence in infancy: A model of parent–infant interaction. *Merrill–Palmer Quarterly, 23,* 163–177.

Goldberg, S., Brachfield, S., & DiVitto, B. (1980). Feeding, fussing, and play: Parent–infant interaction in the first year as a function of prematurity and perinatal medical problems. In T. M. Field, S. Goldberg, D. Stern, & A. M. Sostek (Eds.), *High risk infants and children* (pp. 133–154). New York: Academic Press.

Goldberg, S., Perrotta, M., Minde, K., & Corter, C. (1986). Maternal behavior and attachment in low-birth-weight twins and singletons. *Child Development, 57,* 34–46.

Greenberg, M. T., & Crnic, K. A. (1988). Longitudinal predictors of developmental status and social interaction in premature and full-term infants at age two. *Child Development, 59,* 554–570.

Grigoroiu-Serbanescu, M. (1984). Intellectual and emotional development and school adjustment in preterm children at 6 and 7 years of age. *International Journal of Behavioral Development, 7,* 307–320.

Grunau, R. V. E. (1986). Educational achievement. *Clinics in Developmental Medicine,* 95–96. Sequelae of low birthweight: The Vancouver Study. (Chapter 11, pp. 179–204).

Hack, M., & Fanaroff, A. A. (1988). How small is too small? Considerations in evaluating the outcome of the tiny infant. Current controversies in perinatal care. *Clinics in Perinatology, 15,* 773–788.

Hirata, T., Epcar, J. T., Walsh, A., Mednick, J., Harris, M., McGinnis, M. S., Sehring, S., & Papedo, G. (1983). Survival and outcome of infants 501 to 750 gm: A six-year experience. *Journal of Pediatrics, 102,* 741–748.

Horgan, M., Perlman, M., Sonnekalb, M., & Testi, N. (1984). Morbidity and mortality in infants with birthweights between 501 and 1,000 grams. *Journal of Perinatology, 6,* 243–250.

Hoy, E. A., Bill, J. M., & Sykes, D. H. (1988). Very low birthweight: A long-term developmental impairment? *International Journal of Behavioral Development, 11,* 37–67.

Hunt, J. V., Cooper, B., & Tooley, W. H. (1988). Very low birth weight infants at 8 and 11 years of age: Role of neonatal illness and family status. *Pediatrics, 82,* 596–603.

Hunt, J. V., Tooley, W. H., & Harvin, D. (1982). Learning disabilities in children of birthweight under 1501 grams. *Seminars in Perinatology, 6,* 280–293.

Kitchen, W., Ford, G., Orgill, A., Rickards, A., Astbury, J., Lissenden, J., Bajuk, B., Yu, V., Drew, J., & Campbell, N. (1987). Outcome in infants of birthweight 500 to 999 g: A continuing regional study of 5-year-old survivors. *Journal of Pediatrics, 111,* 761–766.

Kitchen, W. H., Ford, G. W., Rickards, A. L., Lissenden, J. V., & Ryan, M. M. (1987). Children of birthweight less than 1000 g: Changing outcome between ages 2 and 5 years. *Journal of Pediatrics, 110,* 283–288.

Klein, N. K., Hack, M., & Breslau, N. (1989). Children who were very low birthweight: Development and academic achievement at nine years of age. *Journal of Developmental and Behavioral Pediatrics, 10,* 32–37.

Klein, N., Hack., M., Gallagher, J., & Fanaroff, A. A. (1985). Preschool performance of children with normal intelligence who were very low-birth-weight infants. *Pediatrics, 75,* 531–537.

Klein, P. S., Raziel, P., Brish, M., & Birenbaum, E. (1987). Cognitive performance of 3-year-olds born at very low birthweight. *Journal of Psychosomatic Obstetrics and Gynecology, 7,* 117–129.

Kopp, C. B. (1983). Risk factors in development. In M. M. Haith & J. J. Campos (Eds.), *Infancy and developmental psychobiology* (pp. 1081–1188). New York: Wiley.

Kopp, C. B., & Parmelee, A. H. (1979). Prenatal and perinatal influences on infant behavior. In J. D. Osofsky (Ed.), *Handbook of infant development* (pp. 29–75). New York: Wiley.
Korones, S. B. (1981). *High-risk newborn infants* (3rd ed.). St. Louis, MO: C. V. Mosby.
Landry, S. H., & Chapieski, M. L. (1988). Visual attention during toy exploration in preterm infants: Effects of medical risk and maternal interactions. *Infant Behavior and Development, 11,* 187–204.
Landry, S. H., Chapieski, L., Fletcher, J. M., & Denson, S. (1988). Three-year outcomes for low birthweight infants: Differential effects of early medical complications. *Journal of Pediatric Psychology, 13,* 317–327.
Landry, S. H., Fletcher, J. M., Zarling, C. L., Chapieski, L., Francis, D. J., & Denson, S. (1984). Differential outcomes associated with early medical complications in premature infants. *Journal of Pediatric Psychology, 9,* 385–401.
Landry, S. H., Leslie, N. A., Fletcher, J. M., & Francis, D. J. (1985). Visual attention skills of premature infants with and without intraventricular hemorrhage. *Infant Behavior and Development, 8,* 309–321.
Lasky, R. E., Tyson, J. E., Rosenfeld, C. R., Krasinski, D., Dowling, S., & Gant, N. F. (1987). Disappointing follow-up findings for indigent high-risk newborns. *American Journal of Diseases of Children, 141,* 100–105.
Lefebvre, F., Bard, H., Veilleux, A., & Martel, C. (1988). Outcome at school age of children with birthweights of 1000 grams or less. *Developmental Medicine and Child Neurology, 30,* 170–180.
Lloyd, B. W. (1984). Outcome of very-low-birthweight babies from Wolverhampton. *The Lancet,* 739–741.
Lloyd, B. W., Wheldall, K., & Perks, D. (1988). Controlled study of intelligence and school performance of very low-birthweight children from a defined geographical area. *Developmental Medicine and Child Neurology, 30,* 36–42.
McCarthy, D. A. (1972). *Manual for the McCarthy scales of children's abilities.* New York: Psychological Corporation.
McCarton, C. M., & Vaughan, H. G. (1984). Perinatal variables and neurodevelopmental outcomes with preterm births. *Clinical Obstetrics and Gynecology, 27,* 664–671.
McCormick, M. C. (1985). The contribution of low birthweight to infant mortality and childhood morbidity. *New England Journal of Medicine, 312,* 82–90.
Meisels, S. J., Plunkett, J. W., Pasick, P. T., Stiefel, G. S., & Roloff, D. W. (1987). Effects of severity and chronicity of respiratory illness on the cognitive development of preterm infants. *Journal of Pediatric Psychology, 12,* 117–132.
Michelsson, K., Lindahl, E., Parre, M., & Helenius, M. (1984). Nine-year follow-up of infants weighing 1500 g or less at birth. *Acta Paediatric Scandanavia, 73,* 835–841.
Miller, G., Dubowitz, L. M. S., & Palmer, P. (1984). Follow-up of pre-term infants: Is correction of the developmental quotient for prematurity helpful? *Early Human Development, 9,* 137–144.
Minde, K., Trehub, S., Corter, C., Boukydis, C., Celhoffer, L., & Marton, P. (1978). Mother–child relationships in the premature nursery: An observational study. *Pediatrics, 61,* 373–379.
Minde, K., Whitelaw, A., Brown, J., & Fitzhardinge, P. (1983). Effect of neonatal complications in premature infants on early parent–infant interactions. *Developmental Medicine and Child Neurology, 25,* 763–777.
Neligan, G. A., Kolvin, I., Scott, D., & Garside, R. F. (1976). *Born too soon or born too small: A follow-up study to seven years of age.* London: William Heinemann.
Nelson, K. B., & Ellenberg, J. H. (1982). Children who "outgrew" cerebral palsy. *Pediatrics, 69,* 529–536.
Nickel, R. E., Bennett, F. C., & Lamson, F. N. (1982). School performance of children with birthweights of 1000 grams or less. *American Journal of Diseases of Children, 136,* 105–110.
Nilsen, S. T., Finne, P. H., Bergsjo, P., & Stamnes, L. (1984). Males with low birthweight examined at 18 years of age. *Acta Paediatric Scandanavia, 73,* 168–175.

Noble-Jamieson, C. M., Lukeman, D., Silverman, M., & Davies, P. A. (1982). Low birthweight children at school age, neurological, psychological, and pulmonary functions. *Seminars in Perinatology, 6,* 266–273.

O'Connor, M. J. (1980). A comparison of preterm and full-term infants on auditory discrimination at four months and on Bayley scales of infant development at eighteen months. *Child Development, 51,* 81–88.

O'Connor, M. J., Cohen, S., & Parmelee, A. H. (1984). Infant auditory discrimination in preterm and full-term infants as a predictor of 5 year intelligence. *Developmental Psychology, 20,* 159–165.

Papile, L., Burstein, J., Burstein, R., & Koffler, H. (1978). Incidence and evolution of intraventricular hemorrhage: A study of infants with birthweights less than 1,500 gm. *Journal of Pediatrics, 92,* 529–534.

Papile, L., Munsick-Bruno, G., & Schaefer, A. (1983). Relationship of cerebral intraventricular hemorrhage and early childhood neurologic handicaps. *Journal of Pediatrics, 103,* 273–277.

Parmelee, A. H., & Sigman, M. D. (1983). Perinatal brain development and behavior. In M. M. Haith & J. J. Campos (Eds.), *Infancy and developmental psychobiology* (pp. 95–156). New York: Wiley.

Rantakallio, P., & Von Wendt, L. (1985). Prognosis for low-birthweight infants up to the age of 14: A population study. *Developmental Medicine and Child Neurology, 27,* 655–663.

Rickards, A. L., Ryan, M. M., & Kitchen, W. H. (1988). Longitudinal study of very low birthweight infants: Intelligence and aspects of school progress at 14 years of age. *Australian Paediatric Journal, 24,* 19–23.

Rose, S. (1989). Measuring infant intelligence: New perspectives. In M. H. Bornstein & N. A. Krasnegor (Eds.), *Stability and continuity in mental development. Behavioral and biological perspectives* (pp. 171–188). Hillsdale, NJ: Lawrence Erlbaum Associates.

Rose, S. A., & Wallace, I. F. (1987). Visual recognition memory: A predictor of later cognitive functioning in preterms. *Child Development, 58,* 779–786.

Ross, G., Lipper, E. G., & Auld, P. A. M. (1985). Consistency and change in the development of premature infants weighing less than 1,501 grams at birth. *Pediatrics, 76,* 885–891.

Rothberg, A. D., Maisels, M. J., Bagnatao, S., Murphy, J., Gifford, K., & McKinley, K. (1983). Infants weighing 1,000 grams or less at birth: Developmental outcome for ventilated and nonventilated infants. *Pediatrics, 71,* 599–602.

Ruff, H. A. (1986). Components of attention during infants' manipulation exploration. *Child Development, 57,* 105–114.

Saigal, S., Rosenbaum, P., & Stoskopf, F. (1984). Outcome in infants 501–1000 grams birthweight delivered to residents of the McMaster health region. *Journal of Pediatrics, 105,* 969–976.

Sameroff, A. J., & Chandler, M. J. (1975). Reproductive risk and the continuum of caretaking casualty. In F. D. Horowitz, M. Hetherington, S. Scarr-Salapatek, & G. Siegel (Eds.), *Review of child development research* (Vol. 4, pp. 187–244). Chicago: University of Chicago Press.

Shucard, D. W., Shucard, J. L., & Thomas, D. G. (1988). Neurophysiological studies of human cognitive development in premature infants: An approach to the study of maturational brain processes. *Neurotoxicology, 9,* 299–316.

Siegel, L. S. (1983a). Correction for prematurity and its consequences for the assessment of the very low birthweight infant. *Child Development, 54,* 1176–1188.

Siegel, L. S. (1983b). The prediction of possible learning disabilities in preterm and fullterm children. In T. Field & A. Sostek (Eds.), *Infants born at risk: Physiological, perceptual and cognitive processes* (pp. 295–315). New York: Grune & Stratton.

Siegel, L. S. (1984). Home environmental influences on cognitive development in preterm and fullterm children during the first 5 years. In A. W. Gottfried (Ed.), *Home environment and early cognitive development* (pp. 197–234). Orlando, FL: Academic Press.

Siegel, L. S., Saigal, S., Rosenbaum, P., Morton, R., Young, A., Berenbaum, S., & Stoskopt, B.

(1982). Predictors of development in preterm and full-term infants: A model for detecting the at risk child. *Journal of Pediatric Psychology, 7,* 135–147.

Sigman, M. (1983). Individual differences in infant attention: Relations to birth status and intelligence at five years. In T. Field & A. Sostek (Eds.), *Infants born at risk: Physiological, perceptual, and cognitive processes* (pp. 295–315). New York: Grune & Stratton.

Sigman, M., Beckwith, L., Cohen, S. E., & Parmelee, A. H. (1989). Stability in the bio-social development of the child born preterm. In M. H. Bornstein & N. A. Krasnegor (Eds.), *Stability and continuity in mental development* (pp. 29–42). Hillsdale, NJ: Lawrence Erlbaum Associates.

Sigman, M., Cohen, S. E., Beckwith, L., & Parmelee, A. H. (1986). Infant attention in relation to intellectual abilities in childhood. *Developmental Psychobiology, 22,* 788–792.

Skouteli, H. N., Dubowitz, L. M. S., Leven, M. I., & Miller, G. (1985). Predictors for survival and normal neurodevelopmental outcome of infants weighing less than 1001 grams at birth. *Developmental Medicine and Child Neurology, 27,* 588–595.

Sostek, A. M., Smith, Y. F., Katz, K. S., & Grant, E. G. (1987). Developmental outcome of preterm infants with intraventricular hemorrhage at one and two years of age. *Child Development, 58,* 779–786.

Sternberg, R. J. (Ed.) (1985). *Beyond IQ: A triangle theory of human intelligence.* New York: Cambridge University Press.

Stewart, A. (1983). Severe perinatal hazards. In M. Rutter (Ed.), *Developmental neuropsychiatry* (pp. 15–31). New York: Guilford Press.

Stewart, A. L., Reynolds, E. O. R., Hope, P. L., Hamilton, P., Baudin, J., Costello, A. M., Bradford, B., & Wyatt, P. (1987). Probability of neurodevelopmental disorders estimated from ultrasound appearance of brains of very preterm infants. *Developmental Medicine and Child Neurology, 29,* 3–11.

Stewart, A. L., Reynolds, E. O. R., & Lipscomb, A. P. (1981). Outcome for infants of very low birthweight: Survey of world literature. *Lancet, 1,* 1038–1041.

Terman, L. M., & Merrill, M. A. (1960). *Stanford–Binet intelligence scale.* Boston: Houghton Mifflin.

Ungerer, J. A., & Sigman, M. (1983). Developmental lags in preterm infants from one to three years of age. *Child Development, 54,* 1217–1228.

Uzgiris, I. C., & Hunt, J. (1975). *Assessment in infancy: Ordinal scales of psychological development.* Urbana: University of Illinois Press.

Van de Bor, M., Verloove-Vanhorick, S. P., Baerts, W., Brand, R., & Ruys, J. H. (1988). Outcome of periventricular-intraventricular hemorrhage at 2 years of age in 484 very preterm infants admitted to 6 neonatal intensive care units in The Netherlands. *Neuropediatrics, 19,* 183–185.

Vohr, B. R., Coll, C. G., & Oh, W. (1988). Language development of low-birthweight infants at two years. *Developmental Medicine and Child Neurology, 30,* 608–615.

Vohr, B. R., & Garcia-Coll, C. G. (1985). Neurodevelopment and school performance of very low birthweight infants: A 7 year long study. *Pediatrics, 76,* 345–350.

Wallace, I. F., Escalona, S. K., McCarton-Daum, C., & Vaughan, H. G. (1982). Neonatal precursors of cognitive development in low birthweight children. *Seminars in Perinatology, 6,* 327–333.

Washington, D. M., McBurney, A. K., & Grunau, R. V. E. (1986). Communication skills. *Clinics in Developmental Medicine,* 95–96. Sequelae of low birthweight: The Vancouver Study. (Chapter 10, pp. 168–237).

Weisglas-Kuperus, N., Uleman-Vleeschdrager, M., & Baerts, W. (1987). Ventricular hemorrhages and hypoxic ischaemic lesions in preterm infants: Neurodevelopmental outcome at $3\frac{1}{2}$ years. *Developmental Medicine and Child Neurology, 29,* 623–629.

Werner, E. E. (1989). High-risk children in young adulthood: A longitudinal study from birth to 32 years. *American Journal of Orthopsychiatry, 59,* 72–81.

Werner, E. E., Bierman, J. M., & French, F. E. (1971). *The children of Kauai: A longitudinal study from the prenatal period to age 10.* Honolulu: University of Hawaii Press.

Werner, E. E., & Smith, R. S. (1982). *Vulnerable but invincible: A study of resilient children.* New York: McGraw-Hill.

Wilson, R. S. (1985). Risk and resilience in early mental development. *Developmental Psychology, 21,* 795–805.

Zubrick, S. R., McCartney, H., & Stanley, F. J. (1988). Hidden handicap in school-age children who received neonatal intensive care. *Developmental Medicine and Child Neurology, 30,* 145–152.

CHAPTER 3

Malnutrition and Cognitive Development: Research-Policy Linkages and Current Research Directions

HENRY N. RICCIUTI
Cornell University

The question of the possible influence of malnutrition on the mental development of young children has attracted a great deal of attention from researchers in the behavioral, social, and biomedical sciences during the past 25 years. It is a significant research issue because it forces us to deal with the influences of interrelated biological and environmental risk factors that may threaten early cognitive development, particularly in poor populations. At the same time, of course, the problem is one of very great concern from a public health and social policy perspective, both nationally and internationally. It is fair to say that research in this area over the past 2 decades has not been particularly free of ambiguity or inconsistency, in terms of empirical findings as well as their interpretation. At the same time, there have been some significant shifts in research emphasis and direction in recent years worth noting.

A number of critical reviews of the extensive research literature on malnutrition and mental development have appeared in recent years (Galler, 1984; Levitsky & Strupp, 1985; Pollitt, 1988; Ricciuti, 1981b), consequently another such overall review would not be particularly useful at this point. The present chapter therefore focuses selectively on two general issues:

1. First, the discussion examines some of the special problems raised, both for science and public policy, when a research area such as that of malnutrition and mental development has such obvious and important implications for currently prominent social policy and legislative initiatives. For example,

what is the influence of public policy pressures on the choice of topics investigated, and on the reporting and interpretation of research results? Does it make any difference in the long run if the research knowledge base used to advocate desirable social programs is highly ambiguous, with questionable or perhaps even unwarranted conclusions being drawn from it? What is the responsibility of scientists who regard this as being the case in any particular instance? Such questions can meaningfully be addressed here because of the very close linkages, during the past 25 years, between research on malnutrition and mental development, and heightened public efforts to alleviate hunger and malnutrition in poor populations in third world countries, as well as in the United States.

2. Second, the chapter discusses promising recent research directions and needs in two general areas: (a) the role of protein-energy malnutrition (PEM)[1] in children's mental development, and (b) the influence of a specific nutritional deficiency, namely iron deficiency, on the development of cognitive competencies.

MALNUTRITION AND MENTAL DEVELOPMENT RESEARCH: LINKAGES TO SOCIAL POLICY AND POLITICAL ADVOCACY

Beginning in the early 1960s, the possibility that early malnutrition might produce significant and possibly irreversible impairment of children's intellectual development became a matter of increasing concern to researchers as well as to policymakers. The rapidly increasing research interest in this particular issue was triggered in large part by the growing public attention being directed by various international bodies toward the extreme conditions of poor sanitation, disease, and malnutrition characterizing the environments of millions of children in the world's poor populations. Also, beginning in the middle 1960s in the United States, the heightened social and political concerns of the so-called War on Poverty focused attention on the potential adverse effects of malnutrition among U.S. children living in poverty. These public policy concerns were in turn reinforced by early research reports suggesting an association between childhood malnutrition

[1]Protein-energy malnutrition (PEM) is a broad category representing the most common nutritional problem worldwide. Severe or *clinical* malnutrition, usually occurring in the first few years of life, may take the form of *marasmus,* involving chronic deficiencies in both protein and calories, or of *kwashiorkor,* representing primarily an acute protein deficiency. Both require early treatment, often including hospitalization, and in practice, mixtures of the two forms are common. Mild-to-moderate malnutrition, or undernutrition, is by far the most widespread form of PEM, involving less than optimal intake of both protein and calories. It is typically identified in terms of height, weight, and/or head circumference below norms for age.

and impaired mental development among poor children in third world countries.

In this atmosphere of heightened social and political concern about the growth and development of poor children, it is perhaps understandable that both researchers and policymakers tended to come to the rather premature and overstated conclusion that early protein-calorie malnutrition represented a major and direct cause of impaired mental development in young children, including irreversible mental retardation. This view was relied on heavily and effectively as a basis for much social and political advocacy directed toward improving the lot of young children in poor populations, and it led to the natural assumption that improving poor children's dietary intake should prevent mental retardation and enhance intellectual development.

What was the research knowledge base used to support these views? Briefly stated, they included the following: (a) animal and human studies indicating that severe, early malnutrition led to reduction in brain size and number of brain cells; (b) animal studies reporting impaired learning and heightened emotionality, mainly in rats; (c) significantly reduced IQ levels of preschool and school-age children with a history of early clinical malnutrition; and (d) lower IQ levels for short versus tall children in populations characterized by chronic, mild-to-moderate undernutrition (Ricciuti, 1979).

There are a number of important methodological problems that significantly limit the interpretation of these types of data as evidence for a direct causal link between early malnutrition and impaired mental development; these problems have been thoroughly discussed in a number of detailed review papers (Barrett, 1984; Martorell, 1984). In the human studies, the major problem involves the difficulty of separating out the role of the adverse social and environmental conditions typically associated with endemic malnutrition, which are capable of exerting significant influences on mental development in their own right. Moreover, even where the cognitive development of malnourished children is compared with that of nonmalnourished children from the same low-income neighborhoods, this does not rule out the presence of important differentiating features of the home and family environments that are capable of affecting the child's health and nutritional status, as well as mental development. These may include maternal attitudes and knowledge, effective utilization of available resources, quality of early child care, amount and quality of stimulation provided, and so forth. With regard to the question of the permanence of adverse effects on mental development, available evidence was particularly weak. Such evidence was based mainly on continuing low IQ levels of school-age children clinically malnourished early in life who, after treatment, had returned to the same adverse home environments that produced clinical malnutrition in the first place.

In the case of the animal studies of early malnutrition, although there was considerable evidence of adverse effects on brain size and structure, corresponding evidence for permanent impairment of learning was not consistent (Levine & Wiener, 1976; Levitsky, 1979). Moreover, as early as 1972, Levitsky and Barnes (1972) showed that the potential negative behavioral effects of early malnutrition could be significantly attenuated, if not eliminated, by enrichment of the animals' learning environment.

Based on a careful review of the research carried out during the 1970s (Ricciuti, 1981a, 1981b), and generally confirmed during the 1980s, what can we conclude with some confidence about the association between protein-energy malnutrition and cognitive development? In the case of mild-to-moderate, chronic undernutrition, which is the major type of malnutrition in poor populations worldwide, there is essentially no evidence of a direct influence on mental development, apart from the influence of the social and environmental conditions typically associated with endemic undernutrition, either in the family or in the larger social environment.

Aside from the many correlational studies of this issue, additional evidence casting significant doubt on the causal link between malnutrition and cognitive development comes from the results of several major nutritional supplementation studies undertaken in the late 1960s and early 1970s in third world settings where children grow up at risk of mild-to-moderate undernutrition. These interventions were based on the strongly held view that improving the nutritional status of such children, particularly through enhanced protein intake, should have a significant impact on their cognitive development. The overall results of these major intervention research studies suggest that simply increasing dietary intake in mildly to moderately malnourished children has little meaningful impact on intellectual functioning (Bejar, 1981; Joos & Pollitt, 1984). It can be argued that these minimal effects of supplementation on cognitive development should not be surprising, because it is likely that the major sources of influence on cognitive development in these mild to moderately undernourished children were primarily socioenvironmental and genetic rather than nutritional.

With regard to children experiencing clinical malnutrition in the first several years of life, here too it was difficult to find clear evidence of direct, long-term effects on cognitive development, independent of the influence of unfavorable characteristics of the home and family environments in which clinical malnutrition is likely to occur. At the same time, persuasive evidence was beginning to appear suggesting that favorable developmental environments later in childhood could significantly attenuate or eliminate the potentially unfavorable effects of early clinical malnutrition on cognitive development, while continuing adverse environments might accentuate such effects. Finally, it was becoming increasingly apparent, on the basis of both animal and human studies, that if malnutrition does play a role in impeding intellectual development, it may exert some influence indirectly by altering the child's curiosity, responsiveness to the environment, and motivation for learning, as well as maternal responses to the child, rather than through brain changes leading to permanently impaired learning and cognitive competencies.

In more recent years, there has been a growing recognition of the view that malnutrition should be seen as one of a variety of adverse health and environmental factors that may be involved in preventing young children in poor populations from reaching their developmental potentials, both physically and intellectually (Pollitt, in press). Preventive and remedial efforts, therefore, need to be aimed at enhancing the overall developmental environments and health of such children in their families, neighborhoods, and day-care or school settings. It does not seem realistic to expect that we can significantly raise the IQ levels of children in deprived environments simply by providing better nutrition.

Given this brief overview, let us return to a somewhat more detailed analysis of the interplay between malnutrition/mental development research and related social policy initiatives, as this evolved during the late 1960s and the 1970s. This recent history provides an instructive example of the difficulties that may be generated, both for science and public policy, when socially committed investigators become involved in research with obvious implications for social policy or legislative decisions, particularly at a time when such decisions are of widespread public and political concern. Under such circumstances, social advocates and policymakers are naturally anxious to assemble factual data and research findings that provide maximum support for their particular social policy position. At the same time, scientists who may be strongly committed to the long-range goals of a particular policy or legislative initiative are put under considerable pressure to help marshal such evidence, either through their own research or their interpretation of the research literature.

The social and political climate of the late 1960s and 1970s put many behavioral and biomedical researchers under exactly these kinds of pressure. This period was marked by widespread efforts to mobilize public support for programs aimed at improving the lot of children living in poverty, with particular reference to hunger and malnutrition. In 1968, for example, the magnitude of these problems was effectively highlighted in the widely publicized "Hunger USA" report of the Citizens Board of Inquiry into Hunger and Malnutrition in the US (1968), and also in the CBS television documentary by Charles Kuralt on "Hunger in America" (1968). A White House conference on nutrition held in 1970 continued these extensive advocacy and public information activities, which began to build great public and political pressure during the 1970s to enlarge federal programs to feed hungry children and improve the nutrition of pregnant women. As one might expect, in this climate of heightened advocacy for social programs for poor children and families, the implications of available research on malnutrition and mental development tended to be oversimplified and exaggerated, to some extent in the scientific community, but especially in the popular press and among political advocates.[2]

It is interesting to note how heavily the rationale presented in support of such programs relied on the argument that malnutrition was a major cause of impaired mental development and mental retardation among poor children, over and above the obvious health and nutritional advantages of these programs for both mothers and young children. For example, both in 1967, during the Johnson administration, and in 1969 during the early months of the Nixon administration, support for the Supplemental Food Program and its expansion was heavily influenced by administration reports emphasizing the links between prenatal and infant malnutrition and mental retardation or permanent brain damage (Hayes, 1982, pp. 97–102).

These same purported links were boldly emphasized in the headline of a Medical News Report (1968) in the prestigious *Journal of the American Medical Association:* "MENTAL RETARDATION FROM MALNUTRITION: 'IRREVERSIBLE'." Even the highly regarded Special Supplementary Food Program for Women, Infants, and Children (WIC), signed into law in 1972, was originally heavily inspired by the growing body of research purportedly relating malnutrition to mental development (Hayes, 1982, pp. 102–105). In fact, as late as 1978, in supporting the Carter administration's plans to cut 3- and 4-year-olds from the WIC program, according to Hayes (1982), Assistant Secretary of Agriculture Foreman argued that "research on malnutrition and brain development had demonstrated that critical cellular growth occurred prior to a child's third birthday . . . and children under three were therefore the most vulnerable to permanent neurological damage from malnutrition" (p. 124). This statement is particularly remarkable, because by 1978 a great deal of research evidence challenging the view of permanent retardation resulting from early malnutrition had been reported.

As a final example (Hayes, 1982, pp. 105–106), it is interesting to note the compelling and emotional arguments presented by Senator Hubert Humphrey on the floor of the Senate in support of the WIC program during the discussions preceding its final approval in August 1972. These arguments made effective use of vivid photographic displays of malnourished infants and their undeveloped brains, reinforcing testimony presented at earlier hearings emphasizing the permanent brain damage and mental retardation that could result from malnutrition.

It is particularly interesting that during this period, as noted earlier, the

[2]See Hayes (1982) for a systematic analysis of the utilization of research in the formation of federal policies and programs affecting children and families.

strong doubts about a direct causal relationship between mild-to-moderate malnutrition and impaired mental development, and the arguments against permanent brain damage and mental retardation resulting from early clinical malnutrition, were being reported in the literature and at conferences by a good many investigators. In 1973 the respected Food and Nutrition Board of the National Research Council issued a position paper warning against overly simplistic misinterpretations of cause and effect in popularized summaries of research on the effects of malnutrition on brain development. However, these views do not appear to have emerged very noticeably in the many public hearings and legislative discussions such as those just summarized. In the policy arena throughout this period, and to some extent in the 1980s as well, there has tended to be a reluctance to emphasize the more moderated hypotheses being articulated concerning the probable role of malnutrition, and a strong adherence to the questionable view that malnutrition sufficient to affect children's physical growth could also be a direct cause of significantly impaired cognitive development.[3]

Why was this the case? Several factors were probably involved. First of all, given the value that American society places on intellectual competence, the assumption that improved nutrition can enhance brain growth and raise IQ levels of poor children, and even prevent mental retardation, made a very compelling argument for policy and legislative advocates—more compelling than the more modest assumption that improved nutrition and health are important to promote children's overall growth and development, school attendance, work efficiency, and so forth. In third world countries as well, the notion that simply increasing poor children's protein intake could raise IQ levels had dramatic potential implications for national development. It is understandably difficult to attenuate or qualify such politically compelling arguments for clearly much needed nutrition programs.

Second, if there is strong political and public pressure in support of particular legislative or policy recommendations, there is a tendency not to solicit contrary views when organizing public hearings and documenting the facts in support of the proposed policy recommendations (Hayes, 1982, p. 52). Also, in the case of programs that may be of considerable help to thousands of children and families, and are unlikely to do any harm, scientists who may regard the initial scientific justification for the programs to be very weak or highly questionable are unlikely to insist on being heard in the political arena.

---

[3]An impressive 1989 booklet on nutrition and learning prepared for the National Education Association by the Food Research and Action Center (FRAC) as a guide for school employees states, with regard to the negative impact of mild undernutrition on learning, that "the consensus of researchers in the area is that undernutrition does have an independent effect on learning and behavior" (National Education Association, 1989, p. 8).

Let us examine more closely some of the effects of these public policy pressures on research and researchers in the field. The high degree of public and political concern about malnutrition and cognitive development during this period, both nationally and internationally, tended to place investigators in the fields of nutrition, pediatrics, and related social and behavioral sciences under considerable pressure to strengthen the research basis for programs and policies intended to prevent malnutrition and promote mental development. Particularly during the 1970s and early 1980s, a variety of government agencies and private foundations in the United States and elsewhere, as well as international bodies, actively solicited, encouraged, and supported a great deal of research concerned with relationships between malnutrition and intellectual development, including the major nutritional supplementation studies previously alluded to.

In such an atmosphere, there is a natural tendency for many investigators to be especially alert to data suggesting causal relationships between malnutrition and impaired cognitive development, and to be less attentive and open to contrary findings or hypotheses. During this period, when there were many international conferences on malnutrition and mental development, to question the direct causal relationship between malnutrition and cognitive development seemed to be perceived by many as tantamount to arguing against the importance of good nutrition for young children in poor populations. Thus, there tended to be subtle but nevertheless quite real social pressures not to raise such questions too publicly, particularly in the presence of policymakers.

It is interesting to note that during this period and more recently as well, observed associations between malnutrition and mental development continued to be reported by investigators as suggestive of a causal relationship, often quite uncritically (e.g., Ashem & Janes, 1978; Natesan & Devadas, 1981), despite methodological critiques emphasizing the ambiguity and difficulties of interpreting such findings. Moreover, critiques of this sort, as well as empirical research raising significant questions about the direct causal influence of malnutrition on intellectual development, tended to be less visibly reported and less frequently cited (e.g., Das & Soysa, 1978; Hansen, Freesemann, Moodie, & Evans, 1971; Moodie, Bowie, Mann, & Hansen, 1980).

Viewing this overall background in perspective, it can be argued that the prevailing social policy and public pressures during this period appreciably constricted the breadth, objectivity, and openness with which the scientific questions concerning malnutrition and intellectual development were addressed.

What should be the scientist's responsibilities, if any, under circumstances of the sort just described? Does it matter in the long run, for science and social policy, if apparently worthy social programs are advocated and subsequently implemented on the basis of ambiguous, highly questionable, or perhaps even misleading research findings? Does it matter, particularly if such programs may eventually turn out to be of considerable benefit, although perhaps in terms of outcomes other than those originally emphasized? According to the argument here, it does matter in the long run, both from the perspective of science as well as that of social policy development.

It should be recognized, of course, that in the final analysis, the social policies and programs developed by a particular society will depend heavily on that society's dominant values and ideologies. Thus, for example, to the extent that we consider it our moral obligation to ensure that all children are well-fed and healthy, it is not necessary to have an unambiguous research base to justify policies aimed at this objective. For example, it should not have been necessary to justify the WIC program on the basis of the expectation that it would prevent permanent mental retardation. However, to the extent that research findings are employed as an argument for implementing a particular social policy or program, then it is important that the knowledge base be clearly and objectively articulated, including the ambiguities and negative findings, even though this may be considered politically undesirable by advocates of the program, including scientist-advocates.

It seems obvious that in the long run, social policies and programs are likely to be sounder and more effective if from the outset, planning decisions are made on the basis of a clear understanding of the research knowledge base, including both its strengths and its limitations.[4] Therefore, it is important that scientists assume some responsibility for clarifying the relevant available research knowledge not only through reports in the research literature, but also in the arena of public policy deliberations. This responsibility is particularly important if it is apparent that the knowledge base is being overstated or inappropriately utilized in the advocacy or political process.

In terms of more pragmatic long-term considerations, it seems reasonable to assume that if costly social programs or policies have been justified and directed at specific outcomes, largely on the basis of questionable or unwarranted assumptions derived from research, and if these programs subsequently prove to be ineffective, this may seriously weaken the credibility of researchers and increase policymaker's skepticism concerning the value of science in shaping social policy.

Thus far the discussion has centered on some of the problems generated

[4]For example, if discussions were being organized in support of expanded early childhood intervention programs, one would hope that serious attention would be given to the recent paper by Woodhead (1988), which raises important questions about the validity of the generalizations about cause and effect inferred from recent research on the long-term effectiveness of such programs.

when research on protein-energy malnutrition and intellectual development has been utilized by social and political advocates in support of policy or legislative agendas. We turn next to a consideration of important research questions currently being examined or still to be addressed, first in regard to protein-energy malnutrition, and then with respect to iron deficiency.

MALNUTRITION AND COGNITIVE DEVELOPMENT: CURRENT RESEARCH DIRECTIONS

Protein-Energy Malnutrition

Clearly, there is not much additional understanding to be gained through further studies using the traditional methodologies of comparing IQ or other cognitive scores of children having a history of malnutrition with those of nonmalnourished children from the same general population. As indicated earlier, such children are very likely to come from family environments that differ significantly in factors capable of influencing both nutritional status and intellectual development. Also, it is not particularly meaningful to continue to attempt to determine statistically whether malnutrition or the social environment has a greater independent influence on children's cognitive development. Typically, such estimates of independent effects vary greatly depending on within-sample homogeneity or heterogeneity in regard to nutritional or environmental variation (Galler, Ramsey, Solimano, Lowell, & Mason, 1983; Richardson, 1976). Moreover, in the real world where children grow up at risk of malnutrition, socioenvironmental and nutritional influences operate jointly, not independently.

Among the most important research questions that warrant continued and more systematic attention, therefore, is the issue of how malnutrition might combine or interact with related socioenvironmental variables in jointly influencing the course of cognitive development (Pollitt, 1988; Ricciuti, 1979, 1981a). In one of the earliest analyses of this sort, Richardson (1976), working in Jamaica, found that poor school-age boys with a history of clinical malnutrition who came from relatively more favorable home environments showed only a minimal IQ reduction at 6 to 10 years of age, in contrast to the larger IQ deficits of previously malnourished children from the same neighborhood, who lived under more adverse home and family circumstances. On the other hand, Galler (1984) did not find such an interaction in her study of school-age children in Barbados who had been clinically malnourished early in life. In a recent urban Guatemalan study of poor school-age children at risk of mild-to-moderate undernutrition, Johnston, Low, De Baessa, and MacVean (1987) found, rather surprisingly, that malnutrition was more related to IQ levels in the socioeconomically somewhat better-off families than in the poorest. Inconsistencies of this sort should be clarified by further research and analyses addressed to the issue of interaction between nutritional and socioenvironmental conditions within poor populations.

If one considers the broader range of socioeconomic levels represented in most societies, there are several additional examples of the importance of the child's social environment in determining the long-term behavioral outcomes of early clinical malnutrition. This point is illustrated clearly in a study of Korean orphan children who were judged to have been either severely or moderately malnourished at 2 to 3 years of age, just prior to adoption by middle-class U.S. families (Winick, Meyer, & Harris, 1975). At follow-up in Grades 1 to 8, these previously malnourished children achieved levels of intellectual and school achievement clearly within the normal range for U.S. children. Similarly, middle-class U.S. children suffering from early malnutrition because of disease generally show no significant long-term impairment of intellectual functioning (e.g., Klein, Forbes, & Nader, 1975).

In recent years, there has been a growing interest among developmentalists in the general question of how multiple risk factors and so-called *counter-risk* or protective factors operate as interrelated influences on early behavioral development (Ricciuti & Dorman, 1983; Werner & Smith, 1982). It would be important to address such issues more incisively in future research on malnutrition and cognitive development, particularly within poor populations where malnutrition is endemic. More specifically, it would be valuable to examine in a more fine-grained fashion than has typically been the case, those features of the home and family environment, and of the child's experience in that environment, which might make a difference in the cognitive development of children with an early history of malnutrition.

In addition to helping us understand the interactions between early malnutrition and the social environment as joint influences on later cognitive development, fine-grained analyses of the home environments of children at risk of malnutrition can serve another important purpose. That purpose is to achieve a greater understanding of maternal and environmental antecedents of variations in the quality of early child care, which have implications for growth and development. A number of studies of poor families have emphasized the importance of such variations in specific features of family environments, family functioning, or quality of care, which may increase or decrease the risk of malnutrition as well as delayed mental development occurring in some families rather than others in the same at risk population. Based on research done in Jamaica (Richardson, 1974), Mexico (Cravioto & DeLicardie, 1976), and more recently in Barbados (Galler & Ramsey, 1985), these differentiating features seem to center in general on what might best be viewed as the primary caregiver's "mothering competence," broadly defined, or the degree to which child-care practices provide adequate nurturance and support for development, even under the adverse conditions these families confront.

These types of findings can be illustrated briefly in Cravioto and DeLicardie's (1976) prospective longitudinal study of several hundred infants born in a rural Mexican village, 22 of whom were treated for severe clinical malnutrition some time during the first few years of life. At 5 years of age, these children had lower IQ levels than comparison children. The families of these previously malnourished children did not differ from comparison families on such demographic factors as parental literacy, education or income level, family size, or parental age. However, as early as the first year of life, the homes of the malnourished children were observed to be generally lower in the quantity and quality of social, emotional, and cognitive stimulation provided. Also, mothers of the malnourished children were less likely to be in contact with the outside world (e.g., through radio listening), less open to modernization, and were more passive and less sensitive to the young child's needs. It is important to note that these same features of the home environments were related to 5-year IQ levels among children without a history of severe malnutrition. A more complete understanding of such maternal and environmental characteristics, which may increase or decrease the risk of malnutrition and also of impaired intellectual development in populations at risk, would obviously be of great value as background for the development of preventive intervention strategies best suited to particular ecological settings.

In the case of both mild-to-moderate undernutrition and early clinical malnutrition, it can be argued that it is best to view malnutrition as an important component of the complex of significant health problems that are endemic in poor populations, and can produce adverse effects on developmental and educational outcomes (Pollitt, in press). In these environments, the "ecology of malnutrition" is typically characterized by such conditions as absence of a clean water supply, poor sanitation and health care, inadequate food supply and feeding practices, and so forth, leading to widespread infection, parasitic disease, diarrhea, malnutrition, and high infant mortality rates. Moreover, it has been pointed out that in such settings there tends to be a synergistic relationship between malnutrition and disease (Scrimshaw, 1988; Scrimshaw, Taylor, & Gordon, 1968).

Under such circumstances, children's physical growth and development can obviously be significantly compromised. At the same time, it is reasonable to assume that young children in these settings who are chronically ill and malnourished are likely to be less curious about their social and physical environment, and less responsive to opportunities for learning from that environment, whether at home or in school, in part because activity levels may be reduced in order to maintain physiological energy balance (Beaton,

1983). Mild-to-moderate undernutrition in the absence of chronic disease may also be associated with significantly reduced attention and activity levels in young children for the same reason (Sigman, Neumann, Jansen, & Bwilbo, 1989).

Given these leads, it would be particularly valuable at this point to carry out detailed prospective studies of infants and young children at risk of malnutrition, which closely monitor the child's health, nutritional status, and energy levels, both biochemically and behaviorally. The aim here would be to closely examine the links between these characteristics and observational measures of curiosity, exploratory behavior, motivation, and learning. In addition, it would obviously be important to link these latter variables to measures of cognitive development. Research of this sort could also reveal to what extent significantly impaired health or chronic illness, in the absence of clinical malnutrition, may also influence these same behavioral characteristics as well as mental development and school performance.

Studies of the sort just described would permit systematic empirical testing of the previously mentioned hypothesis: If malnutrition influences mental development, it may do so indirectly through lowering the child's responsiveness to his environment and reducing opportunities for learning, thus leading to a slower rate of cognitive development than might otherwise have been the case. Because curiosity and interest in learning can often be enhanced through appropriate enrichment of the child's social and learning environment, this conception of the possible role of malnutrition leads to a far less pessimistic view of the likelihood of remediation than that implied in the assumption of brain-mediated, irreversible impairment of cognitive functioning.

In recent studies of malnutrition and mental development, there has been a growing tendency to move beyond overall infant development tests or standard IQ measures, in the direction of assessing more specific cognitive competencies. For example, some studies have incorporated measures of short-term memory, sustained attention, language, incidental learning, and so forth. This increased concern with the theoretical relevance and specificity of measures of potential cognitive outcomes of malnutrition represents a significant and promising advance that clearly needs to be continued. At the same time, however, it would be particularly important to incorporate culturally appropriate measures of various adaptive, problem-solving, or learning competencies manifested in real-life settings, building on recent efforts to assess what has come to be called "every day intelligence" (Sternberg & Wagner, 1986).

There have been a number of reports indicating that the malnourished child may be responded to quite differently by primary caregivers early in life, so that early social and learning experiences may be more limited than those available to a nonmalnourished sibling (Galler, Ricciuti, Crawford, &

Kucharski, 1984). Further research dealing with this issue certainly would be very worthwhile, particularly if one could demonstrate linkages between such altered social interactions and concurrent or subsequent cognitive development (e.g., Sigman, Neumann, Baksh, Bwilbo, & McDonald, 1989).

Finally, in addition to reports of effects on caregiver–infant interaction, there are a few reports in the recent literature suggesting that variations in nutritional status may be associated with altered social behavior of school-age children, either in the family (Galler, Ramsey, & Solimano, 1985) or in interaction with peers (Barrett, Radke-Yarrow, & Klein, 1982). Although it is not yet clear whether these associations represent a causal relationship, further investigations of possible effects of malnutrition on social behavior certainly would be worth pursuing, on the assumption that some patterns of altered social behavior may have significant implications for cognitive development. Such studies would be particularly valuable if they concurrently examined the roles of chronic illness, parasitic infections, and energy levels, along with nutritional status.

Iron Deficiency and Cognitive Development

Some of the most interesting and significant recent research on malnutrition and cognitive development deals with the role of iron deficiency. During the period of heightened interest in protein-energy malnutrition and mental development in the 1970s, a number of investigators began to examine the influence of specific nutritional deficiencies on mental development and school achievement, particularly that of iron deficiency. This initial interest was based in part on the prevalence of iron deficiency among protein-energy malnourished children, and also on the characteristics of breathlessness, poor concentration, and fatigue typically associated with anemia in children. Some of these early reports (see Evans, 1985) suggested that iron deficiency anemia was associated with lowered measures of school achievement and cognitive functioning in preschool and school-aged children. However, these early studies, which were largely cross-sectional or epidemiological in nature, were plagued by many of the same methodological and interpretive problems characterizing research on protein-calorie malnutrition. Thus, it was not possible to evaluate the influence of iron deficiency apart from that of the generally adverse environmental circumstances under which iron-deficient children tend to live, and from the influence of protein-energy malnutrition, which is common among such children.

During the past 10 years or so, research on iron deficiency and cognitive development has become considerably more sophisticated. It thus represents a potentially significant area for future interdisciplinary research, for a number of reasons:

1. Recent research has led to the development of more precise methods for assessing children's iron status;

2. advances in nutritional and brain biochemistry have made it possible to specify several hypothesized biological mechanisms through which the effects of iron deficiency on cognitive functioning may be mediated; and

3. the possibility of inferring the causal influence of iron deficiency has been greatly enhanced by the increasing utilization of stronger experimental designs involving the measurement of behavioral changes resulting from carefully monitored iron treatment. (Similar conditions have not been as readily available to investigators conducting research on the broader problem of protein-energy malnutrition.)

Specification of Iron Deficiency. In the early studies of iron deficiency, the main strategy involved comparisons of the performance of children classified either as anemic due to iron deficiency, or as nonanemic, typically on the basis of iron levels reflected in hemoglobin values less than or greater than accepted norms (approximately 10.5–12 gm/dL). Through the use of multiple biochemical indicators, modern assessment techniques are capable of differentiating several levels of iron deficiency anemia as indicated primarily by hemoglobin levels, which are indicative of the oxygen-carrying capacity of the blood. At the same time, these indicators are being utilized to differentiate among nonanemic children with varying iron stores at the cellular level throughout the body, including brain cells (Beaton, Corey, & Steele, 1989). It has thus become possible to measure variations in children's iron status from the mild or moderate deficiencies insufficient to cause anemia, through the increasing levels of deficiency that are reflected in iron deficiency anemia.

Despite these significant advances in the specification of levels and types of iron deficiency in children, modern investigators are well aware of various confounding factors that can interfere with accurate measurement of iron status. These include the presence of infection, parasitic disease, or other specific nutritional deficiencies, diurnal variations in individual iron levels, and interindividual variability in what can be considered normal levels.

Mechanisms Mediating Influence of Iron Deficiency. Recent research has been characterized not only by more precise specification of children's iron deficiency, but by a clearer articulation of the possible mechanisms through which variations in iron status might influence cognitive development. The refinements just described, permitting measurement of iron status at the cellular level in nonanemic children, are considered particularly important because there is considerable evidence from animal studies to suggest that reduced iron in brain cells may lead to a decline in the kinds of neurotransmitter activity assumed to be behaviorally relevant for normal attention and learning (Youdim, Ben-Shachar, & Yehuda, 1989). One of the important theoretical issues being addressed by contemporary researchers, therefore, is the question of whether observed behavioral "effects" of iron deficiency in children are attributable primarily to anemia, or to alterations in brain iron metabolism affecting neurotransmitter activity.

Research Strategies. It is not possible to determine causality from the essentially correlational designs used in most earlier studies, so contemporary investigators have leaned increasingly on randomized, double-blind experimental designs in which measures of iron status as well as cognitive performance are made before and after specified periods of iron treatment. Some studies have been able to employ treatment and placebo groups in both iron-deficient and normal children, although it is not always ethically feasible to withold treatment from iron-deficient children.

This experimental treatment approach has the advantage that one can determine whether changes in cognitive measures parallel measured changes in iron status following treatment. Analyses of this sort are made feasible by the fact that children's iron status can be substantially improved over relatively short periods of iron therapy (1 to 3 months). In contrast, nutritional supplementation aimed at ameliorating mild-to-moderate protein-calorie malnutrition takes substantially longer to produce observable effects, and is very difficult to monitor objectively.

What are some of the major findings of recent studies of the association between iron deficiency anemia and intellectual development, carried out for the most part in third world populations?[5] Generally speaking, evidence from this growing body of research is pretty consistent in indicating that prior to treatment interventions, children with iron deficiency anemia do less well in school, and tend to score somewhat lower than nonanemic children on tests of infant development or IQ measures, as well as on a number of more specific cognitive measures. It should be pointed out, however, that these differences tend to be rather small and within the normal range of intellectual functioning. Thus far, differences in iron levels among nonanemic children do not appear to be associated with IQ or cognitive performance measures.

A majority of the studies just alluded to have also included an evaluation of the effects of iron treatment, using the kinds of experimental designs previously described. Let us briefly review these general findings, first in regard to studies of iron deficiency in infants and toddlers, undertaken in part because of the prevalence of iron deficiency in this age group. To evaluate behavioral outcomes, most of these studies have used the Bayley

[5]For detailed recent reviews see Evans (1985) and Lozoff (1988).

Scales, which provide useful measures of overall development in the first 2 years of life, but do not yield assessments of specific cognitive competencies. Because of the relative rapidity of anemic infants' responsiveness to iron treatment, a good many of these studies focused on the evaluation of developmental changes occurring after 7 to 10 days of therapy. Also, detection of such rapidly occurring developmental changes would be of considerable theoretical interest because this would suggest that the corrected behavioral effects were due to iron deficiency at the cellular level rather than to anemia; typically anemia would not be reversed by such short-term treatment.

Although several of these studies suggest that these short-term iron treatments may produce significant improvement in Bayley Developmental Quotients (Oski, Honig, & Helu, 1983; Walter, Kovalskys, & Stekel, 1983), investigations that systematically employed both treatment and placebo groups generally indicate that rather similar gains tend to occur in both groups (e.g., Lozoff, Brittenham, & Viteri, 1982), so that the changes cannot readily be attributed specifically to the iron treatment.

What about the effects of longer periods of treatment of anemic infants? Several studies have examined the behavioral outcome of up to 3 months of iron treatment in children under 24 months of age (Aukett, Parks, & Scott, 1986; Lozoff, Brittenham, & Wolf, 1987). The results generally indicate that the test performance of the majority of anemic infants is not significantly improved following such treatment, thus raising some question as to whether the initial differences in infant behavioral development were perhaps attributable to factors other than iron deficiency anemia as such.

There have been a good many studies of the treatment of iron deficiency in preschool and school-age children, utilizing experimental designs with random assignment of anemic and nonanemic children to treatment and placebo groups. These studies generally report somewhat lower pretreatment intellectual, cognitive, or school performance measures for anemic children. Although a good many investigations also report improvement in cognitive measures following iron treatment, there is still some inconsistency in the findings concerning the behavioral effects of iron treatment.

For example, in a study of school-aged boys in India, Gopaldas, Kale, and Bhardwaj (1985) found evidence of significant improvement in the cognitive functioning of anemic boys treated with the higher of two iron dosages over a 60-day period, in comparison with a placebo group. The cognitive measures employed were visual memory, auditory memory and attention (digit span), maze performance, and a clerical task. Somewhat less encouraging results concerning the reversibility of effects of iron deficiency anemia were reported by Soemantri, Pollitt, and Kim (1985), who studied changes in school achievement test scores of anemic and nonanemic Indonesian children following 3 months of iron therapy. Whereas the scores of anemic iron-treated boys improved significantly over those of untreated anemic children, the achievement scores of the anemic children remained lower than those of the nonanemic children even after treatment, so that the initial differences in achievement were not eliminated. Finally, in a carefully designed study of 1,358 school children in Thailand, Pollitt and associates (1989) evaluated changes in IQ level as well as language and mathematics achievement following 16 weeks of iron treatment in three groups of children initially classified as anemic, iron-deficient but not anemic, and normal. Although iron treatment produced significant improvement in the hemoglobin levels of the anemic children, there was no corresponding improvement in the intellectual or achievement outcomes measured, even when adjustments were made for differences in general nutritional status and disposable income among the three groups.

The variations in the findings of research on the effects of iron treatment are probably due, at least in part, to variations in particular conditions characterizing the samples and treatments utilized. These include such factors as the initial severity of the iron deficiency as well as its duration or chronicity, the presence or absence of disease or malnutrition, duration and levels of iron treatment employed, and so forth. Issues of this sort, as well as a careful review of problems of research design, and important lines of research needed in the light of our present state of knowledge, are systematically addressed in the report of a recent interdisciplinary conference on iron deficiency and behavioral development (Pollitt, Haas, & Levitsky, 1989).

In summary, there is substantial evidence indicating that iron deficiency anemia is associated with moderately lowered performance on developmental tests in infancy, as well as on various intellectual measures in school-age children, including IQ, school achievement, and a number of more specific cognitive competencies such as attention and short-term memory. However, as in the case of protein-energy malnutrition, it is not yet clear whether these associations represent a causal relationship between iron deficiency and behavior. This issue of causality is being currently addressed through the increasing utilization of more refined experimental designs evaluating the effects of iron treatment. Although the behavioral response to treatment in these studies for the most part suggests that iron deficiency may indeed play a causal role, this conclusion must be considered tentative pending further replication of these findings in future research.

Although there is little or no evidence thus far that iron deficiency without anemia is associated with lowered intellectual functioning, this does not rule out the possibility that reduced iron levels at the cellular level may be involved through alteration of significant neurotransmitter activity in the brain. This issue is also one that is continuing to be addressed in contemporary research.

To return briefly to the issues discussed at the outset of this chapter, what can we say about the policy implications of recent research on iron deficiency and intellectual development in children? From a policy perspective, the summary report of the recent conference on iron deficiency (Pollitt, Haas, & Levitsky, 1989) provides a good example of a balanced overview of the conclusions that can be drawn from available research findings, including the uncertainties, along with a statement of the importance of treating and preventing iron deficiency, which is a worldwide public health problem. As such, treatment and prevention need not be justified primarily on the expectation that they will raise IQ levels and improve school achievement.

SUMMARY AND CONCLUSIONS

Research reporting observed associations between protein-energy malnutrition and mental development emerging in the late 1960s and the 1970s was heavily relied on in efforts to advance social policies and programs intended to promote the health, nutritional status, growth, and development of young children in poor populations. In this process of social and political advocacy, the role of early malnutrition as a direct cause of permanent brain damage, mental retardation, or impaired mental development tended to be heavily overstated, given the research evidence available. When investigators are placed under heavy social and political pressures to marshall evidence supporting desirable social programs, as in this case, there may be unfavorable consequences both for science and the development of sound social policies.

In recent years, it has been increasingly recognized that the relationships between childhood malnutrition and mental development are complex, requiring that one take account of the concomitant role of important adverse health and socioenvironmental circumstances typically associated with endemic malnutrition. Significant lines of current and prospective research dealing with malnutrition and cognitive development include (a) continued examination of how malnutrition functions as one of a complex of biological and environmental risk conditions threatening early development; (b) gaining a better understanding of detailed features of the home and child-care environment that may contribute to significantly reduced or heightened risks of malnutrition as well as suboptimal mental development occurring in poor populations; and (c) more sophisticated investigations of the causal role of iron deficiency in observed associations with reduced IQ levels and cognitive functioning in children, with special emphasis on experimental studies of the effectiveness of iron treatment in reversing or preventing these outcomes.

From a policy perspective, research thus far suggests that preventive programs need to be directed at amelioration of the overall health and developmental environments of poor children, whether in homes, neighborhoods, day-care centers, or schools. Such efforts are likely to be more effective in promoting children's mental development than those that focus narrowly on nutritional or dietary intervention.

REFERENCES

Ashem, B., & Janes, M. D. (1978). Deleterious effects of chronic undernutrition on cognitive abilities. *Journal of Child Psychology and Psychiatry, 19,* 23–31.

Aukett, M. A., Parks, Y. A., & Scott, P. H. (1986). Treatment with iron increases weight gain and psychomotor development. *Archives of Diseases of Childhood, 61,* 849–857.

Barrett, D. E. (1984). Methodological requirements for conceptually valid research studies on the behavioral effects of malnutrition. In J. Galler (Ed.), *Human nutrition. Vol. 5, Nutrition and behavior* (pp. 9–36). New York: Plenum.

Barrett, D. E., Radke-Yarrow, M., & Klein, R. E. (1982). Chronic malnutrition and child behavior: Effects of early caloric supplementation on social and emotional functioning at school age. *Developmental Psychology, 18,* 541–556.

Beaton, G. (1983). Energy in human nutrition: Perspectives and problems. *Nutrition Review, 41,* 325–340.

Beaton, G. H., Corey, P., & Steele, C. (1989). Conceptual and methodological issues regarding the epidemiology of iron deficiency: Implications for studies of functional consequences. *American Journal of Clinical Nutrition (Supplement), 50,* 575–585.

Bejar, I. I. (1981). Does nutrition cause intelligence? A reanalysis of the Cali experiment. *Intelligence, 5,* 49–68.

Citizens' Board of Inquiry into Hunger and Malnutrition in the United States. (1968). *Hunger, U.S.A.*. Washington, DC: New Community Press.

Cravioto, J., & DeLicardie, E. R. (1976). Microenvironmental factors in severe protein-calorie malnutrition. In N. S. Scrimshaw & M. Behar (Eds.), *Nutrition and agricultural development: Significance and potential for the tropics* (pp. 25–35). New York: Plenum.

Das, J. P., & Soysa, P. (1978). Late effects of malnutrition on cognitive competence. *International Journal of Psychology, 13,* 295–303.

Evans, D. I. (1985). Cerebral function in iron deficiency: A review. *Child Care, Health, and Development, 11,* 105–112.

Food and Nutrition Board. (1973). *The relationship of nutrition to brain development and behavior.* Washington, DC: National Research Council.

Galler, J. R. (1984). Behavioral consequences of malnutrition in early life. In J. R. Galler (Ed.), *Human nutrition. Vol. 5: Nutrition and behavior* (pp. 63–117). New York: Plenum.

Galler, J. R., & Ramsey, F. (1985). The influence of early malnutrition on subsequent behavioral development: VI. The role of the microenvironment of the household. *Nutrition and Behavior, 2,* 161–173.

Galler, J. R., Ramsey, F., & Solimano, G. (1985). Influence of early malnutrition on subsequent behavioral development: V. Child's behavior at home. *Journal of the American Academy of Child Psychiatry, 24,* 58–64.

Galler, J. R., Ramsey, F., Solimano, G., Lowell, W. E., & Mason, E. (1983). The influence of early malnutrition on subsequent behavioral development I. Degree of impairment in intellectual performance. *Journal of Child Psychiatry, 22,* 8–15.

Galler, J. R., Ricciuti, H. N., Crawford, M. A., & Kucharski, L. T. (1984). The role of mother–infant interaction in nutritional disorders. In J. R. Galler (Ed.), *Human nutrition: A comprehensive treatise. Vol. 5: Nutrition and behavior* (pp. 269–304). New York: Plenum.

Gopaldas, T., Kale, M., & Bhardwaj, P. (1985). Prophylactic iron supplementation for underprivileged school boys: II. Impact on selected tests of cognitive function. *Indian Pediatrics, 22,* 737–743.

Hansen, J. D. L., Freesemann, C., Moodie, A. D., & Evans, D. E. (1971). What does nutritional growth retardation imply? *Pediatrics, 47,* 299–313.

Hayes, C. D. (Ed.) (1982). *Making policies for children: A study of the federal process.* Washington, DC: National Academy Press.

Johnston, F. E., Low, S. M., De Baessa, Y., & MacVean, R. B. (1987). Interaction of nutrition and socioeconomic status as determinants of cognitive development in disadvantaged urban Guatemalan children. *American Journal of Physical Anthropology, 73,* 501–506.

Joos, S. K., & Pollitt, E. (1984). Effects of supplementation on behavioral development in children up to 2 years: A comparison of four studies. In J. Brozek (Ed.), *Malnutrition and behavior: Critical assessment of key issues* (pp. 507–519). Lausanne, Switzerland: Nestle Foundation.

Klein, P. S., Forbes, G. B., & Nader, P. R. (1975). Effects of starvation in infancy (pyloric stenosis) on subsequent learning abilities. *Journal of Pediatrics, 87,* 8–15.

Levine, G., & Wiener, S. (1976). A critical analysis of data on malnutrition and behavioral deficits. *Advances in Pediatrics, 22,* 113–136.

Levitsky, D. A. (1979). *Malnutrition, environment and behavior.* Ithaca, NY: Cornell University Press.

Levitsky, D. A., & Barnes, R. H. (1972). Nutritional and environmental interactions in behavioral development of the rat: Long term effects. *Science, 176,* 68–71.

Levitsky, D. A., & Strupp, B. J. (1985). Nutrition and the behavior of children. In W. A. Walker & J. Watkins (Eds.), *Nutrition and pediatrics: Basic science and clinical application* (pp. 357–372). Boston: Little, Brown.

Lozoff, B. (1988). Behavioral alterations in iron deficiency. *Advances in Pediatrics, 35,* 331–360.

Lozoff, B., Brittenham, G. M., & Viteri, F. E. (1982). The effects of short-term oral iron therapy on developmental deficits in iron deficient anemic infants. *Journal of Pediatrics, 100,* 351–357.

Lozoff, B., Brittenham, G. M., & Wolf, A. W. (1987). Iron deficiency anemia and iron therapy effects on infant developmental test performance. *Pediatrics, 79,* 981–995.

Martorell, R. (1984). Issues in design and data analysis. In J. Brozek (Ed.), *Malnutrition and behavior: Critical assessment of key issues* (pp. 556–575). Lausanne, Switzerland: Nestle Foundation.

Medical News Report. (1968). Mental retardation from malnutrition: "Irreversible." *Journal of American Medical Association, 206,* 30–31.

Moodie, A. D., Bowie, M. D., Mann, M. D. & Hansen, J. D. (1980). A prospective 15-year follow-up study of kwashiorkor patients. *South African Medical Journal, 58,* 677–681.

Natesan, H., & Devadas, R. (1981). Measurement of mental abilities of well-nourished and malnourished children. *Journal of Psychological Researches, 25,* 121–124.

National Education Association. (1989). *The relationship between nutrition and learning: A school employee's guide to information and action.* Washington, DC: National Education Association.

Oski, F. A., Honig, A. S., & Helu, B. (1983). Effect of iron therapy on behavior performance in nonanemic, iron deficient infants. *Pediatrics, 71,* 877–880.

Pollitt, E. (1988). A critical view of three decades of research on the effects of chronic energy malnutrition on behavioral development. In B. Schurch & N. Scrimshaw (Eds.), *Chronic energy deficiency: Consequences and related issues* (pp. 77–92). Lausanne, Switzerland: Nestle Foundation.

Pollitt, E. (in press). *The impact of poor nutrition and disease on educational outcomes.* Geneva, Switzerland: UNESCO.

Pollitt, E., Haas, J., & Levitsky, D. (Eds.). (1989). International conference on iron deficiency and behavioral development. *American Journal of Clinical Nutrition (Supplement), 50* (3).

Pollitt, E., Hathirat, P., Kotchabharkdi, N. J., Missell, L., & Valyasevi, A. (1989). Iron deficiency and educational achievement in Thailand. *American Journal of Clinical Nutrition (Supplement), 50,* 687–696.

Ricciuti, H. N. (1979). Malnutrition and cognitive development: Research issues and priorities. In J. Brozek (Ed.), *Behavioral effects of energy and protein deficits* (pp. 297–313). Washington, DC: National Institutes of Health. (NIH Publication No. 79-1906.)

Ricciuti, H. N. (1981a). Adverse environmental and nutritional influences on mental development: A perspective. *Journal of the American Dietetic Association, 79,* 115–120.

Ricciuti, H. N. (1981b). Developmental consequences of malnutrition in early childhood. In M. Lewis & L. A. Rosenblum (Eds.), *The uncommon child: The genesis of behavior* (Vol. 3, pp. 151–172). New York: Plenum.

Ricciuti, H. N., & Dorman, R. (1983). Interaction of multiple factors contributing to high-risk parenting. In R. A. Hoekelman (Ed.), *Minimizing high-risk parenting* (pp. 187–210). Media, PA: Harwal Publishing.

Richardson, S. A. (1974). The background histories of school children severely malnourished in infancy. In I. Schulman (Ed.), *Advances in pediatrics* (Vol. 21, pp. 167–192). Chicago: Yearbook Medical Publications.

Richardson, S. A. (1976). The relation of severe malnutrition in infancy to intelligence of school children with differing life histories. *Pediatric Research, 10,* 57–61.

Scrimshaw, N. S. (1988). Integrating nutrition into programmes of primary health care. *Food and Nutrition Bulletin, 10,* 19–28.

Scrimshaw, N. S., Taylor, C. E., & Gordon, J. E. (1968). *Interactions of nutrition and infection.* Geneva, Switzerland: World Health Organization.

Sigman, M., Neumann, C., Baksh, M., Bwilbo, N., & McDonald, M. A. (1989). Relationship between nutrition and development in Kenyan toddlers. *Journal of Pediatrics, 115,* 357–364.

Sigman, M., Neumann, C., Jansen, A. A. J., & Bwilbo, N. (1989). Cognitive abilities of Kenyan children in relation to nutrition, family characteristics, and education. *Child Development, 60,* 1463–1474.

Soemantri, A. G., Pollitt, E., & Kim, I. (1985). Iron deficiency anemia and educational achievement. *American Journal of Clinical Nutrition, 42,* 1221–1228.

Sternberg, R. J., & Wagner, R. K. (Eds.). (1986). *Practical intelligence: Nature and origins of competence in the everyday world.* New York: Cambridge University Press.

Walter, T., Kovalskys, J., & Stekel, A. (1983). Effect of mild iron deficiency on infant mental development scores. *Journal of Pediatrics, 102,* 519–522.

Werner, E. E., & Smith, R. S. (1982). *Vulnerable but invincible: A longitudinal study of resilient children and youth.* New York: McGraw-Hill.

Winick, M., Meyer, K., & Harris, R. C. (1975). Malnutrition and environmental enrichment by adoption. *Science, 190,* 1173–1175.

Woodhead, M. (1988). When psychology informs public policy: The case of early childhood intervention. *American Psychologist, 43,* 443–454.

Youdim, M. B. H., Ben-Shachar, D., & Yehuda, S. (1989). The putative biological mechanisms of the effect of iron deficiency on brain biochemistry and behavior. *American Journal of Clinical Nutrition (Supplement), 50,* 607–615.

PART II

Social Factors Influencing Cognitive Development

CHAPTER 4

Culture and Cognitive Development

EDMUND W. GORDON
Yale University

ELEANOR ARMOUR-THOMAS
Queens College, CUNY

Human cognition is an extraordinarily complex phenomenon. The collection and transformation of sensory input into secondary signals, schemata, and concepts—that is, into symbolic representations of the external world—is a sophisticated process accomplished by even the youngest of the species. Of possibly greater significance and consequence is the fact that human thought can be symbolic of actual events, imaginary phenomena, and speculative relationships between phenomena that have been experienced, heard of, or of which humans have conceived. It is the ability to manipulate symbolic representations in order to achieve transformative acts whereby existing phenomena take on new characteristics, serve different purposes, or come to be and represent other things, that makes cognitive behavior so unusual.

What is the genesis of human cognition? Because it is present in some form in all human beings and is typical of the human species, it is difficult to dismiss the possibility that cognitive behavior is the product of some unique potential intrinsic to the species and reflective of organic matter organized in ways specific to human biology. It has been argued by some that whatever is common in the cognitive behavior of human beings is biological in origin, and biological phenomena are genetically transferred from one generation to the next.

But there is wide variation in the content, complexity, purpose, form, and style of human cognition. To the extent that these variations are clustered in human groups known to share the same gene pool (e.g., ethnic and racial groups), some investigators are content to rely on biogenetic explanations, not only for the origins of cognitive function, but also for the characteristics and limitations of cognitive behavior. Following in the tradition of the French philosopher LaMarc, some researchers have further posited that some behaviors with origins in biological phenomena and that have been further shaped by social/cultural experience are transmitted in their altered forms to subsequent generations via heredity (Zirkle, 1946). There are, however, other explanations. In this chapter, we propose that the human social experience is a powerful correlate and possible cause of human behavior and, in large measure, it is the human social experience interacting with whatever is the given in human biology to which the origins, nature, quality, and limitations of human cognitive behavior are to be attributed. This chapter is divided into four sections. First, we seek to understand the nature of human social interactions by looking at the elements of human cultures. Second, we consider neurobiological evidence that suggests mechanisms by which human experience shapes neurological functioning. Third, we argue that current conceptions of cognition and cognitive development rely on the shaping of cognitive behavior by social experience. Finally, we conclude that culture and cognition are interdependent constructs that cannot be fully understood apart from each other.

THE STRUCTURE AND MEANING OF CULTURE

To understand the mechanisms and meanings of these human social interactions, we begin by turning to the study of human cultures. The construct *culture* has a wide variety of definitions, but at the core, when we speak of culture, we are referring to both a cause and a product of human behavior. Geertz (1973) provided a widely accepted conception of culture as an "historically transmitted pattern of meanings embodied in symbolic form by means of which men communicate, perpetuate and develop their knowledge about and attitudes toward life" (p. 89).

Geertz placed a heavy emphasis on language and the nonmaterial aspects of culture—that is, culture as shared ideas, concepts, values, and belief systems. But culture also includes structured relationships, which are reflected in institutions, social status, and ways of doing things, and objects that are manufactured or created, such as tools, clothing, architecture, and interpretative and representational art. Culture is a multidimensional construct consisting of at least five dimensions: (a) the judgmental or normative, (b) the cognitive, (c) the affective, (d) the skill, and (e) the technological. We consider each dimension in turn.

Normative Dimension

The judgmental or normative dimension of culture refers to social standards and values—to those behavior patterns that, according to Berry (1976), people regard as right, proper, and natural. Although this normative dimension is often dominated by religious institutions or beliefs, it is also informed by mores, traditions, a sense of the feasible, even by what the traffic will bear. With respect to cognitive behavior, the normative dimension often provides the constraints within which thought is enabled. For example, one way of interpreting *mind set* is to assume it is a reflection of a way of thinking that is born of accepted cultural practice. Within a given mind set, one might be unable to conceive of a universe without a God because deistic thought is the norm for so many human groups.

Cognitive Dimension

The cognitive dimension relates to social perceptions, conceptions, attributions, and connotations, all of which are categories of human cognition that may be expressed through language. This dimension therefore involves the communicative functions and structures of a social unit and is exemplified by what Berry (1976) described as "group habits of thought." The cognitive dimension obviously overlaps with the judgmental dimension, but goes beyond it to include not only what one thinks about, but how one thinks. More simply, although all people may be capable of thinking in any number of ways, people in different cultural groups tend to adopt certain modes of thinking. Linear and sequential thought, the search for causal relationships, the tendency to generate abstractions, and a focus on the gestalt rather than on the details that make up the whole are examples of ways of thinking that have been adopted by different cultures. In addition to these general ways of thinking, one's culture dictates the taxonomies or categories that are functional within that culture, the allowable metaphors, the connotations, and the functions served by language. Moreover, as some have argued, the cognitive domain may be the most critical dimension of culture because it is both the vehicle for and the product of language development.

Affective Dimension

By affective dimension we refer to the emotional structure of a social unit, including its common feelings, its sources of motivation, joy, and sorrow, and its sense of value. Berry suggested that human beings have "group habits of feeling." According to his notion, there are both emotions that are common to the group and specific stimuli that commonly arouse these emotions within the group members. For example, a nation's flag might commonly arouse feelings of patriotism and nationalism. Similarly, there are shared objects of affection and sentimentality, sources of comfort, and sources of anxiety or fear that bind members of a group together. That is, one's cultural context shapes one's emotions, feelings, and sentiments.

Skill Dimension

The skill dimension signifies those special capabilities the members of a culture develop in order to meet the demands of their social and techno-economic environment (Ogbu, 1978). For example, in nonindustrialized societies where farming, hunting, and gathering activities are important for sustaining the economy, children are socialized to develop related skills. By contrast, in highly industrialized societies where emphasis is given to human-to-machine interactions, we see the demand for socialization toward the skills of commerce and machine production, such as literacy, numeracy, repetitious routinization, and precision. The skills needed for survival and success within each culture varies, and children are trained from an early age to acquire these skills.

Technological Dimension

Finally, we address the technological dimension, the notion of culture as accumulated artifacts, instrumentation, and techniques. We include the objects that are made and used, as well as the manner in which they are used. Here, for instance, it is useful to contrast the processes of information exchange in the less technologically advanced parts of the world with those in the countries with more highly developed technology. When we consider, for example, that for some people news of a disaster in one area can reach others who are thousands of miles away almost as the event occurs versus a transmittal of information taking days or weeks, we see not simply different practices, but the different impact of the available technology on the cognitive and affective behaviors of people.

Culture as an Explanatory Construct

Thus far our definition of culture has primarily emphasized those characteristics by which a culture may be identified or by which the culture of a group may be characterized. The five dimensions of culture—judgmental, cognitive, affective, skill, and technological—however, also indicate ways in which culture shapes behavior. Culture is not merely a descriptive construct. As Harrington (1988) cautioned, culture is not simply a product of human action: "observe the action and you can label the culture" (p. 6.2). Culture also influences human action and must therefore be regarded as an explanatory as well as a descriptive concept. Human action is a product of culture. Some cognitive developmentalists have posited that the development of cognition is a natural consequence of being human as "intendedly rational and scientific . . . striving to adapt or accommodate intelligence to the demands of common reality" (Piaget, as cited by Shweder & LeVine, 1984, p. 49). Other cognitive developmentalists see the genesis of human thought in the social interactions between the developing organism and its environment. Rather than Piaget's conception of self-constructed knowledge, D'Andrade (1980) attributed cognition to "other-dependent learning." D'Andrade asserted that "much of what we know is learned from other people. . . . People are very good at discovering what they must learn under conditions of informally-guided discovery" (p. 186). Whether we refer to mental behaviors or any of the nonreflex and otherwise organized human behavior, it is the context and content prided by one's culture that shapes human behavior. This dual nature of culture—to be descriptive and explanatory—not only is important to our understanding of it as a phenomenon, but is crucial to the use of information concerning culture to inform knowledge production, knowledge utilization, knowledge transfer, and other manifestations of human cognition.

When we use cultural information to describe and identify an individual, we are being sensitive to culture as a status phenomenon. Such information can help us determine people's position, place, and role in the social order, the opportunities and rewards to which they will be exposed and, to some extent, how the people are perceived. From such information we might even predict how the person or the group is likely to behave. However, in order to make accurate predictions, and to understand behavior, we must use information relative to culture as an explanatory concept, as a functional phenomenon. We want to know what this information tells us not simply about status, but about the consequences of the phenomenon for the functioning of the person. How does a particular aspect of culture influence the behavior of the person? What does the symbol or the tool enable the person to do? What societal capabilities are provided by the existence of the language? How do specific belief systems influence individual behavior or patterns of social organization? Questions like these explore the ways in which culture functions to shape individual and group behaviors rather than to describe simply the cultural experience or the status of specific members. Kluckholn (1965) captured the dual nature of culture:

> Culture consists of patterns, explicit and implicit, of and for behavior acquired and transmitted by symbols, constituting the distinctive achievement of human groups. . . . Culture systems may, on the one hand be considered as products of action, on the other hand as influences upon actions. (p. 73)

Thus we suggest that not only does culture describe the thought and behavior of a group of people, but it also shapes their behavior. Culture defines what one does and how one does it. It also provides the schemata that frame and enable the feelings and thoughts about what one does. We assert that cognition is dependent on culture, because it is one's culture that provides the content and the context of thought, even though the process may be enabled by biological capacity and physiological function.

Mechanisms of Cultural Influence

Although we might logically accept that culture dictates both the content and context of cognition and thereby influences cognitive processing, we still can legitimately ask: Is there any evidence that the individual's external context affects the development of the brain or the internal functioning of the brain? In this section, we examine a possible explanatory model.

Hebb (1949) advanced a structural paradigm for understanding the relation between brain function and experience. According to Hebb, it is the function of experience to enable the differentiation of neural cells in their associations, one with the other, to produce what he called *cell assemblies.* A single cell may belong to multiple assemblies, but once so associated, under appropriate patterns of stimulation (extrinsic or proprioceptive) a particular constellation of cells (i.e., cell assembly) is formed or a specific constellation of assemblies is called into operation. Using this perhaps overly simplistic model, we propose it is culture that provides the stimuli, the models, and the contexts by which experience comes to be reflected in organization or differentiation of brain cells. It is a further function of the culture to give meaning to, to set standards for, to systematize, to mediate, and to reinforce the overt expression of the behavioral products of these constellations of cell assemblies. However, it is the unique transformative capacity of the human brain in interaction with its environment that enables these cells and their assemblies to rearrange or respond in new ways to provide the atypical reaction.

Recently, advances in neuroscience have led to new perspectives for understanding the interrelationships among neural activity, experience, and behavior. *Synaptogenesis* is a type of neural change in which initially there is overproduction and later pruning of synaptic connections that occur during the late prenatal and early postnatal periods of development. Greenough,

Black, and Wallace (1987) theorized that although the overproduction of synapses is maturationally regulated, the process of pruning (i.e., which ones are pruned) seems to be a function of experience. According to this perspective, experience triggers neural activity that commits a set of synapses to a particular organization. Synapses not needed for that organization are pruned away, and those synapses that are maintained are those involved in subsequent relevant neural activity.

According to this theory, cultural context can directly affect cognitive processing by influencing synaptogenesis because the density of early synaptic connections, particularly in the prefrontal cortex and its environs, has been linked to the development of ability to solve cognitive problems. For example, Goldman-Rakic's (1987) findings of human infants' ability to solve A-not-B object permanence and delayed response tasks, Fisher's (1987) research on use of single words in infancy, and Brody's (1981) evidence of changes in infants' short-term cued recall have all been explained in terms of synaptogenesis during early infancy. And, the type and density of these synaptic connections do not occur independent of experience.

Greenough and colleagues (1987) used the concepts of *experience-expectant* and *experience-dependent* processes to account for the relation between synaptic connections and experience. According to the experience-expectant notion, relevant or normal experience during an early sensitive period results in normal neural activity that maintains typical synaptic connections, whereas lack of experience or unusual experience leads to atypical neural activity that results in atypical synaptic connections. In a number of animal research studies, we find reports that the absence of relevant visual experience during the period of synaptic overproductions results in severe visual impairment in kittens (Hubel & Wiesel, 1970; Mower, Christen, & Caplan, 1983). Thus, it would appear that although synaptic overproduction is maturationally regulated, the overlapping of relevant experience during the occurrence of synaptic overproduction is necessary for normal development.

According to the experience-dependent hypothesis, every new attempt of the organism to process information gives rise to specific neural activity that results in the formation of synapses. There is some evidence that the formation of synapses occurs as quickly as 10 to 15 minutes following a new experience (Chang & Greenough, 1984). Other studies point to the localization of synaptic generation to the site of the previous information processing. For example, Turner and Greenough (1985) found that rats reared in environments filled with various objects that they were free to explore, generated 20%-25% more synapses per neuron in the upper visual cortex than those reared in impoverished environments. Similarly, Chang and Greenough (1982) found that rats with severed corpus callosa, when provided with monocular experience, generated more extensive dendritic fields in the occipital cortex within a month's time than those animals that did not receive such experience.

In short, there is evidence that the degree of localization, density, and typicality of synaptogenesis all depend on the nature, quality, and timing of environmental input, and in turn, that synaptogenesis affects behavior. Although these findings were derived from nonhuman animal species, they are consistent with the knowledge base concerning the importance of dynamic interaction with the environment for human development. We argue that cultural experience is the vehicle for the environmental inputs that seem to be so critical for cognitive development.

CONCEPTIONS OF COGNITION AND COGNITIVE DEVELOPMENT

To this point, we have attempted to show that (a) culture sets the content and context of human cognition, and (b) cultural experience affects cognitive processing, in part by providing the environmental input that shapes the development of the brain. We now want to consider current perspectives of cognition and the relation between cognition and culture that cognitive psychologists posit to exist.

During the course of the 20th century, competing perspectives have sought to explain the mechanisms that produce change in the structure and/or process of thought in human beings. We focus on two major theoretical perspectives on cognitive development—the *cognitive-structural* and the *contextual* paradigms. Theorists working within these frameworks acknowledge the interplay of biological and environmental forces in the development and manifestation of human cognition. Where they differ, however, is in the relative emphasis given to one source rather than the other and in the mechanisms by which these sources interact to cause development. In this section we examine each perspective's explanation of how development occurs and the role context/culture play in the explanation.

Cognitive–Structural Perspective

The cognitive-structural perspective on cognitive development emphasizes the structural nature of human cognition, and the ordered sequences of increasingly sophisticated logical mental structures that are genetically programmed to unfold in response to experiences over significant periods of life (e.g., Case, 1985; Feldman, 1980; Piaget, 1952). Piaget, perhaps the most celebrated proponent of this view, maintained that there are four major stages of cognitive development and each stage is characterized by unique structural features that enable qualitatively different modes of cognitive functioning. To account for the mechanisms through which development occurs, Piaget posited four concepts: schema, assimilation, accommodation, and equilibration.

In his writings with Inhelder (1969), Piaget referred to a *schema* as a mental structure that serves as a blueprint for action by the individual in analogous or similar situations. Existing schemata are strengthened or transformed into new schemata through two adaptational processes: assimilation and accommodation. *Assimilation* involves taking in experiences from the environment and fitting them into existing schemata. In contrast, *accommodation* allows for the organism to take in new or sufficiently different experiences from the environment and to modify existing schemata in response to these new environmental demands. Herein lies the crux of Piaget's interactional model. The organism is continually interacting with the environment and seeking a "fit" between its existing schemata and new environmental experiences. This interaction is under the control of the equilibration principle.

For Piaget, *equilibration* is the primary mechanism that accounts for developmental change. He described it as a constant tug-of-war between the two adaptational processes—assimilation and accommodation—striving for a balance. The achievement of a balance between the two dynamic processes ushers in a new level of development. This balance is only temporary, however, for tension between biological maturation and the accumulation of new environmental experiences inevitably produces disequilibrium, which sets in motion the assimilation and accommodation processes once again. Throughout this process, Piaget assumed that children play a pivotal role as active constructors of their own development. Furthermore, he contended that this striving to construct higher levels of development is a universal phenomenon, though the rate and form of development depend on both individual variations in environmental experiences and differences in biological maturation.

The cognitive-structural perspective views biological and environmental factors as reciprocal processes determining cognitive development. Furthermore, it is difficult to establish the primacy of one over the other. For example, Piaget, a biologist by training, argued that a certain continuity exists between cognitive development and the purely biological processes of morphogenesis and adaptation to the environment: "Mental growth is inseparable from physical growth. . . . Maturation of the nervous and endocrine systems, in particular, continues until the age of sixteen" (Piaget & Inhelder, 1969, p. vii). At the same time, however, Piaget (1973) stressed the role of environment in cognitive development:

> The human being is immersed right from birth in a social environment which affects him just as much as his physical environment. Society, even more, in a sense, than the physical environment, changes the very structure of the individual. . . . Every relation between individuals literally modifies them. (p. 156)

A vast number of studies that have used the cognitive-structural perspective have reported cultural variation in cognitive development (e.g., Cole, Gay, Glick, & Sharp, 1971; Cole & Scribner, 1974; Laboratory of Comparative Human Cognition, 1983; Rogoff & Waddell, 1982), lending credence to the notion that contextual forces shape the development of cognition and influence its manifestation in idiosyncratic ways. More specifically, what appears as the crystallization of a new form of thought at different periods over the lifespan depend on the kinds of activities to which children are exposed, the age at which they are given the opportunities for the development of cognition related to such activities, and perhaps most importantly, the extent to which experienced significant others mediate the child's experiences with such activities.

In conclusion, the cognitive-structural perspective posits mechanisms by which individuals interact in meaningful ways with the environment in order to develop and/or change their cognitive structures. Furthermore, the evidence of differential patterns of cognitive development in different sociocultural milieus makes the explanation vulnerable to the role of culture in shaping the timing, form, and expression of human cognition.

Contextual Perspective

The Vygotskian tradition purports that nascent cognitive abilities emerge, develop, and are displayed within a sociocultural milieu (e.g., Bronfenbrenner, 1979; Gardner & Rogoff, 1982; Palinscar & Brown, 1984; Wertsch, 1979; Whiting, 1980). This notion of contextual cognition is not new. A noted anthropologist, Clifford Geertz (1962), assumed an interdependence of context and cognition when he stated that "the human brain is thoroughly dependent upon cultural resources for its very operation; and those resources are, consequently, not adjuncts to but constituents of mental activity" (p. 730). These notions suggest that context is not simply the physical setting in which interactions unfold, but encompasses what people are doing with each other, as well as the location and time of their interactions. The contextual perspective emphasizes the centrality of social interaction in the development of human cognition. We now consider the mechanisms by which culture is thought to shape cognitive development.

Vygotsky's (1978) cultural–historical theory posits four concepts that are critical to the thesis that culture shapes cognitive development—transmission of knowledge, transmission of cognitive skills, cultivation of nascent cognitive abilities, and encouragement of cognitive abilities. First, knowledge in one's culture is socially transmitted by adults and capable peers to children. Second, joint participation in the range of activities determined by the culture allows for certain cognitive skills to be practiced and demonstrated by adults so that the children's current cognitive functioning may be modified or strengthened. In this way, the adult helps to shape the children's existing skills to better suit the demands of the culture. Third, new cognitive abilities are cultivated when the adult or capable peer shares in the responsibility for the task with the children. Assuming the role of an expert tutor, the adult models, corrects, clarifies, and explains concepts to the children in order that they attempt and complete the task according to the criteria established by the culture. Finally, the independent use of new cognitive abilities is encouraged when the adult or more capable peer works with the children on challenging tasks that they could not have successfully completed without guidance. Working with the children in their "zone of proximal development," the adult models the task-appropriate behaviors, directs the child's attention to alternative procedures or approaches to the task, and encourages the children to try out their embryonic skills on some portion of the task. As children's ability develops, the adult gradually reduces instructional support and allows them to assume greater independence in task solution. It is this type of *social scaffolding* that Vygotsky suggested as the mechanism for change in cognitive development. In a somewhat similar vein, Nelson (1978; Nelson & Gruendel, 1981) proposed the role of "generalized event representations" or scripts in social interactions to account for changes in cognitive development.

The concept of generalized event representations is similar to the Piagetian concept of schemata, but from a contextual perspective. These mental representations are conceived as being interwoven with specific events in the environment. According to Nelson and Gruendel (1981; Nelson, 1986), representations include the following characteristics of an event: its temporal-causal structure, the people who participate and the social roles they play, its obligatory and optional components, the sequence of actions, and the objects used. At a very early age, children seem predisposed to make sense of activities in which they participate and readily construct schematic representations of events that form the basic building blocks for subsequent cognitive development. In other words, schematic representations, because of their inherent structure, allow for the incorporation of new information about a particular kind of event, and also enable gradual refinement and elaboration of event knowledge. But what circumstances determine whether children will encounter the kinds of experiences critical for cognitive growth and development?

Anthropologists and contextual psychologists (e.g., Barker, 1968; Berry, 1976) contend that the human environments wherein cognition develops are not random events, but rather are highly organized ecological and sociocultural circumstances. In extrapolating from Vygotsky's sociohistorical perspective, the Laboratory of Comparative Human Cognition (1983) identified four ways by which culture influences the organization of children's environments:

1. by arranging the occurrence or nonoccurrence of specific problem-solving environments;
2. by arranging the frequency of the same kinds of events in these learning environments;
3. by shaping the patterning or co-occurrence of events; and
4. by regulating the level of difficulty of the task.

Several investigations have documented the gradual evolution of cognition when adults organize the learning environments of children using the principle of social scaffolding. For example, in the studies conducted by Palinscar and Brown (1984) and Wertsch (1979), the adult was able, through different levels of interaction over time, to socialize the development of self-regulatory skills in children. It was this type of dynamic progression of cognitive functioning that led Vygotsky (1978) to hypothesize that psychological processes begin as interpsychic functions shared on an external and interpersonal plane. Later, through extensive practice of cognitive skills with a significant other, the child is enabled to execute these skills on an intrapsychic plane.

If we accept the primacy of social interaction in the emergence and nurturance of children's cognitive abilities, then we must also consider the implications of negative or different social interactions on cognitive growth and development. In this regard one may hypothesize that within or across cultures, to the extent that the organization, form, style, and content of social interactions may be less than optimal, uneven, or less than optimal, cognitive development can be predicted. Also, to the extent to which variation in the organization and quality of social interactions exist within and across cultures, one may hypothesize variations in cognitive development.

In summary, researchers who espouse the contextual perspective suggest that the mechanisms of cognitive development lie outside the individual and occur in two ways. First, at the societal level, culture provides the norms, conventions, and values of socializing the process and products of cognition (e.g., Lave, 1977; Rogoff & Morelli, 1981; Sharp, Cole, & Lave, 1979). Second, at the interpersonal level, experienced significant others mediate the child's experiences. They provide culturally appropriate contents and strategies for understanding, which in time are internalized by the children and become part of their individual cognitive repertoire and functioning (e.g., Cazden, Cox, Dickinson, Steinberg, & Stonce, 1979; Gardner & Rogoff, 1982; Palinscar & Brown, 1984; Wertsch, McNamee, Budwig, & McLane, 1980).

Obviously considerable progress has been made in the understanding of the mechanisms that contribute to the development of human cognition. Both the cognitive-structural and the contextual approaches have each focused on a different explanation for change: structural transformation versus contextualized variation. It is entirely possible that each of these conceptions is partially correct. The construct must have structure. The diversity in the manifestations of the construct and the conditons under which it develops make obvious the relevance of contextual variance. It is possible that an examination of the relation between culture and cognition may allow for an informative integration of these approaches and may result in a fuller understanding of both culture and cognitive development. Efforts at addressing the mechanisms of cognitive change can be facilitated by thinking of cognitive development as operating within a specific cultural context. Within this view, it is the context that could influence the emergence of cognitive structure or process as well as the achievement of cognitive competence.

CULTURE AND COGNITION: A JUXTAPOSITION OF THE CONSTRUCTS

We begin with the notion that human beings are uniquely social animals, so much so that our very existence depends on social interactions with our environments, but primarily on interactions with each other. We humans are born incapable of independent life. We are socialized in symbiotic relationships from which the capacity for relatively independent action is achieved, but we never seem to lose the need for social interaction. Segall (1979) reminded us that "it is the nature of humans to be socially docile . . . responsive to socioculturally mediated reinforcements, . . . reinforcements dispensed by other people or otherwise stemming from the behavior of others" (p. 5). Gergin (1990) raised the possibility that understanding (i.e., cognition) itself is a social process that occurs exclusively within the individual. According to this view, information, knowledge, understanding, technique, even feeling are social products that come to be reflected in the behavior of individuals and groups of persons and can only be cognitive because of their socialized referents. Thus, any notion of cognition as a process essentially localized within individuals provides limited understanding of the mechanisms by which its ontogeny can be explained. Recognizing cognition as a person–environment transactive, as well as a transducive, process, Gergin (1990) used the term *relational adjudication* to make cognition vulnerable to cultural explanations of its genesis and functioning. It is this cultural vulnerability of cognition that both makes cultural explanations of its genesis so critical and cultural referents essential to the understanding of its functioning.

What then are the mechanisms by which cultural experiences enable biological potentials to emerge and develop into highly organized and differentiated cognitive functions? An understanding of the nature and function of the sociocultural context at both macro- and microlevels is critical for addressing this question. At the macrolevel, the sociocultural context, mediated through institutional structures, provides the value, beliefs, norms, conventions, and technological devices that serve to organize and govern the cognitive and conative behaviors of its members. More specifically, cultural institutions transmit information to its members with regard to what is worth knowing, imitating, and doing. It is through these institutions (i.e., family, religious institution, school, media) that members learn who are the significant others responsible for knowledge and skill transmission; from whom significant reinforcements flow; how knowledge and skills are to be transmitted; the types of activities to be practiced to enable acquisition, application and extension of acquired knowledge and skill; and finally, the standards against which such knowledge and skills are to be judged.

At the microlevel, the sociocultural context, mediated through personal social interactions, provides the opportunity to develop the personal attributions, dispositions, and motivations to behave in existentially appropriate ways. An analysis of the reciprocal behaviors of learners and experienced significant others in teaching–learning transactions provides useful insights with reference to the mechanisms by which experiences are transformed into intrapersonal psychological processes. Experienced significant others make available for learners culturally appropriate tasks to be learned, often under conditions in which the significant other's interest in the learner and/or the task may be more important than interest in the task itself to the learner. In such situations, significant others model behaviors to be imitated and make salient the critical elements of the tasks to be mastered. In addition, they describe, interpret, and explain events relevant to task mastery. They regulate the learner's problem-solving efforts through cues, questioning, feedback, and social reinforcement. In turn, learners imitate modeled behavior, recognize the relationship between the significant other's cues, questions, explanations, and the task situation, respond to questions, modify behavior following feedback and social reinforcement, practice new behavior, and eventually regulate their own behavior without the support of the significant other. Over time, through these reciprocal processes between an experienced other and learners, learners develop a system of knowledge structures and affective cognitive skills that are congruent with the values, beliefs, and conventions of their sociocultural group. These culturally coded knowledge structures are used as interpretative frameworks for assimilating familiar information and accommodating new information into existing knowledge structures.

Developmentally, it is the institution (i.e., family, school, church, peer group, community or social group) that gradually replaces, or at least parallels, the significant other as a source of reinforcement but also as the vehicle for the normative or judgmental dimension of culture. We argue that the institution may have gained significance for the learning person and thus emerges as a major socializing force, or it may simply be so ubiquitous in its presence as to become a primary source of enculturation. High degrees of dissonance in this relationship can result in failure to learn or distortion of the learning process. It may well be that the primary process of cultural transmission is represented by the acquisition and imitation of stimulus-response-situation triads that gain cognitive and conative significance through the processes of accommodation and adaptation.

Accommodation is the process by which the acquisitions and their replications are related to existing schemata (emerging conceptual frames). This process involves making sense of or deriving meaning in terms of the extant situation. It is probable here that a concurrent process occurs, namely, conation (labeling, marking), by which that which is acquired and imitated is symbolized by a name or word or number symbol. On the other hand, *adaptation* is the process by which that which has been accommodated or made a part of one's cognitive repertoire is adapted or adjusted to the demands of the currently perceived or changing conditions. With time, adaptation is enabled to proceed more speedily and to be applied to a broader range of situations because of the process we call *schematization*, the development of conceptual structures that represent the coming together of cognitive, conative, and affective components or aspects of phenomena experienced.

Culture then is the source of much of that which is experienced and provides the meaning for all experiential encounters. It provides the context for stimulus-response-situation replication and accommodation. It provides the situational demand for adaptation. It is the source of the attributions which form the social basis for affect—feelings and personal meaning. It is the orchestration of these factors that emerges as cognition, which we see as rooted in cultural experience, and may help us to understand how it is that such referents for cultural identity, like class, ethnicity, and gender, come to be so powerfully associated with developed cognitive activity.

REFERENCES

Barker, R. G. (1968). *Ecological psychology*. Stanford, CA: Stanford University Press.

Berry, J. W. (1976). *Human ecology and cognitive style*. New York: Sage-Halsted.

Brody, E. B., & Brody, N. (1976). *Intelligence, nature, determinants, and consequences.* New York: Academic Press.

Brody, L. R. (1981). Visual short term cued-recall memory in infancy. *Child Development, 52,* 242–250.

Bronfenbrenner, U. (1979). *The ecology of human development.* Cambridge, MA: Harvard University Press.

Case, R. (1985). *Intellectual development: A systematic reinterpretation.* New York: Academic Press.

Cazden, C. B., Cox, M., Dickinson, D., Steinberg, Z., & Stonce, C. (1979). "You all gonna hafta listen": Peer teaching in a primary classroom. In W. A. Collins (Ed.), *The Minnesota symposium of child psychology* (Vol. 12). Hillsdale, NJ: Lawrence Erlbaum Associates.

Chang, F. L., & Greenough, W. T. (1982). Lateralized effects of monocular training on dendritic branching in adult split-brain rats. *Brain Research, 232,* 283–292.

Chang, F. L., & Greenough, W. T. (1984). Transient and enduring morphological correlates of synaptic activity and efficacy change in the rat hippocampal slice. *Brain Research, 309,* 35–46.

Cole, M., Gay, J., Glick, J. A., & Sharp, D. W. (1971). *The cultural context of learning and thinking.* New York: Basic Books.

Cole, M., & Scribner, S. (1974). *Culture and thought.* New York: Wiley.

D'Andrade, R. (1980). The cultural part of cognition. *Cognitive Science, 5,* 179–196.

Feldman, D. (1980). *Beyond universals in cognitive development.* Norwood, NJ: Ablex.

Fisher, K. W. (1987). Relations between brain and cognitive development. *Child Development, 58,* 623–632.

Gardner, W., & Rogoff, B. (1982). The role of instruction in memory development: Some methodological choices. *Quarterly Newsletter of the Laboratory of Comparative Human Cognition, 4,* 6–12.

Geertz, C. (1962). The growth of culture and the evolution of mind. In J. M. Scher (Ed.), *Theories of the mind* (pp. 123–126). New York: Free Press.

Geertz, C. (1973). *Interpretation of cultures.* New York: Basic Books.

Gergin, K. J. (1990). Social understanding and the inscription of self. In J. W. Stigler, R. A. Shweder, & G. Herdt (Eds.), *Cultural psychology* (pp. 470–606). New York: Cambridge University Press.

Goldman-Rakic, P. S. (1987). Development of cortical circuitry and cognitive function. *Child Development, 58,* 601–522.

Greenough, W. T., Black, J. E., & Wallace, C. S. (1987). Experience and brain development. *Child Development, 58,* 539–559.

Harrington, C. (1988). Culture as a manifestation of human diversity. In E. W. Gordon & Associates (Eds.), *Human diversity and pedagogy* (pp. 6.1–6.51). New Haven, CT: Institution for Social Policy Studies.

Hebb, D. O. (1949). *The organization of behavior: A neuropsychological theory.* New York: Wiley.

Hubel, D. H., & Wiesel, T. N. (1970). The period of susceptibility to the physiological effects of unilateral eye closure in kittens. *Journal of Physiology, 206,* 419–436.

Klatsky, R. (1980). *Human memory* (2nd ed.). San Francisco, CA: W. H. Freeman.

Kluckholn, C. (1965). *Culture and behavior.* New York: Free Press.

Laboratory of Comparative Human Cognition. (1983). Culture and cognitive development. In W. Kessen (Ed.), *Handbook of child psychology: History, theory, and methods.* (Vol. 1, pp. 294–356). New York: Wiley.

Lave, J. (1977). Tailor-made experiments and evaluating the intellectual consequences of apprenticeship training. *Quarterly Newsletter of the Laboratory for Comparative Human Cognition, I,* 1–3.

Lave, J., Murtaugh, M., & de la Roche, O. (1984). The dialectic of arithmetic in grocery shopping. In B. Rogoff & J. Lave (Eds.), *Everyday cognition: Its development in social context.* Cambridge, MA: Harvard University Press.

Mower, G. D., Christen, W. G., Caplan, C. J. (1983). Very brief visual experience eliminates plasticity in the cat visual cortex. *Science, 221,* 178–180.
Nelson, K. (1978). How young children represent knowledge of their world in and out of language. In R. Siegler (Ed.), *Children's thinking: What develops?* (pp. 184–217). Hillsdale, NJ: Lawrence Erlbaum Associates.
Nelson, K. (1986). *Event knowledge: Structure and functions in development.* Hillsdale, NJ: Lawrence Erlbaum Associates.
Nelson, K., & Gruendel, J. M. (1981). Generalized event representations: Basic building blocks of cognitive development. In M. Lamb & A. L. Brown (Eds.), *Advances in developmental psychology* (Vol. 1). Hillsdale, NJ: Lawrence Erlbaum Associates.
Ogbu, J. (1978). *Minority education and caste: The American system in cross cultural perspective. New York: Academic Press.*
Palinscar, A. S., & Brown, A. L. (1984). Reciprocal teaching of comprehension-fostering and comprehension-monitoring activities. *Cognition and Instruction, 1,* 117–175.
Piaget, J. (1952). *The child's conception of number.* New York: Norton.
Piaget, J. (1973). *The psychology of intelligence.* Totowa, NJ: Littlefield & Adams.
Piaget, J., & Inhelder, B. (1969). *The psychology of the child.* New York: Basic Books.
Rogoff, B., & Morelli, G. (1989). Perspectives on children's development from cultural psychology. *American Psychologist, 44,* (2), 343–348.
Rogoff, B., & Waddell, K. J. (1982). Memory for information organized in a scene by children from two cultures. *Child Development, 53,* 1224–1228.
Segall, M. H. (1979). *Cross cultural psychology.* Monterey, CA: Brooks/Cole.
Sharp, D., Cole, M., & Lave, C. (1979). Education and cognitive development: The evidence from experimental research. *Monograph of the Society for Research in Child Development, 44* (1-2, Serial No. 178).
Shweder, R. A., & LeVine, R. A. (1984). *Culture theory: Essays on mind, self, and emotion.* London: Cambridge University Press.
Turner, A. M., & Greenough, W. T. (1985). Differential rearing effects on rat visual cortex synapses per neuron. *Brain Research, 329,* 195–203.
Vygotsky, L. S. (1978). *Mind in society.* Cambridge, MA: Harvard University Press.
Wertsch, J. V. (1979). From social interaction to higher psychological processes: A clarification and application of Vygotsky's theory. *Human Development, 22,* 1–22.
Wertsch, J., McNamee, G., Budwig, N., & McLane, J. (1980). The adult–child dyad as a problem-solving system. *Child Development, 51,* 1213–1221.
Whiting, B. (1980). Culture and social behavior: A model for the development of social behavior. *Ethos, 8,* 95–116.
Zirkle, C. (1946). Early history of the idea of the inheritance of acquired characteristics and pangenesis. *Transactions of the American Philosophical Society, 35,* 91.

CHAPTER 5

Cultural and Parental Influences on Cognitive Development

LYNN OKAGAKI
ROBERT J. STERNBERG
Yale University

In this chapter, we propose that cultural socialization in general and parental socialization in particular affect intellectual development. We argue that parental beliefs and behaviors affect (a) the timing at which particular skills develop, (b) academic achievement, (c) individual differences in intellectual ability, and (d) the development of specific cognitive skills.

In chapter 1, Scarr and Ricciuti persuasively and eloquently argued that it is the child's genotype that drives environmental influences. They provided evidence suggesting that children select and shape their environments in such ways that individual differences in performances will ultimately be obtained. We hope to show not that genotype is irrelevant, but that social context matters in some very important and very concrete ways. We believe parents do affect their children's cognitive development, and that although genetic constraints exist, we do not yet know the boundaries of parental influence.

We have divided this chapter into two sections. First, we address the question: How does general cultural context affect cognition? Second, we discuss specific ways in which parents influence cognitive development.

WHAT EFFECT DOES CULTURAL CONTEXT HAVE ON COGNITION?

In 1974, Urie Bronfenbrenner wrote that developmental psychology had become the study of "the behavior of children in strange situations with strange adults" (p. 3). That is, researchers were studying children's behavior out of their natural context. Psychologists had assumed that a given skill, for example, categorization, could be studied by giving children novel or abstract items to categorize, and in doing so, they could control for differences in prior experiences. Psychologists expected that if individuals knew how to categorize objects according to similarities and differences, then they could apply that process to any type of stimulus. According to our thesis for this section, context and cognitive functioning are intricately interwoven and we cannot consider cognitive functioning without considering contextual influences.

Functional Context of Objects in the Setting

Cultural context determines the ways in which objects are regularly used by the people in the setting. First, the context provides specific objects on which to act and defines the ways in which these objects are used. Reasoning with one set of objects is not necessarily the same as reasoning with a different set of objects. For example, in a study of rural, unschooled and schooled Indian children and U.S. school children, Lantz (1979) found that a simple change from thinking about one set of objects (an array of colors) to thinking about a different set of objects (an array of grains and seeds) dramatically affected performance. Children were asked to describe the items so that each item could be distinguished from the other items in the array by another child later on. Both the rural unschooled and schooled Indian children were able to provide specific descriptions of the grains and to interpret a given description accurately. Both Indian groups scored significantly higher on this task than the U.S. children. However, the U.S. children did much better with the color array than the Indian children. Lantz explained that the Indian children provided less specific descriptions of the colors because in their culture colors could often be substituted for one another with little or no negative consequences. On the other hand, grains and seeds were very important to their communities. And, although the children were being asked to do the same thing with the seeds as with the colors, in this instance, the content of the task affected performance.

It is important to note that Lantz's explanation of performance differences was not based on simple physical familiarity with objects. It was not that the unschooled Indian children were unfamiliar with colors. Rather, the key was the *functional familiarity* or functional context of the objects. Recognition and accurate description of grains and seeds were vitally important to the Indian community's economy. Thus, the Indian children in the experimental task could draw on their agricultural expertise. This notion of functional context accords with results from expert–novice studies. This is illustrated by Chase and Simon's (1973) expert–novice study of recall for configurations of chess pieces in which expert chess players outperformed novices when the chess pieces were arrayed in meaningful chess patterns, but not when the pieces were randomly arrayed on the chess board. Even though the expert chess players were familiar with the chess pieces in both instances, only when the objects were arrayed in patterns that were functionally consequential did they outperform novices.

Sensitivity to the functional context of objects is part of considering changes in the task itself. We must consider not only what objects and concepts children normally encounter in their immediate environments, but also the ways in which those objects and concepts are used. Consider two studies of children's performance on Piagetian conservation tasks. One study (Price-Williams, Gordon, & Ramirez, 1969) compared children from two Mexican villages. In both villages, people made pottery using a process in which balls of clay are pressed into molds. When a mistake is made, the clay is simply taken out of the mold, rolled back into balls, and then pressed back into the mold. Thus, the process models conservation of matter—the shape of the clay changes, while the amount of the clay remains constant. In one village, children were actively involved in making pottery. These children did better on the conservation of matter task than children from the other village who did not routinely work with clay.

A later study by Steinberg and Dunn (1976) involved children of potters in another Mexican village. These children also actively participated in making pottery. However, they did not do better on conservation of matter tasks than children with no pottery making experience. What explains the different results? Villagers in the Steinberg and Dunn study made their pottery by rolling the clay into long coils that were placed one on top of the other to form the pot. For these children, the functional context for working with clay did not involve transforming the shape of the clay from one form to another and then back again. Although they were "familiar" with clay, the way in which they used clay did not require them to notice that a given amount of clay could be formed and reformed into different shapes.

Social Context

When thinking skills are learned in particular contexts, expectations about appropriate behaviors, response choices, and social roles are also established, and these expectations can become part of the supporting context that the child sees as necessary for implementing that skill. When the behaviors and expectations in one's regular social context do not sufficiently match those of a new setting, then the skill may be present, but individuals may be confused as to what is being required of them. In an ethnographic study of three communities in the Piedmont Carolinas, Heath (1983) described a community in which children are rarely asked to answer questions from adults. Children do not take the role of an information-giver. Heath suggested that as a result, these children are confused when they are constantly asked to respond to questions from adults in school—particularly when the adult already knows the answer to the question. The children may in fact know the answers to the questions, but the school context is not giving them the necessary cues so that the children know they are supposed to say what they know.

In the 1930s, Luria (1976) posed the opposite task to a group of Russian peasants. The experimenter wanted the participant to ask three questions about anything. Thirteen of the 21 illiterate peasants simply refused to formulate any kind of question. "I can't imagine what to ask about—I only know about spadework, nothing else. . . . To ask questions you need knowledge, and all we do is hoe weeds in the fields. . . . It would be better for you to ask me" (Luria, 1976, p. 138). In the social context of an experimental interview, these Russian peasants were unable to spontaneously generate questions. Whether or not these adults had a role in their society in which they spontaneously sought information from authority figures is unclear. Certainly it was the case that they did not normally assume the role of the experimental participant who performs odd tasks for no apparent reason, and the expectations and behaviors that they carried with them from their regular social environments did not give them any clues to help them decipher the experimenter's request.

Cultural Values

Cultural context also shapes cognitive development by establishing the criteria for what is accepted as a "good" answer or as "good thinking." For example, Cole, Gay, Glick, and Sharp (1971) presented Kpelle farmers with a set of 20 items, five each from four categories: food, clothing, tools, and cooking utensils. The subjects were asked to sort the objects into groups of objects that go together. Instead of putting objects into the four taxonomic categories, the Kpelle subjects would, for example, put the potato with the pot. After all, one needs the pot to cook the potato. Subjects indicated that a wise man would put things together in this manner. Finally, when the experimenters asked how a fool would do the task, they got the answer they originally expected. Obviously, the Kpelle did have the ability to do the taxonomic classification, but a taxonomic classification was not a sensible response according to Kpelle standards. Luria (1976) found similar responses to classification tasks from unschooled Russian peasants, who although they could identify the correct general categories (e.g., tools, weapons or vessels) would reject the answer as not being sensible according to their cultural perspective.

Typical Problem-Solving Strategies to Use

When faced with a problem or task, does one have a repertoire of typical strategies to use for approaching the task? Are there known appropriate ways for solving the problem? For example, is primacy in problem solving given to speed, to least effort, to efficiency, or to "satisficing" (any solution that satisfies the problem constraints regardless of the speed, efficiency, or elegance of the solution)? Several psychologists (e.g., Goodnow, 1976; Laboratory of Comparative Human Cognition, 1982, 1986; Rogoff, 1981; Rogoff & Morelli, 1989) have argued that the ways in which people approach problem solving are shaped by their culture, and in particular, by schooling. For example, the previously mentioned work by Cole and associates (1971) and by Luria (1976) indicate that when presented with a categorization task, many people choose a functional categorization system. Similarly, when presented with syllogisms, many people draw on their natural experience rather than on logical reasoning skills. For instance, consider Sharp, Cole, and Lave's work with Mayan peasants in Mexico (1979). Experimenters presented their unschooled Mayan participants with the syllogism: "All of the women from Mexico City are beautiful. I have a woman friend from Mexico City. Is my friend beautiful?" The typical response was: "Of course your friend is beautiful. You always like beautiful women no matter where they come from!" Their strategy for solving the "problem" was to draw from their own experience. What kind of woman friend would someone have? Why a beautiful woman friend—of course. Barbara Rogoff (1981) suggested that such problem-solving strategies are typical of nonschooled populations. She proposed that schooling is a powerful cultural tool for shaping problem-solving strategies and identified five consequences of schooling:

1. to obtain skills in "the use of graphic conventions to represent depth in two-dimensional stimuli and in the fine-grained analysis of two dimensional patterns";
2. to improve one's ability to remember unrelated pieces of information;
3. to learn how to organize unrelated items;
4. to learn to organize on a taxonomic basis, rather than on a functional basis; and
5. to learn how to verbalize one's categorization strategies.

Moreover, Rogoff (1981) observed that "schooling appears to have no effect on rule learning nor on logical thought as long as the subject has understood the problem in the way the experimenter intended. Nonschooled subjects seem to prefer, however, to come to conclusions on the basis of experience rather than by relying on the information in the problem alone" (p. 285). Her point was not that schooling is unimportant, but that many skills learned in school are very specific cultural strategies for approaching problems that may not make sense to people from nonschooled backgrounds.

In summary, to understand the way children develop, we cannot simply look at the task that the child is given to do and the child's resulting performance. Instead, we must look carefully at the context in which the child is asked to perform and then look beyond that context for other influencing factors. The way the child understands the task—what the child sees as the goal of the problem, what the child believes are appropriate responses to make—is affected by the roles, activities, and patterns of behaviors the child routinely does in that setting and by behaviors and expectations children carry with them from other settings.

The empirical evidence reviewed in this section indicates that the context in which cognitive processes develop

1. dictates what objects and ideas we normally think about,
2. provides the "function" or ways in which these objects and ideas are normally used,
3. provides the social situations in which we act and shape our roles, actions, and expectations within these settings, and
4. specifies what an acceptable answer or response would be.

Hence, we suggest that, in some very concrete ways, contextual factors influence cognitive development.

FAMILY CONTEXT AND THE DEVELOPMENT OF COGNITIVE ABILITIES

Although one might accept that cultural context influences the cognitive development of all children in that context, one could dismiss the notion that family context could affect the development of specific cognitive abilities and lead to individual differences in performance. In this section, we propose that family context and more specifically, parents, can impact the age at which a skill is acquired, academic achievement, individual differences in cognitive performance, and the development of specific cognitive skills.

Developmental Expectations

Parents' ideas about child development generally include some basic beliefs about when a child should be able to acquire different skills. Although parents' expectations may be readjusted with feedback related to their child's actual performance (e.g., Entwisle & Hayduk, 1978), we suggest that parents' expectations can influence when skills are acquired.

Robert Hess and his colleagues (1980) compared the expectations held by 58 mothers in Japan and by 67 Caucasian mothers in the United States and looked at the relation between expectations and the behavior of the first-born child. The families in both countries included families from lower, middle, and upper socioeconomic groups. Thus, both within country and across the two countries, one would expect to find a broad range of variation in family environments. Mothers were given a set of items related to academic skills, verbal assertiveness ("can explain why he thinks so" or "asks for explanation when in doubt"), obedience or compliance ("comes or answers when called"), social courtesy, emotional maturity, instrumental independence (practical skills), and social skills, and were asked to indicate whether they thought a child should master the skill before age 4, sometime between ages 4 and 6, or after age 6.

As compared to Japanese mothers, U.S. mothers expected their children to be verbally assertive and to have social skills with peers at an earlier age. Japanese mothers, on the other hand, expected their children to be emotionally mature, obedient, and courteous at an earlier age. Over a 3-year period, children were given several tasks and tests to measure cognitive performance, including school aptitude tests at ages 5 and 6, and ability tests at age 6. For both mother–child groups, the overall mean developmental expectations were positively related to children's cognitive performance. In particular, mothers' expectations about verbal assertiveness were most strongly correlated with children's performance in both countries.

Academic Achievement

Cultural groups differ in their expectations related to the academic achievement of their school children. In what areas should children achieve? What factors contribute to achievement?

Harold Stevenson and his colleagues (Stevenson & Lee, 1990; Stevenson, Lee, & Stigler, 1986) reported on cross-national studies of children's academic achievement. For example, they reported that mathematics achievement in Chinese and Japanese school children is superior to mathematics achievement in U.S. school children at Grades 1 and 5, and moreover, Japanese school children in kindergarten do better in mathematics than U.S. children. In contrast, however, scores on reading achievement tests showed a different pattern. Chinese students somewhat outperformed U.S. students, who in turn, did better than Japanese students. To test whether performance differences could be attributed to differences in general intelligence among the children, the researchers compared scores on a set of cognitive tasks (including spatial, perceptual speed, coding, vocabulary, verbal memory, and general information). These tests did not reflect the same patterns of differences across countries. In fact, there was basically no overall difference among the three groups on the cognitive tasks. Instead, the researchers provided strong evidence for differences in the amount and type of instruction in math and reading that could contribute to these results. Furthermore, in addition to differences in schooling, the researchers also indicated their contention that parents' beliefs play a role in these performance differences. First, the U.S. mothers overwhelmingly stated the schools were doing a good job in educating their children. When asked if there were any improvements that could be made in their children's schooling, the subject mentioned most often was reading. Less than 6% of the suggestions were for more emphasis on mathematics or science. The Japanese mothers mentioned reading and mathematics most frequently as subjects in which more instruction time could be devoted. Interestingly, Chinese mothers wanted more emphasis on music, art, and gym. However, the researchers noted that in fifth grade, Chinese students spend 91.5% of their school time on academic activities (reading, math, science, and social studies); as compared to U.S. students, who spend 64.5% of school time on academic activities. Stevenson and his colleagues commented that unless parents were concerned about or dissatisfied with achievement in a particular area (e.g., U.S. mothers and their children's math achievement), it was unlikely that schools would make changes in their curriculum and that children's performance in that area would improve.

A second difference among the parents' beliefs concerned parents' attributions for academic success. Mothers indicated how much they thought effort, natural ability, difficulty of the schoolwork, and luck contributed to academic success. U.S. mothers rated effort and ability almost equally. In contrast, both Japanese and Chinese mothers placed much greater emphasis on effort than on ability. All mothers gave relatively little weight to task difficulty and luck.

In a recent follow-up study, Stevenson and Lee (1990) reported similar findings with respect to what improvements mothers suggest for their children's schooling and what factors mothers believe contribute to achievement. They posited that in cultures that place more weight on effort than on natural ability as a contributor to achievement, both parents and teachers may perceive themselves as having a greater effect on influencing children's development and achievement, and thereby do more to effect achievement in children's lives.

Robert Bradley and Bettye Caldwell (1984) examined the importance of early parenting to children's later school achievement. Children's home environments include both direct parenting behavior (e.g., verbal interaction between parent and child) and indirect parenting behavior (e.g., parent's organization of the physical environment and the family's daily schedule). Bradley and Caldwell used the infant and preschool versions of the Home Observation for Measurement of the Environment (HOME Inventory; Caldwell & Bradley, 1984) to assess children's home environment at 12-, 24-, and 36-months. The two versions of the HOME Inventory include subscales measuring

1. maternal responsivity,
2. maternal acceptance of child,
3. organization of the environment,
4. provision of appropriate play materials,
5. maternal involvement with child,
6. variety of stimulation,
7. language stimulation, and
8. encouragement of social maturity.

Children were given the Mental Development scale (MDI) of the Bayley at 12 months, the Stanford–Binet at 3 years, and the SRA Achievement Tests in first grade.

Several HOME subscales at 12 months were significantly related to first-grade achievement test scores. For example, provision of appropriate play materials at 12 months was significantly related to first-grade reading, language, and math achievement scores (r's from .44 to .58). When MDI and 3-year IQ scores were controlled for, the provision of appropriate toys subscale was still significantly related to first-grade reading scores ($r = .36$).

In a similar longitudinal study, Bradley, Caldwell, and Rock (1988) looked at the relation between early home environment (6 and 24 months) and school achievement and classroom behavior at age 10. In this case, there was little relation between 6-month home environment and school achievement. However, several HOME subscales at 6 months were moderately and significantly related to classroom behavior (r's from .29 to .38). The 24-month HOME scores showed several significant correlations to school achievement test scores and to classroom behavior at age 10. When HOME scores at age 10 were controlled for, several of these 24-month HOME scores were still significant, thus providing some support for the importance of general home environment on children's cognitive development.

In our own work on the relation between parental beliefs and children's cognitive development (Okagaki, Sternberg, & Divecha, 1990), we have found that parental beliefs are related to children's school performance. We examined parental beliefs about child rearing and intelligence in families from different cultural groups, but whose children attended the same school in California. Included in our study were Anglo-American, Cambodian,

Filipino, Mexican immigrant, Mexican-American, and Vietnamese families.[1]

We found that parents have different views of what characterizes an intelligent first-grade child. For example, for the Asian parents, the noncognitive attributes (i.e., motivation for school tasks, self-management skills, and social skills) were more important than the cognitive skills (i.e., problem-solving skills, verbal skills, and creative skills). Particularly for the Filipino and Vietnamese parents, motivation—the drive to do well—was most important to their conceptions of intelligence. To be intelligent is to work hard at achieving one's goals. The emphasis on motivation among Filipino and Vietnamese parents is similar to the Japanese and Chinese mothers' emphasis on effort as the primary factor contributing to school achievement in Stevenson and colleagues' study. This picture of intelligence is fundamentally different from a model of intelligence based on innate cognitive abilities (i.e., a model that says children are intelligent because of their cognitive abilities, regardless of current levels of performance).

For Mexican-American and Mexican-immigrant parents, the noncognitive aspects were as important to their conceptions of intelligence as the cognitive aspects, and among the three noncognitive aspects, social skills were rated as important as the other two attributes. Thus, for the Hispanic parents in our study, the importance of the noncognitive attributes was not simply because the more academically oriented motivation and self-management were highly valued. General social skills were very important to their conception of intelligence.

For the Anglo-American parents in our study, intelligence reflected natural cognitive abilities more than factors such as motivation and hard work. Thus, for Anglo-American parents, a child could be intelligent, that is, have a high degree of cognitive ability, but not be performing well in school because she happens not to be motivated to do schoolwork. In addition, for the Anglo-American parents, the more academically oriented noncognitive attributes—that is, motivation for school tasks and self-management skills—were more important to their conception of intelligence than social skills.

With respect to child-rearing beliefs, we found that the parents in our study expressed very different beliefs about promoting independent behaviors versus promoting conforming behaviors in their children. Both Anglo-American and Mexican-American parents indicated that encouraging independent behaviors was more important than developing conforming behaviors in their children. In contrast, for all of the foreign-born parents, promoting conformity was more important than promoting independence. However, all of the parents believed that developing independent thinking—

[1]To distinguish U.S.-born parents from foreign-born parents, we have designated the two groups of U.S.-born parents as Anglo-American and Mexican-American. Foreign-born parents are identified by their country of origin.

problem-solving and creative skills—was more important than encouraging the development of independent practical skills (e.g., being able to fix one's breakfast) for first graders. Finally, we found that U.S.-born parents emphasized developing creative skills over general problem-solving skills for their young children. In contrast, the immigrant parents rated promoting problem-solving skills to be as important or more important than developing creative skills.

In addition to looking at the differences in parental beliefs, we examined the relation between parental beliefs and children's school achievement test scores. With respect to parents' conceptions of intelligence, we found that the importance of verbal skills to parents' conceptions of intelligence was positively related to school achievement test scores. In contrast, we found that the importance of social skills to parents' conceptions of an intelligent first grader was negatively related to children's school achievement scores. That is, the more important parents believe that social skills are to a child being an intelligent individual, the lower children's scores.

Child-rearing beliefs and children's school achievement scores were also related. For all groups of parents, beliefs about promoting conforming behaviors were negatively related to children's performance. This result is not surprising in light of previous research on parents' beliefs about autonomy and conformity and children's behavior. However, it was particularly interesting that this negative relation held for groups in which parents did not place a high value on promoting conforming behaviors (e.g., Anglo-Americans) and for those groups who placed a comparatively high value on promoting conforming behaviors (e.g., Filipino and Vietnamese parents). This leads us to ask if there are different aspects of conformity—for example, conforming to parents' values (e.g., children sharing parental values and religious beliefs) and conforming in academic skills (e.g., doing homework neatly, emphasis on rote memory of facts). An emphasis on conforming to parents' values could lead to school achievement if school achievement is something that the parents value.

In summary, we suggest that social environment does play a role in school achievement. Our study indicates that parental beliefs are related to level of school achievement. Stevenson and his colleagues showed that parental values and probably broader cultural values have an important impact on the areas in which children achieve. Bradley and Caldwell's work indicates that early home environment is, at least, related to early school performance. But, of course, we recognize that correlation does not mean causation. As Seginer (1983) noted in her review of research on parents' educational expectations, although a majority of studies do report a correlation between parents' educational expectations for their children and children's school achievement, the causal direction between the two variables is unclear. For example, Entwisle and Hayduk's 2-year study (1978) of parents' expectations and school achievement indicated that parents adjusted their expectations about what grades their children would receive after receiving feedback from the school (via school report cards) about their children's progress. However, Seginer observed that parallel research on teacher expectations and children's performance suggests that parental expectations could indirectly influence children's school performance if achievement supporting behaviors by parents, like teachers' behaviors, depend on parents' expectations.

Intellectual Ability

To this point, we have presented evidence that cultural context affects cognitive development in some very important ways and family context can influence the areas in which children achieve and is correlated to the ages at which children acquire skills. But, probably the more critical question to most parents is whether parenting can affect the development of intellectual abilities.

First of all, there is certainly evidence that parenting is related to the development of intellectual abilities. For example, Schaeffer and Edgerton (1985) contrasted two parenting styles: a traditional *authoritarian* style and a more progressive, *democratic* style. Beliefs associated with the authoritarian style include ideas such as: (a) children learn passively, (b) all children should be treated in a uniform manner, and (c) the primary goal of education is to instill knowledge. Beliefs attributed to the progressive democratic style include notions such as: (a) children are active learners, (b) the primary goal of education is to teach children how to learn, and (c) knowledge is relative, rather than static. Over a series of studies, they consistently found that traditional authoritarian beliefs were negatively correlated with children's ability test scores and with teacher ratings of children's creativity and curiosity, whereas progressive democratic beliefs were positively related to children's cognitive performance.

Taking a different approach, Jeanne Brooks-Gunn (1985) did some very interesting research on maternal sex-typed beliefs and behaviors and their relation to children's cognitive development. Mothers completed a sex-typing measure in which they indicated whether a particular behavior was more likely to occur in boys or girls or was equally likely to occur in boys and girls. On the basis of their responses, the mothers were divided into three groups: low sex typing (0%–35% of the items were marked as sex-linked), moderate sex typing (41%–66% of the items were sex-linked), and high sex typing (67%–100% of the items were sex-linked). Children were given the Bayley Scale of Infant Intelligence at 24 months and the Stanford–Binet at 36 months. In addition, mothers and children were observed in a free-play situation during the 24-month test session.

An examination of mothers' beliefs and behaviors indicated that mothers who were classified as low in sex-typed beliefs did more active toy play with their daughters than mothers who were high in sex-typed beliefs. In contrast, the high sex-typed belief mothers of boys did more active toy play with their sons than the low sex-typed group.

At 24 months, there was a significant gender X belief interaction. Girls scored higher on the Bayley when their mothers were low in sex-typed beliefs, but there was no relation between mothers' beliefs and boys' scores. At 36 months, there was a similar, but nonsignificant interaction. Although, at 36 months, both sons and daughters of mothers in the low sex-typed groups scored higher on the Stanford–Binet than did children whose mothers were strong in sex-typed beliefs, the effect of parental belief was stronger for girls.

Although the relationship is complex, Brooks-Gunn demonstrated that mothers' beliefs are related to children's cognitive performance. In addition, she provided evidence suggesting that the relation between maternal beliefs and children's cognitive performance may be mediated through maternal behavior toward the child.

Another approach to studying parental beliefs is the examination of parents' ability to accurately assess their child's ability. There is an underlying assumption that parents who can more accurately judge their children's ability levels are better able to encourage and support their children's development. This assumption accords with, for example, Vygotsky's notion of a zone of proximal development or the distance that is bounded by what the child currently knows and by what is too difficult for the child to comprehend and in which the child, with help, can learn something new.

Hunt and Paraskevopoulos (1980) looked at how accurately mothers could predict their preschool children's performance on a series of IQ items and found the correlation between child's performance and inaccurate predictions to be $-.80$. Similarly, Miller (1986) reported moderate to strong correlations between children's performance and mothers' predictions of children's performance on both IQ-test items ($r = .49$) and Piagetian tasks ($r = .85$).

In his extensive review of the parental beliefs literature, Miller (1988) acknowledged that, although there is support for the hypothesis that more accurate mothers have children who perform better on ability test items and on Piagetian tasks and that this effect could be the result of accurate mothers being better able to teach their children, there are other explanations. For example, perhaps more capable children give better cues as to what they are able to perform and, as a result, their mothers are more accurate judges.

Up to this point, we have reviewed evidence that parenting is related to children's intellectual ability. As we stated in our introduction, our objective is not to show that genetic factors are irrelevant, but to show that environment also makes a difference. We now turn to research that includes measures of parents' intelligence, children's intelligence, and home environment in order to examine the relative importance of genetic and environmental influences.

In her recent review of research on parental effects on children's development, Clarke-Stewart (1988) pointed out that multivariate analyses of data that include both parental genetic factors (e.g., mother's IQ) and parental environmental factors (e.g., parenting behavior as measured by Caldwell and Bradley's HOME scales) indicate that both are important. She cited research demonstrating that mothers' IQ scores predict children's IQ scores after HOME environment has been accounted for and scores on the HOME scales predict children's IQ after mothers' IQ has been accounted for (Wilson, 1983; Yeates, MacPhee, Campbell, and Ramey, 1983, as cited by Clarke-Stewart, 1988).

Luster and Dubow (1989) observed that studies in which home environment was used to predict younger children's IQ levels (e.g., Yeates et al., 1983) were more likely to find effects of home environment when maternal intelligence was controlled for than studies in which the relation between home environment and older children's intelligence was considered (e.g., Longstreth et al., 1981). To test their hypothesis, they utilized the National Longitudinal Survey of Youth (NLSY) data on over 2,000 children and their parents. The NLSY sample included 1,336 preschoolers and 832 early elementary school children. Maternal intelligence was measured by the Armed Forces Qualification Test, which includes four subscales—vocabulary, math reasoning, reading comprehension, and numeric operations. Caldwell and Bradley's HOME scale was used to assess home environment, and the Peabody Picture Vocabulary Test was used as an indicator of children's intellectual ability. They found that for both preschool and early elementary school children, HOME scores contributed significantly to explaining children's ability scores after the variance explained by maternal intelligence had been partialled out. For preschool children, home environment accounted for 7% of the variance after maternal intelligence. For school children, home environment explained only 2% of the variance beyond maternal intelligence. These results lend support to our contention that home environment is an important influence on children's cognitive development, especially early on when the child is not as exposed to other contextual factors.

In her review of the parenting literature, Clarke-Stewart (1988) also argued that adoption studies find significant correlations between HOME scores and child-development measures with parents' IQ partialled out (Plomin et al., 1985, as cited by Clarke-Stewart, 1988). In her words,

> Adoption designs do more than demonstrate the heritability of intelligence; they also provide evidence for the effects of parents' *behavior* on children's

> development. This evidence comes from examining the mean differences in cognitive levels between adopted and nonadopted children. In the Texas adoption study, for example, Horn found that the mean IQ of the adopted children was the same as the mean IQ of the adoptive parents (112), whereas the mean IQ of the biological parents from whom the adopted children had been taken was significantly lower (108). . . . Clearly, the home environment does matter. In fact, in Plomin, Loehlin, and DeFries' study, there were two HOME factors that predicted children's IQ and showed no genetic mediation: variety of toys and experiences and maternal involvement with the child. In adoptive families as well as biological ones these factors were significantly correlated with children's IQ scores. (Clarke-Stewart, 1988, p. 60)

We also note that in most adoption studies, because adoptive families are screened before they are eligible to receive a child, the range in family environments is most likely to be less than in the general population. Consequently, the importance of the environmental influence may be underestimated in adoption studies. In the French adoption study reported by Schiff and his colleagues (Schiff et al., 1978), working-class children adopted early into upper middle-class families were compared to their nonadopted half-siblings (i.e., both sets of children had the same biological mothers) and to selected samples of children from the general population. The average IQ score of the adopted children was 110.6 ($SD = 11.3$), whereas the average IQ score of their nonadopted siblings was 94.5 ($SD = 11.3$). Comparisons of school failure rates indicated that the adopted children performed much better than their nonadopted counterparts and very much like other children from upper middle-class homes. In this study, the differences in the home environments between adopted and nonadopted children were substantial and the differences in their intellectual performance were also substantial, even though the children had the same biological mothers.

In short, we find that although parent socialization is not the sole influence on children's intelligence, it is important. When the effect of parents' IQ is taken into consideration, home environment still predicts children's intelligence.

Specific Cognitive Processes

The previously discussed research primarily employed broad measures of parental beliefs and global measures of cognitive development, such as school achievement test scores. Another approach is to consider the relation between specific beliefs and theoretically relevant cognitive skills. For example, the work by Sigel and his colleagues at the Educational Testing Service (ETS) examines the extent to which constructivist beliefs and practices are incorporated into parents' implicit theories of child development, and in turn, affect children's representational competence (e.g., McGillicuddy-DeLisi, 1985; Sigel, 1982).

To measure parental beliefs about constructivist notions, short vignettes describing situations involving a parent and a 4-year-old child were presented to the parents, and parents answered open-ended questions, such as "Does a 4-year-old know which things float and which don't?" (McGillicuddy-DeLisi, 1985, p. 12). In addition, parents were observed while they helped their children do a paperfolding task. Children's cognitive performance was assessed on several tasks, including memory, conservation, and categorization tasks. The results indicated that both mothers' and fathers' beliefs, and mothers' use of distancing strategies were significantly correlated with children's representational competence.

We conclude this section with discussion of an interesting, albeit speculative, analysis by Sternberg and Suben (1986) on the way specific constraints in the home environment might affect cognitive processing on school tasks. Intrigued by ethnographic studies of children's behavior in home and school settings (e.g., Heath, 1983), Sternberg and Suben (1986) applied the triarchic theory of human intelligence (Sternberg, 1985) to the ethnographers' descriptions of children's cognitive behavior as a first step in identifying possible cognitive processes involved in children's adaptation to school. They matched descriptions of children's behaviors to specific aspects of the triarchic theory to show how cognitive processing may be influenced by early socialization. For example, according to Sternberg's theory, a critical metacomponent concerns the ability to allocate one's resources in an efficient and effective manner. For much of our society, time is one of the resources most carefully apportioned. However, in the Piedmont Carolinas, Heath (1983) studied a community in which very few time limits were placed on tasks and very few activities were actually scheduled. A child of this community may have had literally no experience with being timed in the performance of a cognitive task prior to school. Hence, to say that one has 30 minutes in which to complete a test may have no functional meaning to the child. Sternberg and Suben suggested that such a child's metacognitive processes may be as well-developed as those of a child from a middle-class home, for example, but the rules this child uses to make metacognitive decisions (e.g., when given a task to do, the time involved in doing the task is not an important aspect to consider) do not match the implicit rules that govern school settings.

Similarly, performance-componential functioning may be shaped by one's home environment. For example, Heath (1983) described a community in which children seemed to have developed a holistic approach to examining objects—comparing the objects as wholes rather than attribute-by-attribute. Although these children may be sensitive to shape, color, size, and so on, they did not use these attributes to make judgments as to how two objects might be similar or different. It is not that these children lacked the ability to compare stimuli, but rather, the implicit rules governing object comparisons that had been acquired at home were not the same as the rules assumed by their teachers. Sternberg and Suben argued that the task that children thought they were supposed to be doing was not the "same" task that the teachers had presented to them. This misunderstanding can result in poor performance on a task, which unfortunately may be attributed to a lack of ability on the child's part, rather than to an unfamiliarity with the strategies used to approach the task.

Even though the ethnographic studies Sternberg and Suben examined were not conducted to specifically study the effects of contextual factors on intellectual development, their analyses do identify potential problems in the development of specific cognitive processes that may contribute to poor school performance.

Summary

In this section, we have presented empirical evidence that family context influences the development of children's cognitive abilities. Parents expect children to learn and teach children specific skills at different ages. Parents encourage achievement in different academic areas both directly through interaction with their children and indirectly through interaction with their children's schools. Home environment predicts children's intellectual ability after parents' intelligence has been taken into account. And finally, when specific abilities such as representational competence are considered, parental differences on theoretically relevant beliefs and behaviors are related to children's performance.

CONCLUSION

In this chapter, we have presented two major theses. First, cultural context shapes cognitive functioning in some very specific ways. That is to say, cultural context affects the development of all children's thinking because cognitive processing is intricately intertwined with context. We posited that context constrains the objects of our thought, the ways in which we view these objects (or their functional context), the problems and the problem-solving strategies available to us, and the solutions considered acceptable. Second, we proposed that parenting has an important influence on children's cognitive development. When children learn a skill, which skills children learn, and even the level of expertise children achieve are influenced by parental actions.

We do, however, strongly agree that children have an active part in determining their cognitive development. In almost all of the recent reviews that we read, researchers acknowledged that causal direction cannot be determined because the evidence is correlational, and behavioral scientists have neglected to consider the importance of the children's role in shaping their environment. Children—perhaps because of natural abilities, motivation, curiosity, or social skills—elicit certain responses, behaviors, interactions, and encouragement from parents. In essence, children shape the parents' behavior and thereby facilitate their own development in a particular area. But, if we believe in the power of the child to shape the environment and to evoke particular responses from the parent, should we not also believe in the power of the parent to shape the environment and to encourage the development of specific abilities in the child?

ACKNOWLEDGMENTS

Preparation of this chapter was supported in part by a grant from the Spencer Foundation.

REFERENCES

Bradley, R. H., & Caldwell, B. M. (1984). The relation of infants' home environments to achievement test performance in first grade: A follow-up study. *Child Development, 52,* 708–710.

Bradley, R. H., Caldwell, B. M., & Rock, S. L. (1988). Home environment and school performance: A ten-year follow-up and examination of three models of environmental action. *Child Development, 59,* 852–867.

Bronfenbrenner, U. (1974). Developmental research, public policy and the ecology of childhood. *Child Development, 45,* 1–5.

Brooks-Gunn, J. (1985). Maternal beliefs about children's sex-typed characteristics as they relate to maternal behavior. In I. E. Sigel (Ed.), *Parental belief systems: The psychological consequences for children* (pp. 319–344). Hillsdale, NJ: Lawrence Erlbaum Associates.

Caldwell, B. M., & Bradley, R. H. (1984). *Home observation for measurement of the environment.* Little Rock: University of Arkansas.

Chase, W. G., & Simon, H. A. (1973). Perception in chess. *Cognitive Psychology, 4,* 55–81.

Clarke-Stewart, K. A. (1988). Parents' effects on children's development: A decade of progress? *Journal of Applied Developmental Psychology, 9,* 41–84.

Cole, M., Gay, J., Glick, J., & Sharp, D. W. (1971). *The cultural context of learning and thinking.* New York: Basic Books.

Entwisle, D. R., & Hayduk, L. A. (1978). *Too great expectations: The academic outlook of young children.* Baltimore: Johns Hopkins University Press.

Goodnow, J. J. (1976). The nature of intelligent behavior: Questions raised by cross-cultural studies. In L. B. Resnick (Ed.), *The nature of intelligence* (pp. 169–188). Hillsdale, NJ: Lawrence Erlbaum Associates.

Heath, S. B. (1983). *Ways with words.* New York: Cambridge University Press.

Hess, R. D., Kashiwagi, K., Azuma, H., Price, G. G., & Dickson, W. P. (1980). Maternal expectations for mastery of developmental tasks in Japan and the United States. *International Journal of Psychology, 15,* 259–271.

Hunt, J. McV., & Paraskevopoulos, J. (1980). Children's psychological development as a function of the inaccuracy of their mothers' knowledge of their abilities. *Journal of Genetic Psychology, 136,* 285–298.

Laboratory of Comparative Human Cognition (1982). Culture and intelligence. In R. J. Sternberg (Ed.), *Handbook of human intelligence* (pp. 642–719). New York: Cambridge University Press.

Laboratory of Comparative Human Cognition (1986). Contributions of cross-cultural research to educational practice. *American Psychologist, 41* (10), 1049–1058.

Lantz, D. (1979). A cross-cultural comparison of communication abilities: Some effects of age, schooling and culture. *International Journal of Psychology, 14,* 171–183.

Longstreth, L. E., Davis, B., Carter, L., Flint, D., Owen, J., Rickert, M., & Taylor, E. (1981). Separation of home intellectual environment and maternal IQ as determinants of child IQ. *Developmental Psychology, 17* (5), 532–541.

Luria, A. R. (1976). *Cognitive development: Its cultural and social foundations.* (M. Lopez-Morillas & L. Solotaroff, Trans., and M. Cole (Ed.) Cambridge, MA: Harvard University Press.

Luster, T., & Dubow, E. (1989). *Home environment and maternal intelligence as predictors of verbal intelligence: A comparison of preschool and school age children.* Unpublished manuscript, Michigan State University, East Lansing, MI.

McGillicuddy-De Lisi, A. V. (1985). The relationship between parental beliefs and children's cognitive level. In I. E. Sigel (Ed.), *Parental belief systems: The psychological consequences for children* (pp. 7–24). Hillsdale, NJ: Lawrence Erlbaum Associates.

Miller, S. A. (1986). Parents' beliefs about their children's cognitive abilities. *Developmental Psychology, 22,* 276–284.

Miller, S. A. (1988). Parents' beliefs about children's cognitive development. *Child Development, 59,* 259–285.

Okagaki, L., Sternberg, R. J., & Divecha, D. J. (1990, April). *Parental beliefs and children's early school performance.* Paper presented at the Annual Meeting of the American Educational Research Association, Boston, MA.

Plomin, R., Loehlin, J. C., & DeFries, J. C. (1985). Genetic and environmental components of "environmental" influences. *Developmental Psychology, 21,* 391–402.

Price-Williams, D., Gordon, W., & Ramirez, M. (1969). Skill and conservation: A study of pottery-making children. *Developmental Psychology, 1,* 769.

Rogoff, B. (1981). Schooling and the development of cognitive skills. In H. C. Triandis & A. Heron (Eds.), *Handbook of cross-cultural psychology* (Vol. 4, pp. 233–294). Boston: Allyn & Bacon.

Rogoff, B., & Morelli, G. (1989). Perspectives on children's development from cultural psychology. *American Psychologist, 44* (2), 343–348.

Schaefer, E. S., & Edgerton, M. (1985). Parent and child correlates of parental modernity. In I. E. Sigel (Ed.), *Parental belief systems: The psychological consequences for children* (pp. 287–318). Hillsdale, NJ: Lawrence Erlbaum Associates.

Schiff, M., Duyme, M., Dumaret, A., Stewart, J., Tomkiewicz, S., & Feingold, J. (1978). Intellectual status of working-class children adopted early into upper-middle class families. *Science, 200,* 1503–1504.

Seginer, R. (1983). Parents' educational expectations and children's academic achievements: A literature review. *Merrill–Palmer Quarterly, 29* (1), 1–23.

Sharp, D. W., Cole, M., & Lave, J. (1979). Education and cognitive development: The evidence from experimental research. *Monographs of the Society for Research in Child Development, 44* (1-2, Serial No. 178).

Sigel, I. E. (1982). The relationship between parental distancing strategies and the child's cognitive behavior. In L. M. Laosa & I. E. Sigel (Eds.), *Families as learning environments for children* (pp. 47–86). New York: Plenum.

Steinberg, B. M., & Dunn, L. A. (1976). Conservation competence and performance in Chiapas. *Human Development, 19,* 14–25.

Sternberg, R. J. (1985). *Beyond IQ: A triarchic theory of human intelligence.* New York: Cambridge University Press.

Sternberg, R. J., & Suben, J. G. (1986). The socialization of intelligence. In M. Perlmutter (Ed.), *Perspectives on intellectual development. Vol. 19. Minnesota symposia on child psychology* (pp. 201–235). Hillsdale, NJ: Lawrence Erlbaum Associates.

Stevenson, H. W., & Lee, S. (1990). Contexts of achievement. *Monographs of the Society for Research in Child Development, 55* (1-2, Serial No. 221).

Stevenson, H. W., Lee, S., & Stigler, J. W. (1986). Mathematics achievement of Chinese, Japanese, and American children. *Science, 231,* 693–699.

Wilson, R. S. (1983). The Louisville Twin Study: Developmental synchronies in behavior. *Child Development, 54,* 298–316.

Yeates, K. O., MacPhee, D., Campbell, F. A., & Ramey, C. T. (1983). Maternal IQ and home environment as determinants of early childhood intellectual competence: A developmental analysis. *Developmental Psychology, 19* (5), 731–739.

CHAPTER 6

Socialization of Representational Competence in the Family: The Distancing Paradigm

IRVING SIGEL
ELIZABETH T. STINSON
JAN FLAUGHER
Educational Testing Service

The primary mission of this chapter is to discuss the significance of the family as a socializing agent of the child's *representational competence.* Representational competence refers to the child's ability to manipulate and use symbols in the service of thinking, reasoning, and problem solving. In this chapter we address the current state of the field in terms of concepts employed in family studies. We then present our comprehensive model, evolved over the past 15 years, examining family influences on the development of children's representational competence and subsequent school functioning. Finally, we conclude with a statement advocating future directions of research needed to elaborate the pivotal role of the family in the development of this fundamental competence.

Socialization of the developing child is largely a family affair with parents functioning as the primary agents and overseers of the learning process. Long recognized as the pivotal organization for development of intelligent behavior, the family environment constitutes the most pervasive experiential milieu of the young child, influencing virtually every facet of development (Laosa & Sigel, 1982). Moreover, the family is embedded in a larger, complex social network comprising many significant individuals who provide an array of experiences that influence the child as the child influences others (Cochran, 1988; Powell, 1988).

SOURCES OF FAMILY INFLUENCE

As the only social unit in which biogenetic and social factors merge, the family has provided a central focus for researchers from diverse disciplines seeking to explain behavioral variations among individuals, particularly those relating to intelligence and academic achievement. Aspects of family structure thought to affect the intellectual environment of the child, such as family size, birth order, and spacing of children, have variously been proposed as predictors.

Yet, results derived from these studies using family structural variables are more suggestive than definitive. With respect to family size, several studies have reported declines in children's intellectual ability and academic performance as families get larger (Schooler, 1972; Zajonc, 1976). Moreover, it would appear that earlier predictions of trends in Scholastic Aptitude Test (SAT) scores based on fluctuating family patterns in the U.S. population have been borne out (Zajonc, 1986). Social class, however, has frequently been observed interacting with family size and ability (Marjoribanks, Walberg, & Bargen, 1975), family constellation (Marjoribanks, 1979), family ontogeny (Featherman, Spenner, & Tsunematsu, 1988), and sibling relations (Brody & Stoneman, 1990).

Although contradictions and inconsistencies in the literature on birth order effects evoke comparisons to "a hall of mirrors" (Chittenden, personal communication, November 1989), there is some evidence suggesting that a child's ordinal position may influence intellectual development, particularly when birth spacing between siblings is taken into account (Cicirelli, 1978; Sigel, McGillicuddy-DeLisi, & Johnson, 1980). Our own research in which comparisons were made between one-child families and three-child families with near and far spacing demonstrated significant relationships between family constellation, parents' teaching strategies, and children's representational competence (McGillicuddy-DeLisi & Sigel, 1991). These studies, as a whole, point to important sources of variation in children's cognitive development that are intuitively compelling, albeit methodologically difficult to substantiate.

Aside from these relatively few family sources of influence on children's intellectual growth, developmental psychologists have tended to minimize, or even overlook, the role of the family as a socializing agent in terms of developing cognitive competence. Rather, when considering family influences on cognition, the focus has been on intelligence (IQ), heritability, and social status factors. Structural or configurational family variables are usually not included. In fact, it is interesting that in most literature reviews of cognitive development, in general, and representation in particular, virtually no attributions are made to the role of sociohistorical and family variables. The child just seems to grow in a decontextualized world defined by the methods of the experimenter (e.g., Mandler, 1983; Perlmutter, 1988; Sternberg, 1982).

HEREDITY OR ENVIRONMENT?

The role of parents as active facilitators of children's cognitive development is of relatively recent interest. Prior to the "cognitive revolution," research efforts were primarily directed toward understanding parents' genetic contribution to their children's intelligence as expressed in IQ. However, as controversial hereditarian arguments were eclipsed by the environmentalist position, the nature–nurture pendulum swung away from genetic explanations of individual differences. Now with the emergence of behavioral genetics as a respectable and significant area of study (Plomin, 1989; Scarr & Weinberg, 1990; Sternberg, 1982), developmental psychologists are accommodating the roles of environment and heredity into their conceptual frameworks.

There is a distinction to be made, however, between studies of mental processes that focus on intelligence and those that focus on cognition. Historically, the former have conceptualized intelligence as a measurable index of one's capacity for reasoning, problem solving, and knowledge acquisition (Weinberg, 1989). The study of cognition, on the other hand, encompasses a broader band of intellectual functioning in its emphasis on the mental mechanisms underlying skill acquisition and environmental adaptation (Anderson, 1981; Siegler, 1978).

Although there is considerable overlap in these conceptually different perspectives, it is noteworthy that investigations of parental influence on children's intelligence have essentially been in the nature–nurture tradition, whereas cognition has been studied in the expanded context of socialization (Wertsch, 1985). Current renewed research interest in the sociocultural context of development has gained impetus from cross-cultural studies (Rogoff & Morelli, 1989) reexamining the theoretical integration of cognitive and social processes.

FAMILY SOCIALIZATION OF COGNITION

As indicated earlier, the role of family configurational and structural variables has received short shrift by developmental psychologists relative to cognitive development. Yet, parents function as the child's primary interaction partners and socialization guides. Their roles as enhancers of cognitive development and facilitators of academically relevant skills are presumably integral to the child's successful school adaptation. Academic achievement, after all, represents aspects of both intelligence and cognition and provides an index of the child's competence in a societal institution. Moreover, as cognition increasingly becomes defined as the understanding of social or emotional events as well as physical events (Goodnow & Warton, in press), the socialization process occurring within the family context assumes even greater prominence.

This more comprehensive view of cognition requires a reexamination of the parental role, particularly as it relates to socialization of cognition and subsequent academic achievement, a proxy for cognitive functioning. Whereas earlier studies of parental influence tended to emphasize effects of maternal attitudes and behaviors on the young child's developing intelligence, relatively little attention has been given to how both parents' efforts contribute to short- and long-term developmental outcomes (Clarke-Stewart, 1988; Sigel, Dreyer, & McGillicuddy-DeLisi, 1984). Additionally, while interest in the relation between parental beliefs and early childhood development is substantial (McGillicuddy-DeLisi, 1985; Miller, 1988; Sigel, 1985), less is known about the cognitive framework guiding parents' achievement-related behavior toward their children (Holloway & Hess, 1985). There is reason to believe, however, that children's self-perceptions of academic competence are related more to parents' achievement expectancies than to the child's actual ability (Parsons, Adler, & Kaczala, 1982). Thus, parental beliefs about their children's competencies function as mechanisms of socialization because they provide children with the feedback they use to construct their self-perceptions (Phillips, 1987).

However, the missing longitudinal linkages in the socialization process remain to be established between early parent–child interactions and children's cognitive functioning and subsequent school functioning (Fowler, 1986). If intelligence is defined as the capacity to adapt to one's environment, then academic achievement may be viewed as an indication of the children's utilization of their intellectual competence outside of the home.

In terms of the child's academic competence, parents' achievement expectations (Parsons et al., 1982), performance attributions (Hess & McDevitt, 1986), and developmental beliefs (Stinson, 1989) have all been found to moderate successful school functioning (Featherman et al., 1988; Kellam, Ensminger, & Turner, 1977; Seligman, Kamen, & Nolen-Hoeksema, 1988).

On the other hand, it has been argued that it is how these beliefs are conveyed, that is, parental behavior, which affects the child's intellectual development (Sigel, 1986). Presumably, parental behaviors that facilitate the young child's intellectual growth should enhance that child's subsequent achievement in school. Yet little empirical data have been obtained in support of this premise. To further our understanding of the effects of parents as socializers of cognition, it is necessary to generate a conceptual model that integrates parental beliefs and behaviors within a developmental perspective. By doing so, we can advance our search for a common substrate between early family interactional experiences and later intellectual capabilities.

REPRESENTATIONAL COMPETENCE

Before proceeding to our elaboration of a microgenic behavioral model to examine the development of cognition, let us begin by identifying the cognitive target of concern. We propose that primary cognitive function, rooted in the family context, undergirds subsequent cognitive ability in *representational competence.* Representational competence refers to the child's ability to understand that experience can be transformed into some symbolic mode. Furthermore, it refers to the ability to manipulate symbols mentally, and in so doing, perform mental operations that organize, reorganize, integrate, and elaborate physical and social events into internal representations. Representational competence also involves mental operations that influence how assimilation of external events is transformed and internalized.

The experiential world of children is a microcosm of their culture, including the language, customs, symbols, and all the other artifacts that define the larger society. The culture also defines how the individual reflects on and evaluates experience. To be sure, there are usually idiosyncratic ways of thinking that evolve in the course of development, but even these individualized patterns are in the context of the broader culture.

Representational competence necessitates an implicit understanding that the meaning of events and objects can be re-presented in ways that are essentially abstractions, condensations, and/or selected components of the referent. For example, a word or picture can convey the concept of "catness" if one knows that the various representations of "catness" are transmutations of the same reality. Humans develop a general understanding of transformational rules for representing the world, for establishing equivalences and differences between representations, and for communicating with each other. In a sense, the underlying competence to engage in all of these mental activities requires an awareness that an event retains its identity despite obvious differences in representation. We refer to this knowledge as the *conservation of meaning* in the Piagetian tradition because it is logical to expect the concept of conservation to apply over and above physical characteristics. Moreover, we propose that this aspect of conservation is a requisite for subsequent representational competence (Piaget, 1947/1950).

In summary, generalization of knowledge, application of knowledge, and performance on verbal and mathematical tasks require three interrelated mental functions: understanding of the representational rule, representational competence, and conservation of meaning. Competence with these three functions empowers individuals to communicate experiences both to the self and to others, to solve problems using the symbols and codes of the physical world, and to decipher the more subtly encoded "conversation of gestures" encountered in the social world (Mead, 1934).

Social Origins of Representational Competence

Although there is compelling evidence of a biological base for these cognitive abilities (Plomin, 1989), their subsequent development and behavioral expression are products of social interactions (Doise & Mugny, 1984). The social nature of children's intellectual development has been investigated since the 1920s by theorists working from diverse models (Doise & Mugney, 1984; Luria, 1978; Vygotsky, 1978).

The development of representational competence is no exception. Beyond the neurological givens, we argue that the child's ability to engage in and use representations or cultural symbols is acquired through social experiences that occur initially within the family. Specifically, actualization of the child's inherent abilities is thought to be facilitated by a particular class of parenting strategies we call *distancing behaviors* (Sigel, 1982). Distancing refers to placing a cognitive demand on the child to separate the self mentally from the ongoing present. When used by parents or other family members, distancing strategies create a cognitive environment in which the child is stimulated to reconstruct past events, anticipate the future, or assume alternate perspectives on the present, all of which serve to foster representational thinking. Accordingly, the degree to which parents employ distancing strategies should relate to their children's cognitive development and subsequent school functioning.

Asking children what they did yesterday or what they will do tomorrow, or requesting some type of reflective abstraction—for example, "Do you remember how you felt when . . . ?"—are distancing behaviors that place cognitive demands on the child mentally to reconstruct prior events. Distancing strategies also require the child to employ imagination, to picture objects "in the mind's eye," and to regard them as equivalent to their three-dimensional forms. During these verbal exchanges children are also in a position to internalize the social aspects of the interaction, thereby establishing a basis for the acquisition of social knowledge.

Levels of Distancing

Distancing strategies vary from *low-level,* that is, demanding attention to the ongoing concrete situation, to *high-level,* that is, demanding a maximal separation from the immediate present. In the course of several empirical studies examining the distancing model, three levels of distancing strategies were identified (Sigel, 1986):

Level 1 distancing strategies represent mental demands for associations, visual observations or automatic, routinized information. These low-level strategies, which may be in the form of a question or a statement, make little demand for active, strategic or reflective thought. For example, in both the question, "What is the name of this . . . ?" and the statement, "This is a boat."; minimal demands are made for the child to separate self from the ongoing present.

Level 2 distancing strategies represent cognitive demands on the individual to classify and/or relate disparate events. While these are cognitive demands to transcend what is observable in the immediate environment, visual objects still form the basis for the mental operation to be performed. For example, the child may be asked to classify a group of objects spread out on a table, or be asked to make comparisons between geometric forms.

Level 3 distancing strategies represent cognitive demands to engage in causal inferences, to predict outcomes, and to employ hypothetical reasoning. Again, the form may be a question, e.g., "Can you show me some different ways to illustrate the concept of . . . ?" or a statement, "Cold nights and warm, sunny days help the leaves change colors in the fall" (see Table 6.1).

TABLE 6.1
Types of Distancing Strategies Categorized by Levels

High-level Distancing	*Medium-level Distancing*	*Low-level Distancing*
Evaluate consequence	Sequence	Label
Evaluate competence	Reproduce	Produce information
Evaluate affect	Describe similarities	Describe, define
Evaluate effort and/or performance	Describe differences	Describe—interpretation
Evaluate necessary and/or sufficient	Infer similarities	Demonstrate
Infer cause-effect	Infer differences	Observe
Infer affect	Symmetrical classifying	
Generalize	Azymmetrical classifying	
Transform	Enumerating	
	Synthesizing within classifying	
Plan		
Confirmation of a plan		
Conclude		
Propose alternatives		
Resolve conflict		

Distancing and Disequilibrium. Why should distancing behaviors have the predicted influence on cognitive development? One of the major functions of the distancing strategy is to generate discrepancies between what is experienced and what is expected, creating disequilibrium in the listener. Disequilibrium promotes tension, which, by its discomforting nature, demands resolution. It is the resolution of the discrepancy that impels the individual to reconsider prior knowledge, reexamine assumptions or try out alternatives, and in so doing, restructure the ongoing schema.

This restructuring process involves representational thinking and presumably transforms the child's response. It is the parent's distancing strategy that sets the chain of events in motion. For example, if the child is working on a problem and the parent becomes aware that the child is having difficulty, the parent may ask the child to generate some alternative strategies, for example, "How else might you approach this task?" Or, the parent may encourage the child to make inferences by asking, "Why do you think your approach isn't working?" These distancing strategies, especially when phrased as inquiries, create disequilibrium and children are now in a position to refocus or restructure their approach. The argument follows that such experiences serve to promote representational competence because the children must mentally produce alternative options or reconstruct events in order to respond.

There are two levels of representational thought: figurative and operative (Piaget, 1950). At the *figurative* level, thinking is in concrete terms, as when the child creates an image of an event. In contrast, *operational* processes involve the ability to think in procedural terms, as in mathematical calculations and classification tasks (Sigel & Cocking, 1977). In either event, it is maintained "that the level (i.e., figurative or operative) of representational thinking that an individual will present is a function of the quantity and quality of distancing experiences" (Sigel, 1979, p. 71). For example, we hypothesize that the child who has more frequent experiences with high-level strategies should be more successful in employing planning in the solution of problems.

The Role of Parental Beliefs

We operate on the assumption that the kinds of behaviors we employ are in part an expression of our culture and our view of the other in social interactions. Traditionally, in the developmental field, concern with motivations of parents' behaviors toward children was defined in terms of their child-rearing attitudes (Schaefer & Bell, 1958) and values (Kohn, 1977). More recently, some researchers have suggested that parental attributions about children's behavior are determinants of parenting responses (Dix & Grusec

1985; Holloway & Hess, 1985), whereas other researchers have turned their attention to parental conceptions of children's cognitive abilities (Miller, 1986). These diverse efforts share a common goal, that is, to understand the covert mechanisms driving child-rearing behaviors.

Although each of these approaches represents useful ways of categorizing parent characteristics, we have elected to view parents' beliefs as determinants of distancing behaviors. Beliefs are defined as truth statements, that is, what the individual believes to be true. In effect, beliefs are cognitive representations of reality (Sigel, 1985). Accordingly, beliefs about children as learners comprise one aspect of parents' representational system of children. We assume that how a parent thinks a child learns will influence how the parent chooses to teach the child.

Based on this reasoning, we contend that parents' socialization actions derive from their beliefs and values regarding the parental role and the nature of children. In turn, these cognitions intersect with what parents believe to be true about how their own children learn about their environment. Parents are embedded in the culture, thus child-rearing beliefs are presumably shared by members of their cohort group. But, because parents have their own idiosyncratic set of experiences within the broader culture, there is some variability in parents' constructions.

In our model we incorporate the idea that the nature of the child's response to the parent's distancing strategy may influence the subsequent behavior of the parent or alter beliefs about the child. In this sense, we are constructing a social-interactive model in which distancing behaviors are viewed as social events. The growing competence of children to formulate increasingly more complex responses to the cognitive demands placed on them provides feedback to the parents who, in turn, may reorganize their own representations of the learning process.

Linkages Between Beliefs and Behavior. To this point we have alluded to the hypothesis, broadly speaking, that parental beliefs are guides to actions as well as determinants of the choice of events to which one reacts. That is to say, the type of event and the decision as to what and how to act are outcomes of underlying beliefs and values (Sigel, 1986). Beliefs, in general, are assumed to be always tied to actions in some context, that is, "apparent inconsistencies in manifestations of belief are reconciled when we acknowledge the extent to which situation and belief are tied to each other" (Schiebe, 1970, p. 35). To predict the situation, it is necessary to know the individual's beliefs in conjunction with contextual factors.

Parents as Teachers. A second-grade teacher has commented that "Parents are the real teachers of their children. . . . We (educators) merely refine what they have established" (personal communication).

Underlying parents' socialization functions is their primary responsibility of serving as teachers in the broadest sense of the term. They may approach this role in a formal or informal way. Yet, whether the parent instructs the child directly or provides information informally through books, activities, and experiences, these types of engagements influence the child's developmental course and subsequent achievement.

Generally speaking, verbal exchanges between parents and children occur in two contexts: discipline/management and teaching encounters. In both situations parents are essentially fulfilling the role of teacher. However, in our construction, the teaching situation differs from management encounters in that the focus of the interaction is on intellectual problem solving as opposed to social or personal behavior (Sigel, 1960). In the latter case, parents deal with what to do and what not do and what is right and what is wrong, as they help the child learn the social requirements for functioning in a particular environment. In the former case, the parent's aim is to help children learn about the world they live in, the world of objects, of people, and of events. Granted the line between these interaction contexts may be fine, (yet) our coding schemes have been able to differentiate between the two. In either instance, the parent functions as a socializer.

These conceptualizations of the parental role are consistent with current notions of the socialization functions. In his definition of socialization, Damon (1977) made reference to cognitive terms, for example, understanding, reconstructing, evaluations of similarities and differences. These are the types of distancing experiences children have with their parents that provide the primal socialization environment. It is in this context, we argue, that cognition is socialized; hence, the construct, socialization of cognition.

The Family as a Cultural Conduit. As socialization agents, parents function as cultural filters and conveyers of meta-messages about how children are expected to accommodate their behavior to meet societal expectations (Block, 1983; Hoffman, 1988). Parents overtly and covertly convey messages to their children regarding their overall social and intellectual functioning. In our culture family organization is circumscribed by gender roles; mothers and fathers presumably differ in terms of the beliefs and values they communicate to their sons and daughters. Consequently, early on in the socialization process, parents begin to treat boys and girls differently, especially in terms of their achievement emphases and performance expectations. So, as we began to develop our developmental model of parents' socialization efforts relative the child's representational competence, we built in our concern with differential treatment of boys and girls within the family. Support for this attention to gender differential socialization experiences of children is evidenced in the burgeoning research interest and public speculation regarding girls' and boys' academic performance

(Jacklin, 1989). Gender-stereotyped beliefs held by parents about ability attributes of girls and boys have been shown to directly relate to math achievement in particular (Parsons et al., 1982). Yet, although performance differences between males and females have been extensively researched (Jacklin, 1989) and sex-differentiated parent–child interactions behaviors documented (Block, 1983; McGillicuddy-DeLisi, 1982), parents' beliefs as sources of influence on representational competence as they relate to girls' and boys' achievement have not been addressed. Accordingly, in each of our research projects we made every effort to balance or control for gender. This enabled us to examine the differential effects of parents' beliefs on their sons' and daughters' representational ability and academic achievement as moderated through their distancing behaviors (Sigel, 1985; Sigel et al., 1980; Sigel, McGillicuddy-DeLisi, Flaugher, & Rock, 1983; Stinson, 1989).

EMPIRICAL ORIGINS OF THE DISTANCING PARADIGM

The conviction that representational competence evolves through social interactions within the family context is empirically rooted in earlier research on parent–child communication patterns in impoverished households (Sigel, Secrist, & Forman, 1973). Children coming from homes with limited verbal interaction between family members and little parent–child dialoguing had difficulty performing certain classification tasks. Specifically, tasks in which they had to classify pictures as opposed to three-dimensional objects seemed to baffle them. Their difficulty was apparently due to an inability to comprehend that an item retains its meaning irrespective of an alteration in its presented form. However, following remediative training, children who had initially demonstrated limited competence in representational thinking were able to perform ably in classification tasks requiring mental transformations (Sigel, Anderson, & Shapiro, 1966; Sigel & McBane, 1967; Sigel & Olmsted, 1970). Sigel (1970) maintained that such observed discrepancies in children's ability to conserve meaning and think in representational terms might well be a function of differential use of distancing strategies on the part of parents.

OVERVIEW OF THE DISTANCING RESEARCH PROGRAM

Given our premise that the child's cognitive development and comprehension of the representational rule evolve in the family context, we examined the influence of parental distancing behaviors in relation to (a) family constellation, (b) parents' beliefs about learning, (c) the young child's representational competence, and (d) the preadolescent child's academic achievement.

The initial set of studies examined these questions in the context of the family, with particular focus on parents as teachers of their children. As mentioned earlier, we discovered that birth order and spacing are familial structural factors that result in differential parent interactions and consequences for children. Specifically, one-child families were found to differ from three-child families in terms of parents' beliefs about how children learn, that is, the former favored adult instruction and guidance more than the latter, who expressed more beliefs in the self-regulatory capabilities of the child (Sigel et al., 1980). Spacing of children had little effect on parenting beliefs, but level of education was highly related to how parents thought children learn.

We were encouraged to find that distancing variables measured during parent–child interaction tasks related in the expected directions to children's representational ability on a variety of Piagetian tasks. As predicted, mothers' verbal disapproval of the child's problem-solving attempts were negatively associated with cognitive and social outcomes.

Findings obtained from interview and observation data indicated that what parents said they did in teaching and management situations differed from what they actually did during parent–child interaction tasks. However, parents' self-reported beliefs regarding child development obtained in the same interview did relate to their observed behavior. These data suggested to us that the parents' view of the children, that is, their beliefs concerning the nature of children and how they learn, might be more salient predictors of how parents will behave with their children than self-reports of preferred behaviors.

Distancing and Cognitive Functioning

For the next phase of our ongoing research effort we studied 240 middle-class, suburban families with children between the ages of $3\frac{1}{2}$ and $7\frac{1}{2}$. Only those two-parent families in which both parents agreed to participate were included.

Using observational data derived from videotaped interactions of each parent working individually with the child in two contextually varied tasks (e.g., storytelling and paperfolding), we found that parents' low-level distancing strategies that were closed-ended and didactic, offering the child few options or alternatives, tended to relate negatively to children's cognitive functioning, particularly reconstructive memory. Conversely, parents' use of high-level distancing strategies that require the child to infer, compare, or abstract, were positively associated with children's memory for sentences, anticipatory imagery on a Piagetian task, and overall IQ (Sigel et al., 1983). Clearly, we had begun to demonstrate the connection between the child's representational competence on cognitive tasks and parental distancing behaviors.

Moreover, we were clarifying the psychological characteristics of different types of teaching techniques as we considered our findings. For instance, didactic-controlling strategies (e.g., structuring, attention-getting behavior, statements, commands) afford children little opportunity to think for themselves. Basically, they reflect an authoritarian orientation that does not promote the child's own exploration of options and alternatives. On the measures of representational ability used in this study, the child is required to be an active problem-solver. Preschool children exposed to predominantly didactic-controlling strategies at home are at an intellectual disadvantage because they have had limited experiences with self-determined problem resolution and fewer opportunities to acquire confidence in their own competence. Others too, have reported the negative consequences for children's cognitive and affective development when the significant adults in their lives employ control strategies as opposed to favoring the child's autonomy (Baumrind, 1978; Grolnick & Ryan, 1989). As we had anticipated, relationships between parents' teaching strategies and children's outcomes were clearly dependent on the task involved. Also, mothers' and fathers' behaviors were found to differ to the extent that fathers took longer to complete tasks and used more imperatives (e.g., Do it this way . . .") than mothers while working on paperfolding with the child. Even more intriguing was the related finding that the children's competence on the paperfolding task varied with the sex of the parent working with them, indicating that mothers' and fathers' teaching strategies differentially influence children's spontaneous problem-solving capabilities (Sigel et al., 1983).

The hypothesized link between parents' beliefs about how children learn and their observed teaching strategies proved to be elusive in that findings varied by parent gender. For example, we had expected that the more parents viewed children as active learners, the more likely they would be to employ high-level distancing behaviors during teaching–learning tasks. Yet, whereas mothers' use of high-level cognitive demands related positively to their beliefs in the child's capacity for self-regulation, for fathers' it did not. Conversely, paternal beliefs in direct instruction were positively linked to nondistancing (e.g., didactic, structuring) teaching behaviors, as expected, but this pattern did not hold for mothers.

These inconsistencies were troubling because we had reason to expect a higher degree of concordance between parents' beliefs about how children acquire knowledge and how they go about facilitating that process (McGillicuddy-DeLisi, 1982). We had anticipated that reciprocal belief–behavior relationships would prevail for mothers and fathers. Unfortunately, we had to conclude that, in addition to tapping parents' global beliefs about child development, we had to examine the belief structure underlying everyday teaching situations more directly. Nevertheless, we had confirmed our hypothesis of a positive relationship between parents' use of high-level distancing strategies and their children's representational competence.

Five-Year Follow-Up Study

The next logical step in our research effort was to determine the stability and change of parents' beliefs and behaviors over the 5-year period. We also wanted to examine the long-term relationships between these belief/behavior variables and children's academic performance and self-perceptions. The reader should be reminded that academic performance is used here as a proxy for representational competence.

With a subsample of the two-parent families who participated 5 years earlier, we obtained up-to-date reports from parents regarding their socialization strategies and beliefs relative to their preadolescent children.

Parent Interview. Building on the results of the previous study, we refined our structured interview to take into account parents' behavior-specific rationales relative to typical interactions with their children. We asked parents questions about how they helped their children acquire knowledge in 12 different situations common to this age group. Applying our earlier findings regarding the salience of context in parent–child interactions, we categorized our interview items into knowledge domains to see if mothers' and fathers' self-reported beliefs and behaviors varied accordingly. The domains of interest included the physical world, as well as the social, the moral, and the intrapersonal (emotions).

The following is an example of a situation from the interview:

> You see (child's name) copying someone else's homework and you establish that she/he plans to turn it in tomorrow as her/his own. You want to help (child) learn not to cheat.
>
> First, to elicit parental teaching strategies, the parent is asked what she/he would do to help the child learn not to cheat. Then, to tap parental beliefs, the parent is asked how she/he thinks the reported strategy will help the child learn not to cheat.[1]

Recall that we had originally designed our 12 interview situations to reflect issues pertinent to four different learning domains. Confirmatory factor analyses, however, revealed the presence of only three distinct con-

[1]The interview schedule and coding information are available from the authors.

tent areas because moral and social domain responses loaded on one factor. Subsequently, these three domains were labeled: *physical knowledge, intrapersonal,* and *moral/social.*

While parents were interviewed, children were administered a series of subtests from the Woodcock–Johnson Psycho-Educational Battery (WJPB) to measure their broad cognitive ability and achievement in mathematics and reading. We also assessed children's self-evaluations of their school functioning and self-worth with the Harter Self-Perception Profile (Harter, 1982).

According to distancing theory, representational thinking is stimulated by the degree of cognitive demand parents place on their children to reason, reflect, and generate their own solutions. Presumably, these parental efforts that encourage the child's intrinsic capacity for self-directed as opposed to other-directed learning are guided by beliefs in cognitive processes. Academic subjects such as math and reading, which require abstraction and transformation of information, should thus be positively associated with beliefs mediated by strategies that further the development of representational thought. With these premises in mind, we focused on the following areas:

1. nature of parents' beliefs in different knowledge domains as children approach adolescence;
2. connections between parents' self-reported beliefs and their preferred teaching behaviors;
3. comparisons of parent–child task observations obtained during this follow-up study and when these same children were younger;
4. relationships between parents' earlier beliefs and teaching strategies and children's current school functioning; and
5. concurrent associations between parents' distancing behaviors and children's achievement and scholastic self-perceptions.

The Nature of Parents' Beliefs

Based on our previous study (Sigel et al., 1983), we theorized that parents would express a number of different beliefs regarding how their children learn and become socialized. Yet, we found that four major categories apparently accounted for 87% of all stated beliefs defined as follows: *cognitive processes, direct instruction, positive* and *negative feedback* (see Table 6.2).

The learning perspectives of parents as reported in the interview basically represent two dichotomous views of how individuals acquire knowledge, that is, internally versus externally. Of these two perspectives, the former reflects a freedom dimension (i.e., cognitive processes) where children are encouraged to think and solve problems through their own reasoning and

TABLE 6.2
Definitions of Parental Beliefs

Parental Belief	*Definitions*
Accumulation (ACC)	child learns through practice and additive experiences.
Activity (ACT)	child learns by doing, through hands-on experience.
Cognitive processes (CP)	child learns through thinking and reasoning, considering options, drawing inferences, and weighing of consequences.
Direct instruction (DI)	child learns from being told what to do, from explanations or advice.
Experimentation (EXM)	child learns by trying out alternate solutions in problem solving, trial and erro.
Exposure (EXP)	child learns through imitation and modeling
Manipulation of the environment (ME)	child learns through adult structuring of activities and learning tasks.
Negative feedback (NF)	child learns through being punished or criticized for behavior.
Positive feedback (PF)	child learns through experiencing success, approval, and support.
Self-regulation (SR)	child learns through figuring out own solutions.

initiative, whereas the latter reflects an authoritative dimension characterized by directives, reinforcement, and control by the parent or adult authorities (i.e., direct instruction, positive and negative feedback).

We also anticipated that the situational context of the parent–child interaction would be important to the types of beliefs elicited. This supposition was subsequently borne out in our interviews. Parents most frequently said that they believed children learned about physical concepts, such as measurement, through direct instruction; about feelings and emotions through their own thought processes; and about moral and social behavior from negative feedback. This is not to say that a substantial proportion of parents did not endorse different beliefs from the previously reported pattern, but it serves to highlight the variation in beliefs across different content domains.

Belief-Behavior Response Patterns. Another aspect of the belief–behavior question tapped by our interview data concerned the connections made by parents themselves between their preferred teaching strategies and the beliefs guiding their actions. Through examination of paired (belief–behavior) response frequencies, we found variations in the behavioral expression of mothers' and fathers' four core beliefs. For example, beliefs in direct instruction (see Table 6.2) were acted on differently by mothers and fathers. Mothers tended to use directives alone as their preferred teaching strategy as compared to their husbands, who preferred to provide reasons with information. As anticipated, however, irrespective of gender or domain, parents who held the belief that children learn optimally by using their own thought processes (cognitive processes), were most likely to report using high-level distancing strategies in interview situations.

Parent–Child Interactions Across Time

In addition to interviewing parents about their preferred teaching strategies, we also wanted to directly observe parents "in vivo" behaviors as they worked with their children on problem-solving tasks similar to those in our previous study. Children were 5 years older now, so we substituted knot-tying for paperfolding (origami) and replaced storytelling with a family dilemma scenario that parent and child could read and solve together. As before, we instructed parents to "teach the child" how to do each task in videotaped, 10-minute interactions.

We were now in a position to compare parent–child interactions at two points in time, focusing on continuity of parental teaching strategies across time and the nature of children's responses to parents' distancing behaviors. Examining parent behaviors observed at each time period, we noted a significant decrease in parents' use of inquiry strategies with their pre-adolescents, but a sharp increase in the number of times parents offered information to these older children. The children themselves were now much more active participants in the problem-solving process and were asking their own questions of parents as well as providing information to promote task resolution. In some cases, children took over the knot-tying task and taught their parents how to proceed. Both appeared quite comfortable with this role reversal.

Relationships Between Parents' Early Distancing Behaviors and Children's Current School Functioning

On this descriptive level, it was evident that parent–child interactions at this later point in time were qualitatively quite different from those we had observed when children were younger. Given the developmental changes that had taken place, and the increasing competence of the child to engage in joint problem-solving tasks with adults, we expected a more egalitarian interaction. We wondered, however, if individual differences in current competence levels of children in our sample were a function of parents' beliefs and teaching behaviors when their children were small or now that they were approaching adolescence. Of additional interest was whether children's self-perceptions about their school functioning at this point in time were more closely associated with parenting data obtained earlier or at follow-up.

Multivariate analyses confirmed a basic premise of the distancing model, that is, the parent's early use of high-level distancing strategies in the service of problem solving with the young child contributes positively and significantly to the child's subsequent academic achievement and overall intellectual ability. And as expected, scholastic areas requiring the highest degree of representational competence, for example, mathematics and reasoning, were most strongly associated in a positive direction with high-level distancing strategies. Yet, given the literature on maternal influences on achievement, it came as somewhat of a surprise to find that it was fathers' earlier distancing behaviors with their young children, and not mothers', which proved to be the significant influence on children's later school achievement.

With respect to how parents thought children would acquire knowledge about the world when they were still relatively young, we found correlational evidence to indicate that these early beliefs do impact later school functioning. For example, mothers' beliefs in the effects of positive feedback on the child's learning and fathers' beliefs in getting children to think on their own, both yielded positive relationships with children's academic performance.

Concurrent Parental Influences on Children's Academic Functioning

At the time of the follow-up study, the children in our sample were preadolescents (mean age = 11) and the issue before us was whether the parent variables of interest to us, specifically distancing behaviors and attendant beliefs, were still salient for our theory. Given the developmental changes in the child and the expanded socialization parameters of potential influence, it was reasonable to expect that the magnitude, if not the direction, of correlational relationships between parent and child variables might decrease at this juncture. We were also not surprised to find that spouses were now more similar than different in levels of distancing employed in problem-solving tasks and in beliefs expressed about children's learning. Parents, after all, learn from each other as well as from their children as they coordinate their child-rearing efforts, and assumedly come to share each other's perspective on the parenting process in time. Yet, patterns of concurrent associations between parent and child variables using the total sample of children led us to conclude that we were dealing with phenomena other than across time variability.

It became increasingly clear through subsequent analyses that parent and child gender interact to a significant degree. Patterns of cross-sex influence were evident in correlations between distancing and school functioning where fathers' behaviors related significantly to their daughters' achievement in reading and mothers' related to sons' math achievement. As predicted by the model, associations between distancing and achievement were positive in both instances.

Gender differential patterns of correlations were obtained relative to parental beliefs, as well. However, in this case, mothers' beliefs in their daughters' competence to engage in abstract reasoning and think on their own (cognitive processes) were highly related to daughters' math achievement and self-perceptions of scholastic ability. These same beliefs in cognitive processes, held by fathers, related positively to their sons', but not to daughters', verbal ability and reading achievement.

These findings indicate that gender differences must be considered in family data analyses. We suggest a cautionary note for those who are tempted to combine scores of groups where no mean differences exist. We have demonstrated clearly in our work that even though mean differences do not exist between parents on the variables we measured, correlations between their scores and dependent measures do differ. Why this is the case is not clear, but our results suggest that the belief and behavior variables employed in this study function differently within gender differential family dyads. For example, fathers' distancing behaviors and/or beliefs about their sons' competence seem to play a distinctive role with their sons compared to their daughters. Identifying this phenomenon in our work highlights a significant dimension that must enter into data analysis procedures in future family research.

CONCLUSIONS

We have presented an overview of the workings of the distancing model in the context of the family. In particular, our focus has been on parental socialization of children's representational competence and subsequent academic achievement. Toward this end we conceptualized a social interaction model incorporating parents' beliefs mediated by behaviors that link to children's representational ability. Initially, for methodological purposes, we had to determine the degree to which fathers and mothers agree on beliefs and behaviors. We undertook a series of comparative analyses and found that parent scores on belief and behavior measures did not reach statistical significance. However, despite their lack of statistical difference, we felt that there was sufficient evidence to continue to analyze mothers' and fathers' effects on children separately rather than as a family aggregate. In fact, this approach yielded patterns of significant findings that supported our componential analyses of the family.

Teasing out the individual and joint contributions of the parents relative to the child's cognitive socialization poses conceptual and methodological challenges. Therefore, on the basis of what we have found, it may be premature to overlook individual differences within family constellations relative to the development of children's representational competence.

The results of our analyses of differences between parents led us to examine whether the obtained differences were a function of differences due to the gender of the child. We found that mothers and fathers differ in terms of the nature of their influence on children. This finding points out the significance of gender of children as well as parents as sources of influence on representational and academic competence. Consequently, generalizations we make about parental effects must be qualified on the basis of parent and child gender.

The studies we have referred to, and those we have done ourselves, point to the complexity of the research questions relative to children's cognitive development. In spite of the large variety of factors that function in the daily lives of individuals, there is enough evidence to warrant some optimism in devising and modifying our models of research. However, a major problem in the field of family research concerns the fact that a variety of methods are employed. For example, we have used interviews and observations, others have used questionnaires, and still others use rating scales and neither interviews nor questionnaires. To complicate the matter further there are differences in concept as well. Thus the task before us is to glean similarities and overlap among the diverse data sets. In doing so we can work toward developing some common set of concepts and procedures so the optimal translation from one study to another can occur. As we proceed in this fashion, there will probably be a increasing coherence among the findings. For example, at this point there is considerable agreement that irrespective of how the variable of parental acceptance is defined and assessed, there is a high probability that the more accepting the parents of the child's ideas, the more positive the outcome in terms of the child's perception of self as a competent individual. Other themes of that type have been addressed in the chapter.

One area that still needs considerable attention has to do with the question of developmental changes. One basis of our research, comparing two time points with very discrete variables, it is clear that to expect a simple Time 1–Time 2 correlation is naive. The child is a changing individual, responding differently to similar parental interventions. Moreover, parents also change in the how and the when of their engagement. In the intervening time period as children evolve a new set of understanding and abilities they are organizationally and cognitively different from the earlier status.

Which then is the more predictive, the early cognitive organization, or the latter? Our results indicate that early experiences of the child enveloped in their current cognitive organization do predict current achievement levels.

Thus, it is how younger children understand the world around them, and how they are able to think and reason early on that will relate to subsequent school functioning. The challenge is to work out a developmental model of the changing mind of the child and hence articular sources of influence relative to their time of intervention.

There is still a lot of important conceptual and empirical work to be done, but the state of the art is moving away from the simplistic notions of the previous 2 decades to an awareness of and attention to the complexities of untangling the webs of influence on children's intellectual growth.

ACKNOWLEDGMENTS

Part of the research reported in this chapter was supported by the National Institute of Child Health and Human Development Grant No. R01-HD10686 to Educational Testing Service, National Institute of Mental Health Grant No. R01-MH32301 to Educational Testing Service, and Bureau of Education of the Handicapped Grant No. G007902000 to Educational Testing Service.

We gratefully thank Linda Kozelski for her help in manuscript preparation and editorial assistance, and Myung-in Kim for his statistical assistance.

REFERENCES

Anderson, J. R. (Ed.). (1981). *Cognitive skills and their acquisition.* Hillsdale, NJ: Lawrence Erlbaum Associates.

Baumrind, D. (1978). Parental disciplinary patterns and social competence in children. *Youth and Society, 9,* 239–276.

Block, J. H. (1983). Differential premises arising from differential socialization of the sexes: Some conjectures. *Child Development, 54,* 1335–1354.

Brody, G. H., & Stoneman, Z. (1990). Sibling relationships. In Sigel, I. E., & Brody, G. (Eds.). (1990). *Methods of family research: Biographies of Research projects: Vol. 1. Normal families* (pp. 189–212). Hillsdale, NJ: Lawrence Erlbaum Associates.

Cicirelli, V. G. (1978). The relationship of sibling structure to intellectual abilities and achievement. *Review of Educational Research, 48,* 365–379.

Clarke-Stewart, K. A. (1988). Parents' effects on children's development: A decade of progress? *Journal of Applied Developmental Psychology, 9,* 41–84.

Cochran, M. (1988). Generic issues in parent empowerment programs: A rejoinder to Mindick. In D. R. Powell (Ed.), *Advances in applied developmental psychology: Vol. 3. Parent education as early childhood intervention: Emerging directions in theory, research, and practice* (pp. 67–78). Norwood, NJ: Ablex.

Damon, W. (1977). *The social world of the child.* San Francisco: Jossey-Bass.

Dix, T. H., & Grusec, J. E. (1985). Parent attribution processes in the socialization of children. In I. E. Sigel (Ed.), *Parental belief systems: The psychological consequences for children* (pp. 201–233). Hillsdale, NJ: Lawrence Erlbaum Associates.

Doise, W., & Mugny, G. (1984). *The social development of the intellect* (A. St. James-Emler & N. Emler, Trans.). New York: Pergamon Press.

Featherman, D. L., Spenner, K. I., & Tsunematsu, N. (1988). Class and the socialization of children: Constancy, change, or irrelevance? In E. M. Hetherington, R. M. Lerner, & M. Perlmutter (Eds.), *Child development in life-span perspective* (pp. 67–90). Hillsdale, NJ: Lawrence Erlbaum Associates.

Fowler, W. (Ed.). (1986). *Early experience and the development of competence. New directions for child development, no. 32.* San Francisco, CA: Jossey-Bass.

Goodnow, J. J., & Warton, P. M. (in press). The social bases of social cognition: Interactions about work and their implications. *Merrill–Palmer Quarterly.*

Grolnick, W. S., & Ryan, R. M. (1989). Parent styles associated with children's self-regulation and competence in school. *Journal of Educational Psychology, 81,* 143–154.

Harter, S. (1982). The Perceived Competence Scale for Children. *Child Development, 53,* 87–97.

Hess, R. D., & McDevitt, T. M. (1986). Some antecedents of maternal attributions about children's performance in mathematics. In R. D. Ashmore & D. M. Brodzinsky (Eds.), *Thinking about the family: Views of parents and children* (pp. 95–118). Hillsdale, NJ: Lawrence Erlbaum Associates.

Hoffman, M. L. (1988). Moral development. In M. H. Bornstein, & M. E. Lamb (Eds.), *Developmental psychology: An advanced textbook* (2nd ed., pp. 497–548). Hillsdale, NJ: Lawrence Erlbaum Associates.

Holloway, S. D., & Hess, R. D. (1985). Mothers' and teachers' attributions about children's mathematics performance. In I. E. Sigel (Ed.), *Parental belief systems: The psychological consequences for children* (pp. 177–199). Hillsdale, NJ: Lawrence Erlbaum Associates.

Jacklin, C. N. (1989). Female and male: Issues of gender. *American Psychologist, 44,* 127–133.

Kellam, S., Ensminger, M., & Turner, R. J. (1977). Family structure and the mental health of children. *Archives of General Psychiatry, 34,* 1012–1022.

Kohn, M. (1977). *Class and conformity: A study in values* (2nd ed.). Chicago: University of Chicago Press.

Laosa, L. M., & Sigel, I. E. (Eds.). (1982). *Families as learning environments for children.* New York: Plenum.

Luria, A. R. (1978). *The making of the mind: A personal account of Soviet psychology.* Cambridge, MA: Harvard University Press.

Mandler, J. M. (1983). Representation. In P. H. Mussen (Ed.), *Handbook of child psychology* (4th ed., pp. 420–494). New York: Wiley.

Marjoribanks, K. (1979). *Families and their learning environments: An empirical analysis.* London: Routledge & Kegan Paul.

Marjoribanks, K., Walberg, H. J., & Bargen, M. (1975). Mental abilities: Sibling constellation and social class correlates. *British Journal of Social and Clinical Psychology, 14,* 109–116.

McGillicuddy-DeLisi, A. V. (1982). Parental beliefs about developmental processes. *Human Development, 25,* 192–200.

McGillicuddy-DeLisi, A. V. (1985). The relationship between parental beliefs and children's cognitive level. In I. E. Sigel (Ed.), *Parental belief systems: The psychological consequences for children* (pp. 7–24). Hillsdale, NJ: Lawrence Erlbaum Associates.

McGillicuddy-DeLisi, A. V., & Sigel, I. E. (1991). Family environment and children's representational thinking. In S. Silvern (Ed.), *Development of literacy* (Vol. 6). Greenwich, CT: JAI Press.

Miller, S. A. (1986). Parents' beliefs about their children's cognitive abilities. *Developmental Psychology, 22,* 276–284.

Miller, S. A. (1988). Parents' beliefs about children's cognitive development. *Child Development, 59,* 259–285.

Parsons, J. E., Adler, T. F., & Kaczala, C. M. (1982). Socialization of achievement attitudes and beliefs: Parental influences. *Child Development, 53,* 310–321.

Perlmutter, M. (1988). Cognitive development in life-span perspective: From description of differences to explanation of changes. In E. M. Hetherington, R. M. Lerner, & M. Perlmutter (Eds.), *Child development in life-span perspective* (pp. 191–217). Hillsdale, NJ: Lawrence Erlbaum Associates.

Phillips, D. A. (1987). Socialization of perceived academic competence among highly competent children. *Child Development, 58,* 1308–1320.

Piaget, J. (1950). *The psychology of intelligence* (M. Piercy & D. A. Berlyne, Trans). London: Routledge & Kegan Paul. (Original work published 1947.)

Plomin, R. (1989). Environment and genes: Determinants of behavior. *American Psychologist, 44,* 105–111.

Powell, D. R. (Ed.). (1988). *Advances in applied developmental psychology: Vol. 3. Parent education as early childhood intervention: Emerging directions in theory, research, and practice.* Norwood, NJ: Ablex.

Rogoff, B., & Morelli, G. (1989). Perspectives on children's development from cultural psychology. *American Psychologist, 44,* 343–348.

Scarr, S., & Weinberg, R. A. (1990). The nature-nurture problem revisited: The Minnesota adoption studies. In I. E. Sigel & G. H. Brody (Eds.), *Methods of family research: Biographies of research projects: Vol. 1. Normal families* (pp. 121–151). Hillsdale, NJ: Lawrence Erlbaum Associates.

Schaefer, E. S., & Bell, R. Q. (1958). Development of a parental attitude research instrument. *Child Development, 29,* 339–361.

Schiebe, K. S. (1970). *Beliefs and values.* New York: Holt, Rinehart & Winston.

Schooler, C. (1972). Birth order effects: Not here, not now. *Psychological Bulletin, 78,* 161–175.

Seligman, M. E. P., Kamen, L. P., & Nolen-Hoeksema, S. (1988). Explanatory style across the life span: Achievement and health. In E. M. Hetherington, R. M. Lerner, & M. Perlmutter (Eds.), *Child development in life-span perspective* (pp. 91–114). Hillsdale, NJ: Lawrence Erlbaum Associates.

Siegler, R. S. (Ed.). (1978). *Children's thinking: What develops?* Hillsdale, NJ: Lawrence Erlbaum Associates.

Sigel, I. E. (1960). Influence techniques: A concept used to study parental behaviors. *Child Development, 31,* 799–806.

Sigel, I. E. (1970). The distancing hypothesis: A causal hypothesis for the acquisition of representational thought. In M. R. Jones (Ed.), *Miami symposium on the prediction of behavior, 1968: Effects of early experience* (pp. 99–118). Coral Gables, FL: University of Miami Press.

Sigel, I. E. (1979). On becoming a thinker: A psychoeducational model. *Educational Psychologist, 14,* 70–78.

Sigel, I. E. (1982). The relationship between parental distancing strategies and the child's cognitive behavior. In L. M. Laosa & I. E. Sigel (Eds.), *Families as learning environments for children* (pp. 47–86). New York: Plenum.

Sigel, I. E. (1985). A conceptual analysis of beliefs. In I. E. Sigel (Ed.), *Parental belief systems: The psychological consequences for children* (pp. 347–371). Hillsdale, NJ: Lawrence Erlbaum Associates.

Sigel, I. E. (1986). Early social experience and the development of representational competence. In W. Fowler (Ed.), *Early experience and the development of competence. New directions for child development, no. 32* (pp. 49–65). San Francisco: Jossey-Bass.

Sigel, I. E., Anderson, L. M., & Shapiro, H. (1966). Categorization behavior of lower and middle class Negro preschool children: Differences in dealing with representation of familiar objects. *Journal of Negro Education, 35,* 218–229.

Sigel, I. E., & Cocking, R. R. (1977). Cognition and communication: A dialectic paradigm for development. In M. Lewis & L. A. Rosenblum (Eds.), *The origins of behavior: Vol. 5. Interaction, conversation, and the development of language* (pp. 207–226). New York: Wiley.

Sigel, I. E., Dreyer, A. S., & McGillicuddy-DeLisi, A. V. (1984). Psychological perspectives of the family. In R. D. Parke (Ed.), *Review of child development research: Vol. 7. The family* (pp. 42–79). Chicago: University of Chicago Press.

Sigel, I. E., & McBane, B. (1967). Cognitive competence and level of symbolization among five-year-old children. In J. Hellmuth (Ed.), *The disadvantaged child* (Vol. 1, pp. 433–453). Seattle, WA: Special Child Publications of the Seattle Sequin School.

Sigel, I. E., McGillicuddy-DeLisi, A. V., Flaugher, J., & Rock, D. A. (1983). *Parents as teachers of their own learning disabled children* (ETS RR 83-21). Princeton, NJ: Educational Testing Service.

Sigel, I. E., McGillicuddy-DeLisi, A. V., & Johnson, J. E. (1980). *Parental distancing, beliefs and children's representational competence within the family context* (ETS RR 80-21). Princeton, NJ: ETS.

Sigel, I. E., & Olmsted, P. (1970). The development of classification and representational competence. In A. J. Biemiller (Ed.), *Problems in the teaching of young children* (pp. 49–67). Ontario, Canada: Ontario Institute for Studies in Education.

Sigel, I. E., Secrist, A., & Forman, G. (1973). Psycho-educational intervention beginning at age two: Reflections and outcomes. In J. C. Stanley (Ed.), *Compensatory education for children, ages two to eight: Recent studies of educational intervention.* Baltimore, MD: Johns Hopkins University Press.

Sternberg, R. J. (1982). Introduction: Some common themes in contemporary approaches to the training of intelligent performance. In D. K. Detterman & R. J. Sternberg (Eds.), *How and how much can intelligence be increased* (pp. 141–146). Norwood, NJ: Ablex.

Stinson, E. T. (1989). *Parental ideology: Implications for child academic achievement and self-concept.* Unpublished doctoral dissertation, University of Pennsylvania.

Vygotsky, L. S. (1978). *Mind in society: The development of higher psychological processes.* Cambridge, MA: Harvard University Press.

Weinberg, R. A. (1989). Intelligence and IQ: Landmark issues and great debates. *American Psychologist, 44,* 98–104.

Wertsch, J. V. (1985). *Vygotsky and the social formation of mind.* Cambridge, MA: Harvard University Press.

Zajonc, R. B. (1976). Family configuration and intelligence. *Science, 192,* 227–236.

Zajonc, R. B. (1986). The decline and rise of scholastic aptitude scores: A prediction derived from the confluence model. *American Psychologist, 41,* 862–867.

PART III

School and Intervention Programs

CHAPTER 7

Making a Difference in People's Abilities to Think: Reflections on a Decade of Work and Some Hopes for the Future

JOHN D. BRANSFORD
SUSAN R. GOLDMAN
NANCY J. VYE
Peabody College, Vanderbilt University

Our goal in this chapter is to argue that it is possible to design educational systems that make a difference in peoples' abilities to become independent thinkers and learners. We also argue that, as a nation, we have not yet reached this goal. Granted, courses designed to enhance thinking currently exist and several appear to be successful (e.g., see Blagg, 1990; Nickerson, 1988; Nickerson, Perkins, & Smith, 1985; Savell, Twohig, & Rachford, 1986; Sternberg & Bhana, 1986). Nevertheless, thinking is not a skill to be learned in a single course; it is a way of life that needs to be practiced daily. Much more can be done and needs to be done. Research on the nature of thinking and learning provides important guidelines for how we might proceed.

Our discussion focuses on important changes in thinking about thinking that have taken place during the past decade. We focus on this time period because it was in 1980 that an influential, national conference on thinking took place. The conference was co-sponsored by the National Institute of Education and the Learning Research and Development Center at the University of Pittsburgh. Groups of researchers were asked to review existing thinking skills programs and evaluate them from the perspective of cognitive psychology. Other researchers were invited to present their own views on how thinking developed and how it might be taught. These ideas are reflected in two published volumes that were based on the papers from the 1980 conference (Chipman, Segal, & Glaser, 1985; Segal, Chipman, & Glaser, 1985). Discussions at the conference prompted a number of researchers to become deeply interested in the issues of thinking and to begin to study them in more detail.

We believe that some important changes have taken place since this conference. To be sure, classics in the field of thinking such as Dewey (1933), Polya (1957), and Wertheimer (1959) remain extremely relevant. Nevertheless, there are also new ideas, programs, and research findings that appear to have the potential to make a difference in people's lives. Our discussion focuses on five areas of change during the past decade that we believe are especially important. We conclude our discussion by looking forward to the 1990s and considering what the future might bring.

FIVE AREAS OF CHANGE DURING THE 1980S

Teaching Thinking: From a Potential Fad to an Enduring Concern

At the 1980 conference it was easy to believe that the "let's teach thinking" spirit might be a short-term fad that would soon change to some other trendy notion. If so, it certainly would not be the first time in history that attempts to emphasize thinking have come and gone (e.g., Cuban, 1984; Presseisen, 1986). As we look back over the past decade, however, it seems clear that interest in teaching thinking has persisted. Indeed, Presseisen (1986) maintained that the interest shown during the 1980s is unprecedented. It is evident at many levels, including basic research on thinking, articles in educational journals for teachers and in the "popular" press for parents, special conferences, and activities by states and local school districts, especially those aimed at teacher education and staff development. There are several interrelated reasons why the emphasis on thinking has become an enduring concern.

Poor Test Scores. One reason for continued concern about the need to teach thinking stems from the fact that our nations' students continue to score poorly on tests that require thinking. Students have difficulty writing persuasive essays, solving mathematical word problems, engaging in formal and informal reasoning, criticizing and devising scientific experiments and so forth (e.g., Cooper, 1989a; Jones & Idol, 1990; NAEP, 1981, 1983; National Commission on Excellence in Education, 1983). Nickerson (1988) summarized the results of national tests: "In the aggregate, the findings from these studies force the conclusion that it is possible to finish 12 or 13 years of public education in the United States without developing much competence as a thinker" (p. 5). Note that the argument is not that people cannot think at all. In many ways the ability to think is naturally human. However, people need instruction in order to think "more deeply, more consistently, more productively, more effectively than they otherwise might" (Nickerson, 1988, p. 4).

Concerns of Business Leaders. The poor test scores of our nations' students seem to correlate with the perceptions of many business leaders about the characteristics of todays' graduates. As Resnick (1987) noted:

> Employers today complain that they cannot count on schools and colleges to produce young people who can move easily into more complex kinds of work. They seem to be seeking general skills such as the ability to write and speak effectively, the ability to learn easily on the job, the ability to use quantitative skills needed to apply various tools of production and management, the ability to read complex material, and the ability to build and evaluate arguments. (pp. 6–7)

Increased Needs for Thinking and Learning in the Future. The concerns of business and education leaders would decrease if predictions for the future involved less reliance on the ability to think and learn. The opposite appears to be the case. It seems that a person can no longer learn the skills of a trade and expect them to be sufficient for a lifetime. Learning to be a car mechanic represents a case in point. Today, the skills required of car mechanics are both complex and rapidly changing. Mechanics have to be retrained almost every year in order to deal with fast-paced, technology-driven changes in design. This means that mechanics must have excellent learning skills, including the ability to learn from texts. The mechanic's job is simply one illustration of jobs that will require increasing amounts of retraining in the future. As a consequence, adult illiteracy and a lack of learning skills are bigger detriments to life success than they used to be.

The problem of teaching thinking is exacerbated by the fact that our work force will be comprised of an increasing number of people whom the school system has traditionally had the highest probability of failing: women and minorities (Cooper, 1989a; Hodgkinson, 1985). We need to do a much better job of helping them prepare for lifelong learning and problem solving than we have done in the past. As Resnick (1987) argued, there have actually been two different traditions in our schools. One emphasized "high literacy" (thinking and reasoning) for a select few, the other emphasized more basic skills (e.g., reading predictable texts; performing simple calculations) for the majority of the students. Predictions for the future note that we need to do a better job of teaching thinking than ever, and that we must successfully reach all students and not just a select few.

National Needs and Personal Rights. The vast majority of the arguments for teaching thinking that we have encountered during the past decade emphasize our nation's need to compete with other countries. If we as a nation cannot "work smarter," we will lose our economic standing in the world. This is an important reason for placing a greater emphasis on thinking. Nevertheless, it is useful to note that there are other reasons as well.

An important concept represented at the 1980 conference that seems even more important as time has progressed involves Machado's arguments about the right to be intelligent (Machado, 1980). According to his basic argument, people have the right to learn to think and learn for themselves and only certain forms of government make it possible for this to happen. As "Minister for the Development of Intelligence" in Venezuela, Machado attempted to put action behind his words (e.g., see Herrnstein, Nickerson, Sanchez, & Swets, 1986). Especially noteworthy is Machado's argument that the chief weapon for protecting people from being used by selfish leaders is their ability to think and learn. He also noted that many leaders do not want their people to be intelligent; otherwise the leaders might lose their power. "The key to the problem (in underdeveloped countries) is that no one wants change. The leaders of underdeveloped countries characteristically function as director of the events and orientation of collective life. But to how many of those leaders is the development of their countries really in their own interests? As their people's intelligence increases, how many will maintain their position as directors?" (p. 48).

Nickerson (1986) provided an additional reason for teaching thinking: Because we cannot afford not to. He argued that the major impediment to peaceful progress in the world is irrational human behavior. Unless we can put a stop to it, everyone is at risk. This is especially important in light of Paul's (undated) argument that the natural mode of thought for human beings is egocentric. Our natural tendency is to defend our own beliefs and it can be extremely difficult to seriously entertain points of view that differ from our own.

Implications for Making a Difference. Improving the outcomes of our educational system remains a critical national priority; in fact, its preeminence as a national goal is stronger than ever before. The need for a populace with adaptive learning skills is stressed by many different groups, an indicator that widespread support for "smarter" schooling will continue in the 1990s. There are already signs that businesses are eager to support well-planned educational interventions (e.g., Kuhn, 1990). Interventions that focus on thinking would seem to be a high priority for most groups who want to improve education. Questions about how to pursue such a goal are addressed in the discussion in the next section.

Changes in Ideas About the Nature of Intelligence and Everyday Cognition

An extremely important development during the past decade involves work that has challenged people's beliefs about the nature of intelligence. Prior to the 1980s it was easy to assume that the goal of improving thinking was equivalent to the goal of "increasing intelligence," where intelligence was measured by standardized IQ tests. This assumption implies that the best way to assess thinking skills programs was to use these tests (e.g., see Whimbey, 1975). Some people have continued this practice in the 1980s. For example, Lewis and Greene (1982) created a program to train people on intelligence test–like items and they argue that improvements in peoples' abilities to solve these problems provides a measure of their "raised intellectual ability" for all types of situations. Nickerson (1988) argued that such a claim goes too far and we agree. For most people, work during the past 10 years has expanded their ideas about what intelligence might mean and hence has affected their instructional and assessment goals.

Missing Ingredients in Standard Intelligence Tests. Work begun by Neisser (1976) laid the groundwork for identifying a number of limitations in the traditional formats for measuring intelligence. Neisser noted that traditional tests of academic intelligence contain items that (a) are formulated by other people, hence they do not test problem identification or problem finding; (b) often have little intrinsic interest; (c) attempt to have all the needed information available from the beginning and hence do not assess information finding and learning skills; (d) tend to be disembedded from an individual's experience and hence provide little information about how people make use of their own personal experiences in solving problems.

Wagner and Sternberg (1986) discussed several additional limitations of academically oriented tests. They note that academic tests tend to (e) be well-defined and hence fail to test people's abilities to solve ill-defined problems; (f) have but one correct answer rather than alternate, multiple answers; and (g) allow but one correct solution method rather than a variety of methods.

Academic Versus Practical Intelligence. Neisser (1976) argued that the concept of academic intelligence needed to be supplemented with another concept that he called "practical intelligence" and defined as "intelligent performance in practical settings." Differences between academic and practical intelligence capture the individuals who seem book smart but who do not function well in the everyday world. Of course, some individuals do well in both domains.

The edited book *Practical Intelligence* (Sternberg & Wagner, 1986) contains a number of articles that provide evidence of the value of the concept. For example, Wagner and Sternberg (1986) noted that the typical correlation between on-the-job performance and performance either on IQ tests or employment tests falls at about the .20 level. They also noted that so-called employment tests correlate higher with people's grades during training than they do with how well they actually perform when they are on the job. Therefore, these tests seem to be assessing book learning. But is it possible to actually predict success in everyday endeavors? Wagner and Sternberg created tests that ask people to perform tasks such as rate priorities and select goals that are relevant to their work situation. The correlations between scores on these tests and assessments of everyday job performance were substantial, ranging from .30 to .50. In addition, scores on the Wagner and Sternberg test did not correlate with scores on traditional intelligence tests.

Multidimensional Conceptions of Intelligence. In response to changing conceptions of intelligence and intelligent thinking, new theories of intelligence place a heavy emphasis on practical as well as academic intelligence. Two of the most noteworthy are those by Gardner (1983) and Sternberg (1985a). Both theories have important implications for ways to help people improve their abilities to adapt to everyday as well as academic life (e.g., Gardner, 1983; Sternberg, 1986, 1987). Furthermore, a shift in the emphasis from academic intelligence to multiple intelligences carries with it the implication that intelligence is not a wholistic trait that characterizes an individual. Thus, an individual might be relatively intelligent in school but relatively unintelligent in other contexts such as the auto repair shop, and vice versa. Recognition of these dimensions of difference creates an atmosphere in which studying thinking becomes a more variegated endeavor, focusing on thinking outside as well as inside formal educational settings. In addition, a shift away from "intelligence as traitlike" has moved the study of intelligence into closer proximity to the study of learning and development.

Peoples' Beliefs About Their Own Intelligence. Broader conceptions of intelligence take on increased importance when one realizes that people's beliefs about the nature of intelligence can have important effects on their assessments of their own capabilities. One type of evidence for this claim is anecdotal yet derived from many years of experience. It involves consultants who work with business executives to help them increase their abilities to succeed. Many of these consultants have emphasized that people often hold themselves back through excuses; a very common excuse is, "But you've got to have brains to succeed." The consultants try to help people change these excuses and find the potential they have overlooked.

Research by Carol Dweck and colleagues provides empirical evidence about the importance of peoples' beliefs about intelligence. For example, in studying task performance, Bandura and Dweck (1985; cited in Cain & Dweck, 1989) found that children who believed intelligence was incremental tended to emphasize developing their skills and improving their abilities. However, children who held an entity view of intelligence were oriented toward demonstrating how smart they were and reacted to the task as a test of ability. In the face of failure, incremental views tended to be associated with "mastery" orientations, whereas entity views tended to be associated with "helplessness" responses (Cain & Dweck, 1989; Dweck, 1989).

Research on Everyday Cognition. The increased emphasis on practical intelligence meshes nicely with work that has focused on the learning and problem solving of children and adults in everyday settings such as getting around their house or shopping in a grocery store (e.g., Bransford & Heldmeyer, 1983; Lave, 1988; Rogoff, 1990; Rogoff & Lave, 1984). As well, children's communication skills frequently are more well-developed when observed in familiar, everyday settings rather than in the experimenter's laboratory (e.g., Chapman, 1978; Shatz, 1982). It is clear now that many aspects of everyday cognition differ from the more formal processes tested on tests and taught in school. Consider a problem like finding the solution to $\frac{2}{3} \times \frac{1}{2}$. In school tasks, we expect people to find these answers by multiplying the fractions and coming up with the correct answer: $\frac{1}{3}$. Lave (1988) showed that very different sets of strategies may operate in real-world settings. She studied a group of adults participating in a dieting program. One adult wanted to eat only half of her daily cottage cheese allotment (two-thirds of a cup). She patted two-thirds of a cup of cottage cheese into a circle, cut the circle in half, put one half away and ate the other.

Related to the focus on everyday cognition is the notion that thinking is being investigated as it occurs on the job and in life; the study of thinking is not confined to the study of how people process intelligence test–like items. For example, a number of researchers have placed a heavy emphasis on the study of informal reasoning about everyday situations rather than only on formal reasoning problems like those found in formal logic texts (e.g., see Ennis, 1986; Paul, 1986; Perkins, 1985, 1986; Voss, Perkins, & Segal, 1990). Similarly, researchers are viewing activities such as reading in order to learn, writing, evaluating data, and learning about areas such as physics and mathematics as illustrations of thinking (e.g., see Jones & Idol, 1990; Nisbett, Fong, Lehman, & Cheng, 1987; Resnick & Klopfer, 1989b). Overall, current perspectives on thinking stress that it is a multifaceted process that manifests itself in a variety of ways (e.g., Johnson-Laird, 1988; Nickerson, 1988; Resnick, 1987).

Implications for Making a Difference. Research on the nature of intelligence and everyday cognition has a number of important implications for the 1990s. First, it shifts attention away from training on intelligence test–like items and moves it toward the kinds of tasks people need to perform to be successful in everyday environments. Second, new conceptions of intelligence provide a mechanism for expanding conceptions of "smart" to include much more than traditional school performance measures. This broader framework can help teachers find multiple areas of strengths in their students and in their students' parents. Similarly, it can assist changes in parents' views of themselves and their children, as well as children's views of themselves and those with whom they interact. In short, the idea of multiple intelligences (or multiple components to intelligence) provides a much-needed framework for helping people think differently about those around them as well as about themselves. The latter seems especially important because peoples' beliefs about themselves can have important effects on their behavior (Cain & Dweck, 1989).

Improved Understanding of the Development of Thinking

Over the past decade, research on everyday cognition and intelligence has been accompanied by a correlative change in conceptions of development and the development of thinking. In 1980, the predominant theory of development in the United States was Piaget's (1952). In its U.S. incarnation, Piagetian theory placed little emphasis on social interaction, focusing mainly on characteristics of the individual child. His theory is still extremely important, especially its emphasis on the constructive nature of knowing (Resnick & Klopfer, 1989a). What has emerged in addition is a view that places greater emphasis on the social context of development; this view has profound implications for understanding thinking and how and when it might be taught.

The Social Nature of Cognitive Development. Piaget's emphasis was almost always on the child in isolation. The child might be playing with blocks, balance beams, clay, and so forth; the emphasis was on how the child's interactions with the materials revealed current levels of understanding and set the groundwork for new cognitive developments. Levels of understanding and changes in cognitive functioning were tied to changes in cognitive structures internal to the child.

During the last decade, ideas from theorists such as Feuerstein and colleagues (Feuerstein, 1979, 1980; Feuerstein, Jensen, Hoffman, & Rand, 1985; Feuerstein, Rand, & Hoffman, 1979; Feuerstein, Rand, Hoffman, Hoffman, & Miller, 1980; Feuerstein, Rand, Jensen, Kaniel, & Tzuriel, 1987) and Vytogsky (1978) have received increasingly greater attention from both practitioners and members of the research community. Both of these theorists emphasize that the development of people's abilities to think and learn is strongly shaped by the social context of the child's environment. Feuerstein developed the concept of *mediated learning* in order to emphasize the social basis of becoming human. It was only through mediators in the children's environment (e.g., parents, peers) that they learned what to notice, how to interpret events, what counted as thinking for the particular culture, and so forth (e.g., see Arbitman-Smith, Haywood, & Bransford, 1985; Feuerstein et al., 1987; Lidz, 1987; Sherwood, Kinzer, Hasselbring, & Bransford, 1987). Similarly, Vygotsky emphasized the social roots of cognition and discussed the importance of the "zone of proximal development" (e.g., Vygotsky, 1978; Wertsch, 1979). Rogoff (1990) pointed out the critical change in perspective: "From the sociohistorical perspective, the basic unit of analysis is no longer the [properties of the] individual, but the [processes of the] sociocultural activity, involving active participation of people in socially constituted practices" (p. 14).

Researchers such as Heath (1983) have documented the important role that social context plays in helping students develop certain kinds of thinking and learning skills—only some of which are compatible with the ideas and presuppositions characteristic of most of our nation's schools. Similarly, researchers have pointed to the large differences in literacy-related activities that are characteristic of many children who begin kindergarten or first grade (e.g., Adams, 1990).

We want to stress that emphasis on the social context of development has, in fact, embellished Piaget's focus on the constructive nature of knowing. Resnick and Klopfer (1989a) noted that the constructivist position becomes more powerful—especially for educators—when it is embellished by an emphasis on the importance of mediators. "Today's cognitive science does not suggest that educators get out of the way so that children can do their natural work, as Piagetian theory often seemed to imply" (p. 4). Rather, the role of the social community in guiding the participation of children in thinking activities becomes an important consideration.

Increasing Evidence of Early Competence. As attention shifted to children's performance in everyday social settings, increasing evidence appeared of early competence in many areas, for example, number, communication, problem solving, search behavior (Gelman & Gallistel, 1978; Gelman, Meck, & Merkin, 1986; Klahr, 1978; Shatz, 1982; Wellman & Somerville, 1982; see Smith, 1988 for a summary). More recently, cognitive scientists interested in concept acquisition have written about children's causal theories in domains such as biology and ethics (e.g., Carey, 1985; Keil,

1989). To be sure, a number of elements have to be properly aligned in order for childrens' competencies to reveal themselves; for example, the context of the task must be familiar to the children, the amount of information must not exceed their working memory capacity, and so forth (e.g., Case, 1985; Smith, 1988). However, children are now viewed as capable of rather sophisticated thinking, limited more by lack of knowledge than by the absence of general logical capacities. The work of Brown and colleagues (Brown & Kane, 1988; Brown, Kane, & Echols, 1986; Brown, Kane, & Long, 1989) demonstrates that when these constraints are not exceeded, preschoolers are quite capable of analogical transfer and learning to learn, competencies previously thought to be beyond their reach.

When Does Thinking Develop? The current emphasis on the social nature of cognition and its importance in developing skills of basic thinking, coupled with the demonstration of early competencies among children, have strong implications for the question of when to teach thinking. In 1980 there was a great deal of discussion of the "back to basics" movement and its implications for a movement that emphasized thinking. It was not difficult to imagine a curriculum that began with the basics (e.g., decoding in reading, fact memorization in history, computation in mathematics) and introduced the skills of thinking only in later grades. Most theorists we know would argue that this approach is misguided and, instead, would concur with the argument of Resnick and Klopfer (1989a):

> One of the most significant ideas emerging from recent research on thinking is that the mental processes we have customarily associated with thinking are not restricted to some advanced or "higher order" stage of mental development. Instead, "thinking skills" are intimately involved in successful learning of even elementary levels of reading, mathematics, and other subjects. . . . Thinking, it appears, must pervade the entire school curriculum, for all students, from the earliest grades. (pp. 1–2)

Changes in conceptions of development and how thinking develops contribute to the view that thinking skills are intimately involved in all content areas and at all levels.

Implications for Making a Difference. Research on the development of thinking has a number of implications for the 1990s. The major implication is the increased awareness of the social nature of cognition and its development. Programs that focus only on a part of the child's school day are almost certain to have fewer benefits than those that also focus on parents and ways to involve them in their children's schooling, and on the effects of peers on one another (e.g., Palincsar & Brown, 1987, 1989). In addition, parents as well as other educators need to see how thinking is manifest in everyday activities and can be developed in the context of those activities. The opportunity to realize the "right to be intelligent" (Machado, 1980) depends on enlisting the commitment of parents as critically important mediators of the development of their children's thinking. Thinking is by no means developed only in formal educational settings such as schools. This realization and its implications must be more widely disseminated.

Better Understandings of What People Do When They Think and Solve Problems

The fourth area of research that has brought important changes in understanding involves in-depth studies of effective thinking. Classic studies in this area (e.g., Chase & Simon, 1973; deGroot, 1965) focused on the domain of chess expertise and were conducted well before 1980. During the past decade an increasing number of researchers have begun to study the nature and development of expertise in a variety of other areas, including physics, mathematics, computer programming, writing, social studies, and teaching (e.g., Berliner, 1986; Bransford, Sherwood, Vye, & Riesser, 1986; Chi, Feltovich, & Glaser, 1981; Chi, Glaser, & Farr, in press; Chi, Glaser, & Rees, 1982; Glaser, 1984; Hayes, 1990; Lesgold, 1988). An important synergy operates between this work and developmental studies of problem solving and thinking. Indeed, many of the same concepts are invoked to explain performance and changes in performance.

The Importance of Specific Knowledge. A major conclusion from the research is that high-level expertise in areas such as chess, physics, social studies, computer programming, and so forth, requires a great deal of domain-specific knowledge. Experts do not simply have more knowledge about an area than novices, they also seem to have organized that knowledge in qualitatively different ways. For example, experts in physics may categorize a set of problems as illustrations of deep principles such as "Newton's second law of motion." In contrast, less experienced individuals may categorize problems according to surface features such as whether they involve inclined planes versus pulleys versus springs (e.g., see Chi et al., 1981). Similarly, experts in different domains need and rely on different types of strategies. For example, Anderson (1987) noted that expert problem solving in physics involves a process of reasoning forward from a goal. In contrast, in computer programming experts generally reason backward from a goal.

The Importance of Routines That are Relatively Automatic. A consistent finding from the expert–novice research points out that many aspects of experts' problem-solving processes have become relatively routine or automatic. Without these routines, attentional capacity would be exceeded and people would feel overwhelmed. For example, when first learning to drive a car, novices must consciously attend to individual components such as turning the wheel, hitting the brake, moving the turn signal, and so forth. For novices, it is impossible to attend fully to one's driving and carry on a deep conversation at the same time. With practice, however, patterns of driving become routine and automatized. This frees attentional capacity so that other activities (e.g., carrying on a conversation) can take place at the same time (e.g., Anderson, 1981, 1982; Lesgold, 1988).

In the case of car-driving, automaticity includes an improved ability to recognize the conditions that signal the need to do something like tap the brake, turn the turn signal, shift from second to third gear, and so forth. This improved pattern recognition ability seems to occur in all domains (e.g., Bransford, et al., 1988). In chess, for example, specific patterns are recognized quite effortlessly as instances from certain well-known game strategies (e.g., Chase & Simon, 1973); in mathematics, many problems are almost immediately recognized as belonging to certain well-known classes of problems such as "river current problems" (e.g., Mayer, 1982, 1985); in teaching, experts who are asked to watch videotapes of classroom situations are much more likely than novices to recognize patterns of behavior that signal potential problems, that involve certain approaches to instruction, and so forth (e.g., Berliner, 1986). In all these cases, novices' attentional capacities are often overwhelmed because there is much too much novel information for them to attend to at any one time.

Clearer Differentiations Among Types of Knowledge. Researchers who have studied relationships between knowledge and thinking have made further contributions during the past decade by helping clarify differences in types of knowledge. For example, Anderson's A Cognitive Theory (ACT*; 1983) attempts to clarify the nature of skill acquisition by focusing on the transition from factual or declarative knowledge (e.g., knowledge supplied by a text or a teacher's instruction) to proceduralized or use-oriented knowledge. Put another way, Anderson's theory attempts to account for the transition from "knowing what" to "knowing how." A key feature in "knowing how" is that people learn not only what is important but also when to do the right thing—that is, they *conditionalize* their knowledge. If they do not know when to apply principles, concepts, and strategies, their knowledge does them little good (see also Larkin, 1979; Simon, 1980).

The importance of conditionalized knowledge can be illustrated by attempting to account for the wisdom of people who make effective decisions and often use proverbs to guide their thinking. What kind of knowledge of proverbs would support such thinking? It is not sufficient for such a person to have only declarative knowledge of facts such as "Too many cooks spoil the broth" and "Many hands make light work." The person must also know when each idea is most applicable. This becomes especially clear when one notes that, taken out of context, many proverbs contradict one another (compare the two proverbs already noted). Wise individuals have conditionalized their knowledge. They know when various types of advice are applicable and when they are not. It is this ability to know when to do what that seems to take much of the time that is required for the development of expertise.

Interplay Between Knowledge and Strategies. Related to the preceding discussion of clarifications in the importance of conditionalized knowledge are advances in our understandings of the interplay between specific knowledge and strategies. As a simple example, imagine teaching people the importance of breaking problems into parts. Without the knowledge necessary to define which parts are important, it is very difficult to employ such a strategy (e.g., Bransford, Stein, Arbitman-Smith, & Vye, 1985). Similarly, imagine teaching a simple memory strategy that involves efforts to rehearse stimuli and mentally organize them into categories. For stimulus lists whose organization is apparent to the learner, this *rehearse and organize* strategy can be quite easy to perform; some of the organizational activities will occur almost automatically because a new stimulus (e.g., dog) will almost automatically reactivate a previously experienced, related stimulus (e.g., cat). With other types of materials, however, the person's ability to utilize a rehearse and organize strategy may be very poor (e.g., Lindberg, 1980). People's abilities to make metacognitive assessments of how well they will learn and remember, or how well they have mastered materials, also seem to be affected by their knowledge of the materials about which they are being asked to make judgments and about the nature of subsequent tests (e.g., Nitsch, as described in Bransford, 1979; Chi, 1978).

Bransford and colleagues (1986) discussed a situation where one of them attempted to use a general strategy during decision making but, because of knowledge-organization problems, ran into difficulty. The case in point was to evaluate the pros and cons of buying a soft-top jeep. The pros that were considered centered around the fact that the jeep was a convertible that would be great in the summer. The cons that were considered included the fact that the top had to be removed by hand and the Jeep might be somewhat cold in the winter. The pros won and the decision was made to buy the Jeep. The next day, an entire dimension of information that had not been evaluated suddenly became apparent: The radio was stolen from the Jeep because the doors could not be locked. The concept of "lockable" had not entered into the original decision-making process because it was not a salient characteristic of Jeeps for the decisionmaker. After the radio incident, the decision-makers' knowledge was reorganized and "lockability" of all vehicles became a very salient feature. We believe that many arguments and decisions suffer from similar failures to access knowledge. Furthermore, many improvements in people's abilities to think about and counter arguments in particular content areas probably have to do with knowledge reorganization as well as with the habit of using general strategies such as "list the pros and cons."

A particularly important set of studies on relationships between strategies and content involves Siegler's work on his strategy choice model (e.g., Siegler, 1988; Siegler & Shrager, 1984). Siegler found that individual children have access to a variety of strategies for solving simple arithmetic problems. For example, consider the child who is trying to solve the problem "What's 5 plus 7?" The child can count on her fingers beginning with 1 and count up to 12. Or the child might begin with the largest number (7) and count 5 more to arrive at the answer 12. Alternatively, the child might simply retrieve the answer from memory. In contrast to earlier work on arithmetic problem solution (e.g., Groen & Parkman, 1972) Siegler (1988; Siegler & Shrager, 1984) noted that children do not always use the same strategy over a set of such problems. The same individual might use all these different strategies depending on the particular type of number problem they are attempting to solve. Furthermore Goldman, Pellegrino, and Mertz (1988; Goldman, Mertz, & Pellegrino, 1989) found that the strategy distribution that characterized a child was a good indicator of the changes that might be expected as a result of practice solving such problems. Several important issues emerge from this work: What factors determine the strategies that children use and the changes in the set of strategies from which they choose?

In general, Siegler observed that memory retrieval strategies are used for those knowledge structures that are well-learned (e.g., $5 + 5 = 10$) in the sense of being well-differentiated from other structures that are wrong but may compete for access (e.g., $5 + 5 = 9$ or 11). For knowledge structures that are not well-differentiated, students generally resort to back-up strategies such as counting on their fingers in various ways. Similar patterns have been found for word recognition and spelling (Siegler, 1988), as well as for strategies used in reading comprehension (e.g., Goldman & Saul, 1990). Research on the acquisition of new strategies indicates the importance of guided participation or mediation by the social environment (e.g., Rogoff, 1990; Siegler & Jenkins, 1989). In general, research on *strategy choice* models is providing important evidence about the intimate relationships between the strategies that people successfully utilize and the specific knowledge they have acquired.

Expertise and Novelty. An additional perspective on knowledge and strategies involves questions about how people deal with novelty. In many of the early expert–novice experiments the experts were described as using schema-driven processing in a relatively effortless, automatic manner; their success in problem solving seemed to be primarily a function of domain-specific knowledge that they had already acquired. However, being an expert involves more than the ability to solve already-familiar problems; it also requires the ability to continually deal with new problems and opportunities. Otherwise, today's expert will be tomorrow's also-ran (Bransford, Nitsch, & Franks, 1977; Sternberg, 1985b). Many studies of expertise have presented experts only with familiar problems and hence have failed to emphasize the fact that experts must also deal with novelty (Bransford & Vye, 1989; Perkins & Salomon, 1989). Unless we present experts with materials that are novel to them, we will fail to see the importance of general learning and problem-solving strategies that they have acquired.

Some theorists (e.g., Brown, Bransford, Ferrara, & Campione, 1983) have postulated the existence of general learning strategies that seem to be available to people with expertise in one domain (e.g., cognitive psychology) who are trying to learn novel (for them) information about a different domain (e.g., physics). Researchers have also begun to study the problem-solving strategies used by experts who are presented with novel (for them) problems in areas such as writing (Scardamalia & Bereiter, 1985), physics (e.g., Clement, in press), and mathematics (Schoenfeld, 1989). These studies with novel tasks are very important because they are leading us away from the belief that expertise in an area is primarily a function of rapid retrieval of previously acquired knowledge. Researchers are beginning to conduct more studies of how experts monitor and regulate their behavior when dealing with novel problems (e.g., Schoenfeld, 1989) and how people at different levels of expertise deal with the problem of learning new information (e.g., Bransford, Vye, Adams, & Perfetto, 1980; Chi, Bassok, Lewis, & Glaser, 1989; Frensch & Sternberg, 1989). Miller (1978) provided a discussion of expertise that we find particularly important. He distinguished two types of experts: artisans and virtuosos. *Artisans* solve problems that are given to them and then generally await the next assignment. *Virtuosos* see every situation as an opportunity to learn something new, hence they attempt to relate specific experiences to more general principles and to rethink situations so that recurring problems can eventually be eliminated. Miller's (1978) discussion of virtuosos describes the kind of goal state that fits well with an emphasis on thinking and learning skills.

Implications for Making a Difference. Overall, the emphasis on the role of knowledge in thinking should have an important impact on programs developed in the 1990s. Many of the thinking skills programs discussed at the 1980s conference tended to use "knowledge-lean" problems that did not presuppose a great deal of content knowledge (e.g., Feuerstein et al., 1979;

Whimbey & Lochhead, 1980, 1982). Students' lack of knowledge was seen as a bottleneck that could interfere with their abilities to learn to think, so problems were constructed (many were visually based) assuming knowledge most students would know. In order to get transfer to content areas such as math, science, reading, and other areas, teachers were expected to form "bridges" for their students that made clear how various strategies might be applied (see Arbitman-Smith et al., 1985). This was often difficult to do, especially when the teacher who taught the thinking skills course did not also teach the content courses such as English, Science, and Math (Bransford et al., 1985).

The trend during the 1980s has been toward the integration of thinking instruction in the content areas (e.g., Jones & Idol, 1990; Paul, Binker, Martin, Vetrano, & Kreklau, 1989; Resnick & Klopfer, 1989b; Schwartz, 1987). In essence, this trend can be viewed as an effort to systematize the "bridging" exercises that theorists such as Feuerstein believe are crucial to overall success. Research suggests that an emphasis on thinking can help students learn new skills and content (Bransford et al., 1986; Minstrell, 1989; Nickerson, 1988); hence, attempts to teach thinking in the content areas should not be at the expense of students learning important concepts. Furthermore, because thinking seems to be inherently motivating (e.g., Brown, 1988), the approach has the potential for increasing students' motivation to learn.

Deeper Understanding of Problems With Traditional Approaches to Instruction and Assessment

In conjunction with research on the nature of the knowledge underlying expert thinking and with the interplay between knowledge and strategies, work conducted during the past decade has helped clarify why many approaches to content area instruction and assessment may fail to develop the kinds of thinking skills most people desire. There are several major assumptions underlying this work. First, people must learn when to use relevant knowledge (see the previous discussion of conditionalized knowledge). In addition, in order to do so, new knowledge; must be actively constructed by learners (e.g., Pea & Soloway, 1987; Resnick, 1987) rather than passively received.

The Problem of Inert Knowledge. Whitehead's (1929) arguments about the problem of inert knowledge have been rediscovered during the past decade and have prompted considerable research (e.g., Adams, et al., 1988; Bereiter & Scardamalia, 1985; Brown & Campione, 1981; Gick & Holyoak, 1980; Novick, 1988, 1990; Perfetto, Bransford, & Franks, 1983;

Perkins & Salomon, 1989). Whitehead argued that, in many cases, information presented to students can easily be recalled by them when they are explicitly asked to do so. Nevertheless, when they are placed in new problem-solving contexts, relevant knowledge will often fail to be spontaneously accessed and hence will remain inert.

Bransford, Franks, Vye, and Sherwood (1989) provided the following illustration of inert knowledge. They described the experience of working with college students who were taught problem solving from the perspective of Bransford and Stein's IDEAL model (1984). This model emphasizes the importance of **I**dentifying and **D**efining problems, **E**xploring strategies for solution, **A**cting on the basis of strategies and **L**ooking at the effects (Bransford & Stein, 1984). Students find that the material is easy to learn; all of them can paraphrase the model and provide examples of its usefulness. They have therefore learned something by being told. Nevertheless, after several years of teaching from this problem-solving model, it has become clear that there are numerous instances in which students could profit from the model yet fail to use it. For example, unless explicitly prompted to do so, students may fail to realize how attempts to formulate the topic of a paper relate to discussions of problem identification and definition. They can think about the model, but they tend not to "think in terms of the model" (Bransford et al., 1977) or "think with" the model (Broudy, 1977). The model has not become a real "conceptual tool."

Several authors have discussed reasons why information that students have learned may tend to remain inert rather than be used when it is relevant (e.g., Bransford, Vye, Adams, & Perfetto, 1989; Nickerson, 1989; Perkins & Salomon, 1989; Sherwood, Kinzer, Hasselbring, & Bransford, 1987). First, students may have simply memorized new information rather than understood its significance or relevance. Imagine a student who memorizes new facts about camels (e.g., that they can close their nose passages and have special membranes to protect their eyes) but fails to understand the relevance of these facts for surviving desert sandstorms. This student should be less likely to use the camel information to help him understand a passage about desert travelers who wear face protectors despite the fact that the desert is so hot. Similarly, students who do not understand the general usefulness of various strategies will be less likely to employ these in relevant situations later on (e.g., see Borkowski, Carr, Rellinger, & Pressley, 1990; Brown et al, 1983; Paris & Winograd, 1990; Pressley & Levin, 1983).

A second reason for inert knowledge is related to the first. It occurs when instruction involving new information does not make contact with the students' preconceptions about the topics being studied and hence fails to change these preconceptions. The student may learn isolated bits of new information (e.g., that the earth is round and spinning on its axis or that travel in space involves non-Aristotelian principles of physics). It may be possible for the student to retrieve this new information in some circumstances (e.g., the student remembers that the earth is round when thinking about a picture of the earth taken from outer space). However, when thinking in a variety of other contexts (e.g., when looking at a wall map or thinking about distances across a long expanse such as an ocean) students may fall back into a mode of thinking that is guided by their previous preconceptions. This is especially likely to occur when the initial instruction has failed to help students see the conflicts between their preconceptions and the new information that is taught (e.g., see Anderson & Smith, 1984; Carey, 1986; Feltovich, Spiro, & Coulson, 1988; Minstrell, 1989; Roth, 1985, 1989).

In addition, access to inert knowledge is restricted because it has been learned as a specific, contextualized example rather than as a more general principle. A student may understand how a camel's features help it survive desert sandstorms yet fail to represent this as an illustration of a larger phenomenon of adaptation. If students are asked to explain something about adaptation, it may not occur to them that their knowledge of camels is relevant. Similarly, students in one of the experimental studies conducted by Gick and Holyoak (1980) appeared to treat a story describing a general's strategy for attacking a fort as something very specific rather than represent it as an illustration of a general "divide and conquer" strategy. When specific information is represented at a broader level, it is more likely to be used in new problem-solving contexts (e.g., Gick & Holyoak, 1983).

Moreover, access to inert knowledge may be inefficient because of a lack of automaticity (Bransford et al., 1988a; Schneider & Shiffrin, 1977). We noted earlier that studies of expert problem solvers illustrate the importance of being able to recognize familiar patterns with relative ease. When pattern recognition is still effortful, one's attention is not freed to think of other aspects of the situation and access to additional, relevant information may suffer.

Furthermore, inert knowledge stems from an overreliance on textual environments that make it difficult for students to learn when to apply their knowledge because they can fail to develop the kinds of pattern recognition necessary for expert performance. Imagine training a clinical psychology student to diagnose problems of clients based on verbal descriptions such as "Sarah is mildly anxious, slightly defensive . . ." Words such as "mildly anxious" and "slightly defensive" are labels for the output of an experts' pattern recognition process. A clinical student who can assign an adequate diagnosis after reading verbal vignettes has not necessarily developed the pattern recognition abilities necessary to recognize these patterns in the absence of verbal cues (e.g., Bransford, Franks, Vye, & Sherwood, 1989). Similarly, teachers who are trained to make decisions based on verbal descriptions of classroom situations may fail to notice relevant patterns in real classroom settings. Modern videodisc technology makes it possible to develop the kinds of pattern recognition training that can improve transfer from the classroom to everyday life (Bransford, Kinzer, Risko, Rowe, & Vye, 1989; Spiro, Feltovich, Coulson, & Anderson, 1989).

Why Traditional Instruction Encourages Inert Knowledge. One way to think about the inert knowledge problem is to analyze it from the perspective of differences between declarative and procedural (conditionalized) knowledge. For example, Simon (1980) emphasized that many forms of instruction do not help students conditionalize their knowledge. He argues that "textbooks are much more explicit in enunciating the laws of mathematics or of nature than in saying anything about when these laws may be useful in solving problems" (p. 29). It is left largely to the student to generate the condition-action pairs required for solving novel problems. Thus, students may learn the definition of statistical concepts such as *mean, median,* and *mode* and learn how to compute them. This knowledge is important, but it provides no guarantee that students will know if a particular statistic is the most appropriate one to use.

Research indicates that, in general, instruction that is problem-oriented rather than fact-oriented is much more likely to produce knowledge that is used spontaneously in new settings (e.g., Adams et al., 1988; Lockhart, Lamon, & Gick, 1989; Perkins & Salomon, 1989). Nevertheless, many ways of presenting problems fail to lead to effective transfer. For example, students are often able to solve the problems at the end of a chapter because the chapter provides clues about which operations to apply. When problems are removed from their chapter setting, students often fail to know when to do what (e.g., Bransford, 1979; Porter, 1989). Similarly, although worked-examples can be useful (Ward & Sweller, 1990; Zhu & Simon, 1987), many students do not use the strategies necessary to learn from such examples (Chi, Bassock, Lewis, & Glaser, 1989). In short, the mere presentation of problems to be solved, and of worked-out examples of their solutions, provides no guarantee that students will learn from the examples and develop skills for guiding their thinking later on. Furthermore, the presentation of problems does not develop the skills of problem finding and problem formulation that seem so important for success in the everyday world (e.g., Bransford et al., 1988b; Sternberg, 1985b).

Because of increased emphasis during the past decade on everyday cognition (see previous discussion), researchers have begun to look closely at the relationship between the kinds of problems that tend to be assigned in the context of school learning and those found in everyday settings. Resnick noted that school learning emphasizes (a) individual work, whereas everyday life emphasizes cooperative ventures; (b) "pure thought" to the exclusion of intelligent uses of tools such as calculators and computers; (c) abstract symbols (e.g., formulas in mathematics) to the exclusion of the manipulation of concrete objects and things; (d) general concepts to the exclusion of the specifics necessary for on-the-job competency. In short, there are large gaps between school tasks and tasks in the everyday world.

Why Traditional Tests Encourage Inert Knowledge. A focus on instructional procedures that seem less-than-optimal inevitably leads to the issue of assessment: What is measured and how is the information used? During the 1980s there has been a great deal of discussion of standardized forms of assessment and how they work against the development of curricula for improving thinking skills.

Major criticisms have been made against standardized testing, in part because overly high stakes have been placed on students' performance on these tests. Decisions about teacher competence and the effectiveness of school systems are often made on the basis of these measures. As a result, schools have adjusted their curricula and teaching practices in order to maximize performance. Many educators are worried that the situation has been taken to the extreme. Teachers have been censored for "teaching to the test"; several have lost their jobs for trying to improve their classes' test scores by cheating. Even the popular press has brought attention to education's obsession with testing. Many articles have appeared where concern is expressed that schools have become test-preparation centers.

Although there is wide consensus on the problems created by the testing movement, most researchers do not take the view that testing ought to be eliminated. As Frederiksen and Collins (1989) emphasized, "Such an approach, however, would deny to the educational system the ability to capitalize on one of its greatest strengths: to invent, modify, assimilate, and in other ways improve instruction as a result of experience. No school should be enjoined from modifying its practices in response to their perceived success or failure" (p. 28).

The problem, according to these authors, is not that teachers teach to the test. Instead, the problem is the type of instruction engendered by standardized tests. Many teachers are teaching concepts and procedures in a superficial way. Schoenfeld (in press) described an extreme case where the structure of the test items on a state-administered geometry test was such that students who had been taught to rote memorize geometric proofs performed best. The test did not require students to justify the steps in their constructions and thereby demonstrate their mathematical reasoning abilities. It merely required their constructions to contain all of the arcs and lines and to be accurately drawn.

Researchers (Cooper, 1989b; Frederiksen & Collins, 1989; Quellmalz, 1986) have suggested that we need to change the types of tests that we use to assess educational outcomes in order to prevent the kind of abuse described earlier. As noted earlier, standardized tests mostly emphasize low-level skills, factual knowledge, and memorization of procedures. Frederiksen and Collins proposed that we endeavor to develop "direct tests"—others use the term *performance-based assessments*—of students' thinking. Direct tests attempt to evaluate students' performance on high-level cognitive tasks over an extended period of time. For example, the task might involve writing a piece of persuasive text or conducting a scientific experiment. Alternatively, students may be asked to formulate and solve a complex problem that emerges from a story posed on a videodisc (Van Haneghan et al., 1989).

Tests such as these are more difficult to score than multiple-choice tests because they involve more subjective judgment and expertise. On the other hand, there is an advantage with the approach because the tasks directly assess the thinking skills and problem-solving strategies that are important for students to master. Tasks on standardized tests are at best proxies of these skills and at worst are not indicators of higher-level thinking at all (the geometry example described earlier is a case in point). Direct testing makes it more difficult for instruction to be subverted; it makes it more difficult to find superficial strategies, such as a memorization strategy, that students could be taught and that would produce excellent performance on the test. Indeed, it has been suggested that by teaching to a direct test, teachers may improve their instruction. This could happen if teachers were to use the standards used to score direct tests as key aspects of their own instruction.

A concept about testing that seems congruent with the arguments of Frederiksen and colleagues and has a number of positive features for apprenticeship models is called *curriculum-based measurement* (Deno, 1985; Fuchs, Fuchs, Hamlett, & Stecker, 1990). In curriculum-based measurement, teachers decide prior to instruction what tasks they want their students to be able to perform by the end of the year (or whatever the length of the instructional period). Samples of relevant knowledge and skills from the entire year-long curriculum occur on tests that take place throughout the school year at regular intervals. This is very different from *mastery* testing in which particular concepts and skills taught during the immediately preceding curriculum unit or lesson are assessed.

With curriculum-based assessment, teachers can look at the trajectories of each student's progress relative to larger time frames and instructional goals. Because students do not receive tests on only those items that occurred in the previous unit, they have the chance to show gains in areas (e.g., in mathematical problem solving) where the effects may be more distal from the actual instructional event. Furthermore, gains are tracked against a standard over the course of the year and children may show improvement in an area at any point during the year. In addition, this type of assessment provides information about individual differences in the maintenance of knowledge and skills.

Of course, one could use curriculum-based assessment to assess only basic skills. One needs to select appropriate types of items in order to assess activities such as writing, problem finding, and so forth. Nevertheless, the idea of sampling from the year-long curriculum provides a way to accommodate individual differences in order of mastery and it allows teachers to assess the degree to which students are able to maintain what they have previously learned. Most beneficial, perhaps, is the fact that it helps one focus on learning over the course of a time period such as one year. By defining the longer-term goal states for students that one finds desirable, one gets a better idea of the overall purpose of the cognitive apprenticeship that is being designed.

Implications for Making a Difference. The research on inert knowledge and assessment that has been conducted during the past decade is important for helping us avoid some serious pitfalls. The research makes it clear that particular patterns of teaching and assessment can result in the illusion of effective learning when, in fact, something less than desirable is taking place. In particular, when teaching is composed of isolated bits of facts and skills and assessments assess those isolated bits, an educational program can look quite successful. In reality, however, this approach to instruction may be instilling knowledge and skills that will remain inert outside the testing context. New approaches to assessment that are being developed are going to play an especially important role in the 1990s. Without them, we cannot see the degree to which we are reaching our desired goals.

LOOKING FORWARD TO THE 1990S

The decade of the 1990s may well provide the greatest opportunity yet for the kinds of innovations that will truly make a difference in people's abilities to become independent thinkers and learners. The pressures to help people develop the ability to "work smarter" will almost certainly continue to operate during the 1990s, and, as we noted earlier, the demographics will change. The 1990s may be the time when state and local governments, business leaders, and parents join forces with educators to make changes at all levels of the curricula, and to connect students' learning in school with the home and community in which they live. To be successful, thinking needs to be part of the child's entire day. Specialized courses that focus specifically on thinking should be offered when possible (e.g., see Nickerson et al., 1985; Segal et al., 1985; Sternberg & Bhana, 1986; Vye, Delclos, Burns, & Bransford, 1988). Nevertheless, thinking provides a foundation for learning so it is imperative that it be involved in content courses from the very beginning of the child's entrance into schooling (see Jones & Idol, 1990; Resnick &

Klopfer, 1989b; Schwartz, 1987). Furthermore, we argued earlier that thinking in the service of meaningful goals is highly motivating and may be the best way to get students engaged (e.g., Brown, 1988).

Crucial to the success of any "thinking in the 1990s" movement is the idea of intelligence as a multifaceted concept. People need to be helped to find both their strengths and weaknesses; they need to develop the self-confidence to persist in the face of difficulty (e.g., Cain & Dweck, 1989; Schoenfeld, 1985, 1989); they need to realize that there are many different ways to be competent and successful. But, because "wisdom can't be told" (Gragg, 1940) students probably can learn this only by actually being successful. We must increase the opportunities for students to achieve and experience success.

Situated Cognition and Apprenticeships

Two concepts that we believe will play an important role in the 1990s are the concepts of "situated cognition" (e.g., Brown, Collins, & Duguid, 1989) and "apprenticeship learning" (e.g., Collins, Brown, & Newman, in press). Proponents of situated cognition question the long-standing assumption that knowledge and action can be separated, and they take a highly critical look at the decontextualized form of instruction found in most schools because it tends to produce inert knowledge (see J. S. Brown et al., 1989). Many are also beginning to notice that the students for whom learning is the most decontextualized are those in special "at-risk" classes who are pulled out of regular classroom discussions in order to receive special attention—usually in the form of drill and practice on fragments of concepts and skills. We may well be making it even harder for these students to impose meaning on their experiences than we make it for students in regular classes.

Studies of the learning that occurs in informal, everyday environments and in organized apprenticeships are providing ideas for models of instruction that are quite different from the decontextualized practices so characteristic of formal schooling. In informal and apprenticeship learning, knowledge is learned in the context of meaningful goals, hence its uses for action are clear rather than obscured (e.g., Bransford & Heldmeyer, 1983; Rogoff, 1990).

Collins, Brown, and Newman (in press) discussed how schools might be restructured to create cognitive apprenticeships that let students engage in authentic, productive mental work. They focused on the creation of meaningful tasks and work environments rather than on lists of specific facts, concepts, and skills that students practice in isolation.

Resnick and Klopfer (1989a) and Rogoff (1990) discussed requirements for creating cognitive apprenticeships. First, they must involve real tasks such as writing for real audiences rather than only for the teacher. Second, cognitive apprenticeships involve contextualized practice rather than exercises involving isolated, component skills. Third, just as real apprentices have the opportunity to observe others performing relevant tasks, cognitive apprenticeships in schools should provide similar opportunities for students to learn from models. Special attention should be paid to making the mental activities of the models overt rather than covert. Examples of attempts to create apprenticelike, thinking-oriented activities in areas such as reading, writing, mathematics, and science can be found in a recent publication of the Association for Supervision and Curriculum Development (see especially Beck, 1989; Hull, 1989; Kaplan, Yamamoto, & Ginsburg, 1989; Minstrell, 1989; Palincsar & Brown, 1989; Schoenfeld, 1989).

Videodisc and computer technologies can help make the goal of creating cognitive apprenticeships more feasible (e.g., Cognition and Technology Group at Vanderbilt, 1990; Collins et al., in press; Larkin & Chabay, 1989; Pea & Soloway, 1987; Sherwood et al., 1987; Spiro et al., 1989). These technologies can be used to anchor or situate instruction in shared environments that permit sustained exploration by students and teachers and enable them to find and understand the kinds of problems and opportunities that experts in various areas encounter and the knowledge that these experts use as tools. In addition, students can be helped to experience the value of exploring the same setting from multiple perspectives (e.g., as a scientist, historian, mathematician, etc.). And as they discover their own issues to explore in these environments, they can communicate with other students about their ideas (e.g., Bransford et al., 1988a; Cognition and Technology Group at Vanderbilt, 1990; Van Haneghan et al., 1989).

Alternate Pathways to Knowing. A concept that we believe should play an important role in guiding thinking about the development of cognitive apprenticeships is the concept of "alternate pathways to knowing." Papert (1980) called attention to this concept when he emphasized how the programming language LOGO could be used as a new way to introduce students to concepts such as geometry (see Mayer, 1988). At a general level this concept reminds us that, for any area, our educational system provides only restricted access to areas of knowledge and, for many people, other pathways to this knowledge might make the difference between failure and success (e.g., Bransford, Sherwood, & Hasselbring, 1988).

Consider the case of a child in the early grades who is a very poor decoder and hence is unable to enter into interesting class discussions because access to the background knowledge needed for discussion is only in the form of print. Rather than remove children from class so they can receive decontextualized decoding practice, one can imagine alternate ways to help children gain access to the background knowledge; perhaps through video or through computer programs that supplement the text. In research conducted at Vanderbilt, we find that the presentation of video-based opportunities for acquiring background knowledge can have very beneficial effects on students' participation in class discussions and, eventually, can lead to improvement in comprehension and writing activities (e.g., Bransford, Franks et al., 1989; Kinzer, Hasselbring, Schmidt, & Meltzer, 1990; Risko, Kinzer, Vye, & Rowe, 1990). Similarly, when video-based problem-solving environments are used in mathematics classes, teachers report to us that students who rarely participate in class (in part because they are such poor readers) come to life (e.g., Van Haneghan et al., 1989).

The idea of creating alternate pathways to knowledge is not restricted to the idea of using multimedia such as video rather than only a single medium such as print. At its broadest level, the idea of creating alternate pathways means that we must rethink the content and structure of what we teach. An example that is salient to us involves the areas of geometry and trigonometry. We did well in these courses in school but never liked them and have avoided them as much as possible during our lives. Recently we have worked with our colleagues to develop our technology center's video-based problem-solving series (Cognition and Technology Group at Vanderbilt, 1990) and in that context have revisited geometry and trigonometry in order to find interesting applications that can be portrayed through stories on videodisc. In doing so, we have come to realize that our school experiences robbed us of a great deal of insight and appreciation. Geometry and trigonometry are fun, highly relevant, and basically quite simple. But we never knew this given the instruction we received in school. And we definitely are not alone.

Many mathematicians we know look down on the idea of beginning with applications and want us to approach mathematics as a formal system. We do too, eventually, but it has become clear to us that we learn best by seeing the need for a construct and working from there. Others may well prefer to begin from the perspective of the abstract systems per se. The point is that we see the need to develop alternate pathways and to let people try them out and decide which ones work best for them. We believe that these alternate pathways can be best created through collaboration among people who are experts in particular areas (e.g., geometry, physics, ecology, engineering, writing) with people who are good learners but novices—we call them *intelligent novices.* We hope to see many such collaborations in the 1990s. We also hope to see more collaboration between people who know about thinking and learning and those who know how to create interesting stories and adventures in both print and video formats. Our experience with such collaborations (e.g., Cognition and Technology Group at Vanderbilt, 1990) convinces us that the time is right to join forces in order to design environments that invite thinking. The passive viewing that seems so characteristic of movies and television certainly competes with education for our students' time, but the video media do not have to be used passively (e.g., Bransford, Franks et al., 1989). Especially with the interactive capabilities of videodiscs, there are new opportunities for the design of instructional materials that were not possible a few years ago.

Beyond the Ivory Tower. We close with the hope that, 10 years from now, people will look back over the decade and note that the 1990s was the time when academicians interested in developing thinking-oriented theories and curricula took giant steps out of the ivory tower and began to work closely with teachers, parents, and students in actual settings. Developers of educational theories and programs have, understandably, tended to shy away from the task of taking their ideas into schools and homes and working with experts there (i.e., the students and the teachers) to refine them. The process is time consuming, but the academic community desperately needs the feedback that such an endeavor can supply (e.g., see Sternberg & Davidson, 1987, for a discussion of one attempt at implementation).

We are hopeful that the 1990s will involve a number of large-scale collaborative experiments that will be centered in schools and communities and will link basic researchers with teachers, business leaders, media specialists, parents, and students who work to refine apprenticeshiplike curricula such as those envisioned by proponents of the concept of situated cognition. These curricula need to be evaluated by innovative new measures and, ideally, can be "growing curricula" that are added to and refined by everyone involved. In this way our students will be producing materials for others to learn from as well as having the opportunity to learn from others. As their tasks become more authentic, we suspect that students' abilities to use what they know and go beyond their knowledge will follow suit.

ACKNOWLEDGMENTS

Preparation of this chapter was supported in part by a grant from the James S. McDonnell Foundation and grant No. R215A93046-89 from the U.S. Department of Education. We thank Beth Leopold, Faapio Po'e, and Allison Heath for their editorial help.

REFERENCES

Adams, M. (1990). *Beginning to read: Thinking and learning about print.* Cambridge, MA: MIT Press.

Adams, L., Kasserman, J., Yearwood, A., Perfetto, G., Bransford, J., & Franks, J. (1988). The effects of facts versus problem-oriented acquisition. *Memory and Cognition, 16,* 167–175.

Anderson, J. R. (1981). *Cognitive skills and their acquisition.* Hillsdale, NJ: Lawrence Erlbaum Associates.

Anderson, J. R. (1982). Acquisition of cognitive skill. *Psychological Review, 89,* 369–406.

Anderson, J. R. (1983). *The architecture of cognition.* Cambridge, MA: Harvard University Press.

Anderson, J. R. (1987). Skill acquisition: Compilation of weak-method problem solutions. *Psychological Review, 94,* 192–210.

Anderson, C. W., & Smith, E. L. (1984). Children's preconceptions and content-area textbooks. In G. Duffy, L. Roehler, & J. Mason (Eds.), *Comprehension instruction: Perspectives and suggestions* (pp. 245–257). New York: Longman.

Arbitman-Smith, R., Haywood, H. C., & Bransford, J. D. (1985). Assessing cognitive change. In C. M. McCauley, R. Sperber, & P. Brooks (Eds.), *Learning and cognition in the mentally retarded* (pp. 433–471). Baltimore: University Park Press.

Beck, E. (1989, October). *On learning subject matter.* Paper presented to the National Academy of Education meeting on Learning and Instruction in School Subject Matter, Pittsburgh, PA.

Bereiter, C., & Scardamalia, M. (1985). Cognitive coping strategies and the problem of "inert" knowledge. In S. Chipman, J. W. Segal, & R. Glaser (Eds.), *Thinking and learning skills: Current research and open questions* (Vol. 2, pp. 65–80). Hillsdale, NJ: Lawrence Erlbaum Associates.

Berliner, D. C. (1986). In pursuit of the expert pedagogue. *Educational Researcher, 15,* 5–13.

Blagg, N. (1990). *Can we teach intelligence? A comprehensive evaluation of Feuerstein's instrumental enrichment programme.* Hillsdale, NJ: Lawrence Erlbaum Associates.

Borkowski, J. G., Carr, M., Rellinger, E., & Pressley, M. (1990). Self-regulated cognition: Interdependence of metacognition, attributions, and self-esteem. In B. F. Jones & L. Idol (Eds.), *Dimensions of thinking and cognitive instruction* (pp. 53–92). Hillsdale, NJ: Lawrence Erlbaum Associates.

Bransford, J., Hasselbring, T., Barron, B., Kulewicz, S., Littlefield, J., & Goin, L. (1988b). Uses of macro-contexts to facilitate mathematical thinking. In R. Charles & E. A. Silver (Eds.), *The teaching and assessing of mathematical problem solving* (pp. 125–147). Hillsdale, NJ: Lawrence Erlbaum Associates.

Bransford, J., Kinzer, C., Risko, V., Rowe, D., & Vye, N. (1989). Designing invitations to thinking: Some initial thoughts. In S. McCormick & J. Zutell (Eds.), *Cognitive and social perspectives for literacy research and instruction* (pp. 35–54). Chicago, IL: National Reading Conference.

Bransford, J., Sherwood, R., & Hasselbring, T. (1988). The video revolution and its effects on development: Some initial thoughts. In G. Foreman & P. Pufall (Eds.), *Constructivism in the computer age* (pp. 173–201). Hillsdale, NJ: Lawrence Erlbaum Associates.

Bransford, J. D. (1979). *Human cognition: Learning, understanding, and remembering.* Belmont, CA: Wadsworth.

Bransford, J. D., Franks, J. J., Vye, N. J. & Sherwood, R. D. (1989). New approaches to instruction: Because wisdom can't be told. In S. Vosniadou & A. Ortony (Eds.), *Similarity and analogical reasoning* (pp. 470–497). New York: Cambridge University Press.

Bransford, J. D., Goin, L. I., Hasselbring, T. S., Kinzer, C. K., Sherwood, R. D., & Williams, S. M. (1988a). Learning with technology: Theoretical and empirical perspectives. *Peabody Journal of Education, 64*(1), 5–26.

Bransford, J. D., & Heldmeyer, K. (1983). Learning from children learning. In J. Bisanz, G. Bisanz, & R. Kail (Eds.), *Learning in children: Progress in cognitive development research* (pp. 171–190). New York: Springer-Verlag.

Bransford, J. D., Nitsch, K. E., & Franks, J. J. (1977). Schooling and the facilitation of knowing. In R. C. Anderson, R. J. Spiro, & W. E. Montague (Eds.), *Schooling and the acquisition of knowledge* (pp. 31–55). Hillsdale, NJ: Lawrence Erlbaum Associates.

Bransford, J. D., Sherwood, R., Vye, N. J., & Rieser, J. (1986). Teaching thinking and problem solving: Research foundations. *American Psychologist, 41,* 1078–1089.

Bransford, J. D., & Stein, B. S. (1984). *The IDEAL problem solver.* New York: W. H. Freeman.

Bransford, J. D., Stein, B. S., Arbitman-Smith, R., & Vye, N. J. (1985). Three approaches to improving thinking and learning skills. In J. Segal, S. Chipman, & R. Glaser (Eds.), *Thinking and learning skills: Relating instruction to basic research* (pp. 133–200). Hillsdale, NJ: Lawrence Erlbaum Associates.

Bransford, J. D., & Vye, N. J. (1989). A perspective on cognitive research and its implications for instruction. In L. Resnick & L. E. Klopfer (Eds.), *Toward the thinking curriculum: Current cognitive research* (pp. 173–205). Alexandria, VA: ASCD.

Bransford, J. D., Vye, N., Adams, L., & Perfetto, G. (1989). Learning skills and the acquisition of knowledge. In A. Lesgold & R. Glaser (Eds.), *Foundations for a psychology of education* (pp. 199–249). Hillsdale, NJ: Lawrence Erlbaum Associates.

Broudy, H. S. (1977). Types of knowledge and purposes of education. In R. C. Anderson, R. J. Spiro, & W. E. Montague (Eds.), *Schooling and the acquisition of knowledge* (pp. 1–17). Hillsdale, NJ: Lawrence Erlbaum Associates.

Brown, A. L. (1988). Motivation to learn and understand: On taking charge of one's own learning. *Cognition and Instruction, 5,* 311–321.

Brown, A. L., Bransford, J. D., Ferrara, R. A., & Campione, J. C. (1983). Learning, remembering and understanding. In J. H. Flavell & E. M. Markman (Eds.), *Carmichael's manual of child psychology* (Vol. 1, pp. 77–166). New York: Wiley.

Brown, A. L., & Campione, J. C. (1981). Inducing flexible thinking: A problem of access. In M. Friedman, J. P. Das, & N. O'Connor (Eds.), *Intelligence and learning* (pp. 515–530). New York: Plenum.

Brown, A. L., & Kane, M. J. (1988). Preschool children can learn to transfer: Learning to learn and learning from example. *Cognitive Psychology, 20,* 493–523.

Brown, A. L., Kane, M. J., & Echols, C. H. (1986). Young children's mental models determine analogical transfer across problems with a common goal structure. *Cognitive development, 1,* 103–121.

Brown, A. L., Kane, M. J., & Long, C. (1989). Analogical transfer in young children: Analogies as tools for communication and exposition. *Applied Cognitive Psychology, 3,* 275–294.

Brown, J. S., Collins, A., & Duguid, P. (1989). Situated cognition and the culture of learning. *Educational researcher, 17,* 32–41.

Cain, K. M., & Dweck, C. S. (1989). The development of children's conception of intelligence: A theoretical framework. In R. J. Sternberg (Ed.), *Advances in the psychology of human intelligence* (Vol. 5, pp. 47–82). Hillsdale, NJ: Lawrence Erlbaum Associates.

Carey, S. (1985). *Conceptual change in childhood.* Cambridge, MA: MIT Press.

Carey, S. (1986). Cognitive science and science education. *American psychologist, 41,* 1123–1130.

Case, R. (1985). *Intellectual development: Birth to adulthood.* New York: Academic Press.

Chapman, R. S. (1978). Comprehension strategies in children. In J. Kavanaugh & W. Strange (Eds.), *Speech and language in the laboratory, school, and clinic* (pp. 308–329). Cambridge, MA: MIT Press.

Chase, W. G., & Simon, H. A. (1973). Perception in chess. *Cognitive Psychology, 1,* 33–81.

Chi, M. T., Bassok, M., Lewis, P. J., & Glaser, R. (1989). Self-explanations: How students study and use examples in learning to solve problems. *Cognitive Science, 13,* 145–182.

Chi, M. T. H. (1978). Knowledge structures and memory development. In R. S. Siegler (Ed.), *Children's thinking: What develops?* (pp. 73–96). Hillsdale, NJ: Lawrence Erlbaum Associates.

Chi, M. T. H., Feltovich, P. J., & Glaser, R. (1981). Categorization and representation of physics problems by experts and novices. *Cognitive Science, 5,* 121–152.

Chi, M. T. H., Glaser, R., & Farr, M. (in press). *The nature of expertise.* Hillsdale, NJ: Lawrence Erlbaum Associates.

Chi, M. T. H., Glaser, R., & Rees, E. (1982). Expertise in problem solving. In R. Sternberg (Ed.), *Advances in the psychology of human intelligence* (pp. 7–76). Hillsdale, NJ: Lawrence Erlbaum Associates.

Chipman, S., Segal, J., & Glaser, R. (1985). *Thinking and learning skills: Current research and open questions* (Vol. 2). Hillsdale, NJ: Lawrence Erlbaum Associates.

Clement, J. (in press). Nonformal reasoning in physics: The use of analogies and extreme cases.

In J. Voss, D. N. Perkins, & J. Segal (Eds.), *Informal reasoning.* Hillsdale, NJ: Lawrence Erlbaum Associates.

Cognition and Technology Group at Vanderbilt. (1990). Anchored instruction and its relationship to situated cognition. *Educational Researcher, 19*(6), 2–10.

Collins, A., Brown, J. S., & Newman, S. E. (in press). Cognitive apprenticeship: Teaching the craft of reading, writing, and mathematics. In L. B. Resnick (Ed.), *Knowing and learning: Issues for a cognitive science of instruction.* Hillsdale, NJ: Lawrence Erlbaum Associates.

Cooper, E. J. (1989a). Toward a new mainstream of instruction for American schools. *Journal of Negro Education, 58,* 102–115.

Cooper, E. J. (1989b). Addressing urban school reform: Issues and alliances. *Journal of Negro Education, 58,* 315–331.

Cuban, L. (1984). Policy and research dilemmas in the teaching of reasoning: Unplanned designs. *Review of Educational Research, 54,* 655–681.

deGroot, A. (1965). *Thought and choice in chess.* The Hague, The Netherlands: Mouton.

Deno, S. L. (1985). Curriculum-based measurement: The emerging alternative. *Exceptional Children, 52,* 219–232.

Dewey, S. (1933). *How we think: Restatement of the relation of reflective thinking to the educative process.* Boston: D. C. Heath.

Dweck, C. S. (1989). Motivation. In A. Lesgold & R. Glaser (Eds.), *Foundations for a psychology of education* (pp. 87–136). Hillsdale, NJ: Lawrence Erlbaum Associates.

Ennis, R. (1986). A taxonomy of critical thinking dispositions and abilities. In J. Baron & R. Sternberg (Eds.), *Teaching thinking skills: Theory and practice* (pp. 9–26). New York: W. H. Freeman.

Feltovich, P. J., Spiro, R. J. & Coulson, R. L. (1988). The nature of conceptual understanding in biomedicine: The deep structure of complex ideas and the development of misconceptions. In D. Evans & V. Patel (Eds.), *The cognitive sciences in medicine* (pp. 113–172). Cambridge, MA: MIT (Bradford) Press.

Feuerstein, R. (1979). *Instrumental enrichment.* Baltimore, MD: University Park.

Feuerstein, R. (1980). *Instrumental enrichment: An intervention program for cognitive modifiability.* Baltimore: University Park Press.

Feuerstein, R., Jensen, M., Hoffman, M. B., & Rand, Y. (1985). Instrumental enrichment, an intervention program for structural cognitive modifiability: Theory and practice. In J. W. Segal, S. F. Chipman, & R. Glaser (Eds.), *Thinking and learning skills* (Vol. 1, pp. 43–82). Hillsdale, NJ: Lawrence Erlbaum Associates.

Feuerstein, R., Rand, Y., & Hoffman, M. (1979). *The dynamic assessment of retarded performers: The learning potential assessment device, theory, instruments, and techniques.* Baltimore, MD: University Park Press.

Feuerstein, R., Rand, Y., Hoffman, M., Hoffman, M., & Miller, R. (1980). *Instrumental enrichment.* Baltimore: University Park Press.

Feuerstein, R., Rand, Y., Jensen, M. R., Kaniel, S., & Tzuriel, D. (1987). Prerequisites for assessment of learning potential: The LPAD model. In C. S. Lidz (Ed.), *Dynamic assessment: An interactional approach to evaluating learning potential* (pp. 35–51). New York: Guilford Press.

Frederiksen, J. R., & Collins, A. (1989). A systems approach to educational testing. *Educational Researcher, 18,* 27–32.

Frensch, P. A., & Sternberg, R. J. (1989). Expertise and intelligent thinking: When is it worse to know better? In R. J. Sternberg (Ed.), *Advances in the psychology of human intelligence* (pp. 157–188). Hillsdale, NJ: Lawrence Erlbaum Associates.

Fuchs, L. S., Fuchs, D., Hamlett, C. L., & Stecker, P. M. (1990). The role of skills analysis in curriculum-based measurement in math. *School Psychology Review, 19,* 6–22.

Gardner, H. (1983). *Frames of mind.* New York: Basic Books.

Gelman, R., & Gallistel, C. R. (1978). *The child's understanding of number.* Cambridge, MA: Harvard University Press.

Gelman, R., Meck, E., & Merkin, S. (1986). Young children's numerical competence. *Cognitive Development, 1,* 1–30.
Gick, M. L., & Holyoak, K. J. (1980). Analogical problem solving. *Cognitive Psychology, 12,* 306–365.
Gick, M. L., & Holyoak, K. J. (1983). Schema induction and analogical transfer. *Cognitive Psychology, 15,* 1–38.
Glaser, R. (1984). Education and thinking: The role of knowledge. *American Psychologist, 39,* 39–104.
Goldman, S. R., Pellegrino, J. W., & Mertz, D. L. (1988). Extended practice of basic addition facts: Strategy changes in learning disabled students. *Cognition and Instruction, 5,* 223–265.
Goldman, S. R., Mertz, D. L., & Pellegrino, J. M. (1989). Individual differences in extended practice functions and solution strategies for basic addition facts. *Educational Psychology, 81,* 481–496.
Goldman, S. R., & Saul, E. U. (1990). *Applications for tracking reading behavior on the Macintosh.* Paper presented at meeting of the American Educational Research Association, Boston, MA.
Gragg, C. I. (1940). Because wisdom can't be told. *Harvard Alumni Bulletin,* pp. 78–84.
Groen, G., & Parkman, (1972). A chronometric analysis of simple addition. *Psychological Review, 79,* 329–343.
Hayes, J. R. (1990). Individuals and environments in writing instruction. In B. F. Jones & L. Idol (Eds.), *Dimensions of thinking and cognitive instruction* (pp. 241–263). Hillsdale, NJ: Lawrence Erlbaum Associates.
Heath, S. B. (1983). *Ways with words: Language, life, and work in communities and classrooms.* Cambridge, MA: Cambridge University Press.
Herrnstein, R. J., Nickerson, R. S., Sanchez, M., & Swets, J. A. (1986). Teaching thinking skills. *American Psychologist, 41,* 1279–1289.
Hodgkinson, H. L. (1985). *All one system: Demographics of education—kindergarten through graduate school.* Washington, DC: Institute for Educational Leadership, Inc.
Hull, G. H. (1989). Research on writing: Building a cognitive and social understanding of composing. In L. B. Resnick & L. E. Klopfer (Eds.), *Toward the thinking curriculum: Current cognitive research* (pp. 104–128). Alexandria, VA: ASCD.
Jefferson, T. (1779). For the more general diffusion of knowledge. In D. B. Tyack (Ed.), *Turning points in American educational history* (pp. 19–67). New York: Wiley.
Johnson-Laird, P. N. (1988). A taxonomy of thinking. In R. J. Sternberg & E. E. Smith (Eds.), *The psychology of human thought* (pp. 429–457). Cambridge: Cambridge University Press.
Jones, B. F., & Idol, L. (1990). Conclusions. In B. F. Jones & L. Idol (Eds.), *Dimensions of thinking and cognitive instruction* (pp. 511–532). Hillsdale, NJ: Lawrence Erlbaum Associates.
Kaplan, R. G., Yamamoto, T., & Ginsburg, H. P. (1989). Teaching mathematics concepts. In L. B. Resnick & L. E. Klopfer (Eds.), *Toward the thinking curriculum: Current cognitive research* (pp. 59–82). Alexandria, VA: ASCD.
Keil, F. C. (1989). *Concepts, kinds and cognitive development.* Cambridge, MA: MIT Press.
Kinzer, C. K., Hasselbring, T. S., Schmidt, C. A., & Meltzer, L. (1990, April). *Effects of multimedia to enhance writing ability.* Paper presented at meeting of the American Educational Research Association, Boston, MA.
Klahr, D. (1978). Goal formulation, planning, and learning by pre-school problem solvers or: "My socks are in the dryer." In R. S. Siegler, *Children's thinking: what develops?* (pp. 181–212). Hillsdale, NJ: Lawrence Erlbaum Associates.
Kuhn, Susan E. (1990, Spring). How business helps schools. *Fortune,* pp. 91–106.
Larkin, J. H. (1979). Information processing models and science instruction. In J. Lochhead & J. Clement (Eds.), *Cognitive process instruction: Research on teaching thinking skills* (pp. 109–118). Philadelphia: Franklin Institute Press.
Larkin, J. H., & Chabay, R. W. (1989). Research on teaching scientific thinking: Implications for

computer-based instruction. In L. B. Resnick & L. E. Klopfer (Eds.), Toward the thinking curriculum: Current cognitive research (pp. 150–172). Alexandria, VA: ASCD.

Lave, J. (1988). *Cognition in practice.* Boston, MA: Cambridge University Press.

Lesgold, A. (1988). Problem solving. In R. J. Sternberg & E. E. Smith (Eds.) *The psychology of human thought* (pp. 188–213). New York: Cambridge University Press.

Lewis, D., & Greene, J. (1982). *Thinking better: A revolutionary new program to achieve peak mental performance.* New York: Holt, Rinehart & Winston.

Lidz, C. S. (1987). *Dynamic assessment: An interactional approach to evaluating learning potential.* New York: Guilford Press.

Lindberg, M. (1980). The role of knowledge structures in the ontogeny of learning. *Journal of Experimental Child Psychology, 30,* 401–410.

Lockhart, R. S., Lamon, M., & Gick, M. L. (1989). Conceptual transfer in simple insight problems. *Memory and Cognition, 16,* 36–44.

Machado, L. A. (1980). *The right to be intelligent.* Oxford, England: Pergamon Press.

Mayer, R. E. (1982). Memory for algebra story problems. *Journal of Educational Psychology, 74,* 199–216.

Mayer, R. E. (1985). Mathematical ability. In R. J. Sternberg (Ed.), *Human abilities: An information-processing approach* (pp. 127–150). New York: W. H. Freeman.

Mayer, R. E. (1988). *Teaching and learning computer programming.* Hillsdale, NJ: Lawrence Erlbaum Associates.

Miller, R. B. (1978). The information system designer. In W. T. Singleton (Ed.), *The analysis of practical skills* (pp. 278–291). Baltimore, MD: University Park Press.

Minstrell, J. A. (1989). Teaching science for understanding. In L. B. Resnick & L. E. Klopfer (Eds.), *Toward the thinking curriculum: Current cognitive research* (pp. 129–149). Alexandria, VA: ASCD.

National Assessment of Educational Progress (NAEP). (1981). *Reading, thinking, and writing: Results from the 1979–1980 national assessment of reading and literature* (Report No. 11-L-01). Denver, CO: Education Commission of the States.

National Assessment of Educational Progress (NAEP). (1983). *The third national mathematics assessment: Results, trends and issues* (Report No. 13-MA-01). Denver, CO: Educational Commission of the States.

National Commission on Excellence in Education. (1983). *A nation at risk: The imperative for educational reform.* Washington, DC: U.S. Government Printing Office.

Neisser, U. (1976). General, academic, and artificial intelligence. In L. Resnick (Ed.), *The nature of intelligence* (pp. 135–144). Hillsdale, NJ: Lawrence Erlbaum Associates.

Nickerson, R. S. (1986). Why teach thinking? In J. Baron & R. S. Sternberg (Eds.), *Teaching thinking skills: Theory and practice* (pp. 27–38). New York: W. H. Freeman.

Nickerson, R. S. (1988). On improving thinking through instruction. *Review of Research in Education, 15,* 3–57.

Nickerson, R. S. (1989). New directions in educational assessment. *Educational Researcher, 18,* 3–7.

Nickerson, R. S., Perkins, D., & Smith, E. E. (1985). *The teaching of thinking.* Hillsdale, NJ: Lawrence Erlbaum Associates.

Nisbett, R. E., Fong, G. T., Lehman, D. R., & Cheng, P. W. (1987). Teaching reasoning. *Science, 238,* 625–631.

Novick, L. R. (1988). Analogical transfer, problem similarity, and expertise. *Journal of Experimental Psychology: Learning, Memory, and Cognition, 14,* 510–520.

Novick, L. R. (1990). Representational transfer in problem solving. *Psychological Science, 1,* 128–132.

Papert, S. (1980). *Mindstorms: Children, computers, and powerful ideas.* New York: Basic Books.

Palincsar, A. S., & Brown, A. L. (1987). Advances in cognitive instruction of handicapped

children. In M. C. Wang, H. J. Wahlberg, & M. Reynolds (Eds.), *The handbook of special education: Research and practice* (Vol. 1, pp. 93–112). New York: Pergamon Press.
Palincsar, A. S., & Brown, A. L. (1989). Instruction for self-regulated reading. In L. B. Resnick & L. E. Klopfer (Eds.), *Toward the thinking curriculum: Current cognitive research* (pp. 19–39). Alexandria, VA: ASCD.
Paris, S. G., & Winograd, P. (1990). How metacognition can promote academic learning and instruction. In B. F. Jones & L. Idol (Eds.), *Dimensions of thinking and cognitive instruction* (pp. 15–51). Hillsdale, NJ: Lawrence Erlbaum Associates.
Paul, R. W. (undated). *Critical thinking and the critical person.* Unpublished manuscript.
Paul, R. W. (1986). Dialogical thinking: Critical thought essential to the acquisition of rational knowledge and passions. In J. B. Baron & R. J. Sternberg (Eds.), *Teaching thinking skills: Theory and practice* (pp. 127–148). New York: W. H. Freeman.
Paul, R., Binker, A.J.A., Martin, D., Vetrano, C., & Kreklau, H. (1989). *Critical thinking handbook: 6th–9th grades.* Rhonert Park, CA: Sonoma State University.
Pea, R. D., & Soloway, E. (1987). *Mechanisms for facilitating a vital and dynamic education system: Fundamental roles for education science and technology.* Unpublished manuscript, New York University, New York.
Perfetto, B. A., Bransford, J. D., & Franks, J. J. (1983). Constraints on access in a problem solving context. *Memory and Cognition, 11,* 24–31.
Perkins, D. N. (1985). Postprimary education has little impact on informal reasoning. *Journal of Educational Psychology, 77,* 562–570.
Perkins, D. N. (1986). Thinking Frames: An integrative perspective on teaching cognitive skills. In J. B. Baron & R. J. Sternberg (Eds.), *Teaching thinking skills: Theory and practice* (pp. 41–61). New York: W. H. Freeman.
Perkins, D. N., & Salomon, G. (1989). Are cognitive skills context-bound? *Educational Researcher, 18,* 16–25.
Piaget, J. (1952). *The origins of intelligence in children* M. Cook, (Trans.) New York: International Universities Press.
Porter, A. (1989). A curriculum out of balance: The case of elementary school mathematics. *Educational Researcher, 18* (5), 9–15.
Polya, G. (1957). *How to solve it.* Garden City, NY: Doubleday/Anchor.
Presseisen, B. Z. (1986). *Critical thinking and thinking skills: State of the art definitions and practice in public schools.* Philadelphia: Research for Better Schools.
Pressley, M., & Levin, J. R. (1983). *Cognitive strategy research: Educational applications.* New York: Springer-Verlag.
Quellmalz, Edys S. (1986). Developing reasoning skills. In J. B. Baron & R. J. Sternberg (Eds.), *Teaching thinking skills: Theory and practice* (pp. 86–105). New York: W. H. Freeman.
Resnick, L. (1987). *Education and learning to think.* Washington, DC: National Academy Press.
Resnick, L. B., & Klopfer, L. E. (1989a). Toward the thinking curriculum: An overview. In L. B. Resnick & L. E. Klopfer (Eds.), *Toward the thinking curriculum: Current cognitive research* (pp. 1–18). Alexandria, VA: ASCD.
Resnick, L. B., & Klopfer, L. E. (Eds.) (1989b). *Toward the thinking curriculum: Current cognitive research.* Alexandria, VA: ASCD.
Risko, V. J., Kinzer, C., Vye, N. J., & Rowe, D. (1990, April). *Effects of videodisc macrocontexts on comprehension and composition of casually-coherent stories.* Paper presented at meeting of the American Educational Research Association, Boston, MA.
Rogoff, B. (1990). *Apprenticeship in thinking: Cognitive development in social context.* New York: Oxford University Press.
Rogoff, B., & Lave, J. (Eds.), (1984). *Everyday cognition: Its development in social context.* Cambridge, MA: Harvard University Press.
Roth, K. J. (April 1985). *Conceptual change learning and student processing of science texts.* Paper

presented at the annual meeting of the American Educational Research Association, Chicago.

Roth, K. J. (1989). Developing meaningful conceptual understanding in science. In B. F. Jones & L. Idol (Eds.), *Dimensions of thinking and cognitive instruction* (pp. 139–176). Hillsdale, NJ: Lawrence Erlbaum Associates.

Savell, J. M., Twohig, P. T., & Rachford, D. L. (1986). Empirical status of Feuerstein's 'instrumental enrichment' (FIE) technique as a method of teaching thinking skills. *Review of Educational Research, 56,* 381–409.

Scardamalia, M., & Bereiter, C. (1985). Fostering the development of self-regulation in children's knowledge processing. In S. F. Chipman, J. W. Segal, & R. Glaser (Eds.), *Thinking and learning skills: Research and open questions* (Vol. 2, pp. 65–80). Hillsdale, NJ: Lawrence Erlbaum Associates.

Schneider, W., & Shiffrin, R. M. (1977). Controlled and automatic human information processing: Detection, search and attention. *Psychological Review, 84,* 1–66.

Schoenfeld, A. (1985). *Mathematical problem solving.* Orlando, FL: Academic Press.

Schoenfeld, A. H. (1989). Teaching mathematical thinking and problem solving. In L. B. Resnick & L. E. Klopfer (Eds.), *Toward the thinking curriculum: Current cognitive research* (pp. 83–103). Alexandria, VA: ASCD.

Schwartz, R. J. (1987). Teaching and thinking: A developmental model for the infusion of thinking skills into mainstream instruction. In J. B. Baron & R. J. Sternberg (Eds.), *Teaching thinking skills: Theory and practice* (pp. 106–126). New York: W. H. Freeman.

Segal, J., Chipman, S., & Glaser, R. (1985). *Thinking and learning skills: Relating instruction to basic research* (Vol. 1). Hillsdale, NJ: Lawrence Erlbaum Associates.

Shatz, M. (1982). On mechanisms of language acquisition: Can features of the communicative environment account for development? In E. Wanner & L. R. Gleitman (Eds.), *Language acquisition: The state of the art* (pp. 102–127). New York: Cambridge University Press.

Sherwood, R., Kinzer, C., Hasselbring, T., & Bransford, J. (1987). Macro-contexts for learning: Initial findings and issues. *Journal of Applied Cognition, 1,* 93–108.

Siegler, R. S. (1988). Individual differences in strategy choices: Good students, not-so-good students, and perfectionists. *Child Development, 59,* 833–851.

Siegler, R. S., & Jenkins, E. (1989). *How children discover new strategies.* Hillsdale, NJ: Lawrence Erlbaum Associates.

Siegler, R. S., & Shrager, J. (1984). Strategy choices in addition and subtraction: How do children know what to do? In C. Sophian (Ed.), *The origins of cognitive skills* (pp. 229–293). Hillsdale, NJ: Lawrence Erlbaum Associates.

Simon, H. A. (1980). Problem solving and education. In D. T. Tuma & R. Reif (Eds.), *Problem solving and education: Issues in teaching and research* (pp. 81–96). Hillsdale, NJ: Lawrence Erlbaum Associates.

Smith, C. (1988, April). *Comprehension-monitoring and memory-monitoring: Two sides of same coin?* Paper presented at the annual meeting of the American Educational Research Association, New Orleans.

Spiro, R. J., Feltovich, P. J., Coulson, R. L., & Anderson, D. K. (1989). Multiple analogies for complex concepts: Antidotes for analogy-induced misconception in advanced knowledge acquisition. In S. Vosniadou & A. Ortony (Eds.), *Similarity and analogical reasoning* (pp. 498–531). Cambridge: Cambridge University Press.

Sternberg, R. J. (1985a). *Beyond I.Q.: Toward a triarchic theory of intelligence.* Mass: Cambridge University Press.

Sternberg, R. J. (1985b). Teaching critical thinking, Part 1: Are we making critical mistakes? *Phi Delta Kappan, 67* (November), 194–198.

Sternberg, R. J. (1986). *Intelligence applied.* San Diego, CA: Harcourt Brace Jovanovich.

Sternberg, R. J. (1987). Teaching Intelligence: The application of cognitive psychology to the improvement of intellectual skills. In J. B. Baron & R. J. Sternberg (Eds.), *Teaching thinking skills: Theory and practice* (pp. 182–218). New York: W. H. Freeman.

Sternberg, R. J., & Bhana, K. (1986). Synthesis of research on the effectiveness of intellectual skills programs: Snake-oil remedies or miracle cures? *Educational Leadership, 44,* 60–67.

Sternberg, R. J., & Davidson, J. E. (1987). Teaching thinking to college students: Some lessons learned from experience. *Teaching Thinking and Problem Solving, 9*(3), 1–11.

Sternberg, R. J., & Wagner, R. K. (Eds.). (1986). *Practical intelligence: Nature and origins of competence in the everyday world.* New York: Cambridge University Press.

Van Haneghan, J., Barron, L., Young, M., Williams, S., Vye, N., & Bransford, J. (1989). *The Jasper series: An experiment with new ways to enhance mathematical thinking.* Unpublished manuscript, Vanderbilt University, Nashville, TN.

Voss, J. F., Perkins, D., & Segal, J. (1990). *Informal reasoning and education.* Hillsdale, NJ: Lawrence Erlbaum Associates.

Vye, N. J., Delclos, V. R., Burns, M. S. & Bransford, J. D. (1988). Teaching, thinking and problem solving: Illustrations and issues. In R. Sternberg & E. Smith (Eds.), *Psychology of human thought* (pp. 337–365). New York: Cambridge University Press.

Vygotsky, L. S. (1978). *Mind in society.* Cambridge, MA: Harvard University Press.

Wagner, R. K., & Sternberg, R. J. (1986). Tacit knowledge and intelligence in the everyday world. In R. J. Sternberg & R. K. Wagner (Eds.), *Practical intelligence: Nature and origins of competence in the everyday world* (pp. 51–83). New York: Cambridge University Press.

Ward, M., & Sweller, J. (1990). Structuring effective worked examples. *Cognition and Instruction, 7,* 1–39.

Wellman, H. M., & Somerville, S. C. (1982). The development of human search ability. In M. E. Lamb & A. L. Brown (Eds.), *Advances in developmental psychology,* (Vol. 2, pp. 41–48). Hillsdale, NJ: Lawrence Erlbaum Associates.

Wertsch, J. V. (1979). From social interaction to higher psychological presses: A clarification and application of Vygotsky's theory. *Human Development, 22,* 1–22.

Wertheimer, M. (1959). *Productive thinking.* New York: Harper & Row.

Whimbey, A. (1975). *Intelligence can be taught.* New York: Dutton.

Whimbey, A., & Lochhead, J. (1980). *Problem solving and comprehension: A short course in analytical reasoning.* Philadelphia: Franklin Institute Press.

Whimbey, A., & Lochhead, J. (1982). *Problem solving and comprehension.* Philadelphia: Franklin Institute Press.

Whitehead, A. N. (1929). *The aims of education.* New York: MacMillan.

Zhu, X., & Simon, H. A. (1987). Learning mathematics from examples and by doing. *Cognition and Instruction, 4,* 137–166.

CHAPTER 8

Parents as Instruments of Intervention in Home-Based Preschool Programs

KATHLEEN MCCARTNEY
ELIZABETH HOWLEY
University of New Hampshire

The history of early childhood intervention in this country can be traced to the day nurseries of the mid- to late-19th century, which were charity institutions run for children of immigrants and poor parents (Steinfels, 1973). However, it was not until the 1960s that planned intensive intervention efforts began. Our nation's War on Poverty captured the interest of legislators, who funded a number of social programs in an effort to prevent what was believed to be a cycle of poverty passed from generation to generation. Part of the solution to problems associated with poverty appeared to be education. Early childhood intervention was considered a fundamental part of a multifaceted education effort that included job training and a variety of community action programs (Zigler & Freedman, 1987).

Early childhood intervention programs were designed to prevent school failure. They have typically been structured in one of two ways: center-based or home-based. In *center-based* programs, children receive educational and social stimulation from teachers in an effort to enrich an otherwise disadvantaged environment. In *home-based* programs, parents receive social support and instruction from trained home visitors. The educational philosophy of home-based interventions is different from that of center-based interventions. Parents become the instruments of intervention in the former and parents are supplemented by teachers in the latter. Although center-based interventions appear more intensive, based on number of contact hours between the service deliverer and the child, home-based programs may prove to be more intensive if the behaviors and attitudes of a parent are changed, such that the intervention continues long after the home visits are over.

Bronfenbrenner's (1974) classic review, titled "Is early intervention effective?" promoted family education generally and parent involvement in intervention specifically through his ecological model of human development. In the review, Bronfenbrenner argued that early childhood intervention cannot exist in a vacuum; that is, without supporting social structures, interventions cannot be effective. Bronfenbrenner, and reviewers who have followed, have nearly unanimously advocated parent involvement in early childhood intervention programs. With respect to Head Start, Zigler and Freedman (1987) wrote that "effective intervention can only be accomplished through involving parents and the community in the intervention effort" (p. 87).

The involvement of parents in their children's education has clear historical roots in the United States. The importance of parent involvement is found in educational literature of all sorts and can be traced to maternal associations of the early 1800s, in which mothers met to discuss the religious and moral education of their children (Goodson & Hess, 1975), and to the establishment of U.S. kindergarten programs, in which the education of young children and their parents was linked (White et al., 1989). Social welfare programs, such as early intervention, are sometimes seen as at odds with individualistic U.S. ideals. It seems likely that involving parents in intervention efforts would help reconcile two conflicting desires, to provide children with educational opportunity and to preserve the autonomy of the family. A belief that parents are ultimately responsible for the welfare of their children may motivate and support the philosophy of home-based approaches (White et al., 1989).

U.S. beliefs may help explain developmentalists' advocacy for parent involvement. Halpern (1986) labeled this advocacy a "paradox," because these programs continue to be recommended and used despite the fact that there is not consistent empirical justification for them. The rationale for home-based programs clearly has face validity, despite the fact that little is known about whether they are effective and about the actual mechanisms of effectiveness.

Although empirical data are lacking, reviews are not. In fact, there are even papers that review the reviews (e.g., White et al., 1989). Evaluation findings on early childhood intervention sometimes seem to serve as stimuli in a projective test for reviewers, in that conclusions about efficacy vary widely. In part, differences among reviewers reflect the fact that there is no consensus for what constitutes program success versus program failure. For some, success is demonstrated by positive parent outcomes, and for others success is demonstrated by sustained differences in children's IQ or improved school achievement. Similarly, there is no consensus for which pattern of results would indicate malleability and which would indicate resiliency.

Humanitarian concerns of reviewers may bias interpretations as well. Because these reviews have been used by legislators to guide social policy, especially the level of funding for programs for poor children, some reviewers have almost certainly been cautious about negative pronouncements (Woodhead, 1988). Yet, there seems to be agreement that the task of early childhood intervention is more difficult than that originally conceived in the naive environmental period of the 1960s. Many remain sympathetic to Scarr and Weinberg's (1978) claim that "we have blithely promised a world of change that we have not delivered" (p. 690).

The goal of this chapter is not to make pronouncements about the success or failure of early childhood intervention generally or of home-based programs specifically. The task of reviewers should be to identify effective components of programs. We believe that home-based programs offer a successful model of early childhood intervention when parents become instruments of intervention through a change in their maladaptive beliefs and behaviors. We turn to a description of the philosophy of home-based intervention programs in which we point to the relevance of recent research on parental beliefs. Then we review the limited data base on experimental evaluations of home-based preschool programs. Finally, we offer some tentative conclusions and suggest directions for future intervention efforts.

THE PHILOSOPHY OF HOME-BASED INTERVENTION PROGRAMS

Powell (1989) outlined three explicit goals of programs that involve parents, particularly of home-based intervention programs. First and foremost, these programs seek to increase child competence through parent education and improved parent–educator cooperation. A related second goal is parent self-development. By participating in intervention programs parents may experience personal development that will enhance their parenting skills as well as their job-related and community skills. Third, many educators hope that with job success parents will gain the confidence and ability to seize political power to initiate social change. Empowerment is often a goal of parent programs, because most program designers do not want to foster a paternalistic attitude toward their clients.

Thus, the goal of all home-based programs is for positive changes in parents to lead to positive changes in their children. For parents to become the instruments of intervention for their children, change must be reflected in parental beliefs and behaviors. There has been recent interest in the diverse literature on parental beliefs and their effects on child development (for a review, see Miller, 1988). To some extent, parental beliefs have a cognitive base. For example, although parents favor environmental over biological explanations of behavior, they recognize that the impact of the environment depends on the child's maturational level and on inherent abilities (Miller, 1988). Beliefs also have a motivational/affective base. For example, mothers attribute school success to their children's ability, but they attribute school failure to their children's lack of effort (Holloway & Hess, 1985).

Despite these commonalities, parents also vary considerably in their beliefs about child development. Some of this variability is related to group differences, which suggests that beliefs are not always personal but rather consist of "ready-made schema" (Miller, 1988). For example, Stevens (1984) found that maternal education and family income were positively associated with responses to a questionnaire designed to assess child development knowledge and parenting skill. Similarly, Sameroff and Feil (1985) found that parents from lower socioeconomic status (SES) groups had "simpler" (less perspectivistic) concepts of development. In general, parents from higher SES groups tend to have beliefs that are, in theory, more adaptive in that they are associated with positive behaviors in the parent and positive child outcomes.

There is also some research to suggest that parental beliefs are related to child development. Clearly, these data are of central importance for intervention efforts. Johnson and Martin (1985) found that parents' cognitive-developmental beliefs were positively correlated with children's academic performance, whereas strictly maturational beliefs were negatively correlated with performance. These data, like data from the parent–child socialization literature, are impossible to interpret. The direction of effects is not clear in parent–child correlations (Bell, 1974). In addition, a likely third variable would appear to be the intelligence of the parent, which would result in a correlation between the genotypes of parents and the environments they provide (Scarr & McCartney, 1983).

Experimental studies are needed to determine the extent to which maladaptive parental beliefs can be altered and the extent to which adaptive parental beliefs and behaviors promote child development. For the most part, intervention studies have not systematically assessed change in parental attitudes, perhaps because evaluations have focused on changes in child outcomes. An exception is Segal's (1985) evaluation of the Ready for School Project, a home visiting program for 3- and 4-year-olds. Like most home visiting programs, the goal of this program was for home visitors to help parents to learn skills that would enable them to become effective teachers of their own children. The intervention changed some parents' attitudes. Parents who initially viewed their role as that of a disciplinarian later viewed their role as that of a teacher. Segal speculated that this change probably resulted from the improvement in parent–child social interaction that the program fostered, but the cause of parents' change in attitudes is not clear.

Prescriptions for attitude change are not easy to make, based on existing data in social psychology (Sigel, 1985). Research has shown that many factors affect attitude change, including appealing to a person's reason, increasing trust in communication, strengthening the persuasive message, and appealing to various needs (Sears, Peplau, Freedman, & Taylor, 1985). No doubt these factors interact in complex ways. However, it is clear from the work on teacher expectancies that changes in a teacher's attitude about a child can lead to large effects on child outcomes (Rosenthal & Rubin, 1978). The question for interventionists is how to induce positive expectancies in parents of program children.

How to structure home-based programs is not clear. Although there is no standard curriculum, there are standard procedures (Halpern, 1986). These procedures include parent–home visitor personal relationship building, information sharing, observation, and perhaps case management and advocacy. Sometimes programs involve direct parent training by a home visitor; other times, there is more of an attempt to foster a professional partnership between the parent and the home visitor as they engage in cooperative problem solving. An implicit curriculum is reflected to some extent in the selection of the home visitor. Home visitors may be nurses, social workers, teachers, other professionals, or paraprofessionals. The more professional training the home visitor has, the more likely the curriculum involves direct parent training as opposed to partnership.

One study has systematically examined how home visits are structured. Meleen, Love, and Nauta (1988, cited in Powell, 1989) observed four home visits at eight Head Start sites to study how time was budgeted. Visits lasted approximately 75 minutes. One-third of the time was spent with home visitors working alone with parents. In contrast, home visitors spent very little time working alone with children. Most of their time was spent with parents practicing activities with the home visitor and/or the child. These activities were typically related to school readiness, although this fact probably reflects the educational focus of Head Start. Sometimes, a small amount of time was spent in social-service activities. For example, parents might request information on adult education, welfare, job training, or legal matters.

To summarize, current theory on parental beliefs and attitude change offers a framework for developing a deductive philosophy of potentially successful home-based programs. Existing evaluation studies offer a data base from which to develop an inductive philosophy of successful home-based programs. We turn now to these data.

INTERPRETING THE EVALUATION DATA

Methodological Issues

There is consensus among reviewers on the methodological limitations of intervention studies. Many point out that there has been an *overreliance on tests of intelligence* and school achievement in outcome assessments (Zigler & Trickett, 1978). The goals of these programs extend beyond intelligence. For example, there were seven original goals developed by the consultants of Head Start. The goals were to improve: (a) physical health and abilities, (b) emotional and social development, (c) mental processes, (d) confidence for future learning efforts, (e) parent–child relationships, (f) attitudes toward society, and (g) sense of dignity and self-worth within children and their families (Cooke, 1965, in Zigler & Freedman, 1987).

In fairness, however, Cicirelli (1984) noted that priorities were set by program designers and intellectual development was a goal of the "highest priority." These programs were designed to help prepare socially disadvantaged children for public school (Ramey, Bryant, & Suarez, 1985). Critics have argued that these goals reflect the middle-class majority culture, although such goals may be necessary for school success. Yet the disparity between the program goals and parent expectations and attitudes may actually lead parents to question their own competence (Halpern, 1986). Parents may then place too much blame on their own inadequacies and not enough on other institutions.

Most likely, evaluators have relied on measures of intelligence because IQ tests are among the most reliable and valid measures of school success. Evaluators may have goals concerning child and family functioning but may not be able to identify or construct appropriate measures.

A second criticism concerns the *lack of rigorous experimental design* in evaluation studies. The majority of studies are nonexperimental or quasi-experimental, in that there is a comparison group rather than a control group. Worse, many evaluations involve only a pretest/posttest design with no comparison group whatsoever. In addition, samples are necessarily restricted by volunteerism, and subject participation rates are sometimes low. Although there is a need for the use of experimental, pretest–posttest designs in evaluation studies, Gray and Wandersman (1980) argued that these designs are too restrictive without the inclusion of data on the ecological surroundings of the child. Essentially, they argue for the need to consider moderating and mediating variables. Yet, there is little evidence for treatment interactions in evaluation studies (Cronbach, 1982).

Even with experimental assignment to treatment and control groups, the administration of the treatment variable in the field is not as precise as that in the lab (Powell, 1989). More specifically, to the extent that home visitors individualize the treatment, it will not be uniformly delivered. In addition, evaluators worry that there will be contamination between the treatment and control families, such that the control families experience certain aspects of the intervention.

It is of course critical that researchers who administer pretest and posttest measures to children and their families are blind to whether families received treatment. This is seldom mentioned in reports. Moreover, it is desirable that the program evaluators and the program deliverers consist of independent groups. Again, it is not always clear from reports if this is the case.

Third, *subject attrition* is often high in these studies, perhaps because the subject population is defined as socially disadvantaged or "at risk." It is not uncommon for attrition rates to constitute one-quarter of the sample (e.g., Epstein & Weikart, 1979; Gordon & Guinagh, 1974; Gray & Ruttle, 1980; Madden, O'Hara, & Levenstein, 1984). Evaluation studies with a pretest are by definition longitudinal studies, in that the child and family are studied over the course of the intervention itself. There is a need to study the long-term effects of interventions. Unfortunately, there are few follow-up studies, not because of a lack of interest among researchers but because of problems associated with the feasibility of longitudinal research in general, for example, location of subjects and continued funding. The need for longitudinal research is necessary both to determine whether any identified effects decrease over time (i.e., a "wash out" effect) and to determine whether previously unidentified effects emerge (i.e., a "sleeper" effect).

Less often discussed is the potential *lack of power* in evaluation studies of early childhood programs. The smaller the effect size, which can be defined as the degree to which the relationship studied differs from zero (Rosenthal & Rosnow, 1984), the lower the power. Effect-size estimates are typically reported in standard deviation units. For example, with a sample size of 100, the probability of discovering a small effect, say .20, is only 29% (Kenny, 1987). When reviewers (e.g., Ramey, Bryant, & Suaraz, 1985; Scarr & Arnett, 1987) claim that various forms of early childhood intervention are ineffective, they essentially fail to reject the null hypothesis. Such claims rest critically on seldom-performed power analyses.

We offer the following review with these important methodological limitations in mind.

Experimental Evaluations of Home-Based Preschool Programs on IQ

Evaluation studies are needed for some program goals but not for others. For example, the goal of a program may be to provide social support for families, which any program will do, by definition. Or the goal of a program may be to provide child-care services for families, which again some programs will do, by definition. However, when the goals of a program involve changing children and/or parents in some way, then evaluations are critical.

As we have seen, program success is typically defined as a significant difference between treatment and comparison groups on an intelligence test. Clearly, other important outcome measures exist, such as school success (i.e., special education referral, attendance, grade retention, and teacher evaluations), self-esteem, and quality of parent–child interaction. Less often, success is defined in terms of change in parental behavior or in terms of family economic and life circumstances (Seitz, 1985). Nevertheless, we focus on intelligence as an outcome variable in this review, because this book concerns cognitive development. Consequently, this review is necessarily limited in scope.

As a first step, we review experimental evaluations of home-based intervention programs in which the child outcome assessment included a measure of intelligence. We define an experimental evaluation as one in which there is random assignment to the treatment and control groups. We identified this data base by two methods. First, we conducted a computer literature search of *PSYCLIT* by crossing the descriptor terms *intervention* with *experimental,* as well as searching the term *home intervention.* Second, we examined the references of several review papers (i.e., Clewell, Brooks-Gunn, & Benasich, 1989; Goodson & Hess, 1975; Ramey, Bryant, Sparling, & Wasik, 1985; White et al., 1989). We have summarized the evaluation studies identified through this search in Table 8.1.

Table 8.1 provides a brief overview of the home-based program, means on IQ for the treatment and control groups, and *d,* an effect-size estimate. In a two-group comparison, *d* is defined as the difference between the means, divided by the standard deviation of the population (i.e., sigma). We have estimated sigma as the standard deviation of the control group, which is typical for evaluation studies. We used *t* and *F* statistics to estimate *d* when standard deviations were not reported (see discussion in Rosenthal & Rosnow, 1984). Sometimes, no test statistics and no standard deviations were reported, in which case an effect-size estimate could not be computed.

Note that there are very few experimental evaluations of strictly home-based intervention programs on IQ in Table 8.1. We were only able to identify 14 such evaluations and 3 of them were evaluations of the Mother–Child Home Program (Levenstein, 1977); thus, there are only 12 evaluations of home-based programs. For this reason, we believe that no definitive conclusions can be made concerning the efficacy of home-based intervention on IQ.

In addition, note that there is great variability among the programs with respect to treatment effects on IQ. Effect sizes range from .007 to .75 and are moderate to large for several of the programs. Unfortunately, there are not

TABLE 8.1
Mean IQ for Treatment and Control Groups From Experimental Evaluations of Home-Based Preschool Programs

Author	*Type of Home Program*	*IQ Measure*	*Mean IQ*		*d*
			Treatment	*Control*	
Field (1981)	Neonatal Behavior Demonstration. One Brazelton Demonstration in the hospital by nurses to mothers. Mother's Assessment Behavior of Infant (MABI) completed weekly by mother.	Bayley (MDI) 1 yr.	127	97	
Field (1981)	Mother's Assessment of Child. MABI completed monthly by mothers.	Bayley (MDI) 1 yr.	122	97	
Field Widmayer, Greenberg, & Stoller (1982)	Home-Visit Intervention. 6 months bi-weekly home visits by Black teenage paraprofessional with Black teenage mothers. Activities based on Bayley and Brazelton scales.	Bayley (MDI) 8 mo. 12 mo. 24 mo.	 112 112 104	 109 105 98	
Gordon[a] (1971)	Florida Parent Project. 2 years of weekly visits by trained parent educators with the mother. Educator modeled Piagetian infant stimulation exercises.	Griffiths 12 mo. Bayley (MDI) 24 mo.	111 85	107 91	
Guttelius & Kirsch (1975)	Infant Education Program with Support Group. 2–6 months clinic prenatal care, counseling & screening available. 3 years of home-based well baby-care visits (21 total) by a pediatrician and nurse, with nurse home visits between peditrician visits. Parents invited to bi-monthly support group sessions.	Stanford–Binet 3 yrs.	102.3	91.5	
Guttelius & Kirsch (1975)	Infant Education Program. Program identical to formentioned, but no support group	Stanford–Binet 3 yrs.	96.0	91.3	

(continued)

TABLE 8.1 *(Continued)*

Author	*Type of Home Program*	*IQ Measure*	*Mean IQ* *Treatment*	*Mean IQ* *Control*	*d*
Lambie, Bond, & Weikart (1974) Epstein & Weikart (1979)	Home Teaching with Mothers and Infants. 16 months of weekly home visits by professionally trained staff 1 (avg 45 visits during project), program individualized.	Stanford-Binet			
		3 yrs	103.9	100.6	
Lambie, Bond, & Weikart (1974) Epstein & Weikart (1979)	Home Teaching with Mothers and Infants. 16 months of weekly home visits by community members, students; with mothers (avg. < 45 visits); support & discuss problems	Stanford–Binet			
		3 yrs.	98.3	100.6	
		Grade K	110.7	110.8	.01
		Grade 1	106.4	105.7	.04
Madden, O'Hara, & Levenstein (1984)	Mother–Child Home Program. 20 months, 46 twice weekly home visits by a toy demonstrator.	Stanford–Binet 6 yrs.			
		Cohort 1	102.8	101.1	
		Cohort 2	103.2	105.3	
		Cohort 3	101.3	108.3	
		Cohort 4	107.0	101.1	
Ramey, Bryant, Sparling, & Wasik (1985)	Family Education. 3 years of visits every days. Curriculum included "Learning Games," and parent problem solving.	Bayley (MDI)			
		6 mo.	107.5	105	.20
		12 mo.	107.8	108.5	−.05
		18 mo.	94.3	103.1	−.68
		24 mo.	88.9	97.4	.69
		36 mo.	88.6	92.9	−.34
Scarr & McCartney (1988)	Mother–Child Home Program. 20 months semiweekly home visits Toys given and demonstrated.	Stanford–Binet			
		4 yrs.	106.6	103.1	.21
Slaughter (1983)	Mother–Child Home Program. 14 months semiweekly home visits. Toys given and demonstrated.	Bayley (MDI)			
		22 mo.	114.3	109.7	.40
		32 mo.	109.6	102	.69
		41 mo.	104.1	96.5	.63
Slaughter (1983)	Mother Discussion Group. 14 months weekly discussion groups conducted by social workers with mothers. Discussed child activities and parenting and other problems.	Bayley (MDI)			
		22 mo.	110.9	109.7	.10
		32 mo.	104	102	.18
		41 mo.	105.6	96.5	.75

(continued)

TABLE 8.1 *(Continued)*

Author	*Type of Home Program*	*IQ Measure*	*Mean IQ* *Treatment*	*Mean IQ* *Control*	*d*
Widmayer, Peterson, Calderson, Korn, Carnahan, & Wingerd (1989)	Haitiani Perinatal Intervention Project. 3 months of bi-weekly home visits during the last trimester of pregnancy and semi-weekly for child's first 2 years by Haitian paraprofessional to Haitian women in Miami; Focus on social support, toys, games, discipline.	Bayley (MDI)			
		6 mo.	113.8	108.5	.40
		12 mo.	110.2	104	.40

Note: Effect-size estimates could not be computed for 8 of the 14 studies, because neither standard deviations nor appropriate test statistics were reported.

[a]Additional results from Gordon (1971) appear in Ramey et al. (1985).

enough studies, and therefore there is not enough power, to compare specific program features through contrast analysis. One can only speculate about program features that might account for the magnitude of effects. Even such speculations are limited by the fact that many studies do not report the data necessary to compute effect-size estimates.

The 12 programs are similar in some fundamental ways. Most involve weekly visits and involve parent training of one sort or another. Sometimes the training is subtle, as when the Brazelton scales are demonstrated for the mother (e.g., Field, 1981) and sometimes the training is more direct, as when mothers are taught learning games (e.g., Ramey et al., 1985a). Most programs encourage home visitors to provide various parent support services, either formally or informally.

There are so few experimental evaluations of home-based preschool programs because home visiting is often just one part of an intervention treatment. For example, a comprehensive intervention might include home visiting, child care, social services, and even medical care. These treatments must be evaluated in toto, and so it is impossible to document the role of the home visiting component and whether it is even an important component.

The Importance of Parent Involvement?

One evaluation study directly compared one form of family education to a comprehensive day-care program with respect to growth in IQ (Ramey et al., 1985b). The investigators conducted this comparison study to assess Ramey and Bryant's (1982) claim that the intensity of an educational treatment, where intensity is defined as the time and types of contact with a child, is directly and positively related to intellectual development in high-risk children. Sixty-four high-risk families were identified and randomly assigned to one of three conditions when target children were approximately 3 months of age: day care and family education, family education, or an untreated comparison group. The family education program consisted of trimonthly visits by a paraprofessional. Children were taught various learning games to facilitate the exchange of information on child development, family problem solving, or the teaching of parenting skills. At 36 months, children in the day-care and family education group had higher IQs than children in the family education group and the control group, by 16 and 12 points respectively. The researchers concluded that this form of parent education alone is "not an intervention of enough intensity" to have an impact on IQ.

In a review of preschool education, Ramey and his colleagues (Ramey et al., 1985a) reported mean group differences between experimental and control groups on IQ. They identified 11 infancy interventions that evaluated children at 2 years and rank ordered programs from those most effective to those least effective. A review of these data revealed that IQ gains for day-care programs were greater than those for home visiting programs. Ramey also offered these data as evidence for an intensity hypothesis. There were no real patterns for curriculum effects, but this probably reflects the limited data base from which patterns could be identified.

White and colleagues (1989) specifically investigated the effectiveness of parent involvement using the data base from the Early Intervention Research Institute at Utah State University. They identified 43 home-based intervention studies in which there was a comparison between an intervention group and a no-intervention group. Only 15 of these studies were judged by the research team as studies of good methodological quality. The degree of parent involvement was major in seven of these programs and minor in eight programs. The effect-size estimate for program effects on IQ was actually somewhat greater for programs with minor parent involvement (.66 vs. .49).

As one can see, there have been a number of efforts to synthesize the results of early childhood intervention programs using statistical techniques, like meta-analysis, including our own Table 8.1. There are several potential problems with the use of these techniques in evaluation studies, in particular. Most important, published studies are likely to be biased toward those obtaining significant findings. This is referred to as the "file drawer" problem, because unpublished reports of insignificant studies can only be found in the file drawers of researchers. Thus, these meta-analysis efforts cannot really estimate any kind of average effect-size estimate unless one specifies a limited population (e.g., published, experimental studies). Meta-analysis can be useful in identifying potential moderating variables for treatment effects, but only given a sufficiently large data base, which we do not have here. For this reason, we proceed by reviewing different programs, in which home-based preschool intervention is a part.

Three Examples of Experimental Evaluations of Home-Based Interventions

Home-based interventions differ in their structures. Differences in structure reflect differences in program goals and philosophies. This is most clearly demonstrated when one considers the role of parents in programs. Programs can be classified as either (a) *home-based focused,* in which a home visitor works with both parent and child, (b) *center-based focused,* in which there is a home visiting component, and (c) *home-based or center-based with parent training.* We have selected three relatively successful programs that exemplify these three models. Each of these programs has been carefully designed and evaluated.

Home-Based Focus. The Mother–Child Home Program (MCHP) is a widely used, well-evaluated, home-based program designed for low-income families at risk for educational disadvantage. The program was designed by Phyllis Levenstein and her colleagues at the Verbal Interaction Project in Long Island, New York (Levenstein, 1970, 1977; Levenstein & Sunley, 1968). The MCHP is designed for children between the ages of 2 and 4 years of age and their parents, typically mothers. Children and their parents receive 46 semiweekly visits from a home visitor for each of the 2 years. The home visitor is called a toy demonstrator, because visits are structured around demonstrations of how to encourage verbal interaction during play. Every other visit, the child receives a new book or toy. These materials in and of themselves are assumed to increase the quality of the home environment.

The toy demonstrators are paraprofessionals—often mothers who have already participated in the program with their children—or volunteers. The curriculum is fairly structured. Toy demonstrators are provided with guide sheets for each toy or book that provide ideas on how and what to model for mothers. Although visits are undoubtedly individualized, toy demonstrators share ideas and experiences with a supervisor during staff meetings.

The MCHP is the prototype of home-based early childhood intervention programs in that it consists of a play-based curriculum. Its main goal is to foster intellectual development through language stimulation, and it attempts to make parents the agents of the intervention so that the intervention will continue.

An early evaluation study, which was quasi-experimental, showed moderate IQ gains (Madden, Levenstein, & Levenstein, 1976). However, a second evaluation study with random assignment to treatment groups showed less favorable outcomes (Madden, O'Hara, & Levenstein, 1984). Data from these studies were included in the meta-analysis conducted by the Consortium for Longitudinal Studies (Lazar, Darlington, Murray, Royce, & Snipper, 1982), which concluded that such programs had lasting effects on school competence.

Several independent evaluations of this program have also been conducted. There are some data to suggest that programs like the MCHP help mothers as well. Slaughter (1983) compared two "parent discussion programs," the MCHP and the Mother Discussion Group Program, to a no-treatment control. The discussion group mothers scored higher on a test of mothers' expressed social values and on an observation measure of maternal teaching style. However, children whose mothers participated in the MCHP scored higher than control children on IQ. The program prevented a decline in IQ for this group; children in the control group showed a decline in IQ that is typical for socially disadvantaged children.

In the most recent study of the MCHP, Scarr and McCartney (1988) conducted an evaluation with a pretest–posttest, experimental design. They studied a representative sample of 125 Bermudian families with 2-year-olds in one of nine parishes on the island. Of identified families, 93% agreed to participate in the study and attrition was low. It is important to consider how this random sample of families compares to the selected disadvantaged families from prior studies by Levenstein and her colleagues. Just 33% of the families in this sample can be characterized as disadvantaged on the basis of parental education and occupational prestige. Because the sample ranged from very disadvantaged to very advantaged, it becomes possible to test for treatment interactions with family background indicators. There were few differences on a wide range of outcome variables between the treatment and control group children at 4 years of age. Children in the treatment group scored better on 2 of 17 variables: They performed better on a toy sorting task following maternal instruction and were rated by their mothers as having better communication skills. The difference between the two groups on IQ was 3.5 points, an insignificant difference favoring the children in the treatment group. A search for treatment interactions with a number of family background variables did not lead to any clear pattern. Thus, Scarr and McCartney concluded that the program was not of "any clear benefit."

Center-Based Focus. Field and her colleagues designed a parent training program for teenage mothers, which compared two types of parent-centered intervention to a control group (Field, Widmayer, Greenberg, & Stoller, 1982). The program was designed to prevent negative child outcomes associated with teenage pregnancy. For example, teenage mothers tend to have unrealistic expectations about developmental milestones, as well as punitive child-rearing attitudes. In all, 120 Black, teen mothers were recruited from a university hospital and randomly assigned to one of the three experimental groups.

In the home-based intervention group, mothers received 6 months of bi-weekly home visits, from a team consisting of psychology graduate students and a Black teenager. As in the MCHP, they demonstrated the child activities and exercises for mothers. This curriculum was based on tasks from developmental assessment scales (e.g., Bayley, Brazelton).

Mothers in the nursery intervention served as teacher trainees in an infant nursery at a medical school. For 6 months, these mothers worked 4 hours a day at the center with their own and center infants, and received teacher training as well as payment for their work.

At 4 months, infants from both intervention groups weighed more and received higher scores on the Denver Developmental Scale than control children. Parents of intervention children also rated them as less difficult on a temperament survey. At 8 months, the intervention group scored higher on the Bayley Physical Development Index (PDI), but there were no group differences on the Bayley Mental Development Index (MDI). At this age, only nursery intervention mothers rated their children as less difficult than control mothers.

At 1 year, the intervention groups scored higher than control groups on both Bayley scales (MDI, PDI). Nursery intervention children scored higher on the Bayley PDI than home-based children. In addition, mothers from the nursery intervention were more likely to have returned to work or school, and less likely to have had repeated pregnancies than home-intervention mothers, who returned to work or school and had fewer repeat pregnancies than control mothers. At the 2-year assessment, many of the 1-year findings were replicated. The nursery group again scored higher on both Bayley scales than home intervention or controls. Home-intervention children scored higher than controls. Mother outcome results were the same as the 1-year findings.

These findings demonstrate that the parent training model was the most effective intervention. Field and colleagues (1982) believed this program's success can be attributed to the fact that mothers used teachers as role models, and were able to practice their skills at work as well as at home. In addition, these mothers earned an income and received job training. Not surprisingly, mothers in this group were significantly more likely to be employed at the 2-year follow-up. We suggest that this program positively changed these mothers' beliefs about themselves and their children, and this is the reason for the program's success.

Home-Based/Center-Based With Parent Training. The Yale Child Welfare Research Program delivered an intensive intervention to impoverished families in New Haven, Connecticut from 1967–1972 (Rescorla, Provence, & Naylor, 1982; Seitz, Rosenbaum, & Apfel, 1985). This intervention was individualized to meet the needs of program families and their healthy newborn infants. This project assumed that chronic stress, like that experienced by inner-city families, is a "significant impediment to effective family functioning" (Seitz et al., 1985, p. 377). The intervention staff included a home visitor, a day-care teacher, a pediatrician, and a developmental examiner. Home visitors met with mothers two times a month for the first year of the project, and once a month for the next 2 years (Rescorla et al., 1982). The home visitors role was similar to that of a social worker. They worked to form supportive relationships with parents, and provided counseling on various subjects (Rescorla et al., 1982).

A second component of the family support service was high-quality day-care center available for project families. Families whose children did not attend the day-care center on a daily basis did attend a "toddler school" 2 days a week (Seitz et al., 1985).

Pediatric care was also provided for intervention families. Each child received from 13 to 17 "well baby exams," each of which permitted an hour of exchange between physicians and parents (Seitz et al., 1985). Pediatricians were also available to parents when their children were ill.

Although it is not clear that this intervention should lead to differences in intelligence between groups, the evaluators did, in fact, include IQ as an outcome variable. There was a nonsignificant trend for IQ favoring the treatment group at 30 months (Rescorla et al., 1982). At 12 years of age, there was a very small, nonsignificant group difference in IQ favoring the control group (Seitz et al., 1985).

However, there were other significant differences between groups reported. Intervention boys received more positive teacher ratings, and required fewer negative school services. The intervention group as a whole had less absenteeism and more students with better school adjustment scores than the control group. Seitz and her colleagues (1985) suggested that these school-related outcomes, favoring intervention families, may represent effects of long-standing group differences in parent–child relationships.

Long-Term Effects

Two recent monographs have raised the hopes of developmentalists that there may be long-term effects of preschool programs for indicators of school success, if not for intellectual and cognitive functioning. The Consortium for Longitudinal Studies (Lazar et al., 1982) was formed to evaluate the long-term effects of pioneer studies of early intervention. They identified 11 well-designed studies of early childhood programs that varied in format. Six were center-based programs, two were home-based programs, and three were center- and home-based programs. Children who had participated in the preschool programs were from poor families and 95% of the children were socially classified as Black. Initial evaluation studies were conducted by the principal investigators of the 11 evaluation studies. The follow-up study was conducted by consortium researchers in 1976, when the children ranged in age from 9 to 19.

The results of the follow-up study are impressive. Children who had participated in preschool programs were less likely to require special education classes and were also somewhat less likely to be retained in grade. These results could not be attributed to pretest IQ scores, gender, or a variety of family background variables. Differences in IQ were found for the 3 years following treatment only. The consortium's analysis of this pattern of findings is convincing. They cited Campbell (1971), who noted that all relationships weaken over time. Thus, one might predict any effects on concrete skills or cognitive functioning to wane. However, to the extent that a program is able to alter the context in which the children operate, then long-term effects would be predicted.

One of the programs studied by the Consortium is particularly noteworthy because of both its extensive evaluation and its provocative findings. David Weikart and his colleagues (Berrueta-Clement, Schweinhart, Barnett, Epstein, & Weikart, 1984) evaluated the results of the Perry Preschool Project on children through age 19. This program consisted of a fairly standard morning nursery-school program and weekly home visits by teachers. There were 123 Black children from low-SES families who participated in the program for the 2 years prior to kindergarten entry. The evaluation study has many advantages. First, children were randomly assigned to treatment and control groups. Second, the attrition rate was low. Third, the evaluators have continued to study the children through childhood and adolescence. Fourth, a wide range of policy-relevant outcome variables was studied. Differences between the preschool and no-preschool groups documented the effects of the program in a number of areas. At age 19, a greater percentage of the preschool group was employed, had earned a high school degree, and/or was enrolled in a college or vocational training program. A lesser percentage of the preschool group had required special education and/or was ever detained or arrested. There were no differences between groups on IQ, however, after second grade.

The Perry Preschool Project has received a great deal of attention from policymakers, who are impressed by the longitudinal findings for policy-relevant variables. Weikart and his colleagues produced a cost-benefit analysis that estimates benefits totaling seven times the cost of the program. The apparent success of the program may in fact lie in the outcome variables selected for study. These results are prototypical of those found by the Consortium.

The Perry Preschool Project has received somewhat less attention from developmentalists than from educators and policymakers, perhaps because results have been reported in project monographs rather than peer-reviewed journals. Certainly, these results need to be replicated, preferably by an independent research group. The High/Scope team functioned as both service deliverers and program evaluators.

CONCLUSIONS

Typically, reviews of intervention programs conclude by either explaining the success or failure of such programs. There is a problem with such pronouncements because they rest critically on how success and failure are defined. Rutter (1982) sensibly pointed out that an effect can be defined as either a significant mean group difference, a moderate effect size, or a raising of a standard. If success of home-based preschool programs is defined as a significant difference in IQ, then some programs would be designated as successful; if success is defined as a significant difference on some index of school functioning, perhaps more programs would be designated as successful.

If success of home-based preschool programs is defined through a moderate effect-size estimate, say .40, then some programs are effective. It is important that our expectations about effects on intelligence be realistic. Scarr and Arnett (1987) argued that adoption studies suggest that the malleability of intelligence may be relatively limited. In Scarr and Weinberg's (1980) Adolescent Adoption Study, the IQ of adopted children was 106, which is about 6 points higher than what would be predicted based on their natural parents' IQ scores and about 6 points lower than the biological offspring of the adoptive families.

If success is defined by long-term effects, then our judgments must await additional data, at least on home-based programs. We agree with Cicirelli (1984) that intervention programs need to be "coordinated with lifelong educational and other relevant experiences and opportunities" (p. 916). In other words, to define success as long-term effects may be unrealistic.

Still, which programs are effective? Woodhead (1988) believed that intervention programs generally must be of sufficient length, of sufficient intensity, and include parental involvement. Of parent programs, Powell (1989) concluded that there do not appear to be any critical features of successful programs, except perhaps intensity. A number of reviewers have suggested that programs must only be of high quality and that a number of differing curricula are likely to be effective. Research on the effects of child care and on the effects of schools have similarly documented the effects of global quality (McCartney & Jordan, in press). Research in both these areas, however, does point to the important role of teacher's behavior in the classroom. It may be that we should be evaluating teachers, child-care workers, and home visitors rather than programs themselves.

It is not clear, however, that we have experimented with differing curricula or that current curricula reflect the underlying philosophy of home-based preschool programs. If the goal of these programs is to use parents as instruments of intervention, then perhaps our curricula should focus on the parents rather than on the children. Currently, most programs are structured around educational activities for children. In our review of the literature on parental beliefs, we have suggested that for home-based intervention to be effective, we must change some of parents' maladaptive beliefs. This is a fundamentally different strategy from suggesting that identified disadvantaged parents emulate the play behaviors of middle-class parents.

Maladaptive beliefs of disadvantaged parents may differ, but some commonalities undoubtedly exist concerning parents' perceptions of their role in their children's education and their educational aspirations for their children. It is not clear how difficult it will be to change maladaptive parental beliefs; neither is it clear that a change in beliefs will result in a change in behavior. Research on changing maladaptive health behaviors, such as smoking and overeating, suggests that the link between a change in beliefs and a change in behavior is tenuous at best (Becker, 1974). Research on teacher expectancy effects suggests otherwise.

The social policy benefits of involving parents in intervention efforts are straightforward. Home-based programs, with home visitors, are less expensive than center-based programs, with teachers. We are sensitive to criticisms that nonintensive programs, sometimes referred to as "inoculation" programs or "magic bullets," are unlikely to be effective. However, we believe that a program that led to a real change in parental behavior would hardly lack intensity. It is time to design home-based programs to reflect their common goal to change maladaptive parental behaviors. Certainly, we must evaluate programs to determine whether parental behavior has been changed before we draw premature negative conclusions about home-based preschool programs.

It is important to remember that research on early childhood intervention is not guided by any theory of the environment. Rather, any developing theory of the environment must be guided by work on early childhood intervention, by the study of other environmental effects, and by family studies, especially behavior genetics studies. The existing data suggest that the effects of intervention efforts on intelligence will be modest and any effects will need to be supported by the continuing environment. It remains to be determined how parents can serve effectively as a part of that continuing environment.

ACKNOWLEDGMENTS

Carolyn Mebert, Lynn Okagaki, and Bob Sternberg provided helpful comments on an earlier draft of this chapter. The first author acknowledges the support of a grant from NICHD (U10-HD25451-01) and a grant from NIMH/NICHD (R01-MH43879-01).

REFERENCES

Becker, M. (1974). *The health belief model and personal health behavior.* New Jersey: Slack.

Bell, R. (1974). Contributions of human infants to caregiving and social interaction. In M. Lewis & L. Rosenbaum (Eds.), *The effects of the infant on its caregiver* (pp. 1–19). New York: Wiley.

Berrueta-Clement, J., Schweinhart, L., Barnett, W., Epstein, A., & Weikart, D. (1984). *Changed lives: The effects of the Perry preschool program on youths through age 19.* Ypsilanti, MI: High/Scope Educational Research Foundation.

Bronfenbrenner, U. (1974). *A report on longitudinal evaluations of preschool programs. Vol. 2: Is early intervention effective?* (DHEW Publication No. OHD 74-25). Washington, DC: Office of Human Development.

Campbell, D. T. (1971). Temporal changes in treatment-effect correlation: A quasi-experimental model for institutional records and longitudinal studies. In G. Glass (Ed.), *The promise and perils of educational information systems: Proceedings of the 1970 Invitational Conference on Testing Problems* (pp. 93–110). Princeton, NJ: Educational Testing Service.

Cicirelli, V. (1984). The misinterpretation of the Westinghouse study: A reply to Zigler and Berman. *American Psychologist, 39*(8), 916–917.

Clewell, B., Brooks-Gunn, J., & Benasich, A. (1989). Evaluating child-related outcomes of teenage parenting programs. *Family Relations, 38,* 201–209.

Cronbach, L. (1982). *Designing evaluations of educational and social programs.* San Francisco, CA: Jossey-Bass.

Epstein, A., & Weikart, D. (1979). *The Ypsilanti–Carnegie infant education project: Longitudinal follow-up.* (Monographs of the High/Scope Educational Research Foundation No. 6). Ypsilanti, MI: High Scope Press.

Field, T. (1981). Intervention for high risk infants and their parents. *Educational Evaluation and Policy Analysis, 3*(6), 69–78.

Field, T., Widmayer, S., Greenberg, R., & Stoller, S. (1982). Effects of parent training on teenage mothers and their infants. *Pediatrics, 69*(6), 703–707.

Goodson, B., & Hess, R. (1975). *Parents as teachers of young children: An evaluative review of some contemporary concepts and programs.* Stanford, CA: Stanford University School of Education.

Gordon, I. (1971). Early child stimulation through parent education. In I. Gordon (Ed.), *Readings in research in developmental psychology* (pp. 146–154). Glenview, IL: Scott, Foresman.

Gordon, I., & Guinagh, B. (1974). *A home learning center approach to early stimulation* (Final report to the National Institute of Mental Health). Gainseville: Institute for Development of Human Resources, University of Florida.

Gray, S., & Ruttle, K. (1980). The family oriented home visiting program: A longitudinal study. *Genetic Psychology Monographs, 102,* 299–316.

Gray, S., & Wanderson, L. (1980). The methodology of home based intervention studies: Problems and promising strategies. *Child Development, 51,* 993–1009.

Gutelius, M., & Kirsch, A. (1975). Factors promoting success in infant education. *American Journal of Public Health, 65*(4), 384–387.

Halpern, R. (1986). Home-based early intervention: Dimensions in current practice. *Child Welfare, 65*(4), 387–398.

Holloway, S., & Hess, R. (1985). Mothers' and teachers' attributions about children's mathematics performance. In E. Sigel (Ed.), *Parental belief systems* (pp. 177–199). Hillsdale, NJ: Lawrence Erlbaum Associates.

Johnson, J., & Martin, C. (1985). Parents' beliefs and home learning environments: Effects on cognitive development. In E. Sigel (Ed.), *Parental belief systems* (pp. 25–50). Hillsdale, NJ: Lawrence Erlbaum Associates.

Lambie, D., Bond, J., & Weikart, D. (1974). *Home teaching with mothers and infants: The Ypsilanti–Carnegie infant education project: An experiment.* (Monographs of the High/Scope Educational Research Foundation, No. 2.). Ypsilanti, Michigan: High/Scope Press.

Lazar, I., Darlington, R., Murray, H., Royce, J., & Snipper, A. (1982). Lasting effects of early education: A report from the Consortium for Longitudinal Studies. *Monographs of the Society for Research in Child Development, 47* (2–3, Serial No. 195).

Levenstein, P. (1970). Cognitive growth in preschoolers through verbal interaction with mothers. *American Journal of Orthopsychiatry, 40,* 426–432.

Levenstein, P. (1977). The Mother–child home program. In M. Day & R. Parker (Eds.), *The preschool in action* (pp. 27–49). Boston, MA: Allyn & Bacon.

Levenstein, P., & Sunley, R. (1968). Stimulation of verbal interaction between disadvantaged mothers and children. *American Journal of Orthopsychiatry, 39,* 116–121.

Madden, J., Levenstein, P., & Levenstein, S. (1976). Longitudinal IQ outcomes of the Mother–child home program. *Child Development, 47,* 1015–1025.

Madden, J., O'Hara, J., & Levenstein, P. (1984). Home again: Effects of the Mother–child home programs on mother and child. *Child Development, 55,* 636–647.

McCartney, K., & Jordan, E. (in press). Parallels between research on child care and research on school effects. *Educational Researcher.*

Miller, S. (1988). Parent beliefs about children's cognitive development. *Child Development, 59,* 259–285.

Powell, D. (1989). *Families and early childhood programs* (Research Monographs of the National Association for the Education of Young Children, Vol. 3, NAEYC No. 142). Washington, DC: NAEYC.

Ramey, C., & Bryant, D. (1982). Evidence for prevention of developmental retardation during infancy. *Journal of the Division for Early Childhood, 5,* 73–78.

Ramey, C., Bryant, D., & Suarez, T. (1985a). Preschool compensatory education and the modifiability of intelligence: A critical review. *Current topics in human intelligence, 1,* 247–296.

Ramey, C., Bryant, D., Sparling, J., & Wasik, B. (1985b). Educational interventions to enhance intellectual development: Comprehensive daycare *vs.* family education. In S. Harel & N. Anastasiow (Eds.), *The at risk infant: Psychological, social, and medical aspects* (pp. 75–85). Baltimore, MD: Paul H. Brookes.

Rescorla, L., Provence, S. & Naylor, A. (1981). The Yale child welfare research program: Description and results. In E. Zigler & E. Gordon (Eds.), *Day care: Scientific and social policy issues* (pp. 183–199). Boston: Auburn House.

Rosenthal, R., & Rosnow, R. (1984). *Essentials of behavioral research: methods and data analysis.* New York: McGraw-Hill.

Rosenthal, R., & Rubin, D. (1978). Interpersonal expectancy effects: The first 345 studies. *Behavioral and Brain Sciences, 3,* 377–386.

Rutter, M. (1982). Social-emotional consequences of day care for preschool children. In E. Zigler & E. W. Gordon (Eds.), *Day care: Scientific and social policy issues* (pp. 3–32). Boston, MA: Auburn House.

Sameroff, A., & Feil, L. (1985). Parental concepts of development. In E. Sigel (Ed.), *Parental belief systems* (pp. 177–199). Hillsdale, NJ: Lawrence Erlbaum Associates.

Scarr, S., & Arnett, J. (1987). Malleability: Lessons from intervention and family studies. In J. Gallagher & C. Ramey (Eds.), *The malleability of children* (pp. 71–84). Baltimore, MD: Paul H. Brookes.

Scarr, S., & McCartney, K. (1983). How people make their own environments: A theory of genotype → environment effects. *Child Development, 54,* 425–435.

Scarr, S., & McCartney, K. (1988). Far from home: An experimental evaluation of the Mother--child home program in Bermuda. *Child Development, 59,* 531–543.

Scarr, S., & Weinberg, R. A. (1978). The influence of "family background" on intellectual attainment. *American Sociological Review, 43,* 674–692.

Scarr, S., & Weinberg, R. (1980). Calling all camps! The war is over. *American Sociological Review, 45,* 859–864.

Sears, D., Peplau, L., Freedman, J., & Taylor, S. (1985). *Social psychology.* Englewood Cliffs, NJ: Prentice-Hall.

Segal, M. (1985). A study in maternal beliefs and values within the context of an intervention program. In I. Sigel (Ed.), *Parental belief systems* (pp. 271–286). Hillsdale, NJ: Lawrence Erlbaum Associates.

Seitz, V., Rosenbaum, L., & Apfel, N. (1985). Effects of family support intervention: A ten year follow-up. *Child Development, 56,* 376–391.

Sigel, I. (1985). A conceptual analysis of beliefs. In I. Sigel (Ed.), *Parental belief systems* (pp. 177–199). Hillsdale, NJ: Lawrence Erlbaum Associates.

Slaughter, D. (1983). Early intervention and its effects on maternal and child development. *Monographs for the Society for Research in Child Development, 48*(4, Serial No. 202).

Steinfels, M. (1973). *Who's minding the children: The history and politics of day care in America.* New York: Simon & Schuster.

Stevens Jr., J. (1984). Child development knowledge and parenting skill. *Family Relations,* 33, 237–244.

White, K., Taylor, M., & Moss, V. (1989, April). *Does research support the claims about the benefits of involving parents in early intervention programs?* Paper presented at the biennial meeting of the Society for Research in Child Development, Kansas City, MO.

Widmayer, S., Peterson, L., Calderon, A., Korn, F., Carnahan, S., & Wingerd, J. (1989). *Intervention with Haitian entrant women and their infants.* Paper presented at the biennial meeting of the Society for Research in Child Development, Kansas City, MO.

Woodhead, M. (1988). When psychology informs public policy: The case of early childhood education. *American Psychologist, 42*(6), 443–454.

Zigler, E. & Freedman, J. (1987). Early experience, malleability, and Head Start. In J. Gallagher & C. Ramey (Ed.), *The malleability of children* (pp. 85–95). Baltimore, MD: Paul H. Brooks.

Zigler, E., & Trickett, P. (1978). IQ social competence and evaluation of early childhood intervention programs. *American Psychologist, 33*(a), 789–798.

Chapter 9

The Long-Term Effects of Model Preschool Programs

RICHARD B. DARLINGTON
Cornell University

THE CONSORTIUM FOR LONGITUDINAL STUDIES

In the 1960s about a dozen investigators around the United States ran well-designed experimental or quasi-experimental studies on the effects of preschool programs on disadvantaged children. Altogether almost 4,000 children participated in these studies. The preschool programs used in these studies served as the models for the Head Start program, which began as part of Lyndon Johnson's Great Society initiative.

At the time, little doubt was expressed that programs like this could increase the school-readiness of disadvantaged children. After all, every major industrialized nation spends billions of dollars on school systems that begin around age 5. With increasing understanding of cognitive development in early childhood, it seemed obvious that educational programs for children 1 or 2 years younger could also be reasonably effective. The benefits of enriched preschool programs seemed obvious to middle-class parents, many of whom spent their own hard-earned money on such programs.

But as the decade ended, two publications in particular called this assumption into question. One was the so-called *Westinghouse Report* (Cicirelli et al., 1969), which used data of questionable scientific validity (see Campbell & Erlebacher, 1975) to conclude that the Head Start program had no long-term positive effects on children's ability to succeed in school.

The other was Arthur Jensen's famous (some would say infamous) monograph, "How much can we boost IQ and scholastic performance?" (Jensen, 1969). Jensen's renowned opening sentence was, "Compensatory education has been tried and it apparently has failed" (p. 2). Four paragraphs later, he argued, "In other fields, when bridges do not stand, when aircraft do not fly, when machines do not work, when treatments do not cure, despite all conscientious efforts . . . , one begins to question the basic assumptions . . . that guide one's work" (p. 3). On the next page he proceeded to challenge the assumption that "those children of ethnic minorities and the economically poor who achieve 'below average' in school" are generally capable of benefiting from compensatory education programs designed to steer them toward the kinds of lives and careers enjoyed by the great middle class.

By 1974 it was apparent that these two challenges to compensatory preschool programs were not going to self-destruct or disappear quietly. Jensen's views were widely discussed in academia, government, and the popular press, and Head Start was slated for elimination by the Ford administration. It was abundantly clear that some kind of analysis of the long-term effects of compensatory preschool programs was badly needed.

For several years, Edward Zigler of Yale University had been arguing that the best way to get this information was to return to the aforementioned studies from the 1960s, find the children who had participated in them—some were as old as 16 years by 1974—and study the success of those children in school and in life. In that year Irving Lazar of Cornell University approached the Administration for Children, Youth, and Families, and offered to coordinate such a followup effort.

Lazar asked a graduate student, Harry Murray, to make a list of the research projects that had worked with low-income children, had moderately large samples, used reasonably well-matched control groups, had demographic data (race, family income, etc.) on their samples, and whose children had completed preschool programs no later than 1972. The resulting list included 12 studies. In 1975 Lazar contacted the researchers heading these studies, and all but one agreed to participate in a collaborative follow-up study coordinated by Lazar. The one holdout later went to federal prison for fraud, so his publications are rarely cited today. Thus for all practical purposes the follow-up study included the entire population of studies meeting the criteria mentioned.

Thus was born an organization first called the Consortium for Developmental Continuity, which was soon renamed the Consortium for Longitudinal Studies. Its members included E. Kuno Beller of Temple University, Martin and Cynthia Deutsch of New York University, Ira Gordon (deceased September 1978), Susan Gray of George Peabody College, Merle Karnes of the University of Illinois, Phyllis Levenstein of the Verbal Interaction Project on Long Island, Louise Miller of the University of Louisville, Francis Palmer of the Merrill–Palmer Institute, David Weikart of High/Scope Foundation,

Myron Woolman of the Institute for Behavioral Research in Vineland New Jersey, and Edward Zigler of Yale University. Robert Jester of the University of Florida joined after Gordon's death to manage the follow up of the Gordon project. And I joined the Consortium in early 1977 to head up the data analysis.

The 11 Consortium projects included 3,656 children. Budget constraints prevented us from even trying to find all these children, particularly those for whom no well-matched comparison group was available. But of those names marked for recovery, 76% were reached. Altogether, 2,008 children were in the first follow-up in 1976–1977, whereas 1,104 were in a second follow-up in 1980. The large difference between these two numbers was caused primarily by the nonparticipation, for practical reasons, of Woolman and Zigler in the 1980 follow-up.

The Consortium's 1976 sample was 94% Black and entirely low income. The children's mothers had completed an average of 10.3 years of school. The average head of household was a semiskilled or unskilled worker. Of the children, 62% were in two-parent families at the time of follow up. The 1980 sample was similar.

The early education programs in the Consortium studies were located in urban and rural sites in the Northeast, Southeast, and Midwest. Curricula included programs based on the Bank Street child development model, on Montessori methods, on Piagetian theory, on the Bereiter–Engelmann method, and on others. Some of the programs were conducted in centers, others consisted of visits to the child's home, and still others used a mixture of home and center contact. All programs worked with a given child at least 1 year; some provided up to 5 years of contact. Children in the various projects were aged 2–5 on entry into the programs. All studies are described in detail, in chapters written by their own staffs, in Consortium for Longitudinal Studies (1983).

Some of the studies used random assignment and some did not; details appear in the next section. Several of the studies had not originally been designed for the purpose to which they were now being put. For instance, Merle Karnes and Louise Miller had used scientifically elegant random assignment in assigning children to different kinds of preschool programs. But when these programs were started there seemed to be little doubt that they would generally have positive effects, so Karnes had used no control group at all, and Miller had used a quasi-experimental control group selected without the scientific benefits of random assignment. And with only one exception (David Weikart), none of the investigators had included a long-term follow-up as part of the original design; it simply had not seemed important enough to justify the cost.

Many papers were written by the Consortium members and staff during the Consortium's existence, but the last and most complete report of the pooled results was by Royce, Darlington, and Murray (1983). Most of the results mentioned here are from that source, which is hereafter referred to as RDM.

THE CONSTITUENT STUDIES

Dr. E. Kuno Beller's treatment group consisted of children in the nursery school run by the Early Education Department of Temple University, serving a low-income, predominantly Black neighborhood in North Philadelphia. The program was designed to promote the social, emotional, and cognitive growth of the child. Children attended the program 4 hours a day, 4 days a week. On the fifth day, school staff received in-service training and made home visits. Random assignment was not used in dividing children into treatment and control groups. Rather, the comparison group consisted of 53 children drawn from the same neighborhood to match the nursery group in age, gender, and ethnicity. Beller found no significant differences between preschool and comparison groups on three different IQ tests taken at entry into the program, or on 10 demographic variables. Beller's subjects were approximately 18 at the time of the first Consortium follow-up in 1976–1977.

One of the best-known programs in the Consortium was the program directed by Drs. Martin and Cynthia Deutsch at New York University's Institute for Developmental Studies. This program included over 1,300 children in eight annual cohorts beginning in 1961. However, this program faced particularly severe problems in collecting follow-up data during the life of the Consortium, so it was not used in any of our pooled analyses.

The Florida Parent Education Program was supervised by Dr. Ira Gordon. When Dr. Gordon died during the follow-up effort, his place in the Consortium was taken by Dr. Robert Jester, who knew the program intimately. This program worked with younger children than most; children in the preschool program were aged 3 months to 3 years. The program was based on weekly home visits by trained paraprofessionals. Program content was based largely on a Piagetian model.

Gordon's assignment of children to preschool or comparison groups illustrates an ambiguity in the phrase *random assignment.* If two very different schools are used in a study, and if a single coin flip determines which school forms the treatment group and which forms the control group, then in the literal meaning of the word, assignment was random for every child, even though the advantages of random assignment are glaringly absent in this fictitious example. The example illustrates that the phrase random assignment is really shorthand for *random and independent assignment.* Children in the Gordon study were assigned randomly but not independently; whole towns or sections of towns were assigned together to one group or another. Preschool and comparison groups ended up being comparable on a number of measures, although random assignment was not used in the technical sense of the term. Gordon's subjects were mostly 10 and 11 years old during the 1976–1977 follow-up.

Dr. Susan Gray and her co-director, Dr. Robert Klaus, used true random assignment on a sample of 65 children aged 4 and 5 when they entered treatment programs. During an intense 10-week summer program, children met in groups of 20 for 4 hours each day, 5 days a week. Each group of 20 was led by a teacher and four assistant teachers. For the rest of the year, a home visitor reached each home for 1 hour each week, primarily to prevent the gains of the summer from eroding away. The program was designed to enhance perceptual and cognitive skills, and also attitudes such as achievement orientation and ability to delay gratification. Gray's subjects were about 19 years of age during the 1976–1977 follow-up.

Dr. Merle Karnes ran a whole series of preschool programs on the main campus of the University of Illinois. The primary purpose of her experiment was to compare several different preschool curricula to each other. But when it became important to find children for a comparison group, after much effort she was able to identify post hoc a group of well-matched children who had not participated in the program. Karnes's subjects were 15 to 16 years of age during the 1976–1977 follow-up.

Dr. Phyllis Levenstein's Verbal Interaction Project, on Long Island near New York City, was so named because it was specifically oriented toward encouraging verbal interaction between mother and child. The program consisted of 92 half-hour visits over two 7-month school "years." The visitor brought a series of toys and games as gifts, and showed the mother (or other primary caregiver) and child together how to play with them. Other family members were also encouraged to join in. The toys and games were all commercially available, and had been selected to encourage verbal interaction between mother and child. Children were 2 or 3 years old during this intervention, and were aged 9–13 during the 1976–1977 follow-up. For our purposes, there was no true random assignment, but treatment and comparison groups were closely matched on demographic measures.

Dr. Louise Miller of the University of Louisville ran a carefully randomized experiment to study differences among four different curricula for preschool programs. The comparison of these children to a comparison group with no preschool exposure was only a secondary goal of her work, so there was no random assignment in this regard. A comparison group was selected, which on the average scored above the preschool groups on mean income, percentage of fathers present, and percentage of Whites. Although regression was used to correct for these differences, this method is known to undercorrect, so the comparisons most important for our purposes contained a substantial conservative bias. During the 1976–1977 follow-up Dr. Miller's subjects had an average age of 13.

Dr. Francis Palmer's Harlem Research Project was directed toward male children 2 or 3 years of age. The treatment program was minimal in terms of exposure time—2 hours a week for 8 months—but perhaps compensated by having teachers work with children one-on-one during those hours. Two different treatments were used; some children were specifically trained in basic concepts (big, little, in, out), whereas others received less structured instruction. For our purposes, these two groups were pooled together as treatment groups.

Palmer's treatment-control comparison did not use true random assignment. Rather, treatment groups were selected from male children born in two Harlem hospitals in the period August–October 1964, whereas comparison children were born in the same two hospitals in November and December 1964. Differences between the two groups were more likely caused by the fact that, in recruiting children for the study, one group could be attracted by the specific offer of an instructional program, whereas the other could not; it is less likely that the difference in birth dates was the cause. Researchers attempted to minimize this difference by emphasizing to comparison-group mothers the educational benefits of the testing program administered to all study participants. Palmer's subjects were about 13 years of age during the 1976–1977 follow-up.

To the general public, Dr. David Weikart's Perry Preschool Project is by far the best-known project in the Consortium; over the years I have lost count of the number of times I have seen it mentioned on the CBS evening news. Alone among Consortium projects, Weikart had been continuing to follow his sample before the Consortium was formed and after its termination. Also unique among the projects, Weikart's attrition was zero; no child was ever lost track of, although one did die during the follow-up period. This project used independent random assignment on a group of 123 Black low-income children, all of whom scored in the educable mentally retarded range (70–85) on the Stanford–Binet Intelligence Test.

In the last sentence I avoided saying "true" random assignment because 5 of Weikart's children were placed initially in the treatment group, but were swapped with matched children in the control group when it was found that their mothers were unable to deliver them regularly to the preschool building. At the time of the preschool program this factor helped produce a significant difference between preschool and control groups on frequency of maternal employment (9% vs. 31%). But the problem seemed minimal because on follow-up at ages 15–19, no significant difference was found between groups on whether the mother had ever been employed.

Weikart's preschool curriculum was based on Piagetian theories. Children entered the program at age 3. The program was intense, meeting 5 half-days a week for 2 school years—mid-October through May. Teachers also visited each home weekly for 90 minutes, where they introduced educational activities involving mother and child together.

Dr. Myron Woolman was a member of the Consortium, but had no control over the selection of a comparison group for his program. This comparison group was selected by the State of New Jersey, using procedures that were never adequately explained. It turned out to differ from Woolman's treatment group on a variety of background measures, so that all of Woolman's data were ultimately excluded from our major analyses.

Dr. Edward Zigler of Yale studied children who had attended Follow Through programs in New Haven and Hamden, Connecticut, run by the Bank Street College of Education. Comparison children were drawn from the same public schools attended by the Follow Through children. Zigler's children were about 13 years of age during the 1976–1977 follow-up.

ANALYTIC METHODS AND PRELIMINARY ANALYSES

Overall, about 76% of subjects sought were found, and only 3% of those contacted refused to participate or to sign the consent forms for us to retrieve their school records. So almost all attrition was due to simple inability to find children within the budget constraints of the project.

Aside from the simple amount of attrition in the follow-up, we were very concerned about the possibility that attrition might be nonrandom. Might an overenthusiastic research assistant somewhere be putting a little extra effort into finding the most promising subjects from the preschool group, or the least promising from the comparison group? Or might some more subtle bias be producing the same effect, despite all best efforts to avoid it? To see how this possibility can be tested, consider a background variable such as mother's education, measured at program entry. Imagine a 2 × 2 table of means on mother's education, in which the two classifying variables are treatment versus comparison group, and found versus not found in the follow-up. There might be some legitimate reason why it is harder to find, 10 years later, families with higher or lower mother's education—for instance, such families might be more likely to move. So we should not be bothered by what is called a *main effect* in analysis of variance—a consistent difference, in both treatment and comparison groups, between the average mother's educations of children found and children not found. But if this difference existed for the one group and not the other, or were larger for one group than the other, that would be evidence that our major analyses were being skewed by nonrandom recovery of subjects. This difference between differences is called an *interaction* in analysis of variance. We searched for such interactions on all the major background variables, such as mother's education, family income, child's IQ score at program entry, and other variables. These analyses gave no evidence that we were recovering different kinds of subjects in preschool and comparison groups.

It would be invalid to pool all subjects into a single large sample. To see why, suppose that Projects A and B are both well-designed, but Project A is conducted in a more disadvantaged geographical region than Project B. Suppose also that Project A has a larger comparison group than B, whereas B has a larger treatment group than A. Then in a pooled sample, most of the treatment group would come from the less disadvantaged region, whereas most of the comparison group comes from the more disadvantaged region.

The problem just described could be handled by controlling statistically for project identity. But the various projects had measured different demographic characteristics (family income, mother's education, etc.) or had measured them in different ways, so that scores on these measures could not be entered into a single analysis. Therefore the estimated effect of each individual program was calculated, and the Stauffer pooled-z technique was used to test the pooled significance of the combined effects. This method consists of converting each significance level to a z value via a standard normal table, summing the z's, dividing by the square root of the number of z's, calling this new statistic a pooled z, and finding its significance from a standard normal table.

The typical analytic method within a single project was multiple regression. This is the standard method for controlling for any background differences that may exist between treatment and control groups. In theory, ordinary multiple regression should be used only when the dependent variable is a continuous variable, and several of ours were dichotomous, as when we measured whether children had ever been held back a grade once they began to attend public schools. We therefore repeated many of our analyses using logistic regression, which is designed for dichotomous dependent variables. But our results were so similar that we ended up reporting primarily the results of ordinary multiple regressions, because these are easier for a broad audience to understand.

We also tested for the interaction of program effect with demographic characteristics. A significant interaction term for, say, sex would mean that programs were more or less effective for boys than for girls. However, after correcting for the fact that many tests were performed, none of these tests were significant. So there is no evidence that these preschool programs were more effective for some kinds of children than for others.

We were concerned that exceptionally positive results in a single project might be given undue weight if we simply averaged the measured effects of the preschool programs. Therefore we deleted from each analysis whichever project had the most highly positive result in that one analysis. This eliminated the possibility that a positive pooled result was caused solely by data from a single project. Results that were still statistically significant after this deletion were said to be "robust." As it turned out, the major results were so consistent across projects that this innovation had little effect on those results, although it did affect our analyses of more peripheral results.

FINDINGS

For a study like this, the most obvious dependent variables to use are scores on the nationally standardized achievement tests administered by the public schools. However, these present several complications. Even children who were in a single project during their preschool years may end up in several different school districts by the time they reach junior high school. Therefore they may take different achievement tests. The standardizations of these tests are not so good that scores on different tests can be made interchangeable. Or children may take the same tests a few months apart, making comparisons difficult. But the most important problem in using nationally standardized achievement tests arises because children placed in special remedial education programs often do not take *any* such test. And children held back a grade may take the same test a year later than their former classmates, thus making the scores noncomparable. Because of all these difficulties, achievement test scores were deemphasized as dependent variables in our analyses.

We used a variety of dependent variables, but three were most important. One was *grade retention*—had the child ever been held back a grade in school? The second was *special education placement*—had the child ever been placed in a special education program for children not progressing normally in regular classes? The third dependent variable, *failure to meet school standards,* was a composite of these two—had the child ever been retained in grade or placed in a special education class? Although different school districts make these decisions in different ways, all make them with considerable care, because placing children in special education, or retaining them, is both serious and expensive. We measured these variables at several times during the child's school career, but here we emphasize the results taken at the end of seventh grade.

In general, the variables controlled statistically by regression included mother's education, family income, race, family size, and child's IQ score measured at program entry. All are not listed in this chapter because they differed from project to project. To understand why, imagine that some of these programs—especially programs that emphasized working with the mother in home visits—might have inspired some of the mothers to complete high school and then find better-paying jobs. So, to properly use variables, like mother's education or family income, as covariates or control variables in a statistical analysis, they must be measured for each family before the family's child enters any program in our study. But the studies had begun as totally independent projects that joined forces only after the children studied had already entered the public schools. So they had measured different covariates or had measured them in different ways. Therefore the precise list of covariates controlled must vary from project to project.

We scored special education placement 0 for children so placed and 1 for other children. After adjustment for demographic differences between treatment and control groups, the average regression coefficient of preschool program was .086 (RDM Table 13.6). This means that the average preschool program reduced by 8.6 percentage points the number of children placed in special education. On the average 34.9% of the children in control groups were placed in special education, so this regression coefficient represents an estimated reduction by 8.6/34.9 or 25% of the children placed in special education.

When a similar analysis was done for grade retention, the regression coefficient was .057 and the average retention rate in control groups was 32.0% (RDM Table 13.7). Thus the regression coefficient represents an estimated reduction by 5.7/32.0 or 18% of the children retained in grade.

The same analysis was done for the composite variable of failure to meet school standards. This is the most important single analysis, so we present its results in more detail. Table 9.1, taken from RDM Table 13.8, shows the results separately for each project for which a meaningful regression coefficient could be derived.

As you can see from the *p* column, only one of these effects is significant individually in this particular analysis, but all are positive. So when the

TABLE 9.1
Estimated Effect of Preschool Program on Ability to Meet School Requirements

	Group Sizes			
Project	*Program*	*Control*	*Effect*	*p*
Beller	44	37	.107	.208
Gordon/Jester	61	12	.088	.705
Gray	41	21	.088	.475
Karnes	102	18	.132	.256
Levenstein	20	26	.129	.330
Miller	127	22	.075	.448
Palmer	161	51	.217	.004
Weikart	58	65	.131	.128
Total/Median	614	252	.118	

Note: Effect = regression coefficient; *p* = two-tailed significance level

pooled-z method was used to test the null hypothesis that the eight effects in this analysis were distributed symmetrically around zero, the null was rejected beyond the .001 level of significance. Table 9.1 shows dramatically the need for a consortium of studies to study the effects of interest. And in this analysis there is absolutely no evidence that positive average results were being produced entirely by exceptionally positive results in one or two projects.

Among control children, the average rate of failure to meet school requirements was 44.6% (RDM Table 13.8). Thus the regression coefficient represents an estimated reduction by 11.8/44.6 or 26% in the number of children failing to meet school requirements. The coefficient of .118 also means that we estimated that 11.8% of all children—almost one in eight children in the total preschool sample—was enabled by the preschool program to meet minimal school standards that they would not otherwise have met. It would be unfair to interpret to this to mean that only one in eight children was helped scholastically by the program. Rather, it is fair to assume that most children who would have met these minimal standards anyway were still helped scholastically by the program.

These positive results were accompanied by less impressive results as measured by Stanford–Binet IQ tests. Immediately after the preschool programs, the treatment and control groups differed by an average of 7.4 IQ points, after correcting for demographic differences. This difference declined to 3.0 IQ points when measured 3 or 4 years after the end of the preschool program. Similarly unimpressive effects on IQ test score have been observed by other researchers. The fact that our results on IQ are similar to those of other researchers supports the view that our design and analysis did not contain some gigantic hidden flaw.

All results mentioned are from our final report published in 1983, but are similar to results we obtained as early as 1977. Some criticisms of these earlier results focused on the fact that the dependent variables showing large effects of preschool programs were all based on subjective judgments by public school teachers and officials. Perhaps these officials knew which children had been in preschool programs, and assumed that those children must be succeeding in school because they had attended a preschool program. Or perhaps the preschool programs produced a temporary artifactual inflation in IQ test scores, and these higher measured IQ's prevented children from being retained in grade or placed in special education classes. Indeed, many states have firm regulations specifying that children scoring above certain levels on IQ tests may not be placed in special education classes no matter how poor their school performance.

The first version of this argument—"Johnny must be doing well because he attended a preschool program"—reflects an extremely negative view of public school personnel. In my opinion, more realistically, when a teacher sees Johnny performing poorly in class despite having attended a preschool program, that teacher is more likely to conclude that Johnny needs special help. Thus if teachers know which children attended preschool programs, if anything, that knowledge should introduce a negative rather than a positive bias into our results.

This latter interpretation is consistent with the results we obtained. The analyses reported for the seventh grade—using dependent variables of special education placement, grade retention, and the composite variable of failure to meet school requirements—were in fact performed separately at the end of each grade from kindergarten through seventh grade. If teachers' knowledge were biasing the results in favor of positive effects, that bias would presumably be strongest in the earliest years; teachers in the sixth and seventh grades are far less likely to know or care that Johnny attended a preschool program. But our positive results were consistently stronger for each passing grade. In fact, results for all three dependent variables were negative at the end of kindergarten, and results for grade retention and the composite were consistently negative through the end of second grade. This is consistent with the view mentioned in the previous paragraph—if a teacher saw Johnny performing poorly in class despite having attended a preschool program, the teachers' knowledge of Johnny's history would make them more likely to recommend some remedial step. So our positive results in later grades apparently arose despite a bias caused by teachers' knowledge of children's preschool backgrounds, not because of that knowledge.

DISCUSSION

The Consortium's work is widely credited with being the most important single thing that "saved" Head Start, which was targeted for elimination both in the Ford administration (1974–1977) and at the beginning of the Reagan administration in 1981. I must therefore emphasize that the projects we studied were not Head Start projects. Rather, they were the experimental projects on which Head Start was modeled. Our results imply not so much that Head Start does work, but that Head Start can work when its programs are well run.

Our findings are specific to a particular nation and era; they are not findings for the ages. I say this because in our dreams, we might hope that by the year 2000, the Consortium's positive findings will have had an enormous positive influence on the way young low-income children are schooled. If so, a similar study repeated in the 21st century on new experimental treatments might find negative results because all children are already receiving schooling so excellent that it cannot be improved. No doubt there will be people in the 21st century arguing that this has in fact happened. If so, there will be no way to settle the question except to repeat the study. For all I know, the argument may surface as early as the 1990s. But I have not heard it yet. Rather, there is general agreement that educational programs for most low-income children are sorely in need of improvement.

The Consortium results say nothing about the relative cost effectiveness of preschool programs versus other programs such as remedial summer school, individual counselors, or more effective motivational programs. However, they do say that low-income children can be helped.

REFERENCES

Campbell, D. T., & Erlebacher, A. (1975). How regression artifacts in quasi-experimental evaluations can mistakenly make compensatory education look harmful. In E. L. Struening & M. Guttentag (Eds.), *Handbook of evaluation research* (Vol. 1). Beverly Hills, CA: Sage Publications.

Cicirelli, V. et al. (1979, June). *The impact of Head Start: An evaluation of the effect of Head Start on children's cognitive and affective development.* (Report No. PB 184 328). Report presented to the Office of Economic Opportunity, pursuant to Contract B89-4536. Westinghouse Learning Corporation for Federal Scientific and Technical Information, U. S. Institute for Applied Technology.

Jensen, A. R. (1969). How much can we boost IQ and scholastic achievement? *Harvard Educational Review,* reprint series no. 2, 1–123.

Royce, J. M., Darlington, R. B., & Murray, H. W. (1983). Pooled analyses: Findings across studies. In the Consortium for Longitudinal Studies, *As the twig is bent . . . last effects of preschool programs* (chap. 13). Hillsdale, NJ: Lawrence Erlbaum Associates.

Chapter 10

School and Family: The Collaborative Way

JOSEPH SHIMRON
University of Haifa

Education is always on the public agenda, but there seems to be a new mood in the air, perhaps a rising optimism. There also seems to be an increasing consensus, not only about the need for a change, but also about its direction. The emphasis in current discussions on educational changes is less on instructional techniques or new curricula, and more on changing the social context of education. One target for such a change seems to be the relationship between the school and the family, particularly the increased involvement of the family in the operation of the school. In a sense, this move completes a cycle. The responsibility for education was once completely within the power of the family, was later taken from the family by public authorities, and is now becoming the mutual responsibility of the public and the family.

We should bear in mind that there are, in fact, two levels of relationships between the school and the family: the relationship between the teacher (as a representative of the school) and the parents; and the relationship between the school as a whole (sometimes the authorities of a school district) and the group of families that sends their children to a particular school (or to a school district). This distinction seems useful because the encounters on the two levels have different social atmospheres and different agenda. On the parent-to-teacher level, the social atmosphere typically varies from alienation and mutual suspicion to blatant conflict (friendly relations are not generally the rule). The agenda in the exchanges on this level involve the whereabouts of a particular child. On the (collective) family-to-school level, the typical social atmosphere varies from passivity to conformity, not a very wide range (collaboration is the exception). The agenda on this level concerns school policies and methods. Of course, the two levels interact. In particular, one would expect that an atmosphere of cooperation on the collective (school–family) level would inspire better relationships on the parent–teacher level.

My intention in this chapter is to analyze central issues regarding both levels of relationships. I hope to show that conflicts between parents and teachers (on a local level), although they certainly exist in many schools, are neither inevitable nor desirable, and can be changed as a result of changes on the global level. I start with a discussion of those views that consider the conflict between parents and teachers as not merely inevitable, but also constructive. Then I deal with the issue of parental passivity or parental conformity with school authorities. In this context, I discuss the role of ideology in explaining parental attitudes. The chapter concludes with a discussion of two educational contexts in which the conflict between the school and the family is avoided, to the benefit of the children, the family, and the entire community.

CONFLICTUAL RELATIONSHIP

A dominant opinion in the literature on school–family relationships (where "family" is to be understood as a single family) notes that this relationship is inevitably conflictual, so much so, that a collaboration between the two institutions is occasionally frowned on or questioned, or even considered as undesirable. In one of the earliest studies of the sociology of teaching, Waller (1932/1967) had this to say about the relationship between teachers and parents:

> The fact seems to be that parents and teachers are natural enemies, predestined each for the discomfiture of the other. The chasm is frequently covered over, for neither parents nor teachers wish to admit to themselves the uncomfortable implications of their animosity, but on occasion it can make itself clear enough. (p. 68)

Four and a half decades later, in another account of the sociology of teaching, McPherson (1972) titled a chapter on the relationship between teachers and parents: "Natural Enemies: Teachers and Parents." In her detailed description of a particular school, she cited one teacher, saying humorously, perhaps, "The only answer is to put children in dormitories and take them over completely from the parents. Then we might get somewhere" (p. 136).

Another author cited the humor of a parent. In talking to one homeroom teacher a mother said, "My husband and I get sick and tired of hearing your name at the dinner table. It is always that you said this or you said that. And no one can disagree with you. You are The Word. We have declared you off limits in the house" (Reichart, 1969, p. 57).

In describing the different roles of mothers and fathers in their relationship to the school, Reichart noted, "Fathers are seldom available to teachers and are usually dragged to school only when it is necessary to defend their wives or to support their wives' positions, which often means fanning flames of already overheated emotions" (p. 58).

Finally, in a book exclusively devoted to school–family relationships, Lightfoot (1978) accepted the existence of the conflict as a fact of life, but added that it actually has a constructive outcome:

> Dissonance between family and school, therefore, is not only inevitable in changing society; it also helps to make children more malleable and responsive to a changing world . . . one could say that absolute homogeneity between family and school would reflect a static, authoritarian society and discourage creative, adaptive development in children. (p. 39)

Clearly, these authors see the relationship between the school and the family as inevitably conflictual. Some, as we have just seen, go to great length to find a constructive outcome to the conflict.

EMBRACING THE CONFLICT AS INEVITABLE AND CONSTRUCTIVE

Waller (1932/1967) was among the first to discuss the conflict between schools and families. He took it for granted that both sides wish the child well, yet he noted that it is such a different kind of well that conflict must inevitably arise over it. One source of conflicting interests is that of part versus whole. Teachers are said to be interested in just one aspect of development—intellectual. And they are ready to take unpleasant measures in order to promote it. Parents are interested in the whole child. In their priorities, the child's happiness tops most other desirable states.

One should be careful not to dismiss the issue as trivial. Indeed, parents are concerned with the child's intellectual development and teachers are not entirely indifferent to the child's overall well-being. Yet the most widely accepted measure of a teacher's success is strictly that which measures intellectual achievements and little else. At the same time, it should be emphasized that the present measure of a teacher's success is not necessarily the most appropriate one, and indeed it has been occasionally replaced due to attitudinal change in the community.

Waller was among the first to suggest that the conflict between the parents and the school may be more or less useful. It may be, he said, that the child develops better if he is treated impersonally in the school. One teacher, he noted, mentioned to him that he needed to be impersonal with students in order to maintain discipline and in order to be fair with all the students. Interestingly, the same teacher admitted that, with time, he learned that these two excuses for being impersonal were wrong, because discipline and friendship can be mixed (and fairness too). Still, Waller insisted that with regard to maintaining discipline and fairness in the school, "the attitudes of parent and teacher come into their most irreconcilable opposition" (p. 74). As before, we should realize that these arguments hold only if the teacher subscribes to a certain attitude or conception. They are not necessarily inherent in the child–teacher relationship. It is not altogether uncommon to find teachers who are strict and fair, but also loving and being loved and admired by their students.

In a similar vein, Lightfoot (1978) attempted to portray positive aspects of the conflict between the school and the family and cited a proposition made by Slater (1968). Slater suggested that changes in U.S. society are anchored in child–adult discontinuity, and that the school serves an important function of regulating and modifying parent–child relationships, thereby making social changes more viable: "One segregates children from adult life because one wishes to do something special with them—to effect some kind of social change or to adapt to one. Such segregation insolates the child from social patterns of the present and makes him more receptive to some envisional future" (p. 40).

Relying on this view, Lightfoot (1978) suggested that "absolute homogeneity between family and school would reflect a static, authoritarian society and discourage creative, adaptive development in children" (p. 39).

I found no evidence to support this claim. Moreover, I intend to show that when the schools are expected to cope with particularly demanding tasks, they have a better chance of success when there is a substantial agreement between the school and the family about educational goals and practices. Thus, the claim that a social change is made possible because children are segregated and insulated from their family, and that this may be a positive aspect of the conflict between parents and teachers, seems to have little support.

SCHOOL AND FAMILY AS SOCIALIZATION AGENCIES

Twenty-seven years after Waller's book, the issue was taken up by Talcott Parsons, a prominent sociologist (1959). Parsons assumed that the school is an agency of socialization. That is, it functions "to internalize in its pupils both the commitments and the capacities for successful performance of their future adult roles . . . and to allocate these human resources within the role structure of the adult society" (p. 297). According to Parsons, in order for the socialization process to work, teachers must treat children distinctively different from the way parents do.

The mechanisms of socialization suggested by Parsons need not raise objections from parents. The first mechanism, the internalization of commitments, inculcates in the individual student commitments to the implementation of the broad values of society and a commitment to the performance of a specific type of role within the structure of society. The second mechanism develops capacities. It develops a competence in a particular skill, to be performed by the individual, and a general capacity to live up to other people's expectations—people with whom the student will be brought into contact.

The third mechanism of socialization, accomplished within the school structure, is the selection process. It works by directing high-performing students to continue their studies in college and to prepare them for professional occupations, and by directing low performers to quit higher studies and to prepare themselves to become workers. In Parsons's opinion, the selection process is essential to the functioning of the school as a socialization agency.

The central criterion in the selection process is the student's performance in school. Although Parsons actually pointed to two factors that correlate with the student's intention to pursue college studies, the father's occupation, and performance in school, he concluded that the main process of differentiation (which from another point of view is selection) occurs during elementary school, and it "takes place on a single main axis of *achievement*" (p. 300).

In order to achieve at their highest level, said Parsons, children must reach a level of independence or self-sufficiency in the sense of developing their capacity to take responsibility and to make decisions in coping with new and varying situations. The school, as portrayed by Parsons, is a proper environment for children to exercise their independence. Moreover, unlike the family, where the status of the individual is ascribed biologically, in terms of generation, sex, and age, so that children never have to earn their status, in the school, the status is not ascribed at all—it is achieved or "earned" by differential performance, set by the teacher who is acting as an agent of the community's school system. Thus, in the school, children transcend their familial identification in favor of a more independent one, and come to occupy a differentiated status within the new system.

Furthermore, the classroom is structured so that opportunity for particularistic treatment is severely limited. Because there are many more children in a school than in a family and they are concentrated in a much narrower age range, the teacher has much less chance than a parent to grant particularistic favors. Yet, in Parson's view, this is not necessarily negative. On the contrary, it is this situation in the classroom that enables the emancipation of children from the primary emotional attachment to their family, and leads to the internalization of societal values and norms that are a step higher than those of the family alone.

Thus, Parsons did not see that the school and the family need to be in conflict. But he also expected no positive results from a collaboration between the two institutions. He implied that the school and the family serve the socialization process best by treating children in inherently different ways. According to Parsons, the relationship between the school and the family need not exceed the sharing of common values. In practice, this is achieved when the family recognizes that it is fair to give differential rewards for different levels of achievement, so long as there has been fair access to opportunity. Clearly, then, Parsons did not share the view that the school and the family are natural enemies. Rather, he described them as two systems that complement each other and work in parallel to socialize children according to common values and agreed means.

CRITICISM OF THE PARSONS'S SOCIALIZATION HYPOTHESIS

In general, the assumptions made with regard to the contribution of the school to socialization (in the sense of developing a person who is well-equipped to live in society) must be empirically tested, both within a particular culture and cross-culturally, by correlating different types of schooling with measures of socialization. Until this is done, the socialization assumption seems too hypothetical. Remember that people were socialized successfully even before the modern school was created, and their socialization was mainly accomplished within the boundaries of the family itself.

As already noted, there seems to be no support for the belief that schools are essential, psychologically, for children to exercise their independence or to gain emancipation from their families. As most parents realize, children exercise their independence and self-efficacy long before they go to school and long after they leave schools. Moreover, there seems to be an individually self-paced process by which a child is gradually detached from the family and exercises independence. Such a process goes on at home, with or without (or against) the parents. It also occurs in schools, with or without (or against) teachers. It occurs in other places too.

There is another difficulty with Parsons's notion of "emancipation of the child from his family." Paradoxically, the children who tend to adjust well to school are often those who come from families that have few differences with the teachers—families who share the teachers' values and goals and agree with them on the means and strategies to reach them. These children do not need much emancipation. Differences between teachers and families may be found particularly in families where children tend to withdraw from schools. Thus, to the extent that the emancipation of children from the family is of any value, it works paradoxically for those who need it the least. It does not work for those who would presumably benefit from it the most.

Several other kinds of criticism can be leveled at Parsons's analysis: First, Parsons turns a deaf ear to the cries of parents and teachers, those articulated by the informants of Waller, McPherson, and Reichart, and cited in the opening of this chapter. Second, on a deeper level of analysis, Parsons seemed to force his underlying assumption about the socialization function of the school on the sometimes chaotic and not nearly functional reality of the school practice. One gets the impression that Parsons conceives of the present state of affairs in the school as if it underwent a long evolutionary process, so that every piece and bit of the system is fully adjusted to the rest and accommodated by it. Considering the fact that the school system, as we know it today, is only about 200 years old, such an approach appears hardly justified.

Another kind of criticism is concerned with the global level of school–family relationship. To the extent that schools are an important factor of socialization, one would always need to take into account that as the economy and public attitude changes, so must the dynamics and the objectives of socialization. Furthermore, for the socialization process to change in a satisfactory manner, so that it operates effectively, the school must welcome input from the families. This is particularly true with regard to the central mechanism of selection-by-achievement. Who defines the objectives and the measurements of achievement? According to Parsons, it would be some central authority of the society at large. But in a multiethnic and pluralistic society (particularly, in the United States), central authorities increasingly incline to relinquish much of their power to local communities. In the end, the parents will have a say in affecting schools' goals and strategies. They will also determine the limits of the contrasts between the school and the family. To the extent that there is still a conflict—rather than collaboration—the parents now have the power to adjust, minimize, or indeed eliminate the contrast altogether.

In addition, several recent studies have questioned the claim that the school fulfills an important role in the society due to its functioning as a socialization agency by maintaining the selection-by-achievement process. Leacock (1969) found that middle-class students are rewarded for individuality, aggressiveness, and initiative, whereas lower-class students are rewarded for passivity, withdrawal, and obedience. Critics of the present school system (e.g., Kozol, 1972) argue that in practice, the selection mechanism achieves its goals not so much by emphasizing achievement, but by perpetuating failures. Carnoy and Levin (1985) proposed that "the educational system taught children to accept failure as the logical result of their own inadequacy, and with that acceptance these children became conforming, passive adults, operating well below their intellectual potential" (p. 18).

If these assertions are true, they may have far-reaching implications. Rist (1970) suggested that how children are treated in their earliest school days affects how well they do from that time forward, because of the school's effect on their self-image and self-expectations. Entwisle and Hayduk (1981) found that even the earliest remarks children receive can be strong determinants of future evaluations and that a teacher's earliest formal evaluations (such as the first report card) may play a leading role in determining achievement levels.

Evidently, schools are not the only factor that act to perpetuate, rather than mobilize, children according to their potential performance. Kohn (1969) and MacKenzie (1973) showed that white-collar workers tend to reinforce self-reliance, independence, and integrity, whereas blue-collar workers emphasize conformity. Carnoy and Levin (1985) described how central authorities of education exhibit different expectations for children from upper and lower class families. They showed that at the state level, "the evaluative mechanisms governing school performance set lower academic standards for schools enrolling children from the lower middle class than they do for schools from the upper middle class" (p. 135). Teachers and school staff adopt these expectations, thereby creating a cycle of self-fulfilling prophecy.

Under these circumstances, individual achievement in the school as a factor in mobility-by-selection is confounded with the characteristics a child brings from home. It seems that the school rarely succeeds in breaking the pattern. Lightfoot (1978) was apparently right in asserting that there is an "illusion of mobility and assimilation through schooling . . . in reality, the educational system serves less to change the results of primary socialization in the home than to reinforce (and denigrate) and render them in adult form" (p. 31). For further criticism of Parsons's views, with some other emphases, see Gouldner (1970).

In summary, although Parsons explicitly denies the existence of any conflict between the school and the family, pointing to the fact that the two institutions share common values and agree on how to reach them, his arguments are aptly interpreted as justifying different orientations and practices for the school and the family. Yet, it is not at all clear how necessary it is for the children to be emancipated from their families by the schools, and it is also unclear that the present selection mechanism indeed works as Parsons said it does. In fact, more and more researchers are convinced that the school does more to perpetuate the current social structure by directing children to walk in the path of their parents, rather than to form the conditions for a fair allocation of its graduates within the social system, according to intellectual achievement.

PARENTAL INVOLVEMENT IN SCHOOL OPERATION

What Do Schools Do?

The formation of the modern secular school in the last two centuries was rarely motivated by aspirations to meet the needs of children. The schools were formed to serve the needs of the modern, industrialized state. In serving the economy, the schools participate in the process of sorting and selecting students to reproduce the hierarchic labor forces (Collins, 1979). They also act to equip the future workers, in all levels of the hierarchy, with basic skills necessary to performing their future jobs. In addition, the schools develop individuals whose role will be to produce more knowledge, so as to enable technological progress, social services, and cultural experience. To the extent that the schools replace (or displace) the role of the church and the role of the family, they assume the responsibility to inculcate in the students an image of the ideal society and an image of the ideal citizen in accordance with an agreed set of values. Related to this responsibility is the school's role in preserving and/or transforming social and cultural values with which students can develop their sense of identity and solidarity.

Religious schools, which preceded secular schools by hundreds (indeed thousands) of years, have different motivations and justifications, but they never intended to educate all children or to develop skills for citizenry in a modern state, or skills needed for performing a job in a workplace. They also never intended to produce new knowledge.

Katznelson and Weir (1985) noted that "the development of government-controlled schooling is part of the larger organizational history of the state's displacing family, church and voluntary association controls over various spheres of life" (p. 31). In Europe, the promoters of school development, in addition to the government, were industrialists, land owners, and the intellectual elite. By and large parents were passive in this development or even resisted it (Maynes, 1985). In the United States, parental resistance was largely absent. The influence of the family on school development was rather indirect, either through working-class organizations or through their participation in the political system.

As I indicated in discussing Parsons's view, there seems to be wide agreement that schools preserve and perpetuate the present social structure—economically, culturally, and ideologically. This perception is supported by a number of empirical studies. The 1966 Coleman and associates study pointed out that neither the quality of education nor the amount of resources invested in education determines the educational outcome. Jencks's (1972) study revealed that, by itself, a more egalitarian school system does little to change the distribution of income or opportunity. Bowles and Gintis (1976) reported several studies showing that although inequality in years of schooling is gradually decreasing, inequality in income is not decreasing.

Parental Conformity: The Ideological Trap

In light of this evidence, from the mid-1960s to this day, the relatively small involvement of parents (particularly those who have good reasons to be dissatisfied) in redefining educational goals and practices needs to be explained. It is unfortunately so that even parents of poorly treated children do not challenge the public school. How can we explain this inaction?

There are many possible types of explanations. Some parents may expect the school system to enable the best future for their children, even if they realize that their chances of achieving this goal with the present school system are slim. Although these parents might be a minority (cf. Brantlinger, 1985), they may be among the more articulate.

The more complete explanation concerns the effect of the ideology factor. At one time most parents were students themselves, and among other things, they learned to respect authority. However, an explanation solely based on the fact that children at school learn the rules of "good behavior" so as to become submissive citizens (and workers) is insufficient. Rather, the conformity of parents seems to result from the success of various mechanisms, acting continuously among people of all classes, to promote ideological commitments to the society as a collective. In general, these ideological mechanisms are successful enough to obscure the gap between what schools are supposed to do and what they are actually doing.

Althusser (1970) discussed these mechanisms in explicit terms. He defined ideology as an underlying belief system—as a representation of "the imaginary relationship of individuals to their real conditions of existence" (p. 162). Individuals are considered "wicked" if they do not subscribe to the ideology or if they act against it. Following Gramsci (1971), he pointed out that even private social institutions function as (what he coined) "Ideological State Apparatuses." The relative unity and independence of at least some of these apparatuses is paradoxically secured by the state, so that people do not usually suspect that the common belief about what social institutions do is promulgated by the ruling class.

Among the ideological apparatuses, Althusser mentioned the school, the church, the family, the parties, the unions, as well as the media. The ideology, Althusser claimed, is always unified, despite the diversity, and it is always the ideology of the ruling class. Nevertheless, it should be added, the principles of the common ideology are phrased in a manner that makes them palatable to everyone. Among other things, these principles define equal opportunities and equity, goals that the present school system, by itself, cannot achieve, even if it were so inclined.

Althusser added that the apparatuses are "multiple, distinct, 'relatively autonomous' and capable of providing an objective field to contradictions" (p. 149). This is an important distinction because it explains the tolerance of the global structure (the state) toward conflicting articulations of ideological exchanges.

Althusser considered the school itself as a dominant ideological apparatus, and indeed one needs only to remember the flag placed in every classroom; the pledge of allegiance every morning; the singing of the national anthem; the rhetoric in major school events, to realize how the school acts as an ideological apparatus, to promote and maintain the prevailing ideology. Recent research reveals many more means by which the school acts as an ideological apparatus, such as the school curriculum, textbooks, and children's fiction stories (Anyon, 1983; Apple, 1979; Taxel, 1983).

The role of ideology in our society may be defined in somewhat different terms. Among other things, ideology provides a theory of how society operates. Such a theory is essential for all members of society as guidance for personal conduct. Every group and individual needs an ideology. Thus, ideology cannot be reduced to a single means for securing the hegemony of the society in the hands of the ruling class.

If Althusser's analysis has at least some validity, however, then the question of parents' conformity (or passivity) may be less puzzling. The democratic capitalistic state tolerates objections and conflicts within the limits set by the common ideology, which is prompted by both state and private institutions. The goals and the principal methods of the schools are deeply rooted in the state ideology. When parents challenge the schools' goals or even its principal methods (as distinguished from having a specific complaint with regard to their own child), they may be seen as denying the basic ideology of the state. Relatively few parents can afford to be seen in this light. Challenging the school system, thus, becomes difficult because of the function of the school as an ideological apparatus that acts to preserve the social structure of the state from any threats of destruction. In light of this analysis, if parents want their children to attain a life different from their own, they will have to shatter the false mirror of reality, which was created by ideological apparatuses.

While admitting the role of ideology in explaining the stability of social structures, we should be careful not to attribute the totality of a parent's passivity (or conformity) in relation to the education of their children to what is called here the *ideological trap.* There seem to be other reasons for passivity, particularly among low-income parents. For one thing, it is probably unfair to describe the parents as completely brainwashed by the prevailing ideology, to the extent that they are unable to sense that they are being mistreated by the ruling class and its ideology. It seems more realistic to assume that many parents understand their predicament, but they are more or less powerless to force a change, unless given the proper guidance. In other words, the ideological apparatuses, powerful as they are, are not the only mechanisms acting to maintain social stability. In a capitalistic society, individual income is a measure of personal success. People of low income are likely to perceive themselves as failures and inferiors. Changing self-perception and low self-esteem takes time. It also requires a support mechanism during the period in which personal attitudes may be changed.

In the two examples discussed later, one group of parents agrees with the school on the educational goals and strategies and is ready, even eager, to participate in the operation of the school, in order to assure the best results. This is a religious community, in which the members and the educators are united in their perception of education. In the second example, parents have had no reason to be satisfied with the results of the school, but with the proper guidance, they involved themselves in the operation of the school, in a joint effort to change the school's outcome. In the course of their action, they seem to have changed the life of the entire community. In both examples, the collaboration of parents and teachers is central.

WHERE CONFLICT IS MINIMIZED

An important distinction in sociological discussions of school functioning is the distinction between (*explicit*) *curriculum,* which is the official list of subject matters to be instructed in the school, and *hidden curriculum,* which consists of the norms and values implicitly taught in the school, even though they are rarely listed as learning objectives (Dreeben, 1968; Jackson, 1968). Appel and King (Appel, 1979) observed how, in kindergarten, the hidden curriculum is reified in children's learning how to distinguish between work and play, how to deal with authoritarian adults (teacher), and how to compete with other children. The rules that constitute the relationship between teachers and children, teachers and parents, and children among themselves, generally belong to the hidden part of the curriculum. Apple aptly noted that it may not be by accident that these rules are tacit. In this way, they are preconceived as if they are above debates and impervious to challenges. Thus, "their potency as aspects of hegemony is enlarged" (p. 87).

In reference to our interest in the school–family relationship, we should note that the hidden curriculum is particularly problematic precisely because (by definition) its elements are not depicted as school objectives and, therefore, are not negotiable. In meetings between school representatives and parents, for example, the representatives of the school would rather discuss new programs of instruction than rules of behavior (e.g., disciplinary actions). These rules are portrayed as being constitutive—not subject to alteration.

Nevertheless, if a hidden curriculum (just like any other hidden agenda) is not openly negotiated, and agreed on, or if it is not accepted as part of a religious faith, then different parties to the encounter may become frustrated, alienated, or even hostile. The improvement of the school, in terms of making it more effective in achieving its agreed on goals, seems to justify an effort to minimize the hidden curriculum, so that school objectives are openly defined, agreed on by all groups, or subject to readjustment by ongoing debate. With this in mind, I turn now to discuss two educational contexts in which these ideals are approximated, in spite of the enormous differences between the two types of education.

THE TRADITIONAL JEWISH EDUCATION

The reality of the religious education to be discussed here is very different from the reality of secular education in modern, urbanized society. There are obvious differences in the educational goals and strategies, as well as in the social and economic input and output. Yet I find two justifications for bringing it up here. First, the psychology of a child, a parent, and a teacher, and the interactions between them are not totally dependent on contextual differences. There are psychological predispositions, drives, and motives, as well as psychological constraints that are fundamental enough to be influential in any educational context. Also, even remote examples are instructive in exemplifying the variety of human possibilities. Second, I believe that, to a certain extent and for a limited purpose, it is useful to consider means and measures of education, independent of educational goals. Some educational arrangements are likely to be effective in remarkably different contexts. With these justifications in mind, I offer the following discussion.

The traditional Jewish education, commonly recognized as the Cheder, today serves less than 15% of the Jewish people. It preserves the goals and practices of an educational system that may be traced back in history some 2,000 years. In this educational system, male children begin formal instruction at the age of 3 or 4. At this age, boys are separated from girls, who stay in kindergarten until entering girls' school, at the age of 6 or 7.

The religious principles that guided the development of Jewish education stem from the biblical tale of Exodus. In this context, the fathers were ordered to "tell" their sons about the events and the lessons of the exile in Egypt, and about the significance of their liberation for their future life as a nation and as individuals (cf., Ex. 13:8, 14). These statements were, apparently, later interpreted to imply that the responsibility for the education of Jewish sons rests on the shoulders of their fathers.

The earliest documentation of institutionalized elementary education in Jewish tradition can be traced in the postbiblical scriptures of Oral Law, the Mishna, and the Talmud (the second century B.C. to the fifth century A.D.). The Talmud (Bava Batra 21:1) tells us about a Rabbi called Joshua Ben Gamla who (about 63 A.D.) was probably the first to put forward a new interpretation of the biblical injunction to the fathers to instruct their sons. According to his interpretation, the fathers' responsibility could be transferred in part to others. Fathers remained responsible for the education of their sons, but the instruction itself could henceforth be done by proxy, that is, by an instructor (*Melamed*).

Elementary education was carried out in the synagogues, which served as community centers, facilitating schooling during morning hours. Under the guidance of the scholars of the yeshiva (the "graduate school" for Jewish studies), any educated adult male could be a teacher. General education was designed not only to prepare a few youngsters for later studies in the yeshiva, but to prepare all male children for participation in the daily affairs of religious practice at home or in the synagogue. An ordinary male adult in a Jewish community had to know how to read in order to take part regularly in the prayers held in synagogues, which entailed reading from prayer books and the Bible.

The Cheder was founded in Europe half a millennium ago and still exists in many communities of Orthodox Jews around the world. Originally, the Cheder was modeled after the Talmudic example, already discussed. The Cheder (otherwise known as Talmud Torah), which in modern times became the equivalent of a kindergarten and primary school, probably started out as a private educational arrangement in small Jewish communities, where several parents would hire an adult male to teach their sons the common prayers and some reading. The Cheder operated at first on a voluntary basis as a place where fathers brought their children to fulfill their responsibility for teaching their sons. (In practice, from what we know, it was usually the mother who saw to it that her son got the best education the family could afford.)

In modern times, most Cheders, although still private institutions, are supervised by officials of the local Jewish communities. In our day they are also subsidized by the allocation of public funds, and they operate as one option of compulsory education for children from the age of 5. My account of the Cheder, in the following section, is based on classroom observations and recordings of extensive discussions with five teachers, in a Cheder run by the Chabad movement in Israel, in the spring of 1989. As I was told by several Orthodox educators, there are no essential differences between the Chabadic Cheders and other Cheders run by other Orthodox groups.

The educational ideology (belief) of the Chabadic teacher stems from the medieval Jewish tradition of the Kabala. In this account, a man (women are disregarded in this context) has dual spirits, the animalistic spirit governed by bodily drives and passions, and the spiritual mind governed by intellect, knowledge, wisdom, and the spiritual drive to reach God through spiritual love. Mental states have different qualities that are hierarchically graded from the more common and simple to the most refined and spiritual. According to this approach, children are obviously at the lowest level of mental development, because their spiritual mind is yet undeveloped. Thus, they are driven by their bodily needs, which distance them from the way toward God. This approach sees no value in childhood as such, because being driven by the animalistic spirit, the child is less able to love God. Like the adult, the child can approach God by both acquiring the proper habits of religious life and developing his spiritual mind. Understandably, in this process, learning has a crucial role.

In practice, the Chabadic educators, particularly those who work with young children, do appreciate the specific needs of early childhood. In their instruction, they make room for singing and playing. They also use both positive and negative reinforcement. The school management attempts to appoint (male) teachers who are able to relate to children with loving and caring.

The Classroom as an Integral Part of the Community

An important facet of the Cheder activity is its close relationship to the community life. The Cheder was actually developed as a microcosmos of Jewish life. As I show elsewhere (Shimron, 1990), the general stream of events of the Orthodox community at large at certain times coregulate the activities of the Cheder. This is most apparent when observing different cycles of the Cheder activity. The most prominent cycles are the day, the week, the month, and the season (which is related to the holidays).

Many of the 613 acts (*Mitzvot*) that an Orthodox male Jew is expected to observe are closely tied to the stream of time. For example, when he opens his eyes in the morning, he has to say a special blessing; before breakfast he is expected to say a set of prayers; before and after every meal he says another set of blessings. There are three periods of prayers during a day, and a certain prayer before he goes to bed. In addition, there are special religious rituals at the beginning and the end of the week, the beginning of the month (of the Hebrew calendar), and the Jewish holidays. Thus, an Orthodox Jew must have a very keen sense of time. Almost every hour of the day has a special meaning.

The activities in the Cheder reflect this rhythm. Most events of the religious life are acted out during the school day. Thus, when children come to the school, they pray the morning prayer, just like the adults at home or at work. Before or after their meal, they pray again and go through the hand-washing ceremony, like other adults. Jewish holidays are central elements of the Cheder curriculum; they are dealt with in the classroom as they occur along the year. In a sense, almost every subject dealt with in the classroom is tied to the superstructure of the time cycle above and beyond the school. Unlike the regular school, in which the curriculum is fixed according to criteria of preferences of subject matters and according to an understanding of child development, the curriculum of the Cheder is determined by the larger timetable of religious life in the congregation at large. This is evident in the daily morning prayer, the time devoted to the weekly portion of the Bible, and in the time devoted to "seasonal" events such as holidays and the beginning of months of the Jewish calendar. As a result, the class periods, to which we are accustomed in the modern school, are regulated by the religious rhythm of the daily events. Thus, if the regular school is often seen as a microcosm that has its own independent pulse and direction, the Cheder resonates to the rhythm of the larger congregation outside the school.

The relationship between the teacher and the parents in this type of religious education appears to be much closer than in the secular public school. These relationships are strengthened due to several factors. First, children start school at the age of 3 or 4. In dealing with children so young, the teacher is directed to consider the individual needs of children as much as possible. Second, many of these schools operate within close communities, of which both the teacher and the parents are members. Therefore, teachers and parents are likely to meet each other in the synagogue or in other places in the neighborhood. Teachers are likely to be genuinely interested in satisfying the parents by making their child reasonably happy. The relationship between teachers and parents may also be strengthened due to the fact that the same teacher will often teach several boys of the same family.

The Rabbi of the community also often plays an important role in smoothing out differences between the families and the school. The Rabbi is a spiritual authority, respected and obeyed by parents and teachers alike. In his capacity, he visits the school periodically. When he does, he is likely to enter classrooms and to examine individual children. Unlike a school superintendent, however, the Rabbi interacts with the families of the community on different matters. Thus, he knows the parents well and is more able to smooth out possible misunderstandings between the parents and the teachers.

As a practical mechanism for institutionalizing parent–teacher collaboration, it is customary in the Cheder for the teacher to circulate a form letter to the families every Friday, after 6 days of study. In the letter the teacher tells the parents what was taught during the week and urges them to test their child on the weekend. The parents return the letter to the school at the beginning of the week (on Sunday morning), together with their comments on the child's progress. This arrangement improves the interrelationship of the school and the family, as the two complementary environments that encompass the child.

As both parents and school personnel are members of the Orthodox community, they share the same convictions (conceived as principles of faith) and agree about their implementation. The parents and the entire community explicitly expect the school to prepare their male children for a religious life. As a result, unlike the modern school in which the curriculum is predominantly determined by a list of selected subjects, the religious school strives to reach a balance between learning its selected subject matter and practicing-by-doing the religious way of life. The teacher and the Rabbi are construed as true role models whose behavior should be imitated. Thus, in this educational system, what was defined earlier as a hidden curriculum is usually made evident and explicit (no longer hidden), due to a wide a priori acceptance by both teachers and parents of educational goals, which encompass individual conduct in a very detailed manner, and the strategies to attain them.

In addition, an analysis of the Orthodox belief system (Shimron, 1990) shows the centrality of learning in their perception of proper living—learning as a way of life, not just storing information or acquiring skills. According to this conviction, one should start learning as early as possible, and continue to learn to the end of one's life.

In sum, time junctures, such as the day, the week, and the year function as means for connecting and integrating the inner structure of the Cheder with other structures—the family, the congregation, the entire Orthodox community, and the Jewish people. As a matter of belief, some of these connect the individual with God. The integration of life in the Cheder with other circles of which the child is part seems to be a factor that ought to be taken into account in explaining how this educational system accomplishes its goals and how it has endured over so many years. Total agreement about school goals and the means to achieve them, and explicit expectation that the role of the school is to inculcate religious conduct in its students, help to minimize what is otherwise known as a hidden curriculum. When the hidden curriculum is minimized and when school goals and strategies are agreed on by all parties of the educational process, the relationship between the school and the family is founded on a solid base of collaboration. The absence of constructive conflicts does not appear to hamper children's development or to worry the parents.

REFORMING URBAN EDUCATION

My second example of school–family relationship is the School Development Program, initiated by the Child Study Center at Yale University. The story of the New Haven school reform, headed by Professor James Comer, is now well-documented and publicized in a book (Comer, 1980), in a number of journal articles (e.g., Comer, 1988a, 1988b, 1986; Haynes, Comer, & Hamilton-Lee, 1988), and in a number of press coverages, from *Newsweek* (Oct. 2, 1989) to the *New York Times* (Jan. 20, 1988; Jan. 24, 1990; June 13, 1990). In spite of the public interest, however, it seems that the academic community is yet to to realize the significance of this large-scale model of school reform, and to come to grips with its practical and theoretical implications. If the reports are valid (as they appear), then it seems that structural change of educational management, coupled with changes in school–family relationship, results not only in significant educational progress, but also in the transformation of community life, from one that was alienated from the school to one that is deeply involved in the school's daily operation.

The project began in 1968, when an intervention research team inspired by Albert J. Solnit at Yale's Child Study Center and headed by James Comer involved itself in two urban schools in order to learn how they function, and then began to develop and implement a model for improving the schools. The team included a social worker, a psychologist, and a special education teacher. The two schools had 300 and 350 pupils each, from kindergarten to the fifth grade. The pupils were almost 99% Black and almost all poor. At the beginning of the project the pupils were ranked near the bottom in achievement and attendance, among the 33 schools in the city of New Haven. The staff's turnover rate was 25%, and the parents, in Comer's words, "were dejected, distrustful, angry and alienated" (1988a, p. 44). The school had no positive effect on the community around it.

By 1975, after some initial difficulties, the project was clearly having an effect. By 1979, without any change in the socioeconomic makeup of the schools, students in the fourth grade had caught up to their grade level. By 1984, they ranked third and fourth highest on the Iowa Test of Basic Skills. The attendance rate in one of these schools became the first or the second in the city. In 1980, the team left the schools as the program was fully integrated into the normal practice of the schools. Since then, the program has spread to other schools in New Haven and to more than 50 schools in several states, where it has achieved a level of success on a par with those of the New Haven schools.

The project appears to have made a remarkable contribution to urban education. To an outside observer, the success of this effort, if continued, appears to have the potential power not only to change the future of the children and the families who are directly affected, but also to have political implications, due to its power to transform social relationships.

As descriptions of this project are readily available, my discussion is brief. I am principally interested in the educational presuppositions of Comer and his group and in the mechanisms they forged to accomplish their goals.

Educational Presuppositions

Comer and his associates assumed that, for elementary school children, the acquisition of knowledge is critically (although not exclusively) mediated by significant adults. This assumption, in fact, seems so obviously true that we tend to ignore it. All too often we think of instruction in terms of knowledge structures or learning and memory processes, and tend to forget that young children will learn best (sometimes, they will learn only) if a personal, affective relationship is established between them and an adult who functions as a source of knowledge. The adult's role in mediating knowledge is absolutely crucial in the early stages of language acquisition, but it goes far beyond. Indeed, the importance of adult mediation in the acquisition of knowledge decreases with age, but it never quite diminishes (even in college and after).

For elementary school learning, this assumption implies that instructors cannot afford to be impersonal in the classroom, without jeopardizing their efficiency as conveyers of knowledge—quite the opposite of what was previously suggested by Waller, Parsons, and Lightfoot. In practice, it implies that to increase their efficiency, teachers would do well to become familiar with each child's background so that they would be able to relate to the child on a person-to-person level. To do that, teachers will have to acquaint themselves with the child's family, and to maintain an ongoing relationship with it.

Moreover, Comer and his group assumed that elementary school children experience difficulties when they encounter conflict, contempt, hostility, or even mistrust between the significant adults in their environment. This implies that for teachers to be effective, they must be on speaking terms with the child's parents. Also, the readiness of the child to be open to the influence of the teacher depends on the children's perception of the respect their parents have for that teacher. Thus, in order to be instructionally effective, the teacher must earn the respect of the children's parents. If not, the teacher stands little chance to become a *significant adult*.

When adults, such as teachers, become significant for a group of children, children imitate them, identify with them, and internalize their attitudes, values, and skills. They also become motivated toward academic learning in the process. Comer (1986) stressed that where motivation to learn does not exist prior to the classroom experience, this process of becoming a significant adult is critically important; where motivation already exists, the interpersonal classroom experience reinforces it. Frustration, disappointment, anger, acting up, friction between home and school, among school staff members, or between staff members and students, all these factors block learning by destroying the learning-conducive interaction between a child and an adult.

Thus, the contrast between a child's (learning) experience at home and in school deeply affects the child's psychosocial development, and this in turn shapes academic achievement (Comer, 1988a). This contrast is particularly sharp for poor minority children from families outside the mainstream:

> A child whose development meshes with the mainstream values encountered at school will be prepared to achieve at the level of his or her ability. In addition, the meshing of home and school fosters further development: When a child's social skills are considered appropriate by the teacher, they elicit positive reaction. A bond develops between the child and the teacher, who can now join in supporting the overall development of the child. (p. 45)

When the contrast between the family atmosphere and the school is particularly sharp, as it seems to be among poor minority families, educational reforms need to treat both sides of the interaction—the attitudinal change at the school must be accompanied by attitudinal change in the family.

Comer (1988a) noted that parents of failing students take the problems as personal failure or as evidence of animosity or rejection by the mainstream. They lose hope and confidence, and become less supportive of the school. Moreover, some parents become defensive and hostile, avoiding contact with school staff. The result is a high degree of mutual distrust between home and school, which makes it difficult to nurture a bond between child and teacher that can support development and learning. Unfortunately, the children of parents who alienated themselves from the school are often the ones most in need of seeing their parents or people like them interact successfully with school staff members in the school setting.

Mechanisms for Change

The reform of the school was carried out by creating three new mechanisms. The first mechanism is the *Governance and Management Team*, which was to become the new center of power in the school. The team included the principal, two teachers elected by all teachers, three parents elected by the parent organization, and a mental health team member. The school principal was the head of the team. In its weekly meetings the team addressed issues such as curriculum development, the social climate of the school, staff development, planning and coordinating group activities.

The second mechanism developed by the project was the *Parent Participation Group.* This mechanism was formed to institutionalized routes for interaction between the school and the families as a group. It enabled democratic election of parent representatives to the new governance team and to other committees controlled by this team. Once organized, parents became active in initiating and implementing broad-based activities. Some parents were also employed as classroom assistants, tutors, or aides.

The third mechanism was the *Mental Health Team.* The team constituted a classroom teacher, a special education teacher, a social worker, and the school psychologist. They consulted the governance and management body in questions of policymaking, in an attempt to foster the development of favorable conditions. The team served individual teachers by suggesting in-classroom ways to manage early or potential problem behaviors. In addition, they trained school personnel to provide a variety of child development and mental health services.

The project posed a challenge and offered help to all parties in the educational process: the school management, the teachers, the families, and, of course, the students. The results were their own reward. The school principals' challenge was to lead in changing the power structure of the school. They were asked to share their power with teachers, parents, and the intervention team in forming the Governance and Management Team. The principals' reward was better cooperation with teachers and families, a change in the school social climate, and, of course, the higher reputation of the school.

The parents' challenge was to organize a parent organization that was to become an independent force, cooperating with others to improve the school. They were expected to intensify their involvement in school activities. The parents were offered a Parent Participation Program and a positive social experience in collaborating with teachers and school authorities. Their direct reward was the improvement of their relationship with the school staff, and, of course, the success of their children.

The teachers' challenge was to adjust to the structural changes and to the new power shift, to intensify their cooperation with the parents, and to become active in new kinds of school activities. They were offered professional help in coping with classroom problems from the mental health team. Their reward was the improvement of the school social climate, which affected their relationship with parents and the students, and a better prospect for overall success.

Much of Comer's rationale for his project was based on his knowledge of school psychology, his experience as a psychiatrist, his personal convictions, and a lot of common sense. It should be interesting and useful to find out which of his assumptions and observations are supported empirically, according to current knowledge in the social sciences. At this moment, one has to accept or reject some of Comer's assumptions at face value. But this is hardly a criticism of Comer's approach. Those who share Comer's sense of urgency and the need to revise the present school system should accept the premise that in acting to change a complex reality such as education, one cannot adopt anything but a comprehensive approach. It is unrealistic, for example, to expect success in changing the attitudes of the students without changing the attitudes of the teachers or the parents. In bringing about such a comprehensive change, there will always be a gap between what we know for a fact (i.e., what has been empirically established) and what we suspect or believe to be true, but, nevertheless, accept as working hypotheses on which to base our action.

Collective Power

In his 1980 book, Comer attributed the reasons for the deterioration of urban education to the erosion of authoritative power of the parents, the teachers, and, most of all, the school management. Yet in reading Comer's reports on the School Development Program, one must ask, is this project really about power? And if it is, where does the new power lie? From the previous discussion it should be clear that the problems approached by Comer's group and the solutions proposed were by no means limited to questions of power or authority. It may be realized that one contributing factor to the success of the project was the improvement of the school social climate, within the school and between the school and the families. The improved social climate made it possible for all individuals to bring forward their better qualities and to accomplish more. But that has little to do with gaining or losing power.

Comer suggested that in the reformed school, the principal at the head of the Governance and Management Team is a more powerful leader than the ordinary principal in other urban schools. But this is quite paradoxical, because, in fact, under the new circumstances, principals share much of their traditional power with their team. Those who gained more power are the parents, the teachers, and the mental health team. Principals, although still at the head of the power structure, owe their remaining power to the goodwill of their team members—to their willingness to cooperate with them. Their new status is more like *primus inter pares.*

Thus, in terms of power-shift, to the extent that the revised school has more power, it is the institution as a whole—the school—that became more powerful. In the end, it is the community around the school that is now more powerful with its children better educated, its parents having a better self-image, and its community-wide membership having a heightened sense of self-efficacy.

CONCLUSIONS

This chapter has focused on the possibility of a collaborative relationship between the school and the family. One may wish to assess the relative weight of improving the school–family relationship in the overall appraisal of the educational systems discussed here. Such an assessment, however, may be difficult in view of the fact that the components of these models work, in reality, as wholes. There may be no meaningful way to assess the importance of one particular element of an educational system, out of its global context (we tend to perceive systems as being modular, but forget that they operate as wholes). How may we sum up the nature and the merit of the collaborative school–family relationship?

Collaboration between the school and the family is not equally important in every educational system. The amount of collaboration in the schools serving the mainstream middle-class or upper class society is relatively low, although the outcomes of these schools are relatively high. Indeed, there are private schools that serve only upper classes in which school–family collaboration is minimal. Yet there seem to be no circumstances under which conflictual relationship between the school and the family are justified. Unlike the suggestions of Waller, Parsons, and Lightfoot, I find no constructive outcomes from school–family conflict or alienation.

There may be different factors that compensate for the absence of collaboration or continuity between the school and the family. In traditional upper classes there seems to be a tacit agreement between the school and the family about the role of the school and a general satisfaction with the school outcomes. As long as the school lives up to parents' expectations, the involvement of the parents may indeed be low. Children of the upper class are generally the most prepared for the demands of the school, thus, school–family collaboration may be less crucial (but see my final remark).

Collaboration between the school and the family becomes critical when schools are not successful or when the task to be performed by the school is particularly demanding. In our first example of early education in a religious school, the task of educating boys as young as $3\frac{1}{2}$ years old for adult Orthodox Jewish life (amidst a secular society) seems quite demanding. It requires collaboration because the educational system may not work if the continuity between the family and the school is not carefully kept, so that the school or the family are seen as extensions of each other. In the case of the Comer project, the task is no less demanding, although for different reasons of course. The task is demanding mainly because the children of low-income parents are often the least prepared for school, their families and communities are not sufficiently supportive, and their schools cannot make up or compensate for all the structural deficiencies. Intensifying the collaboration between the family and the school is in a sense an admission of weakness—a sign of humility, if you wish—which means that neither the school nor the parents, when left to their own, are able to secure successful education for the children.

Finally, from the previous discussion one may get the impression that collaborative effort between the school and the family is only advantageous for problematic schools. This, I think, is wrong. It was often found in education that programs designed for disadvantaged groups benefited all children. True, there are priviledged communities where schools do reasonably well, without collaborating with the parents. Yet I suspect that intensifying the collaboration between these schools and their families will raise the schools to a higher level of performance. Upper class parents who generally enjoyed higher education themselves have more to contribute to the collaboration, and their children are better prepared to take advantage of better education.

ACKNOWLEDGMENT

This chapter is dedicated to Yonat.

REFERENCES

Althusser, L. (1971). Ideology and ideological state apparatuses (Notes toward an investigation). In L. Althusser (Ed.), *Lenin and philosophy and other essays* (pp. 127–186). New York: Monthly Review Press.

Anyon, J. (1983). Workers, labor and economic history, and textbook content. In M. W. Apple & L. Weis (Eds.), *Ideology and practice in schooling* (pp. 37–60). Philadelphia: Temple University Press.

Apple, M. W. (1979). *Ideology and curriculum.* London: Routledge & Kegan Paul.

Brantlinger, E. (1985). What low-income parents want from schools: A different view of aspirations. *Interchange, 16*(4), 14–28.

Bowles, S., & Gintis, H. (1976). *Schooling in capitalist America.* New York: Basic Books.

Carnoy, M., & Levin, H. M. (1985). *Schooling and work in the democratic state.* Stanford, CA: Stanford University Press.

Coleman, J. S., Campbell, E. Q., Hobson, C. J., McPartland, J., Mood, A. M., Weinfeld, F. D., & York, R. L. (1966). *Equality of educational opportunity.* Washington DC: U.S. Government Printing Office.

Collins, R. (1979). *The credential society.* New York: Academic Press.
Comer, J. P. (1980). *School power.* New York: Free Press.
Comer, J. P. (1986). Parent participation in the school. *Phi Delta Kappan, 67*(16), 442–446.
Comer, J. P. (1988a). Educating poor minority children. *Scientific American, 259*(5), 42–48.
Comer, J. P. (1988b). Is 'parenting' essential to good teaching? *NEA Today* (special ed.), *8*(6), 34–40.
Dreeben, R. (1968). *On what is learned in school.* Reading, MA: Addison-Wesley.
Entwisle, D. R., & Hayduk, L. A. (1981). Academic expectations and the school attainment of young children. *Sociology of Education, 54,* 34–50.
Gouldner, A. W. (1970). *The coming crisis of western sociology.* New York: Basic Books.
Gramsci, A. (1971). *Selections from the prison notebooks.* New York: International Publishers.
Haynes, N. M., Comer, J. P., & Hamilton-Lee, M. (1988). The school development program. *Journal of Negro Education,* 57(1), 11–21.
Jackson, P. W. (1968). *Life in classroom.* New York: Holt, Rinehart & Winston.
Jencks, C. (1972). *Inequality: A reassessment of the effect of family and schooling in America.* New York: Basic Books.
Katznelson, I., & Weir, M. (1985). *Schooling for all.* New York: Basic Books.
Kohn, M. L. (1969). *Class and conformity: A study in values.* Homewood, IL: Dorsey Press.
Kozol, J. (1972). *Free schools.* Boston: Houghton-Mifflin.
Leacock, E. B. (1969). *Teaching and learning in city schools.* New York: Basic Books.
Lightfoot, S. L. (1978). *Worlds apart.* New York: Basic Books.
MacKenzie, G. (1973). *The aristocracy of labor.* London: Cambridge University Press.
Maynes, M. J. (1985). *Schooling in Western Europe.* Albany, NY: State University of New York Press.
McPherson, G. H. (1972). *Small town teacher.* Cambridge MA: Harvard University Press.
Parsons, T. (1959). The school class as a social system: Some of its functions in American society. *Harvard Educational Review,* 29(4), 297–318.
Reichart, S. (1969). *Change and the teacher.* New York: Thomas Y. Crowell.
Rist, R. C. (1970). Student social class and teacher expectations: The self-fulfilling prophecy in ghetto education. *Harvard Educational Review, 40,* 411–451.
Shimron, J. (1990). Time perception and time as an organizer in teaching reading in Israeli parochial school. In M. Ben Peretz & R. Bromme (Eds.), *The nature of time in schools.* New York: Teachers College Press.
Slater, P. (1968). Social change and the democratic family. In W. Bennis & P. Slater (Eds.), *The temporary society* (pp. 20–52). New York: Harper & Row.
Taxel, J. (1983). The American revolution in children's fiction: An analysis of literary content, form, and ideology. In M. W. Apple & L. Weis (Eds.), *Ideology and practice in schooling* (pp. 61–88). Philadelphia: Temple University Press.
Waller, W. (1967). *The sociology of teaching.* New York: Wiley. (Original work published 1932)

CHAPTER 11

Schooling, Culture, and Cognitive Development

HAROLD W. STEVENSON
CHUANSHENG CHEN
SHIN-YING LEE
ANDREW J. FULIGNI
University of Michigan

We have many reasons to be interested in the effects of schooling on children's development. There are obvious questions about the types and amount of schooling necessary for individuals to function effectively in their societies. Accordingly, a great deal of attention has been given to studying the influence of time spent in the classroom, the type of school attended, and the mode of instruction on children's scholastic achievement. But there is more to be gained from going to school than academic knowledge and skills. A commonly held hypothesis purports that going to school improves one's cognitive ability. For example, there are long-held beliefs that the study of mathematics teaches us to think logically and that courses in science help us to think abstractly. We do not yet have the firm evidence necessary to support or to refute such beliefs, but they help to motivate the study of the effects of schooling on cognitive development.

There is perhaps an even more fundamental reason why we should study the influence of schooling on child development. It is seldom acknowledged that the information we have about normal child development is based on the study of a special kind of human being—the child in school. When we ask about what types of cognitive tasks 6-year-olds are capable of performing, we really are asking about the competencies of first graders. Typically, 6-year-olds selected for study are all enrolled in school. When psychologists such as Piaget write about the emergence of higher levels of cognitive processes at age 12, they are describing the thought processes of children who have been enrolled in school for 6 years. In short, much of what we consider to be developmental changes in cognitive functions derived from general experience and maturation actually may be due in part to the more specific experiences of attending school. As a result, it is impossible in much of our psychological research to tease apart the effects of chronological age and years of schooling. Despite the fact that this point has been made repeatedly (e.g., Cahan & Cohen, 1989), it is rarely mentioned in theoretical discussions about human cognitive development.

STUDIES OF SCHOOLING, CULTURE, AND COGNITIVE DEVELOPMENT

It is not our purpose here to review the literature on the relations between schooling, culture, and cognitive development because comprehensive reviews are already available (e.g., Anderson, Spiro, & Montague, 1977; Rogoff, 1981; Scribner & Cole, 1973). Nevertheless, it is useful to introduce the topic by outlining some of the methods used by psychologists in their investigations and to briefly describe some of their findings.

Research on schooling and cognitive development has been of two general types. In the first type, psychologists have compared the performance of schooled and nonschooled children. Of course, it is misleading to say that nonschooled children receive no form of education. Children acquire many skills in informal settings through being taught by parents, peers, or employers. Differences have been noted, however, in the ways in which teaching occurs in formal and in informal settings (Greenfield & Lave, 1982). Although teachers in informal settings rely on many different teaching techniques, their teaching is likely to depend more on demonstration and modeling than on the verbal instruction that characterizes teaching in formal settings. Learning in informal settings also tends to have immediate utility. Although the learners may acquire the skills necessary for solving their practical problems, learning in informal settings seldom transcends these needs. In contrast to learning that takes place in formal settings, sophisticated strategies are seldom applied during the course of learning, and little effort is expended in attempts to translate the newly acquired knowledge into some type of abstract representational system.

Studies of informal education have been especially concerned with the kinds of cognitive operations children are capable of performing without the benefit of formal schooling. It is clear from studies such as those described by Scribner and Cole (1973) and by Greenfield and Lave (1982) that complex mental operations can indeed be performed effectively by nonschooled children. An example appears in Saxe's (1988) recent studies of young street vendors in Brazil. These children employ sophisticated means of solving the mathematics problems encountered in their daily sales transactions, even though they have received no formal instruction in mathematics. In fact, even though these children are capable of reaching the correct solution in their heads, they have difficulty in solving mathematics problems "the school way"—which means through the set of formal operations they have been taught in school. Nevertheless, other evidence by researchers such as Wagner (1982) points to the fact that although these complex mental abilities may be found in nonschooled children, they develop at a slower rate than they do in schooled children.

Although the results have rather consistently yielded higher scores on cognitive tasks for children who attend school, reliance on naturally occurring variation in school attendance inevitably leads to problems in attribution. Are the differences due to attending school, or are they due to other factors that co-vary with school attendance? At least two types of factors can be suggested. First, children who attend school may develop test-taking skills, easy rapport with adults, and familiarity with the testing situation and testing materials that help them to obtain higher scores than the less sophisticated unschooled children. Second, children who attend school may display greater cognitive competence, even before they enter school, than those whose schooling is omitted or delayed (Irwin, Engle, Yarbrough, Klein, & Townsend, 1978). The latter effect may occur because parents who choose to send their child to school also tend to provide their children with more stimulating home environments, or parents may simply elect to send only their more able children to school. Moreover, the effects may not be the same in different cultures. Ginsburg (1977), for example, described two African cultures, one agricultural and one involving mercantile trading. Schooling in mathematics played a more important role in the first than in the second culture. Learning mathematics proved to be more dependent on instruction in school for the children in the agricultural culture than in the mercantile culture because in the latter culture children had more opportunities to learn about mathematics through their everyday experiences.

Interpreting the effects of schooling would be clearer if it were possible to conduct controlled studies in which children are arbitrarily assigned to schooled and nonschooled groups. This, of course, is not possible. The only available way to sort out the influences of these various factors is through statistical procedures. Unfortunately, as Super (1977) pointed out, many of the studies fail to gather enough information about the child's home environment so that these influences can be taken into account. In order to understand why parents do or do not choose to send their children to school, it is necessary to have information about the socioeconomic, educational, and motivational characteristics of the families.

A second type of studies dealing with the relation between schooling and cognitive development are those in which the amount or type of schooling received by the children is varied. For example, some investigators have examined the effect of following the regular school year with attendance at summer school. In a review of these studies, Heyns (1987) showed that attending summer school can arrest the declines in achievement scores that often occur during the summer, especially for children from disadvantaged homes. But studies of this type are subject to the same methodological problem that is found in studies of the schooled and unschooled children: The amount of schooling, in this case attendance at summer school, cannot be controlled by the investigator. A partial remedy for this problem has been offered by Cahan and Cohen (1989), who studied the effects of various amounts of schooling by comparing year-end performance by the youngest and oldest children in three successive elementary school grades in Israeli schools. Because assignment to a grade in these schools was based on chronological age, the oldest children in one grade differed in age from the youngest children in the next higher grade by 1 year of schooling but by only a few months of chronological age. Comparisons revealed that 1 year of schooling had a notably greater effect than 1 year of age on the test scores—especially for verbal tests.

Although our conclusions from the aforementioned studies are tenuous, it appears that attending school hastens the rate of cognitive development. This is a very general statement, but it is impossible to be more precise without additional evidence. Nor can we describe the ways in which schooling may have such an influence. Schooling may have many different kinds of effects, such as teaching children how to attend to and carry out instructions, to encode experience into words, to decode abstract visual representations of stimuli, and to develop strategies for learning and remembering. We do not know how different types of schooling may have differential effects on their development or how these effects might operate in different cultures. Attendance at school is not in itself a variable of great specificity, and in order to understand how schooling influences cognitive processes we must understand the social setting and culture in which it occurs.

TWO NEW STUDIES

The remainder of this chapter is devoted to the discussion of data we have obtained about the effects of schooling in two large cross-cultural studies. In the first study we compared schooled and nonschooled children from traditional, indigenous societies on tests of academic achievement and cognitive development. The study departed from most of the earlier studies of this type in providing sufficient information about the children's families to enable us to evaluate not only the effects of schooling but also of a number of other potentially relevant variables on the prediction of children's test scores. We were able to determine whether schooling had an independent effect, or whether its impact on children's development was lost when other variables, such as the educational level of their parents, were taken into consideration.

In the second study we investigated schooling in three industrialized societies. Our interest here was in contrasting the effects of schooling on academic achievement and cognitive development in three societies purposely selected because we believed the levels of academic achievement of the children in the three societies were likely to differ during the early years of elementary school. The major question was whether schooling would have a leveling effect; that is, whether children in the three societies would become more alike in their levels of cognitive development and academic achievement during successive years of schooling.

The final section of the chapter compares the performance on achievement and cognitive tests of first graders from the indigenous societies with that of first graders from the industrialized societies to answer the following question: Is attendance at school associated with greater similarity in academic achievement than in cognitive abilities? In tests of academic achievement, children are directly taught the content on which they were tested, but in tests of cognitive abilities they are not. Whatever effects that might be found in the second case must depend on incidental rather than direct consequences of attending school.

Study 1: Quechua Children of Peru

Peru is an ideal location in which to study the effects of schooling on children's development. All children in Peru are expected to attend elementary school, but only about half of the children in Peru enter school at the appropriate age of 6 years. Enrollment drops rapidly during each subsequent year, so that by the sixth grade only a small percentage of Peruvian children remain in school. These national statistics include data for both the Mestizos (mixed Spanish and Indian) and the indigenous Quechua-speaking Indians. Separate statistics are not available for the two ethnic groups, but it is clear that fewer Quechua than Mestizo children are enrolled in school. Peru also is a country with dramatically different environments: the flat plains of the coast, the high Andean mountains (*sierra*), and the tropical rain forest (*selva*). Quechua children generally live in remote regions of the *sierra* and the *selva,* and in the squatter settlements (*barriadas*) of coastal cities. They are among the poorest citizens of the country. Selection of Quechua children for study thus made it possible not only to study the effects of attending school, but also the generality of these effects across three different environments.

Research Locations

The children were from one urban (Lima) and two rural environments (villages in the regions of Andahuaylas and Lamas). Lima is on the Pacific coast, Andahuaylas is in the *sierra,* and Lamas is in the *selva.*

Lima. Millions of people live in *barriadas* located in the barren, treeless hills on the outskirts of Lima. The inhabitants of these settlements are primarily Quechua peasants who have migrated to Lima from the *sierra* in the hope of finding a better standard of living and greater opportunities for their families in the city. Major migration to the city began several decades ago, when the first squatters took over areas near highways. The lower areas of the *barriadas* contain sturdily constructed homes and are relatively stable communities. But as more and more migrants arrived in Lima, they were forced to settle in higher and higher regions of the hills. As one climbs the hills, the condition of the homes becomes more flimsy, the population becomes more transient, and the living facilities become more primitive.

Most migrants consider themselves temporary residents of the city who will return to the highlands. Nevertheless, they tend to stay in the city once they have moved, but remain in close contact with their relatives and friends in the highlands. El Ermitano, the *barriada* in which we conducted our research, was settled by families that migrated primarily from villages in the region of Andahuaylas. Migrants to the city must adapt to the urban Mestizo culture, which means they must abandon their traditional garments for Western clothing and gradually replace Quechua with Spanish as their daily language. Employment for migrants is generally unstable and residents of El Ermitano are frequently in search of some means to earn money.

Andahuaylas. Andahuaylas was an important area in the Inca empire. Even today, highlands families retain traditional cultural values and the Quechua language. Native dress is worn, holidays and rituals of the past are still observed, and ancient stories continue to be recounted. The primary occupations are farming and herding. Although Spanish is the official language of the country and the legal language of instruction throughout Peruvian schools, all of the teachers in Andahuaylas spoke Quechua as well as Spanish. In Lima, only 20% (16 out of 81) of the teachers could speak Quechua; in Lamas, where a high percentage of teachers are Mestizos, only 1 teacher in the 15 classrooms we visited knew Quechua.

Lamas. The second rural group lived in the area of Lamas, which is located in the *selva* of mid-Northern Peru. This is one of the most remote areas of the country, and access to many of the villages is impossible during the rainy season. The Quechua-speaking families are a minority group in the predominantly Mestizo culture of the region. They are believed to be descendants of the Chancas, a group residing in Andahuaylas that was defeated in a battle with the Incas over 500 years ago. This group migrated to the *selva,* hundreds of miles from their homelands. They did not become assimilated into other indigenous Amazonian groups, and even though they adapted in many ways to the dominant Mestizo culture of the region, they retained their Quechua language and a few remnants of their highlands culture. Studies of blood typing and other biological characteristics support the fact that the Quechua of Lamas and of Andahuaylas have the same genetic background (Frisancho, Borkan, & Klayman, 1975). The families are farmers and exist in a subsistence economy.

The Schools

Schools in Peru are not well-equipped. According to the latest available statistics, the value of the classroom materials and other nonsalary items in Peruvian schools averages approximately $3 per pupil (Heyneman, 1984). In the United States, the average is approximately $220 per pupil. Expenditures for the Quechua schools are likely to be well below the national average. The schools we visited in Lima had little equipment and the school buildings were run down; many windows in the schools were broken and sections of the buildings sometimes were without a roof. Conditions in Andahuaylas were somewhat better; for example, all of the classrooms had a blackboard and in nearly 80% of the classrooms there were pictures and maps. The schools in Lamas tended to be in stark buildings with little equipment or furniture. Not every classroom had a blackboard, fewer than one in five had maps or pictures, and textbooks were not available for every child.

The schools in the El Ermitano *barriada* had many students and many children were enrolled in each class. The average class contained 47 pupils. Individual schools in the less densely populated rural regions enrolled fewer children; nevertheless, the average class size was also large: forty in Andahuaylas and 38 in Lamas. The average educational level of teachers in all three locations was equivalent to a junior college education. It is difficult to lure teachers to the rural schools. As a result, most of the rural teachers (94% in Andahuaylas and 87% in Lamas) were natives of the region. Large cities, in contrast, hold great attraction for teachers from all over the country. This is reflected in the fact that only 31% of the teachers in Lima were natives of Lima.

Recruiting Children

This report describes the performance of 6- to 8-year-olds who had not attended school or who were enrolled in the first grade. The 421 children in the present study were nearly evenly divided according to location of residence, sex, and school attendance. The schooled and nonschooled children differed little in age; the mean age was 7.2 years for the schooled group, and 7.0 years for the nonschooled group. The study began after the children had attended school for approximately 6 months.

In each location we tested as many of the children as we could find who were within the range of ages we included in the study. It is obviously easier to locate children who are enrolled in school than children who are not enrolled. Nevertheless, finding subjects who were not in school was not an unusually arduous task. Our procedure was to send a person to the neighborhoods or villages to locate families with a child of the proper age. Once one child in a village or school had participated in the study, other children were eager to volunteer. The test materials were interesting, the children had the undivided attention of an adult, and they were given snacks and small gifts for their participation. All examiners were Peruvians and, when appropriate, were bilingual in Spanish and Quechua. The examiners lived in the villages during the time they conducted the testing and became familiar figures to the adults and children through daily contact. Residents of El Ermitano were equally familiar with the examiners through their daily visits to the *barriada*.

Parents were asked why they sent their children to school. They explained that their goals were to enable the children to improve their lives by learning to read, write, and speak Spanish, and to learn about numbers and computation so they would be able to function effectively in commercial activities and not be deceived.

Why did some families not send their child to school? The reasons differed in each location. In Lima, the majority of the parents said it was because they thought the child was too young. In Andahuaylas, parents either said they thought the child was too young or the child's help was needed at home. Lamas parents also said they needed their child's help at home, and a few said they thought their child was too young.

The Tests

Achievement Tests. Because there were no standardized achievement tests for reading and mathematics in Peru, it was necessary for us to devise our own. We did this after analyzing the textbooks used in Peruvian schools. The reading test included 49 items of increasing difficulty. The first items required the child to read letters, words, and clauses. Later items tested for comprehension by asking the children to select one of three pictures described by a word or phrase or to answer questions about the content of a few simple sentences. All reading textbooks in Peruvian schools are in Spanish, so the reading test was written in Spanish.

The 30 items in the mathematics test evaluated the child's ability to count, to understand the concept of more and less, to read numbers, and to solve oral word problems and written computation problems.

Cognitive Tasks. Cognitive tasks also had to be constructed. The challenge was to include tasks that covered a broad range of cognitive abilities, that were interesting, culturally appropriate, and reliable. Our final battery contained 21 tasks, but we limit our discussion here to a representative sample of 8. The following paragraphs contain brief descriptions of the tasks.

1. *General information.* The test was similar to the general information tests commonly included in tests of intelligence. The answers to the questions were not necessarily taught directly in the first year of school, but depended on information that could be absorbed from everyday experience.
2. *Concept formation.* The concept formation task consisted of three parts: initial learning, a test for transfer, and a test of whether the child had learned to respond on the basis of a generalized concept rather than to specific stimuli. The stimuli were pictures of familiar fruits, flowers, and birds.
3. *Seriation.* The seriation tasks were of the types commonly used in Piagetian studies; the child was required to organize an array of objects according to one dimension, such as length, and according to two dimensions, such as color and number.
4. *Story memory.* The child heard a short story about two children and then was asked questions about what had been read.
5. *Memory tasks.* In two memory tasks (memory for digits and auditory memory), the child was asked to repeat what the examiner demonstrated—a list of numbers or a series of taps separated by long and short pauses. In the memory for movements task, sequences of bodily movements were demonstrated or described to the child and the child was asked to repeat them. In the visual memory task, the child was shown a scene composed of an array of miniature animals, objects, and people. The scene was then covered with a cloth and the child was asked to recall the items that had been seen. On a second trial with different stimuli the scene was described rather than displayed to the child.

Test Results

Two aspects of the results of the achievement and cognitive tasks are of special interest. We asked if performance differed according to whether or not the children attended school, and then whether the effects were similar among the three locations. We asked these questions initially about the achievement tests and then about the cognitive tasks.

Achievement Tests. All of the nonschooled children in Andahuaylas and Lamas proved to be illiterate. They were unable to read even a few letters of the alphabet. Only in Lima, where there is easy access to printed materials, were any of the nonschooled children capable of reading some of the alphabet or a few words.

Schooled children in both Lima and Andahuaylas responded correctly to some of the items on the reading test. Children in Lima could name many of the letters and some children in both Lima and Andahuaylas were capable of both reading a few words and responding correctly to a few of the comprehension questions. Although the children in Lamas had attended school the same length of time as the children in Lima and Andahuaylas, their knowledge was limited to reading a few letters of the alphabet. The most interesting aspect of the results for the reading test is not the fact that the schooled children in Lima and Andahuaylas were capable of reading as much as they did, but that the instruction received by the children in Lamas proved to be so unproductive. We attribute the low scores of the Lamas children to the generally poor quality of education provided for the Quechua children in the *selva* and to the lack of home support for education. Children in Lamas have limited opportunities to interact with their parents. Quechua farmers must go deep into the rain forest in order to find cultivatable land. As a result, these small plots of land (*chacras*) are far from the villages where they make their homes. Because the *chacras* are so far away, young children are typically left in the village during the week in the care of older siblings or village elders while their parents work on the *chacras*. Consequently, young children generally are able to interact with their parents only on weekends and cannot share their daily school experiences with them.

The children, especially in Lima, were more knowledgeable about the rudiments of mathematics than they were about the fundamentals of reading. This was due in part to the fact that children play a contributing role in the economy of families residing in the *barriadas*. From a young age, children from the *barriadas* in Lima participate in commercial activities that require calculation, such as selling recyclable materials they have collected, or personal items, such as foodstuffs and combs. Thus, even nonschooled children in Lima have some mathematical skills, such as counting, knowing number values, and solving simple word problems. In Andahuaylas and Lamas, nonschooled children could barely count and schooled children could do only the simplest word problems. However, schooling yielded greater benefit for the mathematics scores of the Andahuaylas first graders than for the children in the other two locations. Knowledge of mathematics in the farming communities of the *sierra* apparently more strongly depends on schooling than it does in the rural regions of the *selva*.

Cognitive Tasks. Schooled and nonschooled children differed significantly in their performance on all but two of the cognitive tasks: memory for digits and visual memory. The scores for the children who attended school were higher than those who did not attend school. Performance on all of the cognitive tasks also differed significantly according to where the children lived. The children from Lamas received the lowest scores on every task; only in auditory memory did their scores even approach those obtained by the children in Lima or Andahuaylas. However, the performance of the children from Andahuaylas indicates that rural residence was not consistently associated with lower cognitive scores. Rural children in Andahuaylas were as effective as the urban Lima children on many of the tasks. Furthermore, schooling had a similar effect on cognitive performance in all three locations. That is, after 6 months of attending school, the scores of children in Lamas had increased as much as those of children in Andahuaylas and Lima. This is in contrast with the effect of schooling on academic performance. As discussed earlier, the amount of academic knowledge gained through schooling depended on where the children lived.

Background Factors

Data from the interviews with the children's mothers made it possible to isolate characteristics of the three locations that might be related to the children's performance. Our purpose in presenting these data is to describe differences in background factors in the three locations and then to determine which of the factors, along with school attendance, were predictive of the children's performance.

In general, Lima and Andahuaylas appeared to provide children with more stimulating environments for cognitive development than Lamas. It is not surprising that this should be the case in a large city like Lima, but it is less obvious why this was also true for Andahuaylas. Several lines of evidence indicate that families in the *sierra* maintain a complex indigenous culture that is rich in history, handicrafts, and the arts, and in social and religious practices. Families in the *selva,* however, have retained little of the cultural heritage of the highlands, and they have not created a stimulating new culture. There are several indications in our interviews with the children's parents that the Lamas children encounter a relatively impoverished environment.

We sought to describe the quality of the children's homes by asking the person who interviewed the mother to determine how many of the following 10 items were present in the home: electricity, radio, television, newspapers, books, children's books, machines, pictures, toys, and portraits. Children in Lamas clearly had limited access to these potential sources of stimulation. The mean numbers of items were 6.6 in Lima, 3.6 in Andahuaylas, and 1.3 in Lamas.

Another measure of the potential of the home environment for cognitive stimulation is the parents' level of education. None of the groups of parents had attended school for more than a few years. Mothers spent fewer years in school than the fathers, but neither mothers nor fathers in any of the locations had, on the average, completed elementary school. The range was from an average of .1 year for Lamas mothers to 4.9 years for Lima fathers. The percentage of parents who were literate paralleled the data for attendance at school. Literacy was highest in Lima (98% of fathers and 65% of mothers), lowest in Lamas (60% of fathers and 5% of mothers), and intermediate in Andahuaylas (69% of fathers and 25% of mothers).

In addition to data related to the quality of the home and the educational level of the mothers and fathers, we also obtained information about parental efforts to teach their child. Mothers were asked what things they or other adults had attempted to teach the child from among a list of 9 items described to them. The list included colors, numbers, letters, money, seasons, riddles, games, reading, and stories. The means for the three locations were much more similar than those for the other environmental variables: 6.4 for Lima, 4.8 for Andahuaylas, and 5.7 for Lamas.

The background variables just described are often found in the child development literature to be predictive of children's performance in school and on cognitive tasks. We sought to determine whether this would be the case for the Peruvian children. Regression analyses were conducted, whereby an evaluation was made of the independent contribution of these and other variables to the prediction of the children's scores on the two achievement tests and the eight cognitive tasks. Seven independent variables were included in the analyses. In addition to three of the variables just discussed (quality of the home, father's education, and parental teaching) and whether or not the child attended school, two variables related to the child's residence were included: Lima versus Lamas, and Andahuaylas versus Lamas. Information about one other variable completed the list. This was a measure of the children's nutritional status, a variable that has been found to have a significant influence on cognitive development (see, e.g., Freeman, Klein, Townsend, & Lechtig, 1980). The measure of nutritional status we used was one commonly included in studies of nutrition: the circumference of the upper arm (see Frisancho, 1981).

The regression analyses for the achievement tests and cognitive tasks revealed that among extremely poor children from an indigenous culture in a developing country, macrovariables such as whether or not they attend school, their residence in the shanty-towns of the city or in the remote countryside, and their nutritional status have a stronger relation to cognitive development than more subtle variables, such as parental education and the quality of the home. In fact, none of the partial correlations derived from home quality and father's education were significant, whereas most of the other partial correlations were significant. The cognitive scores of these children were associated with efforts made by adults to provide out-of-school teaching in only three analyses.

These results are only partially in line with those typically found in more developed countries, where variables such as parental education and the quality of the home have strong relationships with children's cognitive development. This situation is not unreasonable. The correlates of cognitive development may not be the same when nearly all children have adequate nutrition and when the conditions for cognitive development are generally more favorable than those that exist among poor residents of third world countries such as Peru. It is to three of these industrialized countries that we now turn. The United States, Taiwan, and Japan have compulsory elementary education, high standards of living, and well-educated adult populations. The conditions under which children live in these three locations provide a striking contrast with those found in the *barriadas* and remote villages of Peru. All but the most severely handicapped children attend elementary school; children have adequate nutrition, clothing, and housing, and daily life in large cities provides a wide array of interesting stimulation.

Study 2: Chinese, Japanese, and U.S. Children

Research Locations

Taipei (Taiwan). Taipei is a modern industrial city whose residents have attained a relatively high standard of living and broad educational opportunities. A blend of both modern and traditional cultures exists in the city. The organization of schools in Taiwan is similar to that in the United States. Children enter school in September after their sixth birthday, and attendance is compulsory through the ninth grade. As in the United States, over 99% of 6-year-olds attend elementary schools to which they are assigned according to the district within which their family resides. The range in socioeconomic status of the families and educational level of the parents included within each school is much greater than in the United States. Although kindergartens and preschools are mainly privately owned and attendance is not compulsory, approximately a third of the children in our Taipei sample had attended preschool and 81% of the children had spent at least 1 year in kindergarten.

Sendai (Japan). Sendai was chosen as the site for our studies because it is a more traditional Japanese city than cities near Tokyo that have been strongly influenced by the West. Also, according to the opinions of individuals who know both Japan and the United States, it is the city that has a cultural and economic status within Japan that parallels that of the city we chose in the United States: Minneapolis. Universal public education is provided. Children spend 6 years in elementary school, followed by 3 years in middle school and 3 years in high school. Kindergarten is not obligatory in

Japan, but 98% of the 6-year-olds in this study attended kindergarten, a percentage similar to that in the United States. Unlike Minneapolis and Taipei, where the school year begins in September and ends in early summer, the school year in Sendai begins in April and continues, with several holidays, until the middle of March of the following year.

Minneapolis. The Minneapolis metropolitan area was chosen as the site of our research in the United States. Minneapolis residents tend to come from White, native-born, English-speaking, middle-class families. We assumed that these factors would provide an advantageous linguistic and cultural environment for cognitive development and academic achievement. If children's scores in Minneapolis compared unfavorably with those of the Chinese and Japanese children, even less favorable comparisons would be likely to be found in other sites in the United States where greater proportions of children speak English as a second language, come from economically disadvantaged homes, and have parents whose cultural backgrounds diverge from the typical middle-class milieu to which U.S. elementary school curricula are addressed.

The Children

It is essential in cross-national studies that the same procedures be used in each culture for selecting the children to be studied. The approach we chose was to sample first by schools and then to sample children within these schools. On the basis of advice from educational authorities in each city, 10 schools were chosen as being a representative sample of schools. From each school, two first-grade and two fifth-grade classrooms were randomly selected to yield the full sample of 20 classrooms at each grade. Tests and interviews were given in each grade to target samples of 240 children and their mothers in each city. These target samples of children were constituted by randomly selecting six boys and six girls from each classroom. The kindergarten children attended 24 kindergartens in each city. For our target sample we randomly chose six boys and six girls from each of the 24 classrooms.

The Tests

Reading and mathematics tests were given to the children at all levels of schooling. The procedure for constructing the tests was the same as that described in the preceding study, but more difficult items were included at the upper levels of the tests. There are no standardized curricula for kindergartens in any of the three locations, thus we used materials that researchers and kindergarten teachers in the three locations agreed were appropriate for testing children of kindergarten age. The items included matching and identifying letters (or symbols for the syllabary of Japanese or for the phonetic system of Chinese), decoding simple words, and comprehending simple phrases and sentences. The reading test for elementary school children included sight reading of vocabulary and comprehension of text. The kindergarten mathematics test evaluated the children's ability to count, to recognize numbers, and to solve simple arithmetic word problems. The mathematics test for the elementary school children included 70 questions, including both computation problems and word problems.

Each phase of the study occurred at the same point in the school year of each city. This is an important factor because only if the length of schooling in elementary schools is comparable in the cities could the performance of children in the three locations be compared meaningfully.

Cognitive Tasks. As in the preceding study, it was necessary to develop our own battery of cognitive tasks. Five tasks were constructed for the kindergarteners and 10 for the elementary school children. Only the tasks given to both kindergarten and elementary school children are discussed here. These are general information, vocabulary, and verbal-spatial skills.

1. *General information.* The test was comparable to the general information test developed for Study 1.
2. *Vocabulary.* Children were asked to define words. The words were obtained from the lexicon compiled by us of all words contained in the readers used in the three cities, popular books and magazines for children from each culture, and the Chinese, Japanese, and U.S. versions of the Wechsler Intelligence Scale for Children-Revised (WISC-R) test of intelligence. The final list contained words that were judged to be of equal difficulty in the three languages, were considered to have precisely the same meaning in the three languages, and could be scored reliably.
3. *Verbal-spatial skills.* The test of verbal-spatial skills was designed to tap children's ability to understand and follow verbal directions. For example, in the kindergarten study the examiner asked the child, "Which one is a picture of a line above three triangles?" (The child had been given practice with the terms before being tested.) The child chose from one of four pictures. In one of the more complex items given to the elementary school children, the child was shown a square and was told, "Inside the square draw a cross that divides the square into four parts. In the upper right box draw a small circle and in the lower left box draw a small triangle."

Test Results

The first comparisons of interest concern the relative status of children in the three locations on the achievement tests and cognitive tasks over the

6-year period. Average scores are not the most effective way to compare scores in different tests given at different periods of development, for the average score and the variability of scores would be expected to differ at different grades. Transforming raw scores into scores with the use of same unit of measurement (standard deviation units) helps to make comparisons across tasks, grades, and cultures easier to understand. These transformations were made for each test at each grade. A child's z score for a test was based on the mean and standard deviation of the distribution derived from the scores of children from all three cultures.

There is little evidence that schooling acted as an equalizer of differences in achievement among children living in these three locations. Reading scores were as widely separated at fifth grade as they had been in kindergarten (see Fig. 11.1), and mathematics scores diverged even more widely at fifth grade than they had earlier. Chinese children received the highest scores in reading, and both Chinese and Japanese children greatly surpassed the U.S. children in mathematics.

The lower panels of Fig. 11.1 illustrate the changes that occurred in the children's scores on the cognitive tasks. Scores for the kindergarten children in the three cities were widely separated, but by fifth grade the differences became much smaller.

What do these data say about the effect of schooling on cross-national differences in achievement and cognitive development? These data indicate that successive years of schooling do not reduce cross-national differences in academic achievement, but do appear to have a leveling effect on cognitive development.

Correlates of Achievement

Variations in the children's nutritional status or in the stimulation available at home from items such as books or radios—at least within the ranges included in the Taipei, Sendai, and Minneapolis families—are unlikely to be strongly related to children's academic achievement or cognitive development. Nearly all children have adequate nutrition and nearly all homes have such items as books and radios. Other variables, including parental education, parental beliefs, and children's motivation, are much more likely to play a significant role in children's development. We have discussed these variables in detail elsewhere (see Stevenson et al., 1990), but for our purposes here we illustrate the effects by reference to only two of these variables: parental education and children's motivation.

Recall that parental education was not significantly related to the Peruvian children's scores on the achievement tests or cognitive tasks. For example, the correlations in Lima between mothers' education and the first graders' reading and mathematics scores were .06 and .08, respectively. The corre-

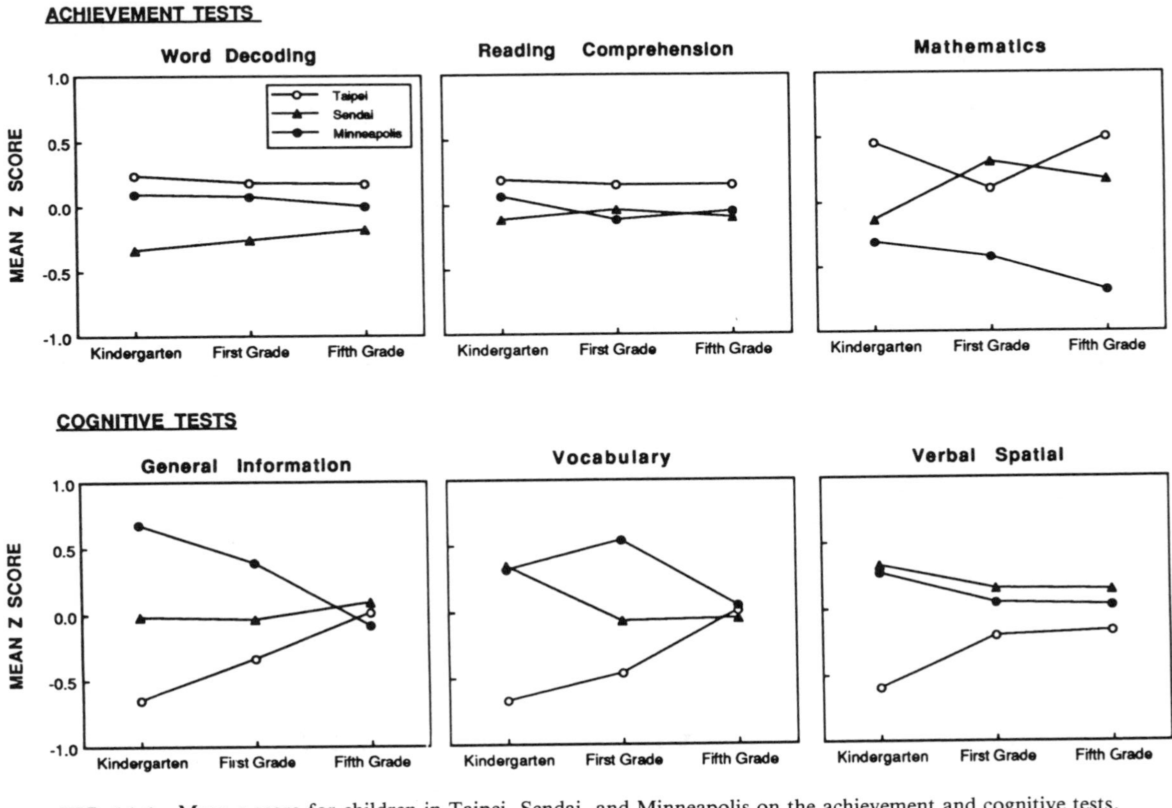

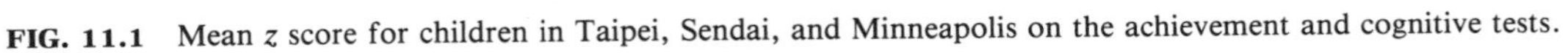

FIG. 11.1 Mean z score for children in Taipei, Sendai, and Minneapolis on the achievement and cognitive tests.

sponding correlations with fathers' education were .17 and .10. Correlations with scores on the cognitive tasks were also very low: the median correlation with mothers' education was −.04, and with fathers' education, .03. These findings were replicated in Andahuaylas and Lamas. However, when the same correlations were computed for first graders in Taipei, Sendai, and Minneapolis, the median correlation was .30 for the achievement tests and .27 for the cognitive scores. Thus, in contrast to the findings for Peru, variation in the educational level attained by the parents was significantly related to children's performance in Japan, Taiwan, and the United States.

Children's motivation for schooling is a second factor that is often found to be predictive of their academic achievement. We obtained two measures of this variable from our interviews with the mothers in Taipei, Sendai, and Minneapolis. Mothers rated their child's motivation for achievement compared to other children and were asked to rate how much their child liked school. A composite variable constructed from these two ratings was correlated with the children's test scores. The correlations at first grade were .33 for Minneapolis, .43 for Taipei, and .22 for Sendai; the corresponding correlations at fifth grade were .18, .26, and .33, p's $< .05$.

Our point in describing these sets of correlations is to illustrate how variables that may describe minimal effects among children within the context of poverty may have significant effect on achievement of children living in more affluent environments. We should also point out that variables such as children's motivation for achievement may not only account for variability in academic achievement within a culture, but may help to explain differences in achievement between cultures. For example, the pattern whereby the scores of U.S. children tended to decline and Chinese children tended to increase between kindergarten and fifth grade is mirrored in the ratings for motivation and liking school. The ratings made by the U.S. mothers declined during these years, whereas those made by the Chinese mothers increased.

Comparisons of Peruvian, Chinese, Japanese, and U.S. Children

When we planned the two studies we did not expect to compare their results, but in assessing academic achievement and cognitive development of young children it is inevitable that the studies would contain tests covering similar topics and comparable material. For example, any evaluation of academic achievement of elementary school children would include a test of reading. Moreover, regardless of the language being read, a reading test must begin with an assessment of the child's knowledge about the simplest elements of the written language and progress to evaluations of the child's comprehension of text. Similarly, analyses of young children's knowledge of mathematics necessarily must contain items tapping fundamental skills, such as the ability to count, perform elementary mathematical operations, and solve simple word problems. The same is true in assessing young children's cognitive abilities; there is a limited number of cognitive processes that can be evaluated.

It turned out that in addition to tests of reading and mathematics, three other tasks in the two studies contained similar, and sometimes identical items: general information, story memory, and auditory memory. It was possible, therefore, to compare the scores of first graders on these tests across the six locations: Lima, Andahuaylas, Lamas, Taipei, Sendai, and Minneapolis. The results appear in Fig. 11.2.

The reading tests had been given to the Taipei, Sendai, and Minneapolis children after 4 months of schooling, and the mathematics tests, after 6 months, which was also the average for the Peruvian testing period. The contrasts between what the Quechua children had learned and what the children in the other cities had learned was startling. First graders in Taipei, Sendai, and Minneapolis were much more capable in reading and in mathematics than the first graders in any of the locations in Peru. This was true for reading whether the subtest involved naming letters, reading words, or comprehending what was read. In mathematics, there were large disparities in knowledge of mathematical concepts and operations. This is evident in the average scores and in the data from items that were similar in the two mathematics tests. The percentage of first graders in each location who were able to respond correctly to each of the 10 similar items is indicated in Table 11.1, where the items from the Peruvian test are listed first, followed by the items (in parentheses) from the test given to the Chinese, Japanese, and U.S. children. Peruvian first graders were less adept than the first graders in Asia or in the United States at counting (Items 1 and 2), making comparisons of number (Items 3 and 4), solving a word problem (Item 5), and in performing the operations of addition, subtraction, and multiplication (the remaining items). Lamas first graders could do none of the problems involving mathematical operations, and the children in Lima and Andahuaylas were much less capable of solving these problems than were the Asian and U.S. children.

A very different picture emerges when comparisons are made of the three cognitive tests, where children from the six locations demonstrated much more similar levels of competence. In fact, the scores of children in Andahuaylas and Lima differed very little from those of children in Sendai and Taipei. Children in Lamas tended to receive lower scores than the other children, and children in Minneapolis tended to receive higher scores. We believe that the Minneapolis first graders did well on general information items because of the greater tendency of U.S. mothers to read to their young children, engage them in social conversation, and to take them on excur-

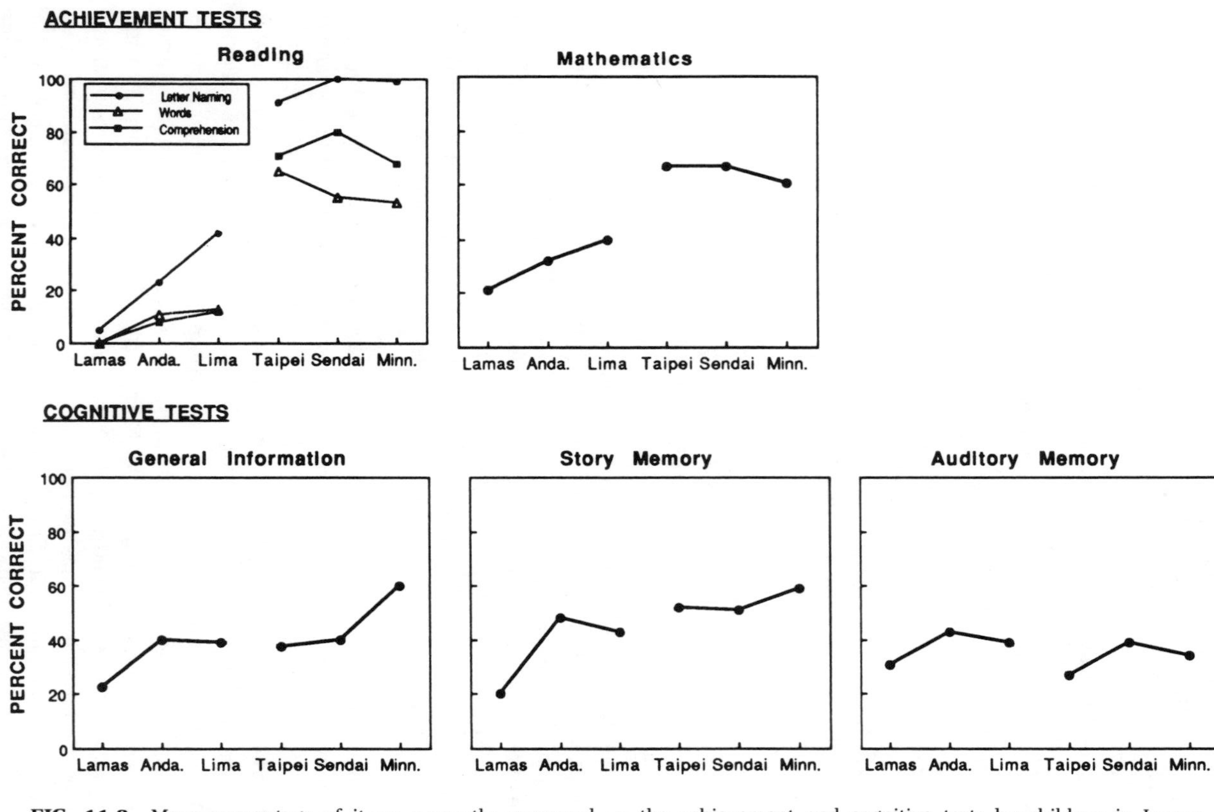

FIG. 11.2 Mean percentage of items correctly answered on the achievement and cognitive tests by children in Lamas, Andahuaylas, Lima, Taipei, Sendai, and Minneapolis.

TABLE 11.1
Percentage of Subjects Responding Correctly to Items on the Mathematics Test

	Lamas	*Andahuaylas*	*Lima*	*Taipei*	*Sendai*	*Minneapolis*
1. Counting 3 cubes (4 dots)	83	85	93	100	100	99
2. Counting 15 cubes (17 dots)	40	55	83	95	87	84
3. 4 pigs vs. 5 chickens (4 vs. 2 dots)	51	77	74	100	100	100
4. 6 vs. 4 (13 vs. 7)	37	54	79	97	99	97
5. 5 + 6 (5 + 7)[a]	0	23	33	61	82	65
6. 6 + 2 (5 + 3)	0	16	25	97	98	94
7. 3 × 3 (3 × 2)[b]	0	4	7	77	69	45
8. 32 + 24 (19 + 25)	0	5	1	34	24	16
9. 4 × 2 (4 × 9)	0	0	4	2	4	4
10. 31-14 (62-36)	0	0	0	8	5	1
N	65	71	71	241	240	237

[a]This item was a word problem in both studies.
[b]This item was a word problem for Taipei, Sendai, and Minneapolis children.

sions—activities in which children are more likely to build up a fund of general information (see Stevenson et al., 1990). As was shown earlier in Fig. 11.1, however, this advantage disappears by the time these children are in the fifth grade.

Items from the general information test can also be analyzed in greater detail; four items were identical on the two versions of the test. As can be seen in Table 11.2, children in Andahuaylas and Lima approached or exceeded the levels of performance of the Asian children on these items. Lamas children did less well. Dogs are common in Lamas, but only half of the children could answer the question of how many legs a dog has. Few Lamas children knew what plants need in order to grow. This finding appears to reflect their limited opportunities to participate in life at the *chacras*.

These two sets of findings are very provocative. The level of cognitive development of first graders from very poor indigenous families in both rural and urban settings in Peru appears to be comparable to that of children

TABLE 11.2
Percentage of Subjects Responding Correctly or Partially Correctly to Items on the Test of General Information

	Lamas	*Andahuaylas*	*Lima*	*Taipei*	*Sendai*	*Minneapolis*
Number of legs a dog has	46	72	89	86	83	97
Things plants need to grow	15	93	69	49	50	98
Why humans can't live under water	34	25	28	15	30	30
What pumps blood	0	17	3	5	8	19
N	65	71	71	241	240	237

in large urban centers of industrialized countries, but their academic achievement does not. In other words, the Peruvian children appeared to possess the requisite cognitive abilities to benefit from schooling, but the academic environment provided by their schools and their homes did not enable them to make the progress in mastering the academic subjects of which they were capable. This conclusion is based on the results of a limited number of tests. Nevertheless, it suggests that, except in the case of the seemingly extreme cognitive deprivation experienced by the children in Lamas, cognitive development of young children proceeds more similarly in widely different environments than formal learning in school.

CONCLUSIONS

The effects we have been discussing are those that occur with small amounts of schooling—about 6 months in the case of the first graders. Even so, schooling showed a significant effect on both the achievement and cognitive scores of children in all of the locations included in the study. The results are therefore in line with those reported in earlier studies. As we have seen, however, it is critical that we consider the influence of culture in interpreting these results.

The children who attended school had learned something about reading and mathematics: a great deal in the case of children in Japan, Taiwan, and the United States, and far less in the case of children from the three locations in Peru. When we examined the differences in scores on the cognitive tasks between schooled and nonschooled children in Peru, we found a smaller effect than appeared for the achievement test scores.

Can we interpret the differences between the scores of the schooled and nonschooled children as being due to the effects of schooling, or were the schooled children brighter than the nonschooled children even before they entered school? We cannot answer the question with complete confidence, but we do know that schooling had a significantly positive relation to the achievement and cognitive scores even after the effects of such variables as home quality, parental education, nutritional status, and parental efforts to teach the child had been accounted for. In view of the nonsignificant contribution of the more subtle environmental variables such as parental education to these children's scores, it seems doubtful that the inclusion of other variables would have reduced the effects of schooling.

Schooling did not have equivalent effects on academic achievement across the different cultural settings. The impact of schooling was much less for impoverished indigenous children living in small villages in the tropical rain forest than for children from the slums of a large city or for children in a society that had preserved many parts of its ancient highlands culture. Similarly, urban children in Taiwan, Japan, and the United States differed significantly in what they had learned about mathematics over the 5 years they had attended school. In other words, the effect of schooling on academic achievement varied according to the culture in which the children lived. The only exception was in the case of reading in the industrialized societies; differences were as great during kindergarten as they were in fifth grade. The different effects of schooling for reading and mathematics may be due to the fact that all three of the industrialized societies give strong emphasis to the importance of reading, but mathematics is much more strongly emphasized in Asian societies than in the United States.

The effects of schooling followed a different pattern when the cognitive tasks were considered. Scores for both the schooled and nonschooled children differed from each other to the same degree in the three indigenous societies. Quite a different effect appeared for the industrialized societies. The greater the amount of schooling, the smaller the differences between the scores of the children from the three societies. Schooling thus had a leveling effect on the cognitive development of children in the large industrialized cities, whereas it did not have this effect on the children in Peru. These comparisons were not strictly analogous; in the one case they were between children who did and did not attend school, and in the second case they were between children who attended school for different amounts of time. Fortunately, we can respond to this point by referring to additional data collected in Peru. An older sample of children—children between 7 and 12 years of age—had attended school for 1, 2, or 3 years (see Stevenson & Chen, 1989). Differences in the achievement scores increased across the 3 years, but differences in the cognitive measures were no greater at third grade than they had been at first grade.

The background factors found to be predictive of children's achievement and cognitive scores were strongly influenced by the society in which the children lived. The factors that were effective in the industrialized societies were much more subtle than those factors in the indigenous societies. Whereas children in poor, indigenous families differ greatly in their nutritional status, differences in factors such as the child's motivation for achievement are more likely to differentiate families in industrialized societies—at least among families of the types included in this study. As a consequence, different sources of variation turned out to be the effective predictors of performance in the two types of societies.

Perhaps the most provocative finding was the equivalence in the cognitive scores of the first graders in Peru and in Taiwan, Japan, and the United States. Despite enormous differences in the environmental conditions under which they lived, the children had similar scores on several measures of cognitive skills. Cognitive skills, it should be noted, can be more readily acquired in an incidental manner than the academic skills that must be learned through formal instruction.

Or, perhaps the Peruvian children performed poorly on the achievement tests because the Quechua families did not perceive the utility of academic skills as readily as families from urban industrialized societies. It is not immediately obvious to poor families from developing countries why children should learn the abstract materials that are taught in the formal school setting. Learning represents not only differences in opportunity but also in perceived need. The need for formal education is more evident to children and parents in urban centers of industrialized societies. What children in less developed societies may learn in school are general skills, such as how to follow verbal instructions and pay attention, rather than the formal content of the curriculum. It does not appear that the Quechua children lacked the cognitive skills necessary for academic success. They possessed the cognitive abilities necessary to benefit from schooling to a greater degree than was evident in their scores on the reading and mathematics tests.

As is the case with many studies of child development, we end with more complexity, but also with greater clarity than we possessed before we began the studies. Schooling is not a simple or readily understood variable, and general discussions of the influence of schooling on cognitive development are meaningless unless cultural factors are taken into account. The correlates and benefits of attending school differ greatly between developing countries and industrialized societies, and examination of these correlates must consider both the physical and cultural environments in which these developments occur. Schooling appears to be of benefit to children both directly in teaching them formal knowledge, but also in hastening their cognitive development. We need to know how these effects occur and whether protracted schooling results in levels of cognitive functioning that would otherwise be impossible. But it is unnecessary to go to other countries to investigate these phenomena. Subcultures within the United States differ greatly in many of the ways that we have found to be important for children's academic achievement and cognitive development. We know that the achievement gap between children in these U.S. subcultures widens as the children grow older. It is critical, therefore, that we have a better understanding of the interplay between home, school, and culture in producing these effects.

ACKNOWLEDGMENTS

We wish to thank our collaborators in each research site, the examiners, research assistants, parents, and their children for their contribution to this research. Study 1 was supported by grants from the W. T. Grant Foundation and the National Science Foundation. Study 2 was funded by the National Institute of Mental Health. The writing of this chapter was supported by a grant from the National Science Foundation (Grant MDR 8751390).

REFERENCES

Anderson, R. C., Spiro, R. J., & Montague, W. F. (Eds.). (1977). *Schooling and the acquisition of knowledge*. Hillsdale, NJ: Lawrence Erlbaum Associates.

Cahan, S., & Cohen, N. (1989). Age versus schooling effects on intelligence development. *Child Development, 60,* 1239–1249.

Freeman, H. E., Klein, R. E., Townsend, J. W., & Lechtig, A. (1980). Nutrition and cognitive development among rural Guatemalan children. *American Journal of Public Health, 70,* 1277–1285.

Frisancho, A. R. (1981). New norms of upper limb fat and muscle areas for assessment of nutritional status. *American Journal of Clinical Nutrition, 34,* 2540–2545.

Frisancho, A. R., Borkan, G. A., & Klayman, J. E. (1975). Pattern of growth of lowland and highland Peruvian Quechua of similar genetic composition. *Human Biology, 47,* 233–243.

Ginsburg, H. (1977). Some problems in the study of schooling and cognition. *Quarterly Newsletter of the Institute of Comparative Human Development, 1,* 7–10.

Greenfield, P., & Lave, J. (1982). Cognitive aspects of informal education. In D. Wagner & H. W. Stevenson (Eds.), *Cultural perspectives on child development* (pp. 181–207). San Francisco: W. H. Freeman.

Heyneman, S. (1984, February). *Two thirds of the world's students: Intellectual development and schools in developing countries.* Talk given at the Center for Advanced Study in the Behavioral Sciences, Stanford, CA.

Heyns, B. (1987). Schooling and cognitive development: Is there a season for learning? *Child Development, 58,* 1151–1160.

Irwin, M., Engle, P. L., Yarbrough, C., Klein, R. E., & Townsend, J. (1978). The relationship of prior ability and family characteristics to school attendance and school achievement in rural Guatemala. *Child Development, 49,* 415–427.

Rogoff, B. (1981). Schooling and the development of cognitive skills. In H. C. Triandis & A. Heron (Eds.), *Handbook of cross-cultural psychology* (Vol. 4, pp. 233–294). Boston: Allyn & Bacon.

Saxe, G. B. (1988). The mathematics of street vendors. *Child Development, 59,* 1415–1425.

Scribner, S., & Cole, M. (1973). Cognitive consequences of formal and informal education. *Science, 182,* 953–959.

Stevenson, H. W., & Chen, C. (1989). Schooling and achievement: A study of Peruvian children. *International Journal of Educational Research, 13,* 883–894.

Stevenson, H. W., Lee, S. Y., Chen, C., Stigler, J. W., Hsu, C. C., & Kitamura, S. (1990). Contexts of achievement: A study of American, Chinese, and Japanese children. *Monographs of the Society for Research in Child Development, 55,* Serial No. 221.

Super, C. (1977, April). *Who goes to school and what do they learn?* Paper presented at meetings of the Society for Research in Child Development, New Orleans.

Wagner, D. A. (1982). Ontogeny in the study of culture and cognition. In D. W. Wagner & H. W. Stevenson (Eds.), *Cultural perspectives on child development* (pp. 105–123). San Francisco: W. H. Freeman.

CHAPTER 12

Directors of Development: A Play in an Unknown Number of Acts

ROBERT J. STERNBERG
Yale University

ACT 1

The Scene: A Classroom in 1965

Professor Heredita walks out on the stage, which is a college classroom. The professor has thick eyeglasses, a long beard, and a decidedly studious look. He turns to his class, consisting of 35 fairly bright, usually hard-working students. He starts to talk:

Professor Heredita: Today we are going to learn about children's thinking, and especially, why it is that some children think better than others. The question is: "What is it that brighter children inherit from their parents that less bright children do not inherit?" The answer is: "Intelligence."

Brighter children are more capable thinkers by virtue of their having higher intelligence quotients, which are measured by IQ tests. IQ tests measure a broad span of abilities to think well, and when these abilities are assessed collectively, we are able to get a very good reading on what that child's potential will be, both as a learner in school and later as a success in life. People's IQs are not equal, of course: They vary considerably. As you may know, the mean IQ is 100, and the standard deviation is about 15, meaning that roughly two thirds of people have IQs between 85 and 115. Some children come into the world with truly superior amounts of intelligence, which are generally indicated by IQs of 130 and above. Other children, unfortunately, come into the world mentally retarded, with IQs below

70. Whereas Francis Galton, Lewis Terman, and others, have shown that intellectual genius is transmitted through families, mental retardation is usually, but not always, transmitted through families. Occasionally, there will be damage to the child, either in the uterus or after birth, such as severe head trauma caused by a near-fatal car accident.

Although intelligence is stable throughout the lifetime, IQ may vary slightly as a function of what we call *errors of measurement.* In other words, on a given day, there may be distracting influences in the testing room, or the person may have had a bad day, or the person may have his mind on something else. But these sources of error are simply *noise* in the equation, and if one were able to give a child an intelligence test over and over and over again, eventually we would obtain that child's *true score,* in other words, the correct measurement of what that child is able to accomplish in his life. In sum, the use of intelligence tests has enabled us to understand why it is that some children think better than others, and thus have put the study of cognitive development on a scientific footing.

ACT 2

The Scene: A Classroom in 1970

Professor Proportio enters the college classroom. He has a dignified but slightly rumpled look. His eyes are deep set and have a penetrating stare. He is an older gentleman, someone who has clearly been doing scholarly work for a very long time. He stands and faces the class:

Professor Proportio: Today we are going to study why it is that some children are brighter than others. In other words, what is it that results in some children thinking more clearly and more deeply than others? The question is: "To what extent is intellectual ability inherited, and to what extent is it environmental?" The answer is: "Intelligence is largely inherited."

Scientists who are interested in what makes some children brighter than others study the extent to which intelligence is inherited and the extent to which it is environmental. We used simply to assume that intelligence is hereditary. For example, as recently as 5 years ago when Professor Heredita taught this course, he simply assumed that intelligence must be inherited. We now no longer assume this, but use precise genetic techniques in order to assess the proportion of variation due to heredity and the proportion due to environment. We now know from studies by Cyril Burt and many others that intelligence is largely inherited. About 80% of the variation across children in their IQ test scores is due to genetic factors. This means 20% is not due to genetic factors. However, within this 20% is error of measurement and other factors that contribute instability, so that by the time we are done with dividing up the 20%, it appears that environment contributes relatively little to children's different performances in intellectual activities. Basically, this means that you are what your genes make you, and there is precious little that you can do about it. That is not to say that one can predict perfectly a child's level of intelligence from parental levels of intelligence. But certainly there is no better predictor.

ACT 3

The Scene: A Classroom in 1975

Professor Enviro enters the college classroom. He is young, bearded, and has a slightly hippy look. He wears sandals and looks like he needs a shave and a face wash. His hair is long and unkempt. The professor looks more like a social activist than a professor, and indeed he is. He turns to face his class and starts to speak:

Professor Enviro: Today we are going to discuss why it is that some children are smarter than others. All of you know that some children seem to be able to do intellectual things better than others: to learn to speak, to understand what is said to them, to read, to write, and so on. But why do we get these differences? The question is: "To what extent is intelligence an inherited attribute and to what extent is it environmentally determined?" The answer is: "Intelligence is determined largely by environmental factors in the child's life."

At one time we thought intelligence was inherited. But Leon Kamin's devastating analytic critique of the work of Cyril Burt and others has shown that there is no basis for the belief that the answer to the heredity–environment question is "heredity." On the contrary, the evidence in favor of the inheritance of intelligence is largely flawed. It appears that the heritability of intelligence is actually quite low, and there is now no real evidence to suggest that it is anything greater than zero. Some children are born into the privileged classes, and have many resources available to them. Others are born into slums and ghettos, and have virtually no resources available to them. Some children are educated in the finest schools, others receive poor educations or no education at all. Some children have parents who push them to read and to learn arithmetic before they ever start school, whereas others have parents who, if anything, discourage them from intellectual attainments before they start school. But, if one looks at the amazing variety of environmental factors that impinge on each child, it is easy to see why we would obtain individual differences in IQ scores. Moreover, many of us are even beginning to question just how much the IQ score tells us. After all, IQ tests themselves are culturally biased in that the people who write the questions themselves come from a certain culture and emphasize in their test questions the skills valued by the culture. So one could argue that not only is intelligence environmentally determined, but even our conceptions of what intelligence is are themselves environmentally determined. Surely we are not going to claim that our conception of what it means to be smart is something that we inherited from our parents and grandparents. In short, one of the surprises of modern psychological research has been that contrary to prior beliefs, intelligence is largely environmentally determined, not genetically determined.

ACT 4

The Scene: A Classroom in 1980

Professor Balanceo enters the typical college classroom. The professor is young, suave, well-groomed, and well-dressed. The 31 students in the class do not look at all like the students of 5 years ago. Their hair is shorter, and they are better dressed. They seem more attentive, and more eager to please the professor. They open their notebooks and get ready to take notes. Professor Balanceo starts to speak:

Professor Balanceo: Today we are going to study what it is that makes some children brighter than others. We all know that children show diverse levels of performance on tests of intellectual abilities. The question we seek to address today is simply why this is so. Let's get specific. The question is: "What proportion of variability in intelligence is inherited and what proportion is environmentally determined?" The answer is: "It appears that the proportions are roughly balanced, although we do not, and arguably cannot, know for sure."

Behavior geneticists are people who seek to understand the extent to which intelligence is inherited and the extent to which it is environmental. Moreover, they seek to give us some understanding of how the genes and how the environment affect intelligence. At one time, we believed that intelligence was almost exclusively inherited, due in part to faulty studies of the transmission of intelligence, and in a limited number of cases, even to falsification of data. Later, many of us came to believe, perhaps in reaction to the hereditarian view, that intelligence is almost exclusively environmental. The latest research shows, however, that the contributions of heredity and environment are roughly equal. In other words, we now understand that intelligence is a balance between the genes and the environment, and not merely a product of one or the other. We are no longer locked into the all-or-none views of the past. We have come a long way in our thinking, embracing a sort of dialectic where the need for extreme views is eventually realized to be unrealistic, and a more balanced viewed replaces both of the extremes.

We also know now that our ability to assess the extent to which individual differences are inherited and the extent to which they are environmental is nowhere near as good as we thought. There are many questions arising about the validity of the intelligence tests on which assessments of hereditary versus environmental contributions have been made. We have realized, for example, that intelligence tests may measure products of intellectual performance, but not the processes that give rise to these products. Different children may arrive at identical answers using different processes of thought, so that the apparent equivalence of their performances is illusory. Moreover, cultural, social-class, and other biases inevitably influence scores on the tests. Thus, although we can apply quite precise statistical measurements to address the question of the extent to which intelligence is inherited and the extent to which it is environmental, we now recognize that the measurements to which we apply these statistical procedures are themselves limited and, in many cases, flawed.

ACT 5

The Scene: A Classroom in 1985

Professor Interactio enters the college classroom. He is a well-groomed, well-manicured man of middle-age. He is dressed in a jacket and tie. His appearance is spotless and flawless, almost like that of a successful business executive rather than a college professor. He is a man on the rise, ambitious and successful. He has a slightly resentful look, almost as though the time he is about to spend teaching is taking away from what he really should be doing with his time in order to achieve the success he craves. He turns to face his class of 28 students:

Professor Interactio: Today we are going to learn about why it is that some children are brighter than others. Put another way, what enables some children to achieve success in school and in their life as they approach intellectual tasks, whereas other children have great difficulty or frequently experience failure. The question is: "To what extent are individual differences in intelligence hereditary, to what extent are they environmental, and to what extent are they an interaction between heredity and the environment?" The answer is: "Individual differences in intelligence are largely a product of the interaction between genes and environment, rather than merely a product of one or the other."

Previously we believed that the question was whether individual differences in intelligence are hereditary or environmental or both. We thought in strictly linear terms, as though simply assigning proportions to inheritance and environment could answer the question of interest. But we were asking the wrong question. We now know that the proper formulation of the heredity–environment issue requires us to take into account interaction between the genes and the environment, and not just one or the other. Obviously, we have come a long way from the days in which we believed that understanding individual differences in intelligence is merely a question of assigning numerical values to each of two partitions.

The meaning of *interaction* is in no way straightforward. According to the basic idea, inheritance may well place some upper limit on the potential level children can achieve, but no children reach the full potential that lies within them. The vagaries of the environment can either result in children coming quite close to their genetic level of endowment, or remaining a far cry from it. Because we are now coming to understand that intelligence is multifaceted, we further recognize that simple coefficients of heritability do not tell us nearly as much as we once thought they did. They may tell us something about the inheritance of that limited proportion of intelligence measured by standard psychometric intelligence tests at the same time that they tell us practically nothing about those aspects of intelligence not measured by these tests. For example, many people now believe interpersonal skills and more creative intellectual skills, or even musical skills, can be understood within the rubric of intelligence. Clearly, none of our tests adequately address these kinds of abilities.

The difficulties of assigning proportions to heredity and environment are not only in the multifaceted nature of intelligence, but in the limitations of the kinds of methods available for assigning these proportions. For example, we now know that h^2, the coefficient of heritability, can vary as a function of population, the point in history at which the population is measured, the geographical localization of the population, and many other factors. There are unexplained differences in h^2 as a function of these sorts of factors, so that the value of the statistic is limited without regard to the kinds of tests one uses in order to assess it. Even worse, we now know that many of the studies that have been done to assess h^2 were inherently broad. For example, in studies of identical twins reared apart, one cannot assume that the identical twins were randomly placed into environments. On the contrary, in many studies children of greater privilege were in fact placed in environments of greater privilege, and vice versa. So we need to be very cautious before jumping to the kinds of supposedly firm conclusions that in the past we thought were possible. Instead of being so concerned about assigning values to each score, we need to know how heredity and environment interact, and to understand that intelligence is not fixed in any case. Children performing at a certain level at one time can perform at a different level at another time as a function of changes in environmental circumstances or training in intellectual skills; consequently, our assessments are inherently limited by the volatility of intelligence, and not only the ways in which it is measured.

ACT 6

The Scene: A Classroom in 1990

Professor Complexa enters the college classroom. A woman in her late twenties, she has a serious, studious look. She also looks tired, as though the sheer complexity of the questions with which she has been dealing has weighted her down. She is a woman who has been through the wars—intellectual wars—and knows there are no easy solutions. She does not seem to have the same psychological distance from the class as the professors of earlier years. She recognizes that her role as a professor is not so different from the role of the student as both the professors and students of earlier years had thought. She knows that her role as a learner is never done; in 5 or 10 years, some other professor will be entering the classroom to give the same lecture, but the content will be different. She turns to face her class of 36 neatly dressed, well-scrubbed students, who look as though they are preparing for job interviews in law or finance firms, rather than to learn about the psychology of cognitive development. Professor Complexa begins her lecture:

Professor Complexa: Today we are going to learn about the directors of development—the kinds of influences that can be observed on children's thinking. In the past, scholars addressing this question were interested in, and sometimes obsessed with, assigning proportions to the contributions of heredity and environment to observed individual differences in intelligence. Today, we are much less concerned with assigning numbers that really tell us very little. We are more concerned with understanding just what the influences are that affect children's cognitive abilities, whether hereditary or environmental. We know that these influences can be of many kinds. Not only do heredity and environment interact, as we well realized even 5 years ago, but hereditary and environmental factors tend themselves to be correlated, making it difficult even to assign proportions to the contributions of each, because in reality, heredity and environment are nonindependent.

Class, a useful source of information on the directors of development is a book by that same name edited by Lynn Okagaki and Robert J. Sternberg. Rather than summarizing the book for you, what I would like to do is to acquaint you with some of the major generalizations that emerge from the book.

First, both biological and environmental factors affect the development of intelligence, both individually and interactively. Biological factors sometimes covary with environmental factors, thus it is difficult, if not impossible, to set a clear percentage of variation in individual differences in intelligence due to the one or the other. If one places the covariation in the biological component, that component's contribution is overemphasized, and similarly for the environmental factor.

Second, the interaction between biology and environment is two-way. First, biology can affect the environment. For example, parents with low biological intelligence may not provide the optimal environment for their children. But conversely, poor nutrition or conditions for mental growth may affect the biology of the organism. Reductionist explanations of the development of intelligence must fall short because they do not recognize the dual directionality of the interaction between biology and environment.

Third, the environment is not merely something that is static and "out there." People actively create portions of their environments, and the ways in which they do so may be affected by earlier environments in which they developed, as well as by biological factors. Two people with identical past experiences may create different environments, just as two people with identical biology may create different environments. In sum, we just cannot clearly separate biological from environmental factors in intellectual development.

Fourth, intelligence is not just a thing "in the head," anymore than the environment is just a thing "out in the world." Different cultural and ethnic groups may have different notions of what it means to be intelligent, and these different notions will affect the ways in which parents from a given cultural or ethnic group socialize their children to be intelligent. If the home and school groups have similar notions of what it means to be smart, then the socialization at home will "pay off" in the school. But if the notions are different, a child may appear to be smart in the home community but stupid in the school, or vice versa. In order to help children maximally exploit their potential, we need to understand the cultural conception of intelligence that has motivated their socialization in the home environment.

Fifth, children will become more successful adults if they not only acquire knowledge, but if they also acquire knowledge for use. But much of the knowledge children acquire is "inert"—that is, children are unable to use it. Effective programs of schooling give attention not only to what is taught, but to how it is taught so that the children will later be able to use it. Programs for developing children's intellectual skills and achievement have had varied success, but in some cases, their success has been underestimated because of the use of narrow criteria for assessing program effectiveness.

Finally, the best results for intellectual development will be achieved if there is a harmony between the goals of the home and the school. Too often, exactly the opposite seems to be true, and parents are in conflict with the values of the school, or simply indifferent to them. Parents need to understand the culture and goals of the school, while teachers need to better understand the home culture and its goals. Many teachers work with children of cultural and ethnic groups without any familiarity with their values and norms. The result is an intolerance that fosters underachievement and despair.

In sum, our emphasis in understanding the directors of development has shifted from assigning numbers to a more qualitative, psychological understanding of the variables—both biological and cultural—that influence children's cognitive development.

We used to think that the important thing was to find answers. We now recognize that the answers we generate are a function of the questions we ask. In a sense then, the question is more important than the answer, because the question dictates the answer. If we ask a suboptimal question, then we may obtain an answer, but an answer to a question that was improperly posed. The question, then, is: "What question should we ask?" The answer to that question changes and will continue to change as we study the directors of children's cognitive development.

ACT 7

The Scene: A Classroom in 5565

Professor Futura enters the classroom. She is dressed in futuristic clothing, of a kind that in the past was only seen in science fiction movies. She seems to glide above the floor, which indeed she is doing. The color scheme of her clothing is elaborate, as is her multicolored hair. Her head seems slightly larger in proportion to her body than was true of the previously described professors. She turns to face her class, which is gazing at her studiously. They, too, are dressed in futuristic clothing. She begins her lecture:

Professor Futura: Today we are going to study why it is that some children are more intelligent than others. We believe this is a question that psychologists have been seeking to address for hundreds and even thousands of years, although our records of past attempts were destroyed in the massive attacks of World War 4. Doubtless, previous attempts were marred by lack of sophistication and ignorance regarding the true nature of human abilities and their measurement. We have moved beyond these primitive attempts at understanding individual differences in cognitive abilities and their development. At last, we are able scientifically and precisely to address the question of why it is that children differ intellectually. The means by which we do this is of extremely recent invention. It is called an IQ test.

ACKNOWLEDGMENTS

Preparation of this chapter was supported by grants from the Spencer and McDonnell Foundations.

Author Index

C

D

E

F

G

K

L

T

Subject Index

A

B

M

N

O

P

W